1 & 2 TIMOTHY AND TITUS

PREACHING THE WORD

1 & 2 TIMOTHY
AND
TITUS

To Guard the Deposit

1 & 2 Timothy
by
R. Kent Hughes

Titus
by
Bryan Chapell

CROSSWAY BOOKS • WHEATON, ILLINOIS
A DIVISION OF GOOD NEWS PUBLISHERS

1 & 2 Timothy and *Titus*

Copyright © 2000 by R. Kent Hughes and Bryan Chapell.

Published by Crossway Books
      a division of Good News Publishers
      1300 Crescent Street
      Wheaton, Illinois 60187

Cover banner by Marge Gieser

Art Direction: Cindy Kiple

First printing, 2000

Printed in the United States of America

Library of Congress Cataloging-in-Publication Data

Hughes, R. Kent and Chapell, Bryan
  [1 & 2 Timothy]
  1 & 2 Timothy and Titus.
    p.   cm. — (Preaching the word)
  Includes bibliographical references and index.
  Contents: 1 & 2 Timothy / by R. Kent Hughes — Titus / by Bryan Chapell.
  ISBN 1-58134-175-X (alk. paper)
  1. Bible. N.T. Pastoral Epistles—Commentaries. I. Title: 1 and 2 Timothy and Titus. II. Title: First and Second Timothy and Titus. III. Chapell, Bryan. Titus. IV. Title.
BS2735.3.H83 2000
227'.8307—dc21
                    99-087971
                      CIP

15	14	13	12	11	10	09	08	07	06	05	04	03	02	01	00
15	14	13	12	11	10	9	8	7	6	5	4	3	2	1	

R. Kent Hughes:
To my son William Carey Hughes
on the occasion of his first pastorate

Bryan Chapell:
To my ministry students
whose zeal for the gospel furthers my own

*Guard the good deposit that was entrusted
to you — guard it with the help of the
Holy Spirit who lives in us.*
2 Timothy 1:14

Table of Contents

Acknowledgments

Once again, thanks to my executive assistant, Mrs. Sharon Fritz, who has seen all the volumes of the Preaching the Word series through to publication — and that includes finding difficult references and verifying the accuracy of materials consulted. Again, thanks to Mr. Herbert Carlburg, who reads everything with an eye for detail. Crossway's Managing Editor, Ted Griffin, always improves his writers. He knows what he has done for this book. Most of all, I want to express deepest appreciation to my wife, Barbara, who weekly listened to my ideas and helped bring them down to earth and out to the congregation.

A Word to Those Who Preach the Word

There are times when I am preaching that I have especially sensed the pleasure of God. I usually become aware of it through the unnatural silence. The ever-present coughing ceases and the pews stop creaking, bringing an almost physical quiet to the sanctuary — through which my words sail like arrows. I experience a heightened eloquence, so that the cadence and volume of my voice intensify the truth I am preaching.

There is nothing quite like it — the Holy Spirit filling one's sails, the sense of his pleasure, and the awareness that something is happening among one's hearers. This experience is, of course, not unique, for thousands of preachers have similar experiences, even greater ones.

What has happened when this takes place? How do we account for this sense of his smile? The answer for me has come from the ancient rhetorical categories of *logos*, *ethos*, and *pathos*.

The first reason for his smile is the *logos* — in terms of preaching, God's Word. This means that as we stand before God's people to proclaim his Word, we have done our homework. We have exegeted the passage, mined the significance of its words in their context, and applied sound hermeneutical principles in interpreting the text so that we understand what its words meant to its hearers. And it means that we have labored long until we can express in a sentence what the theme of the text is — so that our outline springs from the text. Then our preparation will be such that as we preach, we will not be preaching our own thoughts about God's Word, but God's actual Word, his *logos*. This is fundamental to pleasing him in preaching.

The second element in knowing God's smile in preaching is *ethos* — what you are as a person. There is a danger endemic to preaching, which is having your hands and heart cauterized by holy things. Phillips Brooks illustrated it by the analogy of a train conductor who comes to believe that he has been to the places he announces because of his long and loud heralding of them. And that is why Brooks insisted that preaching must be "the bringing of truth through personality." Though we can never *perfectly* embody the truth we preach, we must be subject to it, long for it, and make it as much a part of our ethos as possible. As the Puritan William Ames said, "Next to the Scriptures, nothing makes a sermon more to pierce, than when it comes out of the inward affection of the heart without any affectation." When a preacher's ethos backs up his *logos*, there will be the pleasure of God.

Last, there is *pathos* — personal passion and conviction. David Hume, the Scottish philosopher and skeptic, was once challenged as he was seen going to hear George Whitefield preach: "I thought you do not believe in the gospel." Hume replied, "I don't, but *he does*." Just so! When a preacher believes what he preaches, there will be passion. And this belief and requisite passion will know the smile of God.

The pleasure of God is a matter of *logos* (the Word), *ethos* (what you are), and *pathos* (your passion). As you *preach the Word* may you experience his smile — the Holy Spirit in your sails!

R. Kent Hughes
Wheaton, Illinois

1 Timothy

1

Greetings to All

1 TIMOTHY 1:1, 2

Paul, an apostle of Christ Jesus by the command of God our Savior and of Christ Jesus our hope, To Timothy my true son in the faith: Grace, mercy and peace from God the Father and Christ Jesus our Lord.

There are substantial reasons to be energized by the prospect of studying the Pastoral Letters of St. Paul.

I am filled with pleasant anticipation by the purpose of 1 Timothy as it is variously stated by the apostle. The overarching purpose of the book is to teach the proper ordering and conduct of the church, as Paul so clearly states it to Timothy: "Although I hope to come to you soon, I am writing you these instructions so that, if I am delayed, you will know how people ought to conduct themselves in God's household, which is the church of the living God, the pillar and foundation of the truth" (3:14, 15).

Paul had communicated the essentials of church conduct during his earlier long ministry in Ephesus, but recent events had apparently necessitated his spelling it out again in a letter to Timothy, to whom Paul had charged the care of the churches there. And in respect to Timothy, Paul's instructions about church operations were meant to help him to "hang in there" — "Timothy, my son, I give you this instruction in keeping with the prophecies once made about you, so that by following them you may fight the good fight, holding on to faith and a good conscience" (1:18, 19). So the letter of 1 Timothy provides the exhilarating essentials to both leader and congregation as to how they must conduct themselves to the glory of God. This is cause for marked enthusiasm in our day, when there is so much confusion about what the church ought to be like.

I am also enthusiastic because the teaching of 1 Timothy (and all the Pastorals) about church order and conduct came through *special revelation from Christ to St. Paul*, as is implicit in the stated purpose of this letter, as we will see.

To begin with, when Paul earlier wrote to the Galatians he made it very clear that the gospel had come to him by special personal revelation from Christ himself — "I want you to know, brothers, that the gospel I preached is not something that man made up. I did not receive it from any man, nor was I taught it; rather, I received it by revelation from Jesus Christ" (1:11, 12). Thus we understand that the knowledge of the gospel was not mediated to Paul through any other human being. It came straight from the lips of Christ. The gospel theology that he inscripturated in his writings first came from Christ. Most believe this happened during Paul's three-year sojourn in Arabia (cf. Galatians 1:13-18).

Along with "the gospel," Paul received knowledge of what he called "the mystery," which he referred to as "the mystery made known to me by revelation" (Ephesians 3:3). Evidently Paul was given knowledge of "the mystery" in the same direct manner that "the gospel" had been given to him — straight from Christ.

In the book of Ephesians, which deals so much with "the mystery," Paul indicates that it is revealed in the coming together and ordering of three pairs of relationships: 1) *heaven and earth*, 1:9, 10; 2) *Jew and Gentile*, 2:11 — 3:6; and 3) *husband and wife*, 5:31, 32. All three relationships are joined and ordered under the headship of Christ. And all three (heaven/earth, Jew/Gentile, husband/wife) are joined into one by and through Christ. Each pair reveals a different aspect of the wondrous mystery of Christ's work.[1]

Understanding from Ephesians something of the dynamic union and ordering that comes from the mystery of Christ, the purpose of 1 Timothy (which has to do with church order and conduct) takes on additional importance — because the practical ordering of the church has everything to do with the revelation of the mystery of Christ to the world. We know this because the word *mystery* was in Paul's thinking when he declared the purpose of 1 Timothy. Listen closely to the purpose of 1 Timothy again: "I am writing you these instructions so that, if I am delayed, you will know how people ought to conduct themselves in God's household, which is the church of the living God, the pillar and foundation of the truth. Beyond all question, the mystery of godliness is great" (3:14-16a).

Paul then quotes an excerpt from a creedal hymn about Christ's incarnation. Because the mystery of Christ's incarnation made possible the gospel and the mystery of Christ and the church, the hymn sings of the wondrous reality of the Incarnation: "Beyond all question, the mystery of godliness is great: He appeared in a body, was vindicated by the Spirit, was seen by angels, was preached among the nations, was believed on in the world, was taken up in glory" (v. 16). And now, with Christ ascended, the church (his Body) proclaims the mystery by the way it lives on earth.[2]

The details of proper church life are therefore part of "the administration of this mystery" revealed to Paul directly from Christ, as that apostle explained in Ephesians where he talks about the union of Jew and Gentile:

> *Although I am less than the least of all God's people, this grace was given me: to preach to the Gentiles the unsearchable riches of Christ, and to make plain to everyone* the administration of this mystery, *which for ages past was kept hidden in God, who created all things. His intent was that now, through the church, the manifold wisdom of God should be made known to the rulers and authorities in the heavenly realms, according to his eternal purpose which he accomplished in Christ Jesus our Lord. (3:8-11, emphasis added)*

First Timothy is a letter on order in the church and how it ought to live so as to reveal that "mystery." God tells us in 1 Timothy how the church must look and act if it is to glorify him. It has everything to do with the gospel and the declaration of the revealed mystery. Thus we have in 1 Timothy one of the grand treasures of the church — given directly from Christ to Paul for us. It is of immense value. The final paragraph of 1 Timothy begins with this charge: "Timothy, guard what has been entrusted to your care" (6:20) — (that is, "guard the deposit, the revelation, I have given to you"). And Paul goes on to include in the opening paragraphs of 2 Timothy a further charge: "Guard the good deposit that was entrusted to you — guard it with the help of the Holy Spirit who lives in us" (1:14). This is our happy charge today, and it is grounds for expectant enthusiasm.

First Timothy is incredibly relevant. Philip A. Towner of Covenant Seminary addresses the question of the relevance of the Pastorals, saying:

> What do these three letters have to do with our present situation? Consider the agendas for Christian action and evangelical response being set in many quarters of the church today. At the forefront are a number of very pressing items: the church's role in a changing society, the church's responsibility to the poor and the disfranchised, the Christian message among competing messages, the secularization of Christianity, church and state. Consider some of the perennial issues: a Christian attitude to wealth and materialism, the church's response to the cults, spiritual lifestyle, leadership and authority, the role of women, discipline in the church. Finally, consider some of the items on our personal agendas: the true meaning of godliness, faithfulness to the gospel, suffering and life in the Spirit, responsibility to those in authority, the importance of Christian witness. For the church that seeks to understand its role

in a complex world and for the individual Christian "who wants to live a godly life in Christ Jesus" (2 Tim 3:12) today, the Pastoral epistles make very relevant reading.[3]

Indeed they do.

Paul provides a Biblical worldview for today's culture-bound church. The Pastorals are shocking and disjunctive. There is nothing bourgeois about the Pastorals, as some critics have argued. They are not a tract about middle-class ethics.[4] Certainly they do call the church to a respectable lifestyle, but it is radically respectable, and radically ordered by the most radical of all persons — Christ himself! The Pastorals are also bracing. The church that will ride the high seas of the second millennium will be the one that is biblically defined — by the Pastorals.

The Pastorals are also saving. We will see that Paul tells Timothy in the middle of the first letter, "Watch your life and doctrine closely. Persevere in them, because if you do, you will save both yourself and your hearers" (4:16). That is what I hope for myself and you — to be saved as we study this book. Not saved and re-saved (as in reborn again and again), but saved certainly and securely, and therefore saved from our selfishness and from our carelessness, and then saved and saved and saved and saved from our sins as we give closer attention to our doctrine and way of life.

GREETINGS (vv. 1, 2)

With the purpose of 1 Timothy in mind (the proper order and conduct of the church), let us turn to Paul's carefully phrased greetings to Timothy, which are meant to hearten him in his daunting leadership role.

Paul. Paul's opening self-designation — "Paul, an apostle of Christ Jesus by the command of God our Savior and of Christ Jesus our hope" (v. 1) — is boldly significant because this is the only greeting where he claims that his apostolic position was due to divine command. Here the word is freighted with the nuance of a royal order.[5] Paul regards himself as sovereignly dispatched by the Holy Trinity, as seen by his naming the first two members. His intention here is to convey to embattled Timothy (and perhaps even more to the elders of the church) that his teaching was authoritative.

Paul's indication that his "command," his commission, came from "God our Savior and . . . Christ Jesus our hope" was both emotive and heartening. The phrase "God our Savior" is deeply rooted in the Old Testament and was common in Jewish devotional language, which repeatedly recalled his acts of salvation.[6] Thus the Virgin Mary naturally used it in the *Magnificat*: "My soul glorifies the Lord and my spirit rejoices in God my Savior" (Luke 1:46, 47). Paul was implicitly saying, "Timothy — and whoever else reads this — what I am going to tell you comes from our Savior God, who backs up what he commands. Take heart!" The additional phrase "and of Christ Jesus our hope" makes it even more encouraging, because *hope* in the New Testament means certain hope, fully confident expectation of an as yet unrealized fulfillment.[7]

So from the onset Paul's letter to Timothy was pure offense — confident, authoritative, and encouraging. "Chin up, Timothy! Chin up, all who love the church and desire to see her sail as she should despite rough waters."

Timothy. Paul's heartening introduction was matched by his tender address to Timothy: "To Timothy my true son in the faith" (v. 2a). Timothy came from a mixed (Jew/Gentile) marriage. His godly mother Eunice was Jewish and his pagan father a Greek. They lived in the pagan town of Lystra (cf. Acts 16:1; 2 Timothy 1:5). Most think that Timothy was converted while a boy during Paul's first missionary journey, when the apostle was almost stoned to death in Lystra (Acts 14:8-23; cf. 2 Timothy 2:11).

Paul was delighted with young Timothy and added him to his entourage, possibly as a replacement for John Mark. It was a good choice, apparently confirmed through prophetic utterances by Paul's associates. Timothy was gifted for ministry through the laying on of hands (1 Timothy 1:18; 4:14) and was circumcised, so as not to hinder ministry among Jews, thus becoming a lifelong member of the missionary task force.

When this first letter was written to him, he was still young because Paul advised him, "Don't let anyone look down on you because you are young" (4:12), and in 2 Timothy he warned him, "Flee the evil desires of youth" (2:22). John Stott calculates that he was in his mid-thirties.[8] Not only was Timothy young, he was also timid. So Paul says to him, "For God did not give us a spirit of timidity" (2 Timothy 1:7). Earlier he had encouraged the Corinthians, "If Timothy comes, see to it that he has nothing to fear while he is with you, for he is carrying on the work of the Lord, just as I am" (1 Corinthians 16:10). "Timid Timothy" needed encouragement.

Timothy also appears to have had a fragile constitution and nagging stomach problems, for which Paul advised, "Stop drinking only water, and use a little wine because of your stomach and your frequent illnesses" (1 Timothy 5:23). So we conclude that Timothy, by nature, was not a missionary commando — a C. T. Studd or a "Dr. Livingston, I presume." And this is probably why we find him so endearing. He is one of us. He does not intimidate anyone. He is so un-Paul!

Yet Paul loved him affectionately. The appellation "Timothy my true son in the faith" appears to contain a double balm, gently assuaging the fact that Timothy was regarded as illegitimate by Jewish law, while also affirming the spiritual legitimacy of Timothy's own faith — "my true *son* in the *faith.*" The church was meant to recognize in Paul's affection the stamp of approval, particularly in light of the difficulties Timothy was facing. Paul's other letters also reflect the beautiful depth of his affection for his shy, sometimes frail disciple. To the Corinthians he wrote, "I am sending to you Timothy, my son whom I love" (1 Corinthians 4:17). And to the Philippians he said of Timothy, "As a son with his father he has served with me in the work of the gospel" (Philippians 2:22). And to Timothy himself he would poignantly write at the beginning of his next letter, "Recalling your tears, I long to see you, so that I may be filled with joy" (1:4). How heartening Paul's words were to his reluctant successor.

And Timothy did well. We do not know exactly how it all worked out in Ephesus, but we can be sure he faithfully carried out his duties. We know he was Paul's faithful cohort to the end, through thick and thin. We also know that Timothy himself became a prisoner for a time (cf. Hebrews 13:23). And we know he was mightily used by God. Oswald Chambers could well have had Timothy in mind when he wrote:

> God can achieve his purpose either through the absence of human power and resources, or the abandonment of reliance on them. All through history God has chosen and used nobodies, because their unusual dependence on him made possible the unique display of his power and grace. He chose and used somebodies only when they renounced dependence on their natural abilities and resources.[9]

Triple blessing. Paul now rains a triple blessing in the form of a prayer-wish upon his dear disciple: "Grace, mercy and peace from God the Father and Christ Jesus our Lord" (v. 2b). The standard pagan Greek greeting was simply "Greetings!" (*charein*), which Paul had early changed into "Grace" (*charis*), creating a Christianized greeting that he combined with the standard Hebrew greeting, "Peace" (*shalom*). Thus the typical Pauline greeting was the beautifully nuanced "Grace and peace." But in 1 and 2 Timothy Paul inserts "mercy" between them, creating a triple blessing that is particularly fitting to Timothy's situation.

In invoking God's grace upon Timothy, Paul referenced not only God's *saving* grace (cf. Ephesians 2:8), but even more, God's *continued* grace for living. God is lovingly disposed toward his children, and Paul wishes all the gifts and blessings upon Timothy that naturally fall from a smiling God. It is the "grace upon grace" that John speaks of (John 1:16, Greek) — the "he gives us more grace" of the Apostle James (cf. James 4:6).

The added word *mercy* here carries the idea of God's special care for a person in need.[10] The Old Testament equivalent of this word (*hesed*) is used multiple times in the Psalms, with the idea of help in time of need. Paul may well have used this word because of Timothy's Jewish background,[11] which would bring to mind the rich associations of this word — "help to those who cannot help themselves" — "help to the wretched" — "help to the helpless." Timothy was in a situation that would sometimes bring him to the end of himself in certain relational miseries. But there God's special care would be his.

"Peace" is, of course, first of all peace with God (cf. Romans 5:1) and then inner peace for living (cf. John 14:27). His wish for Timothy was for personal tranquillity and well-being, and also for interpersonal peace as he challenged the church to climb to higher ground.

How beautiful this triple blessing was! The source of grace, mercy, and peace was and is the infinite resources of God. No matter how much God would give the young servant of the Lord, there would always be more. This was Paul's wish for Timothy! Grace upon grace to equip him for ministry. Mercy upon mercy to attend to his distresses. Peace upon peace — tranquillity and well-being — throughout his life.

God would give Timothy the grace, mercy, and peace he needed to teach the Ephesians "how people ought to conduct themselves in God's household, which is the church of the living God" (1 Timothy 3:15). And Timothy would follow Paul's instruction and "fight the good fight" (1 Timothy 1:18). May we do so as well, and in so doing declare the mystery of Christ in the gospel to the world.

2

The Wrong Use of the Law

1 TIMOTHY 1:3-7

As I urged you when I went into Macedonia, stay there in Ephesus so that you may command certain men not to teach false doctrines any longer nor to devote themselves to myths and endless genealogies. These promote controversies rather than God's work — which is by faith. The goal of this command is love, which comes from a pure heart and a good conscience and a sincere faith. Some have wandered away from these and turned to meaningless talk. They want to be teachers of the law, but they do not know what they are talking about or what they so confidently affirm.

The precise beginning of the church in Ephesus is not known. We do know, however, that Priscilla and Aquila were involved very early in its shaping, if not founding, when Paul dropped them off at a brief stopover in Ephesus on his hurried way to Antioch (circa A.D. 52) during his second missionary journey (cf. Acts 18:18-22).[1] Ultimately, when Paul returned, he engaged in a mighty two- to three-year ministry, preaching first in the synagogue and then in the hall of Tyrannus (cf. Acts 19:8-10). His ministry was filled with extraordinary power, so much so that the idol-making industry suffered substantial economic losses that eventuated in the famous Ephesian riot led by the idol-makers' guild (cf. Acts 19).

Those tumultuous years marked the firm establishment of a powerful beachhead in the most important city of the Roman province of Asia. Ephesus became the command center for the evangelization of Asia Minor. The church in Ephesus was supremely crucial to Paul's ministry, and in his poignant farewell address to the Ephesian elders he gave this clear warning:

"Now I know that none of you among whom I have gone about preaching the kingdom will ever see me again. Therefore, I declare to you today that I am innocent of the blood of all men. For I have not hesitated to proclaim to you the whole will of God. Guard your-

selves and all the flock of which the Holy Spirit has made you over-
seers. Be shepherds of the church of God, which he bought with
his own blood. I know that after I leave, savage wolves will come
in among you and will not spare the flock. Even from your own num-
ber men will arise and distort the truth in order to draw away dis-
ciples after them. So be on your guard! Remember that for three
years I never stopped warning each of you night and day with
tears." (Acts 20:25-31)

Now, as he writes this first letter to Timothy, in A.D. 64, some five years
have elapsed since his ministry in Ephesus. Trouble has come to the church
from within — savage wolves are in the very sheepfold. And Paul has
already dispatched Timothy to Ephesus to deal with the problems. It was
imperative that Timothy succeed. So Paul penned specific directions about
church conduct and order in a document that is now known as 1 Timothy.

As mentioned in our study of the apostle's uniquely crafted salutation
to Timothy in verses 1, 2, the greetings were meant to steel and hearten this
timid disciple for his difficult task. At the same time the greetings were
ominous because they did not include Paul's thanksgiving for the church,
as did nearly all his letters. That which was taking place in Ephesus was no
cause for thanksgiving.[2]

THE PROHIBITION (vv. 3, 4a)

Paul, *sans* thanksgiving, went right to the point with a ringing prohibition:
"As I urged you when I went into Macedonia, stay there in Ephesus so that
you may command certain men not to teach false doctrines any longer nor
to devote themselves to myths and endless genealogies" (vv. 3, 4a).

The "certain men" who were teaching false doctrines are unnamed, but
the people knew who they were.[3] They were even elders, as Paul had so
clearly predicted in his farewell to the Ephesian church leaders: "Even from
your own number men will arise and distort the truth" (Acts 20:30). Gordon
Fee convincingly argues that this is evident from 1 Timothy because of: 1)
the fact that they presume to be "teachers of the law" (v. 7) and that teaching in 1 Timothy is a specific responsibility of elders (cf. 5:17; 3:2); 2) the
fact that two are subsequently named, "Hymenaeus and Alexander," and
are excommunicated by Paul rather than by the elders of the church (1:19,
20); and 3) the fact of the repeated concerns expressed about elders in this
letter regarding their qualifications (3:1-7), their discipline, and apparently
their replacement (5:19-25).[4]

The elder problem dominated the entire church landscape. These false
teachers were not from the outside, nor were they individual church members (which would be bad enough). Rather, they were from among the vari-

ous leaders in the house churches. No wonder Paul had to urge Timothy to stay on in Ephesus!

Paul describes the style and motivations of these false teachers within the elders in verses 6, 7: "Some have wandered away from these and turned to meaningless talk. They want to be teachers of the law, but they do not know what they are talking about or what they so confidently affirm." Rabbis were called "teachers of the law" (cf. Luke 5:17; Acts 5:34). These elders in Ephesus aspired to be Christian versions of the rabbis — authoritative interpreters of the deep things of the Old Testament. In imitation of their rabbinic counterparts they spoke with assured confidence and dogmatism, though they did not know what they were talking about. The modern preacher's version of the bluster described here is the marginal note on his preaching manuscript, "Weak point here. Look confident and pound the pulpit!" In grim reality, they had apostatized and wandered away from love into controversy, away from pure hearts and good consciences to duplicity and religious insincerity.

Their method of teaching false doctrine was "to devote themselves to myths and endless genealogies" (v. 4a). The Old Testament is full of genealogies that made perfect fodder for "Jewish myths" (Titus 1:14) — the fanciful allegorical creation of stories about the people in the genealogies. The Jewish tradition included books such as *The Book of Jubilees* (circa 135-105 B.C.), a fanciful rewrite of Old Testament history from creation to Sinai. The later *Biblical Antiquities of Philo* (circa A.D. 70) retells more of the Old Testament story — from creation to the death of King Saul.[5] Thus there were ample allegorical models for the Ephesian elders turned Christian rabbis to imitate.

These errant elders weren't Judaizers like those in Galatia, who taught salvation by obedience to the law. There is not a hint of this in the Pastorals. As John Stott explains, "They were certainly speculators. They treated the law (that is, the Old Testament) as a happy hunting ground for their speculations."[6] It was not so much that they set out to be heretical. They simply wanted to "go deeper" into the Scriptures. They wanted to go beyond the "simple" exegesis of Paul, and by giving people and events allegorical meaning, simple stories would reveal fantastic truths. They did not set out to abandon the gospel doctrine that salvation is by faith alone, but in fact their progressive accretions smothered the gospel.

It was all so appealing, and it fed on the incipient Gnosticism in Ephesus that would flower in the second century. Their style and approach is timeless. It is spoken softly with a distant heavenly look in the moist eye: "What you believe is good — it's a good beginning point. But there is more that those of us who have paid the price of meditation and study can reveal to you. Adam stands for the spirit, Eve represents the flesh. One is good, the other is bad."

And their disciples live on today. Consider the incredible distortions that the number 666 has undergone to spell out the name of every international villain from Caesar to Napoleon to Hitler to Stalin. A few years ago the best-selling book *The Bible Code*, a tendentious interpretation of the Old Testament, claimed that an Israeli mathematician, Dr. Elijahu Rips, has decoded the Bible with a computer formula, unlocking 3,000-year-old prophecies of events such as the Kennedy assassination and the election of Bill Clinton — "everything from the holocaust to Hiroshima, from the moon landing to the collision of a comet with Jupiter."[7] Religious novelties abound everywhere — fantastic claims of new truth about everything from raising perfect children to restraining the aging process. The problem is that these teachings and their systems, while not denying the gospel outright, replace it.

So we see that Paul exhibits a huge concern in the Pastorals for sound doctrine. Paul mentions doctrine (*didaskalia*) seven times in 1 Timothy, not to mention its verbal forms. These seven occurrences are not readily apparent in the *New International Version* because *didaskalia* can be variously translated "doctrine" or "teaching" or "instruction." These references are:

- 1:10, where Paul exalts "sound doctrine."
- 4:6 — "If you point these things out to the brothers, you will be a good minister of Christ Jesus, brought up in the truths of the faith and of the good teaching that you have followed."
- 4:13 — "Until I come, devote yourself to the public reading of Scripture, to preaching and to teaching."
- 4:16 — "Watch your life and doctrine closely. Persevere in them, because if you do, you will save both yourself and your hearers."
- 5:17 — "The elders who direct the affairs of the church are worthy of double honor, especially those whose work is preaching and teaching."
- 6:1 — "All who are under the yoke of slavery should consider their masters worthy of full respect, so that God's name and our teaching may not be slandered."
- 6:3, 4a — "If anyone teaches false doctrines and does not agree to the sound instruction of our Lord Jesus Christ and to godly teaching, he is conceited and understands nothing."

Having observed Paul's repeated emphasis on sound doctrine, we must make this connection: 1 Timothy, with its great emphasis on doctrine, has a basic practical purpose — to teach the people in Ephesus how to live — to "know how . . . to conduct themselves in God's household, which is the church" (3:15). There is a dynamic connection between our doctrine and the way we live. This truth is directly opposite to much contemporary

Christian thinking. Often today we hear people say, "We don't need more doctrine. What we need is practical preaching." Now, we must certainly agree that preaching must be applied. But we must not agree that there is no connection between the doctrinal and the practical. What we know and believe has everything to do with how we live. Doctrine is at the heart of practical living.

Do you love God now? Will you love him less if you learn more about him? Absolutely not! You will love him more. The more you learn of his excellencies, his holiness, his grace, his mercy, his love, the greater will be your grasp of his character, and the closer to him you will draw.

The greatest need of the church today is not less doctrine but *more* doctrine — about God, about salvation, about ourselves, about character, about church, about family. Our greatest need is to know God better — and we can learn more only from his Word.

THE PROHIBITION'S RATIONALE (v. 4b)

Having enjoined Timothy to command these "certain men not to teach false doctrines," Paul briefly stated his rationale behind the command: "These promote controversies rather than God's work — which is by faith" (v. 4b). Arcane, novel interpretations serve only to promote questionings and controversies. They naturally spawn elitism and snobbery. Those who "buy in" think all others are simple or unspiritual or even downright sinful.

The ultimate tragedy of false doctrine is that "God's work — which is by faith" is not promoted. The depth of the tragedy is better understood when we see that the phrase "God's work" literally reads, "the administration of God" and uses the same word as in Ephesians 3:2 ("the administration of God's grace") and 3:9 ("the administration of this mystery"), in both places meaning the responsibility of administering or managing. Here in 1 Timothy 1:4 it refers to *the administration of God which is by faith.* The church and especially its leaders have been given the responsibility (the stewardship) of administering or managing the truth that salvation and Christian living are by faith.[8]

The tragedy in Ephesus was that the false teachers had blocked the faithful discharge of God's administration of this truth. The "by faith" gospel wasn't going out. The very conduct of the people, their confusion, and their wrangling prevented the conduct and church order that would promote the "by faith" gospel. This again goes to the explicitly stated purpose of the book — to teach the proper conduct of God's household, which is the church (cf. 3:15). For Paul, everything rides on the conduct and administration (*oikonomia*) of God's household (*oikas*), the church — because if the church is living as it should, the gospel will spread!

THE PROHIBITION'S PURPOSE (v. 5)

This understanding leads to the positive reason why Paul had Timothy command the false teachers to desist. Paul asserts, "The goal of this command is love, which comes from a pure heart and a good conscience and a sincere faith" (v. 5). If the Ephesian elders would put a stop to the teaching of false doctrine by their deluded eldest colleagues and go back to sound doctrine, that would restore love to God's people — "The goal of this command is love."

What is this "love"? It is love for God first, and then love for those around us — the classic dimensions of love in the Ten Commandments, as Jesus so eloquently proclaimed: "'Love the Lord your God with all your heart and with all your soul and with all your mind.' This is the first and greatest commandment. And the second is like it: 'Love your neighbor as yourself.' All the Law and the Prophets hang on these two commandments" (Matthew 22:37-40). Love for others is made possible and is fueled by love for God. As John Piper has said, "Love is the overflow of joy in God which gladly meets the needs of others."[9] And when this happens, the administration of God by faith given to his people goes into full gear. "All men will know that you are my disciples if you love one another" (John 13:35).

The love described here comes from a dynamic triple inner work.

First, in the *heart* — "which comes from a pure heart." Jesus' beatitude is certainly in view here: "Blessed are the pure in heart, for they will see God" (Matthew 5:8). Blessed is the heart that is pure and is thus focused on him. Rich Old Testament associations are also in the background, such as Psalm 86:11, where David prays, "Give me an undivided heart, that I may fear your name." Or Jeremiah 32:38, 39, which prophesies the effects of the New Covenant: "They will be my people, and I will be their God. I will give them singleness of heart and action, so that they will always fear me for their own good and the good of their children after them." This radical purity and focus in the depth of one's being elicits love from one's heart.

Second, in the *conscience* — "and a good conscience." The essential meaning of *conscience* is one's inner awareness of the quality of one's own actions (cf. Romans 2:15; 9:1; 2 Corinthians 1:12).[10] But in Biblical culture it also meant the sense of one's moral actions as part of a group. The "good conscience" sensed inner moral approval from God and God's people.[11] Such "a good conscience" was innately joyous. Love for others was its boon.

And third, in *faith* — "and a sincere faith" — literally, "a faith without hypocrisy." The way some people live has no relationship to the faith they declare with their lips. Here "sincere faith" means a faith that is really there — an "undissembling faith."[12] Such faith joins naturally with love. In fact, the Pastorals link faith and love eight times (1 Timothy 1:14; 2:15; 4:12; 6:11; 2 Timothy 1:13; 2:22; 3:10; Titus 2:2)!

Never sell doctrine short. False doctrine promotes controversies and strife. Its wranglings, its confusions, its snobbishness, its empty talk bring hatred and distrust. But sound doctrine produces a dynamic love "which comes from a pure heart and a good conscience and a sincere faith" (v. 5). Joyful worship flows up to God. And the overflow gladly meets the needs of others.

Publisher and author Frank Sheed eloquently capsulized the primacy of Biblical, doctrinal knowledge:

> A virtuous man may be ignorant, but ignorance is not a virtue. It would be a strange God Who could be loved better by being known less. Love of God is not the same thing as knowledge of God; love of God is immeasurably more important than knowledge of God; but if a man loves God knowing a little about Him, he should love God more from knowing more about Him: for every new thing known about God is a new reason for loving Him.[13]

What we understand and believe about God (Father, Son, Holy Spirit) is everything!

> *What we believe about ourselves,*
> *What we believe about the cross,*
> *What we believe about the world,*
> *What we believe about our purpose,*
> *What we believe about the church,*
> *What we believe about our relationships,*
> *What we believe about God's Word*
> *is everything!*

3

The Proper Use of the Law

1 TIMOTHY 1:8-11

We know that the law is good if one uses it properly. We also know that law is made not for the righteous but for lawbreakers and rebels, the ungodly and sinful, the unholy and irreligious; for those who kill their fathers or mothers, for murderers, for adulterers and perverts, for slave traders and liars and perjurers — and for whatever else is contrary to the sound doctrine that conforms to the glorious gospel of the blessed God, which he entrusted to me.

A characteristic of the Apostle Paul's writings is digression. In the middle of an argument, a word or allusion will suggest an important thought — and Paul will take off on the subject. But his digressions are always relevant. Paul has been encouraging Timothy to put an end to the work of false teachers in Ephesus, and he says of them, "They want to be teachers of the law, but they do not know what they are talking about or what they so confidently affirm" (v. 7). With this mention of their misuse of the law, he digresses in verses 8-11 on the proper use of the law. A review of Paul's concerns and purpose in writing to Timothy will help us better understand his thinking in this section.

PAUL'S CONCERN

Apostasy's speed. The threat of wholesale apostasy in Ephesus drove Paul at the time he wrote this letter. His concern was well-founded because of the speed with which apostasy had come to some of the elder-led congregations in Ephesus. It had only been four years since his famous farewell address to the Ephesian elders in which he had warned them saying, "After I leave, savage wolves will come in among you and will not spare the flock. Even from your own number men will arise and distort the truth in order to

draw away disciples after them" (Acts 20:29, 30). And now it was dread-
fully true.

Unbelievable! The Ephesian church had drunk from the pure stream of
apostolic teaching. There could be no better water than that! God's Word
from a writer of God's Word! In today's terms they did not drink merely from
the tap but from the apostolic fire hose — for three years. They had even
had the grandest ecclesiastical letter of the New Testament written personally to them. But within forty-eight months of Paul's farewell, apostasy had
come.

Sadly, the Ephesians were not unique on the apostolic landscape. Only
six verses into his letter to the Galatians, Paul had exploded, "I am astonished
that you are so quickly deserting the one who called you by the grace of
Christ and are turning to a different gospel — which is really no gospel at all"
(Galatians 1:6, 7). Perhaps his experience with the rapid demise of the
Galatians fueled his warning to the Ephesian elders.

In any event, both cases make concrete the sobering reality that gospel
ministries nourished from the well of God's Word can become apostate
with amazing speed. This reality is a plaintive refrain in 1 Timothy: "Some
have rejected these and so have shipwrecked their faith" (1:19). "The Spirit
clearly says that in later times some will abandon the faith and follow deceiving spirits and things taught by demons" (4:1). "Some have in fact already
turned away to follow Satan" (5:15). "Some people, eager for money, have
wandered from the faith and pierced themselves with many griefs" (6:10).
And the final verse of the book bemoans those who "have wandered from the
faith" (6:21).

Should our concern be any less today? Absolutely not! If anything, given
Paul's experience, the repeated record of church history, and recent events
in the evangelical church, our vigilance must be even greater. It is a solemn
fact that any given church can depart from the faith in less than a generation. To imagine otherwise is to be so inflated with the helium of naive
pride that we imagine we are above the human condition and that of the
church itself, impervious to what happens in life and history. The truth is,
apostasy can easily happen to any of us if we do not guard against it and
stay close to Christ.

My own evangelical awareness parallels the rise of Evangelicalism in
American culture. In 1948 I was taken by my grandmother to hear Billy
Graham preach in a great tent on Figueroa Street in Los Angeles. I was
born again in 1955 and felt the disdain of my former mainline church. In
retrospect, it was probably more fear than disdain because it, like the other
liberal churches in town, was shrinking as evangelical churches grew. I was
a youth pastor in the 1960s. My uniform was sandals, bell-bottoms, and flow-
ered shirts. "Groovy!" I participated in a huge harvest of souls in those
tumultuous years. 1974 was declared by *Time Magazine* to be "The Year of

the Evangelical." And in the 1980s evangelical Christianity was in the driver's seat of the American Protestant enterprise. Now, in early 2000, with Evangelicalism at its crest, times have clearly changed.

In 1987 the University of Chicago Press published James Davison Hunter's *Evangelicalism, the Coming Generation*, a survey of nine evangelical liberal arts colleges and seven evangelical seminaries that defined many of the changes. Regarding evangelical theology Dr. Hunter wrote: "There is less sharpness, less boldness, and, accordingly, a measure of opaqueness in their theological vision that did not exist in previous generations (at least to their present extent)."[1] Hunter further observes:

> What is happening, however, is an alteration in the cultural meaning of orthodoxy and, accordingly, an alteration in the cultural meaning of specific criteria of orthodoxy. In each case there is a broadening of the meaning of some of Evangelicalism's fundamental religious symbols. The meaning of such doctrines as the inerrancy/infallibility of Scripture, justification through Christ alone, and the nature and purpose of the Christian mission has become more inclusive. They mean more than they did even a generation or two ago. The cognitive boundaries of theological orthodoxy, once narrowly construed, become variously widened. Insofar as this is true, theological orthodoxy is reinterpreted; the tradition is redefined.[2]

A decade later Millard Erickson, Distinguished Professor of Theology at Baylor University's Truett Seminary, wrote *The Evangelical Left: Encountering Postconservative Evangelical Theology*, in which he chronicles a redefining of three essential doctrines by some who wear the label *Evangelical* — namely, the doctrine of Scripture, the doctrine of God, and the doctrine of salvation.

We must take heed not to rest on the evangelical victories and achievements of recent years — history's greatest evangelists, huge churches, overflowing schools and seminaries, cultural influence. We must remember that Ephesus was the lighthouse of Asia Minor. It was up to this point an apostolic success story. It had been evangelical in the purest sense of *evangelion* with its primary emphasis on the gospel and on mission. But the church at Ephesus was beginning to decay from the inside.

We must take to heart that 1 Timothy is imperative for us who know and serve Christ today. Sadly, there is widespread neglect of the Pastorals by evangelicals because of their being so direct in delicate matters such as church discipline, qualifications for leadership, and male and female roles. We evangelicals have also been subtly influenced by liberals' rejection of the Pastorals on the false suppositions that they are "second-century," "middle-class," and "status quo." The resulting neglect of the Pastorals by people of *the* Book is unconscionable. If we do not allow Scripture to define the church, the forces of culture will!

Apostasy's immorality. Why had some of the Ephesian elders become teachers of false doctrine? The answer is implicit in the verse we examined in our last study. Namely, they had abandoned "love, which comes from a pure heart and a good conscience and a sincere faith" (v. 5). Their false teaching had come as a result of their moral decline. Doctrinal departure follows moral departure. Notice in verse 19 that Paul urges Timothy to hold "on to faith and a good conscience" and that "some have rejected these and so have shipwrecked their faith." Also consider 4:1, 2: "The Spirit clearly says that in later times some will abandon the faith and follow deceiving spirits and things taught by demons. Such teachings come through hypocritical liars, whose consciences have been seared as with a hot iron."

How could Christians who had drunk from the supreme stream of apostolic gospel truth leave Christ and the gospel for "myths and endless genealogies" (1:4)? The answer is in verse 5: They had ceased to maintain purity of heart and a clear conscience. I have seen this happen in the lives and walk of friends who were once fellow soldiers but failed to keep their hearts clean, then fell away, and now believe doctrines contradictory to the gospel. When you fail to guard your conscience, you become open to the world, the flesh, and the devil — and thus prey to fanciful theology and heresy.

The battle for orthodoxy is lost not only in the head but in the heart. Apostasy begins at the very deepest level, when we trample our conscience. There is no doubt that some of us have inner places where we have ridden roughshod over our hearts, indulging ourselves at the expense of God's work within us. In time, our love for God will fade, our heart and conscience will give in, and we will be shells of hypocrisy. Maintaining "a pure heart and a good conscience and a sincere faith" is the primary battle for those who want to live for God.

PAUL'S PURPOSE

Paul's concern about apostasy in Ephesus was intimately connected with his purpose in writing to Timothy. The classic statement of his purpose is stated in 1 Timothy 3:15 — "If I am delayed, you will know how people ought to conduct themselves in God's household, which is the church of the living God, the pillar and foundation of the truth." Furthermore, the subject of church conduct and order runs through every chapter of his letter.

But there is also an underlying purpose (which many miss), stated in 2:3, 4 — "This is good, and pleases God our Savior, who wants all men to be saved and to come to a knowledge of the truth." Paul also used the phrase "God our Savior" in his opening greeting, "Paul, an apostle of Christ Jesus by the command of God our Savior and of Christ Jesus our hope" (1:1). On the deepest level, 1 Timothy is not about church order but about the evangelization of the world! It is about a Savior who will save all who believe: "This is a trustworthy saying that deserves full acceptance (and for this we labor and strive), that we have put our hope in the living God, who is the Savior of all men, and especially of those who believe" (4:9, 10). One's *doctrine* and one's *conduct* have everything to do with *evangelism*. "Watch your life and doctrine closely. Persevere in them, because if you do, you will save both yourself and your hearers" (4:16).

When you see that Paul's deepest concern is that "all men to be saved and . . . come to a knowledge of the truth," his digression in verses 8-11 makes sense. These errant, false-teaching elders had abandoned the outward proclamation and defense of the gospel and had turned inward, using, of all things, the law to promote their teaching.

THE USE OF THE LAW

Proper use. Paul opens his digression by saying, "We know that the law is good if one uses it properly" (v. 8). In Romans 7:12 he gave his classic statement of the law's goodness: "So then, the law is holy, and the commandment is holy, righteous and good." Despite the misunderstanding and errant teaching of some, there is no disjunction between the law and the gospel. Law and gospel rest on the same moral base, and they complement each other. People have always been saved by grace, whether living under the law or the gospel.

The law's excellency affords three uses — a *restraining* use, a *condemning* use, and a *sanctifying* use.

The *restraining* use of the law is seen in public life, as an external restraint on wrongdoers (cf. Galatians 3:23 — 4:7). And it does a "good" (literally, *kalos*, "beautiful") job of this. Without law, everyday public life would be impossible.

The *condemning* use of the law involves spiritual guilt and judgment (cf. Romans 7:7-25). Paul described his experience of this in Romans 7:13 — "Did that which is good, then, become death to me? By no means! But in order that sin might be recognized as sin, it produced death in me through what was good, so that through the commandment sin might become utterly sinful." The law hammered Paul down, so that he might see his own sin and open himself to the gospel. John Stott quotes Martin Luther in this respect:

It is a mighty "hammer" to crush the self-righteousness of human beings. For "it shows them their sin, so that by the recognition of sin they may be humbled, frightened, and worn down, and so may long for grace and for the Blessed Offspring [Christ]." It is in this sense that "the law was our schoolmaster to bring us to Christ."[3]

The third use, that of *sanctifying*, involves defining the parameters of a graced life. No one can live up to the law, but it does lay out God's mind as to our moral and ethical responsibilities toward God and man. We especially see its sanctifying work in Christ's enlightening teaching in the Sermon on the Mount about it (Matthew 5:17ff.). That sermon also shows the condemning use of the law, which demands perfection (cf. Matthew 5:48), and calls the Christian to depend fully on God's grace.

Improper use. But the false teachers in Ephesus were not making proper use of the law. Evidently they were abusing the law by making it out to be a means of righteousness.[4] They represented the law's standards as humanly attainable as they mixed the law with "genealogies" and "myths" (cf. 1:4). This caused believers in Ephesus to misunderstand and ignore God's moral demands[5] and, tragically, to abandon the gospel of grace.

In the midst of the darkness of the heathen world, the errant elders should have been using the law to demonstrate to the unrighteous their deep spiritual need. Thus Paul says, "We also know that law is made not for the righteous [i.e., the self-righteous Ephesian Christians[6]], but for lawbreakers and rebels, the ungodly and sinful, the unholy and irreligious; for those who kill their fathers or mothers, for murderers, for adulterers and perverts, for slave traders and liars and perjurers — and for whatever else is contrary to the sound doctrine" (vv. 9, 10). Paul concocted a grotesque list that begins with six general epithets and then luridly references the fifth through the ninth commands, which have to do with the way human beings abuse other human beings, then ends the list with, "and for whatever else is contrary to the sound doctrine" — literally, "healthy doctrine."[7] The world is morally diseased and must be proclaimed to be condemned by the law.

Paul's point is relentlessly clear: If you are going to proclaim the law in this dark, diseased world, do it as an entrance to preaching the gospel. These men were sitting around with a small group of self-righteous believers, weaving endless teachings into an imagined ladder to high spirituality. For these Ephesian elders, the church had become their mission field. This is fatal. When you begin making Christians your unreached people group, something is wrong.

A telling example of this occurred when a friend of mine was in the hospital. She was visited by another woman who, after being marvelously converted, fell into some narrow, cultish teaching. As they were talking, a nurse came in, and the patient began to talk with her. She was very attentive to the nurse and was obviously looking for an opportunity to share her faith. Her guest just sat there. After the nurse left, the visitor turned to the patient and said, "You are attempting to witness to her, aren't you? Well, that's good for you, but not for me. I'm not interested in that because God has given me the burden of helping Christians straighten out their lives."

Certainly we must spend time discipling new believers, but when we lose our concern for the world and become burdened for Christians alone, we are headed for trouble.

Sound doctrine. Having mentioned "sound doctrine" or "healthy teaching" (v. 10), Paul added a description of it — "that conforms to the glorious gospel of the blessed God, which he entrusted to me" (v. 11). The gospel is the ultimate repository and expression of healthy teaching. Anything that moves away from it or dethrones it as the centerpiece of the church is diseased and dangerous. The gospel is especially good news when set against the backdrop of the bad news of humanity's gross sinfulness. The good news is that Jesus died for "lawbreakers and rebels, the ungodly and sinful, the unholy and irreligious; for those who kill their fathers or mothers, for murderers, for adulterers and perverts, for slave traders and liars and perjurers" (vv. 9, 10) — for you and me!

Gresham Machen, the great Princeton theologian and the founder of Westminster Seminary, understood this.

> What good does it do me to tell me that the type of religion presented in the Bible is a very fine type of religion and that the thing for me to do is just to start practicing that type of religion now? . . . I will tell you, my friend. It does not one tiniest little bit of good. . . . What *I* need first of all is not exhortation but a gospel, not directions for saving myself but knowledge of how God has saved me. Have you any good news for me? That is the question that I ask of you. I know your exhortations will not help me. But if anything has been done to save me, will you not tell me the facts?[8]

4

Gratitude for Grace

1 TIMOTHY 1:12-17

I thank Christ Jesus our Lord, who has given me strength, that he consid-ered me faithful, appointing me to his service. Even though I was once a blasphemer and a persecutor and a violent man, I was shown mercy because I acted in ignorance and unbelief. The grace of our Lord was poured out on me abundantly, along with the faith and love that are in Christ Jesus. Here is a trustworthy saying that deserves full acceptance: Christ Jesus came into the world to save sinners — of whom I am the worst. But for that very reason I was shown mercy so that in me, the worst of sin-ners, Christ Jesus might display his unlimited patience as an example for those who would believe on him and receive eternal life. Now to the King eternal, immortal, invisible, the only God, be honor and glory for ever and ever. Amen.

There is embedded in the heart of the present passage one of the great gospel texts of the apostolic church and of the Reformation. The words of that text are familiar to many: "Here is a trustworthy saying that deserves full acceptance: Christ Jesus came into the world to save sinners — of whom I am the worst" (1:15). This single sentence has been used to encourage count-less souls on their way to Christ. It stands as a frontispiece to the English Reformation because of its effect upon Thomas Bilney, the early Reformation martyr.

Thomas Bilney, known as "little Bilney" due to his diminutive stature, was born in 1495. Because he had a scholarly bent, he studied law at Cambridge, becoming a fellow of Trinity Hall in 1520. But neither study nor ordination brought him peace. Then he began to read the Latin transla-tion of Erasmus's Greek New Testament, and as Bilney described it:

I chanced upon this sentence of St. Paul (O most sweet and com-fortable sentence to my soul!) in 1 Timothy 1. "It is a true saying, and worthy of all men to be embraced, that Christ Jesus came into

the world to save sinners; of whom I am the chief and principal."
This one sentence, through God's instruction and inward working
. . . did so exhilarate my heart, being before wounded with the guilt
of my sins, and being almost in despair, that even immediately I
seemed unto myself inwardly to feel a marvellous comfort and
quietness, insomuch that "my bruised bones leaped for joy" (Psalm
51). After this, the Scripture began to be more pleasant unto me than
the honey or the honey-comb. . . .[1]

Bilney immediately became a central figure in a group of theologians
who met at the famous White Horse Inn, which stood on what is now the corner of King's Parade and Rose Crescent in Cambridge. And there this group
prepared for the Reformation in England. Bilney was arrested in 1527 and
was forced to recant. But little Bilney couldn't contain himself and set off
preaching again in 1531. He was again arrested, then tried and burned at
the stake.[2] His most famous convert, Hugh Latimer, who became the most
prominent preacher of the English Reformation, was inspired by Bilney's
courage and reverently referred to him in his sermons as "St. Bilney."[3]
Latimer, too, died at the stake, in Oxford in 1555.

What a monumental effect 1 Timothy 1:15 has had! And well it should,
for it gives us the gospel in miniature. There is no doubt whatsoever that it
can make "bruised bones" leap for joy.

This verse sits in the center of a section of 1 Timothy in which Paul
digresses about his sheer wonder and gratitude over his experience of grace
and what God's undeserved kindness means for the world. "Gratitude for
Grace" is a perfect summary, but the passage is much more that — it is an
expression of the awesome magnitude of the gospel that we preach.

Contextually, Paul's initial digression in verses 8-11 about the proper
use of the law ended with a mention of the "glorious gospel," and that phrase
inspired another digression — on the magnitude of the gospel of grace. It
begins with the apostle's personal testimony about God's grace to him (vv. 12-
14), extends the grace principle even further — to the world (vv. 15, 16),
and then ends with a passionate doxology to the God of grace in verse 17.

THANKS FOR PERSONAL GRACE (vv. 12-14)

Paul the persecutor. This outpouring of gratitude stemmed from Paul's personal history before meeting Christ. Paul, at that time called Saul, hunted
down Christians, desiring to devastate the church. He was a brutal, implacable, bloody man. Paul's personal biographer, Dr. Luke, described him as a
religious predator: "Meanwhile, Saul was still breathing out murderous
threats against the Lord's disciples. He went to the high priest and asked
him for letters to the synagogues in Damascus, so that if he found any there

who belonged to the Way, whether men or women, he might take them as prisoners to Jerusalem" (Acts 9:1, 2). Paul preyed on those "who belonged to the Way" — the followers of Jesus who said, "I am the way and the truth and the life" (John 14:6). His goal was nothing short of the complete extermination of the Way.

Luke's description here of him as "still breathing out murderous threats" literally reads, "breathing in threats and murder." As A. T. Robertson explained, "Threatening and slaughter had come to be the very breath that Saul breathed, like a warhorse who sniffed the smell of battle."[4] He was a frightening, violent enemy. Paul later described his behavior to Agrippa by saying:

> *"I too was convinced that I ought to do all that was possible to oppose the name of Jesus of Nazareth. And that is just what I did in Jerusalem. On the authority of the chief priests I put many of the saints in prison, and when they were put to death, I cast my vote against them. Many a time I went from one synagogue to another to have them punished, and I tried to force them to blaspheme. In my obsession against them, I even went to foreign cities to persecute them." (Acts 26:9-11)*

He was a callous, pious, self-righteous, bigoted murderer hell-bent on a full-scale inquisition. His hatred soon reached well beyond Jerusalem. He sought and received extradition papers from the Sanhedrin so he could go to Damascus and ravage the Christian community there as well. It was 150 miles to Damascus (about a week's travel), but he would have traveled months for the privilege. Saul the hunter! Saul the man of blood!

The rest of the story has become the treasured deposit of the apostolic church and of all who have valued an apostolic life.

> *As he neared Damascus on his journey, suddenly a light from heaven flashed around him. He fell to the ground and heard a voice say to him, "Saul, Saul, why do you persecute me?" "Who are you, Lord?" Saul asked. "I am Jesus, whom you are persecuting," he replied. "Now get up and go into the city, and you will be told what you must do." (Acts 9:3-6)*

Paul, an untamable tiger, met the Lion of the tribe of Judah at the Damascus off-ramp! He renounced persecuting the church to become a major player in the drama of world evangelization.

Thanks for apostleship. This astounding pre-Christian personal history accounts for his burst of thanksgiving: "I thank Christ Jesus our Lord, who has given me strength, that he considered me faithful, appointing me to his

service. Even though I was once a blasphemer and a persecutor and a violent man, I was shown mercy because I acted in ignorance and unbelief"
(vv. 12, 13).

On one level Paul knew exactly what he had been doing. He had been
wreaking violence and even death on the followers of Christ. And he was
responsible for his sin. On another level he was not culpable because he
"acted in ignorance and unbelief." Negatively, he was truly ignorant of Jesus'
real messianic status. Positively, as a sincere Pharisee, he truly believed
that he was serving God by stamping out the false messianic sect called
"Christians."[5] Paul was not saying that his acting "in ignorance and unbelief"
had earned him mercy. Rather, he meant that it did not disqualify him from
receiving mercy. His having sinned while "in ignorance and unbelief" indicates that he had not knowingly defied God with what the Old Testament
calls sins of a "high hand" — purposeful defiance. (For this basic concept
see, for example, Numbers 15:29, 30.)

On the Damascus Road, Paul (Saul) did not deserve mercy — he was
shown mercy. As the Puritan Thomas Goodwin literally translated this, "I
was bemercied."[6] God met him in his sinful, miserable, self-righteous ignorance and "mercied" him. God did not give Paul what he deserved or what
he had coming to him. That would have been death! Rather, he showed him
mercy.

Paul was not only given salvation but apostleship (v. 12). Paul was given
"strength" in the sense of being made "equal to the task" (cf. NEB). He was
considered "faithful" not because he had been faithful, but because the Lord
considered him worthy of trust and therefore as one who would be faithful.[7]
And then Paul was appointed "to his service."

Thanks for grace. Paul sums up his gratitude in the next phrase: "The
grace of our Lord was poured out upon me abundantly, along with the faith
and love that are in Christ Jesus" (v. 14). The words suggest an overflowing
supply. This is, in fact, the verse from which John Bunyan titled his book
Grace Abounding to the Chief of Sinners.

An artist once submitted a painting of Niagara Falls to an exhibition
but neglected to give it a title. The gallery came up with the whimsical words,
"More to Follow."[8] Niagara Falls, which has been spilling over billions of
gallons per year for thousands of years and has more than met the needs of
those below, is a fit emblem for the floods of God's grace. There always is
more to follow, or as James so beautifully says, "he gives us more grace"
(James 4:6a). There always is more grace. Martin Luther wrote:

> Just as the sun is not darkened by the whole world enjoying its light,
> and could, indeed, light up ten worlds; just as 100,000 lights might
> be lit from one light and not detract from it; just as a learned man
> is able to make a thousand others learned, and the more he gives, the

more he has — so is Christ, our Lord, an infinite source of all grace, so that if the whole world would draw enough grace and truth from it to make the world all angels, yet it would not lose a drop; the fountain always runs over, full of grace.

There is no hyperbole here. Paul expressed the facts with careful precision at the end of Romans 5 when he said, "But where sin increased, grace increased all the more, so that, just as sin reigned in death, so also grace might reign through righteousness to bring eternal life through Jesus Christ our Lord" (Romans 5:20, 21). There is no conceivable accumulation of sin that grace cannot overflow. Grace increases the more we need it, and there is always "more to follow"!

God's grace is beautiful, for it not only outstrips our sins, but it instills as its visible expressions "the faith and love that are in Christ Jesus" (v. 14b). When grace abounds, "faith" and "love" likewise abound. Hearts like Paul's, previously filled with unbelief, are now filled with faith; hearts once filled with hatred are filled with love.

A graced life soars on love and faith. Paul is personally thankful — thankful for his salvation — thankful for his apostleship — thankful for mercy — thankful for grace — thankful for faith — thankful for love.

THANKS FOR GENERAL GRACE (vv. 15, 16)

Salvation for the worst. Now Paul's very personal praise for grace widens to praise for its universal significance, beginning with the grand verse that made Thomas Bilney's bones leap for joy: "Here is a trustworthy saying that deserves full acceptance: Christ Jesus came into the world to save sinners — of whom I am the worst" (v. 15).

Some have accused the apostle of being disingenuous and projecting a false humility. The "worst" of sinners? The first (as the Greek says) of sinners? *Numero uno*? "Come on, Paul! There are far greater sinners than you! You never even dreamed of the sins I do." But Paul was utterly sincere. What he says here is in perfect accord with what he says elsewhere of himself (cf. 1 Corinthians 15:9; Ephesians 3:8). This is authentic Pauline psychology and theology.

Also note that he did not say, "I *was* the worst of sinners, but "I *am* the worst." This is the thinking of a healthy regenerate heart. Saving Christianity never endows one with a sense of superiority. Paul knew what he had been and what he was and what he continued to be in himself. This knowledge even increased with the years, as he understood his heart even better than at first. Paul's confession here is no doubt what drew Thomas Bilney, who had been searching so long and so hard. There was hope for little Bilney's dark heart.

This is the very soul of the gospel — "Christ Jesus came into the world to save sinners — of whom I am the worst." This is the awareness of a graced heart.

Hope for the worst. Now comes the great hope: "But for that very reason I was shown mercy so that in me, the worst of sinners, Christ Jesus might display his unlimited patience as an example for those who would believe on him and receive eternal life" (v. 16). If God could and would do this for a man who put Christian believers in prison and cast his vote for their deaths — a man who provided the prototype of the Inquisition — a master of religious thuggery, a Torquemada — there is hope for all of us! Paul calls to us across the centuries, "Don't despair. He saved me, the worst of sinners — a religious sinner who persecuted Christ himself (cf. Acts 9:4) — and he can save you!"

In 1918 in Tokyo Tokichi Ichii was hung for murder. He had been sent to prison more than twenty times. He was as tough as men get. In response to his hatred and violence, on one occasion after attacking a prison guard he was bound and gagged and hung from the ceiling so that his toes barely reached the ground. Before receiving his death sentence, he received a New Testament sent by two Christian missionaries, a Miss West and a Miss McDonald — resulting in the notorious criminal's coming to know Christ. When Tokichi was sentenced to death, he accepted that as "the fair, impartial judgment of God."

During a visit Miss West directed him to read 2 Corinthians 6:8-10, which deals with suffering. There Mr. Ichii noted, among other things, the line "poor, yet making many rich." He wrote of this:

> This certainly does not apply to the evil life I led before I repented. But perhaps in the future, someone in the world may hear that the most desperate villain who ever lived repented of his sins and was saved by the power of Christ, and so may come to repent also. Then it may be that though I am poor myself, I shall be able to make many rich.

Tokichi died on the scaffold with great humility. His last words were, "My soul, purified, today returns to the City of God."[9]

God through his grace had reached a man who called himself "the most desperate villain who ever lived," just as he had reached "the worst of sinners" 1,900 years before. God's grace can reach *anybody*.

What we must grasp here (and grasp it with its full integrity and passion) is that Paul was absolutely convinced of the truth of his words. Christ Jesus' power and his eagerness to save anyone who turned to him both informed and drove Paul's missionary heart. Paul believed this with his whole being. There was no doubt in his mind. Why? Because he knew Jesus' atoning death was sufficient. Why else? Because when he received the Savior, Jesus gave his righteousness to him. As a result Paul knew by experience mercy, grace, love, faith, and apostleship. And he was "the worst"!

This conviction must be ours as well. This is the reality that drives me. God has saved me, and if he can do that in my life, he can do it for anybody. I believe this with all my heart.

No one on this earth is beyond grace, and only divine grace makes the difference. It is all of God — just as it was for Paul on the Damascus Road. The hunter was the hunted. As the Lord told Ananias regarding Paul, "This man is my chosen instrument to carry my name" (Acts 9:15).

"Christ Jesus came into the world to save sinners" — number one sinners like you and me. It is all by his grace. If you have not already come, come now!

PRAISE THE GOD OF GRACE (v. 17)

At this point Paul is ready to explode with a doxology. John Calvin remarks:

> His enthusiasm breaks out into this exclamation, since he could find no words to express his gratitude. These sudden outbursts of Paul's come mainly when the vastness of the subject overpowers him and makes him break off what he is saying. For what could be more wonderful than Paul's conversion? At the same time he admonishes us all by his example, that we should never think of the grace shown in God's calling without being lost in wondering admiration. This sublime praise of God's grace swallows up all the memory of his former life. How great a deep is the glory of God![10]

We should also notice here that though Paul has been emphasizing the work of God in personal, immanent terms of God's mercy, grace, and patience, the doxology speaks of God in awesome, transcendent terms. This is because when the apostle considers what God has done, he can only speak in the most stupendous terms — "Now to the King eternal, immortal, invisible, the only God, be honor and glory for ever and ever. Amen" (v. 17).

We see here four awesome designations for our great God.

  • Paul calls him "the King eternal." God is the King of all ages who sovereignly governs every age before creation, after creation, to the final age, and on into eternity.
  • Paul calls him "immortal." God is not subject to decay or destruction and therefore is in the most absolute sense "imperishable, incorruptible, and immortal."[11]
  • Paul calls him "invisible," for the physical eye cannot see him.

He "lives in unapproachable light, whom no one has seen or can see" (1 Timothy 6:16). All that human beings have ever seen of him (other than the incarnate Christ) are glimpses of his glory.

• Paul calls him "the only God" (*mono theo*). He alone is what he is. Of himself God has declared, "I am the LORD, and there is no other" (Isaiah 45:18).

To this awesome God of grace, Paul invokes "honor and glory for ever and ever. Amen."

In conclusion, our song of grace must follow the same contours as Paul's song.

First, praise for *personal* grace, like that of Paul as expressed in verses 12 and 14. "I thank Christ Jesus our Lord. . . . The grace of our Lord was poured out on me abundantly, along with the faith and love that are in Christ Jesus" (v. 14). Such personal praise for the flood of personal grace that washed over his soul buoyed Paul higher and higher!

Second, praise for *general* grace as expressed in Bilney's life verse: "Here is a trustworthy saying that deserves full acceptance: Christ Jesus came into the world to save sinners — of whom I am the worst" (v. 15).

> *Amazing grace! how sweet the sound*
> *That saved a wretch like me!*
> *I once was lost, but now am found,*
> *Was blind, but now I see.*
>
> *'Twas grace that taught my heart to fear,*
> *And grace my fears relieved;*
> *How precious did that grace appear*
> *The hour I first believed!*
> *("Amazing Grace,"*
> *John Newton, 1779)*

Such amazing grace in the life of John Newton, former slave trader, confirmed the offer of life-changing grace for all who respond to Christ. "But for that very reason I was shown mercy so that in me, the worst of sinners, Christ Jesus might display his unlimited patience as an example for those who would believe on him and receive eternal life" (v. 16).

Our song of grace should end on the same awesome note as Paul's: "Now to the King eternal, immortal, invisible, the only God, be honor and glory for ever and ever. Amen" (v. 17).

5

Fighting the Good Fight

1 TIMOTHY 1:18-20

Timothy, my son, I give you this instruction in keeping with the prophecies once made about you, so that by following them you may fight the good fight, holding on to faith and a good conscience. Some have rejected these and so have shipwrecked their faith. Among them are Hymenaeus and Alexander, whom I have handed over to Satan to be taught not to blaspheme.

As mentioned earlier, the most notable convert of the early English Reformer and martyr Thomas Bilney was Hugh Latimer, who like Bilney died at the stake. Latimer was easily the most popular of the reforming preachers — full of the Word, with a vivid preaching style. He preached justification by faith alone but also preached that a justified man will show it in the way he lives. He was unsparing of other preachers' shortcomings: "Since lording and loitering hath come up, preaching hath come down. . . . They hawk, they hunt, they card, they dice."[1] He accused his fellow preachers of "pampering of their paunches . . . munching in their mangers, and moiling in their gay manors and mansions."[2]

On one occasion he was invited to preach at Hampton Court before Henry VIII, and he predictably offended the king. Henry commanded Latimer to preach again the following Sunday and to make an apology. Latimer addressed himself as he began to preach:

> Hugh Latimer, dost thou know before whom thou art this day to speak? To the high and mighty monarch, the king's most excellent majesty, who can take away thy life if thou offendest; therefore, take heed that thou speakest not a word that may displease; but then consider well, Hugh, dost thou not know from whence thou comest; upon whose message thou art sent? Even by the great and mighty God! who is all present, and who beholdest all thy ways, and who

is able to cast thy soul into hell! Therefore, take care that thou deliverest thy message faithfully.[3]

Then Hugh Latimer preached the same sermon he had preached the week before — with even more energy! What a man of God! There can be no doubt that Hugh Latimer, like his mentor Thomas Bilney, fought the good fight. Those sixteenth-century saints embodied apostolic steadfastness.

FIGHTING (vv. 18, 19a)

A charge to fight well. This steadfastness, this forthrightness, this courage, this ability to carry out one's task — to finish well — is what Paul wished for young, shy Timothy when he gave him this famous charge: "Timothy, my son, I give you this instruction in keeping with the prophecies once made about you, so that by following them you may fight the good fight" (v. 18).

Evidently at some specific time (perhaps at Timothy's commissioning) heartening prophecies had been made about him. Though we do not know when or where this happened, information from other Scriptures allow us to form a picture. We know that when Paul recruited Timothy, "The brothers at Lystra and Iconium spoke well of him" (Acts 16:2). We know that at some point there was an event in which three things happened to Timothy: 1) he was given a spiritual gift; 2) a prophecy was made over him; and 3) the elders laid hands on him. We know this from 1 Timothy 4:14 (italics added): "Do not neglect your *gift*, which was given you through a *prophetic message* when the body of elders *laid their hands* on you."

Very likely the gift he received was that of preaching or exhortation because Paul encouraged him in his second letter, saying, "For this reason I remind you to fan into flame the gift of God, which is in you through the laying on of my hands. For God did not give us a spirit of timidity, but a spirit of power, of love and of self-discipline" (2 Timothy 1:6, 7). Paul's urging Timothy not to succumb to timidity suggests that the gift he was to fan was preaching. And it appears that Timothy was wonderfully stirred by this event and made a memorable confession because in the final chapter of 1 Timothy Paul urges him: "Fight the good fight of the faith. Take hold of the eternal life to which you were called when you made your good confession in the presence of many witnesses" (6:12).

So the picture we get is of a great spiritual event in Timothy's life in which wonderful prophecies were made about his future gospel ministry as various people spoke of his fitness and the powerful voice he would become. At that time the elders solemnly laid their hands on him and prayed over him, and he was remarkably gifted for ministry. It was such a monumental event that normally shy Timothy rose and made a "good confession in the presence of many witnesses."

Paul was inciting Timothy to remember his commissioning and was thus motivating him to carry out "this instruction" (more accurately, "this command"), referring to his charge to "command certain men not to teach false doctrines any longer nor to devote themselves to myths and endless genealogies" (vv. 3b, 4a). The sense is, "This instruction that you are to give to the false teachers to desist from propagating their erroneous ideas is in keeping with the wonderful prophecies made about your spiritual usefulness. Remember these prophecies, Timothy. Live them out. Be strong. Carry out the command. And in so doing, fight the good fight!"

These high spiritual hopes that others held for him constituted a powerful appeal. We have all experienced the pulse-quickening motivation of others' expectations upon our lives. Perhaps it was your grandmother's hopeful belief that because you were the smartest child in your school, you would surely win that spelling bee. Oh, you tried, but *rhinoceros* did you in. Or maybe it was a football game, with the conference championship at stake. When you glanced into the stands and saw your family there, cheering you on, you played harder than ever!

I recall one Sunday morning, about a year after I'd come to College Church (which I still pastor), when the chairman of the Council of Elders ran up to me before the service saying, "Pastor, I have the most wonderful news! Dr. Stephen Olford and Dr. Alan Redpath are here for the service." I felt a twinge in my stomach and smiled weakly. I do not think the sermon was exceptional that morning, but that was not due to a lack of effort!

The expectations voiced for Timothy at his commission were prophetic and from the Lord. And he did live them out and "fight the good fight." Ultimately this charge is for all of us, regardless of our place and calling in life. The martial, fighting language is significant. Paul chose it deliberately and used it more than once, in various forms. We are to *fight*.

Conflict — spiritual warfare — is especially the province of leadership. The evangelical cause owes much to Gresham Machen, the Princeton divine who so brilliantly stood against modernism in the 1930s. Of him Pearl Buck wrote: "I admired Dr. Machen very much while I disagreed with him on every point. And we had much the same fate. I was kicked out of the back door of the church and he was kicked out of the front one. He retaliated by establishing a church of his own. . . . The man was admirable. He never gave in one inch to anyone."[4] Machen's life was that of the consummate Christian gentleman fighting a great fight!

How to fight well. The question we must ask is, how can we fight the good fight? Simply by "holding on to faith and a good conscience" (v. 19a). This short phrase is deceptively comprehensive because, as John Stott points out, it contains what is *objectively* and *subjectively* necessary to "fight the good fight." On the one hand, we must hold on to the *objective* deposit of the "faith," meaning the apostolic faith. On the other hand, we must hold tight to the *subjective* treasure of "a good conscience."[5]

So we see first of all that if we are to fight well, we must have a solid grasp on the objective content of our faith, the essentials. As we asked several chapters ago, *If you love God while knowing little about him, will you love him less by knowing more about him?* Of course not! The deeper the knowledge of our infinite, loving, merciful, gracious, holy God, the deeper our love will become. The sad truth for so many Christians is that their love of God languishes due to their lack of knowledge of him. They simply do not know much about God. They may have a relationship with him, but it is stunted by their ignorance of him.

Evangelical ignorance is a fact. Most Christians cannot name the Ten Commandments. Many cannot even name five of them. Many do not even know where they are found. If we are to love God as we ought, we must know the doctrine of God, the doctrine of Christ, the doctrine of salvation, just to name a few. But our knowledge must not come from textbook dogmatics but from the Bible — its history, its narratives, its poetry, its parables, its didactic passages, its apocalyptic sections. The Bible provides a multifaceted, many-textured, vital knowledge of God that anoints the mind and affections with love. I cannot urge enough the necessity of knowing the Word of God. Begin by learning one book, perhaps Romans. Know its theme, its divisions, its unity. What you know and believe about God is everything, because what you know and believe will determine how you live. Doctrine determines conduct. Right doctrine makes it possible to "fight the good fight."

Second, we see that if we are to fight well, we must hold on to "a good conscience." The conscience was an immense issue for Paul, like a looming planet that filled his whole horizon. Three other times in the Pastorals Paul referenced the importance of a healthy conscience. In 1:5 he told Timothy that the purpose for commanding the elders to stop teaching false doctrine was to bring them back to "love, which comes from a pure heart and a *good conscience* and a sincere faith." In 3:9 he taught that church leaders "must keep hold of the deep truths of the faith with a *clear conscience*." In 2 Timothy 1:3 he substantiated his own ministry, saying, "I thank God, whom I serve, as my forefathers did, with a *clear conscience*."

The rest of the New Testament testifies to Paul's empowerment through "a good conscience." He courageously took his stand before the Sanhedrin, looked them straight in the eye, and declared, "My brothers, I have fulfilled my duty to God in all *good conscience* to this day" (Acts 23:1). Then standing before Governor Felix he confidently declared, "So I strive always to keep my *conscience clear* before God and man" (Acts 24:16). To the Romans Paul voiced his amazing affirmation of love for his people as true because it was spoken with a clear conscience: "I speak the truth in Christ — I am not lying, my *conscience* confirms it in the Holy Spirit" (Romans 9:1). Thus we see that for Paul "a good conscience" is at the very root of fighting the good fight.

Not only that, but by coupling "faith and a good conscience" as he has, Paul was saying that "a good conscience" is key to maintaining a sound "faith." John Calvin put this succinctly: "A bad conscience is the mother of all heresies."[6] That is all too true! I have seen friends with whom I spent a whole night praying for the world, or another who I never dreamed would stray, so chronically violate their consciences that they later gave up the faith. When morals slip, doctrine ebbs, and the fight is soon lost.

The necessity of a clear conscience should loom planet-like on our horizons. Conscious disobedience will kill our spiritual life. Obedience to Christ may appear to be legalistic by society's standards, but our conscience calls out. Some habit may be okay for others, but for you it is wrong because your conscience says so. There may be an attitude or thought pattern that no one else can detect and you are free to nourish — at the expense of your conscience. It may be an attachment that is wrong, but the only voice telling you so is your conscience. If your inner voice calls to you, heed it. Do not sin against your conscience. This is all so hard — especially today when conscience is dismissed as a mere safety device, collectively created to protect civility. But God's Word is clear — we must cultivate "a good conscience."

"A good conscience" is the mother of a sound faith and the wherewithal to fight the good fight. This has been my experience. I can stand up to substantial pressure if my conscience is clear. But without a clear conscience, there is no power to endure or resist.

In the last chapter we considered the early martyr of the English Reformation Thomas Bilney, who was burned in 1531, and also Hugh Latimer, who was burned in 1555. There were also two other martyrs who died within a year of each other — Nicholas Ridley who was burned along with Latimer in 1555 and Thomas Cranmer who died at the stake in 1556.

Thomas Cranmer had served as Archbishop of Canterbury. But he is most remembered for his 1549 and 1552 editions of the Book of Common Prayer. (I had the privilege of viewing the original during a private tour of Jesus College some years ago with my two sons.) Cranmer had been forced to watch the burnings of Latimer and Ridley, and after much pressure he signed a number of recantations. But on the eve of his execution his courage returned as he stood in St. Mary's Church in Oxford. Instead of repeating his recantations, he repudiated them. Why? He said:

> And now I come to the great thing which so much troubleth my conscience, more than any thing that ever I did or said in my whole life, and that is the setting abroad of a writing contrary to the truth, which now here I renounce and refuse as things written with my

hand contrary to the truth which I thought in my heart, and written
for fear of death, and to save my life, if it might be. . . . And foras-
much as my hand hath offendeth, writing contrary to my heart,
therefore my hand shall first be punished; for when I come to the
fire, it shall first be burned.[7]

When he came to the stake the next day, "Then it was, that stretching
out his right hand, he held it unshrinkingly in the fire till it was burnt to a
cinder, even before his body was injured, frequently exclaiming, 'This
unworthy right hand!'"[8] What power there is in faith and a clear conscience!
Thomas Cranmer fought the good fight!

Our warfare is far less dramatic. Nevertheless, God's Word holds true.
There are two necessities for staying on course to the end. First is "holding
on to faith," the objective deposit of the apostolic faith — right doctrine.
Second is "holding on to . . . a good conscience" — the subjective treasure
of a holy life. Armed with faith and a clear conscience the Christian can withstand all Hell! With faith and a clear conscience you will finish the fight well.

FAILING (vv. 19b, 20)

Notable shipwrecks. While some of the elders in Ephesus had fought well,
others had failed miserably, and Paul noted them by name: "Some have
rejected these and so have shipwrecked their faith. Among them are
Hymenaeus and Alexander" (vv. 19b, 20a). Their failure was rooted in the
loss of "a good conscience." The plural in the *New International Version's*
"Some have rejected these" is misleading because "rejected" refers in the
Greek to "a good conscience."[9] Hymenaeus and Alexander willfully and
deliberately rejected their conscience.

And they literally shipwrecked not "their faith" but *the* faith, as Gordon
Fee points out.[10] Their doctrine was on the rocks. We know that Hymenaeus
went overboard on his eschatology because 2 Timothy 2:17, 18 mentions
"Hymenaeus and Philetus, who have wandered away from the truth. They
say that the resurrection has already taken place, and they destroy the faith of
some." Perhaps Alexander was also crazed by this "over-realized" eschatology. The point is, they wandered away from the gospel — and it all began
with the deliberate rejection of their conscience.

Rescuing the shipwrecked. Did Paul write these two men off? Not at
all! Rather, he "handed [them] over to Satan to be taught not to blaspheme"
(v. 20b). The purpose was remedial — so they would learn "not to blaspheme." Paul used the same language in 1 Corinthians 5:5, where he said,
"Hand this man over to Satan, so that the sinful nature may be destroyed
and his spirit saved on the day of the Lord." Here Paul fervently hoped that
both Hymenaeus and Alexander would be restored.

This "hand[ing] over to Satan" was excommunication. Paul cast Hymenaeus and Alexander out of the church — away from God's care and protection and thus under the power of Satan. It was Paul's intention that they be buffeted by Satan and that their separation from God in this way be brought home to them by their forced separation from God's people.

Though it might appear otherwise, Paul's attitude was one of grace, severe grace, as he explained in a different circumstance to the Thessalonians: "If anyone does not obey our instruction in this letter, take special note of him. Do not associate with him, in order that he may feel ashamed. Yet do not regard him as an enemy, but warn him as a brother" (2 Thessalonians 3:14, 15). This is the proper work of the church, and a church that takes its work seriously will do this when the occasion requires.

The message is clear: We, like Timothy, are called to "fight the good fight." Our method is twofold — hanging on to "faith" and hanging on to "a good conscience." This is the way Paul and Timothy fought — as did their Reformation counterparts Thomas Bilney, Hugh Latimer, Nicholas Ridley, and Thomas Cranmer.

Lord! Arm your people with faith and a good conscience. Amen.

6

Praying and Living
for the Gospel

1 Timothy 2:1-10

I urge, then, first of all, that requests, prayers, intercession and thanksgiv-
ing be made for everyone — for kings and all those in authority, that we
may live peaceful and quiet lives in all godliness and holiness. This is good,
and pleases God our Savior, who wants all men to be saved and to come
to a knowledge of the truth. For there is one God and one mediator between
God and men, the man Christ Jesus, who gave himself as a ransom for all
men — the testimony given in its proper time. And for this purpose I was
appointed a herald and an apostle — I am telling the truth, I am not lying
— and a teacher of the true faith to the Gentiles. I want men everywhere
to lift up holy hands in prayer, without anger or disputing. I also want
women to dress modestly, with decency and propriety, not with braided hair
or gold or pearls or expensive clothes, but with good deeds, appropriate for
women who profess to worship God.

On a dangerous seacoast where shipwrecks often occur stood a lifesaving station. The building was just a hut, and there was only one boat, but
the few devoted members kept a constant watch over the sea and with no
thought for themselves went out day and night tirelessly searching for the
lost. Many of those who were rescued and also others from the surrounding
area wished to become associated with the station and to give their time,
money, and effort for the support of its work. New boats were bought and
new crews trained. The lifesaving station grew.

In time some of the crew became concerned that the station was so crude
and poorly equipped. They felt that a more commodious place should be provided as the first refuge of those snatched from the sea. The emergency cots
were replaced with beds, and better furniture was purchased for the enlarged
building. The station became a popular gathering place for its members,

and they decorated it beautifully and furnished it exquisitely. Fewer members were now interested in leaving the plush station to go to sea on lifesaving missions. So they hired surrogates to do that work. However, they retained the lifesaving motif in the club's decorations, and a ceremonial lifeboat lay in the room where club initiations were held.

One dark stormy night a large ship was wrecked off the coast, and the hired crews brought in boatloads of cold, wet, half-drowned people. They were dirty and sick and obviously from distant shores. The station was in chaos. The event was so traumatic that the people contracted for outbuildings to be constructed so future shipwrecks could be processed with less disruption.

Eventually a rift developed in the station. Most of the members wanted to discontinue the station's lifesaving activities as being unpleasant and a hindrance to their normal social life. Some insisted, however, that rescue was their primary purpose and pointed out that they were still called a lifesaving station. But the latter were ignored and told that if they wanted to keep lifesaving as their primary purpose, they could begin their own station down the coast, which they did. Over time those individuals fell prey to the same temptations as the first group, coming to care more about comforting one another than rescuing the perishing. After a while a few, remembering their real purpose, split off to establish yet another lifesaving station. And on and on it went. Today if you visit that seacoast, you will find a number of impressive lifesaving stations along the shore. Sadly, shipwrecks still occur in those waters, but most people are lost.[1]

"The Life-Saving Station" is a parable with deep historical roots that reach all the way back to the coast off ancient Ephesus. Paul's great fear was that the vibrant lifesaving station in Ephesus, the principal lighthouse in Asia Minor, would put out its light or forget its mission. Indeed, there had been shipwrecks from even their own number, men like elders Hymenaeus and Alexander who had abandoned "faith and a good conscience" (1:19). These interior defections so early in the lifesaving ministry of the church at Ephesus were the reason Paul wrote Timothy, who was to "command" such men "not to teach false doctrines" (1:3).

Now at the beginning of chapter 2, Paul gives explicit instructions to the Ephesian churches on how to pray and live so that the lifesaving gospel will continue to go out to all people — praying and living for the gospel. Paul's concern was that false teaching by the likes of Hymenaeus and Alexander was turning the Ephesian congregations into elitist clubs that focused on "myths and endless genealogies" instead of the life-giving gospel (1:4). His concern is easily seen in this section because he uses terms that stress the universal range of the church's responsibility — verse 1, "prayers . . . for *everyone*"; verse 4, the divine desire for "*all* men to be saved"; verse 6, Jesus "gave himself as a ransom for *all* men"; and verse 7, which emphasizes ministry to "the Gentiles" and not just the Jews. The universality of the gospel — the fact that it is for everyone — is Paul's passion.

A CALL TO PRAYER AND HOLY LIVING (vv. 1, 2)

Prayer. Paul begins with a shot at the exclusivist attitudes being taught by the false teachers: "I urge, then, first of all, that requests, prayers, intercession and thanksgiving be made for everyone" (v. 1). Clearly, the scope of Christian prayer is to be expansive and expanding. John Stott, long-time pastor of All Souls in London, has observed how far short of this the church often falls.

> Some years ago I attended public worship in a certain church. The pastor was absent on holiday, and a lay elder led the pastoral prayer. He prayed that the pastor might enjoy a good vacation (which was fine), and that two lady members of the congregation might be healed (which was also fine; we should pray for the sick). But that was all. The intercession can hardly have lasted thirty seconds. I came away saddened, sensing that this church worshiped a little village god of their own devising. There was no recognition of the needs of the world, and no attempt to embrace the world in prayer.[2]

Such restricted sympathies must never be tolerated corporately or privately. Our prayers must embrace the globe as well as our nearest and dearest. I cannot help but recall F. B. Meyer's account of awaking early one morning at a conference with A. B. Simpson (founder of the Christian and Missionary Alliance) and discovering Simpson weeping in prayer as he clutched a globe. May his tribe increase!

Living. Along with this general exhortation to wide-ranging prayer, Paul added, "for kings and all those in authority, that we may live peaceful and quiet lives in all godliness and holiness" (v. 2). This was not a prayer to live a quiet middle-class life, free from stress, as some critics have charged. Paul never encouraged that. Rather, he warned in 2 Timothy, "In fact, everyone who wants to live a godly life in Christ Jesus will be persecuted" (3:12; cf. 2 Timothy 1:8). His prayer here for those in authority implicitly asked for peaceful conditions in which Christians could freely live out exemplary lives, so the unsaved would speak well of Christ and their teaching. Indeed, Paul used identical language in 1 Thessalonians 4:11, 12 exhorting believers "to lead a quiet life . . . so that your daily life may win the respect of outsiders."[3]

The indisputable fact is, the best argument *for* and *against* Christianity is Christianity — or more precisely, how Christians practice their

Christianity! Christianity lived out can make inroads where few other things can.

As far as we know, Thomas Huxley, the famous agnostic, never put his faith in Christ, but he did experience some degree of conviction. Toward the end of his life, Huxley was a guest at a retreat in a country home. Sunday came, and most of the guests went to church. Naturally, Huxley did not go. Alone, he approached a man known to have a simple and radiant Christian faith. Huxley said, "Suppose you don't go to church today. Suppose you stay at home and you tell me quite simply what your Christian faith means to you and why you are a Christian." "But," said the man, "you could demolish my arguments in an instant. I am not clever enough to argue with you." Huxley gently replied, "I don't want to argue with you; I just want you to tell me simply what this Christ means to you." The man stayed and did as Huxley had requested. When he finished, there were tears in the old agnostic's eyes.[4]

When we observe how the church of Christ has prayed and lived down through the centuries, there is little doubt that the slow progress of the gospel is due to prayerlessness more than anything else. God works powerfully through prayer.

In fact, prayer brought down the Berlin Wall. In May 1989 at Leipzig, in the historic Nicolai Kirche (St. Nicholas Church) where the Reformation had been introduced exactly 450 years earlier, a small group began to meet in one of the church's rooms to read the Sermon on the Mount and pray for peace. The group expanded and moved to a larger room and finally began to meet in the church's nave, which began to fill up. Alarmed, the Communist authorities sent officials to attend. They threatened the gatherers and temporarily jailed some. On prayer nights they blocked the city's nearest Autobahn off-ramp. Then on October 9, 1989, some 2,000 individuals crowded in to pray for peace, and another 10,000 gathered outside. And soon the Berlin Wall came down.[5] Coincidence? No. This was the kind response of a caring, all-powerful God to the prayers of his people.

Think what would happen to the witness and power of the church if a great mass of Christians began to pray for everyone with unified passion and focus! Mighty walls of unbelief would fall, and personal witness would penetrate strongholds with incredible power. Lifesaving stations would rescue the perishing.

THE AWESOME GROUNDS BEHIND THE CALL (vv. 3-7)

The grounds for Paul's call to pray for all people are threefold — first, God's desire (vv. 3, 4); second, God's work (vv. 5, 6); and third, Paul's missionary call (v. 7). This triad forms one of the most significant missions and evangelism passages in the New Testament.

God's desire. "This is good," says Paul (referring to prayers "for every-one"), "and pleases God our Savior, who wants all men to be saved and to come to a knowledge of the truth" (vv. 3, 4). Thus Paul assaulted the exclu-sivism that had engulfed some of the lifesaving stations in Ephesus — the "Us Four and No More" clubs. Their mission field had become "the frozen chosen," their mission that of instilling a deeper-life chill, lowering the temperature of their souls. This kind of spiritual elitism feeds on the classism and racism and tribalism and nationalism that comes so naturally to us sin-ful human souls.

It was this kind of thing that so maddened William Carey when his church leadership told him, "Young man, if God is going to convert the heathen, he will do it without your help or ours." That response drove him out of his church and on to India, where he became the father of modern missions. (My wife and I named our youngest son William Carey Hughes in honor of the universality of the gospel and as a hope for his life.)

Now it is a fact that the Scriptures, and Paul in particular, teach divine election. Paul says in various passages: "But we ought always to thank God for you, brothers loved by the Lord, because from the beginning God chose you to be saved" (2 Thessalonians 2:13), "For he chose us in him before the creation of the world to be holy and blameless in his sight. In love he pre-destined us to be adopted as his sons through Jesus Christ, in accordance with his pleasure and will" (Ephesians 1:4, 5). "And those he predestined, he also called; those he called, he also justified; those he justified, he also glo-rified" (Romans 8:30; cf. Matthew 11:25-27; John 6:37-44; Acts 13:48; 1 Peter 1:1, 2).

But the Scriptures also teach the complementary truth so clearly stated in verse 4: God "wants all men to be saved and to come to a knowledge of the truth." This, of course, does not mean that God wills everyone to be saved. If he did, all would be saved because no one can resist his will. What we have here is an expression of the divine desire that brought about the Incarnation and Christ's death on the cross — "For God so loved the world that he gave his one and only Son, that whoever believes in him shall not per-ish but have eternal life" (John 3:16). We see it in the drama on the cross where Jesus, with his arms nailed wide as if to embrace the world, prays over the soldiers who crucified him: "Father, forgive them, for they do not know what they are doing" (Luke 23:34). And later he promised the thief, "Today you will be with me in paradise" (Luke 23:43).

This divine desire informed and drove Paul to engage in a worldwide mission. It is not our responsibility or capability to solve the puzzle of divine sovereignty and human responsibility. It is our task to preach the gospel universally — to every tongue and people regardless of class or rank. It is our mission to proclaim what God wants us to proclaim. Lifesaving was Paul's business — and it is ours.

God's sovereign work. The second ground behind God's call to pray and witness to the lost is the work of God that is here given confessional expression: "For there is one God and one mediator between God and men, the man Christ Jesus, who gave himself as a ransom for all men — the testimony given in its proper time" (vv. 5, 6). Everything rests on God's work.

God's unity. It rests on his unity — he is "one God." This truth has been perverted by some to support their exclusivistic delusion — "He is ours, and not anyone else's!" However, the fact that he is the one and only God supports the universality of the gospel — he must then be the God of both Jews and Gentiles. Our *exclusive* faith (there is one God, and no other) leads necessarily to our *inclusive* mission (the "one God . . . wants all men to be saved").

God the Son's mediatorship. Our exclusive God has an exclusive mediator — "and one mediator between God and men, the man Christ Jesus" (v. 5). Literally this reads, "One also is the mediator between God and man."[6] Jesus is the only go-between. Because he is both God and man, he can represent both sides equally. In effect, Jesus answered in his person the cry of Job, "If only there were someone to arbitrate between us, to lay his hand upon us both" (Job 9:33). Jesus lays one hand, so to speak, on the Father and the other on his children — he is our "mediator."

God the Son's payment. The final element of God's divine work is the infinite ransom paid by God the Son, "who gave himself as a ransom for all men — the testimony given in its proper time" (v. 6). His payment is effectual for all who believe. As Paul says later in 4:9, 10, "This is a trustworthy saying that deserves full acceptance (and for this we labor and strive), that we have put our hope in the living God, who is the Savior of all men, and especially of those who believe."

So we see from this pulsing confessional statement that everything is of God! This inspires us to live a life of prayer and mission. The desire of God — "who wants all men to be saved and to come to a knowledge of truth" — is to be our desire. We are called to be lifesavers.

Third, Paul's commission. As a final argument Paul referenced his own special role in the spread of the gospel — "And for this purpose I was appointed a herald and an apostle — I am telling the truth, I am not lying — and a teacher of the true faith to the Gentiles" (v. 7). The fact that God chose Paul to preach the gospel to the Gentiles is proof that God desires to reach all people and proof of his children's obligation to pray for and reach out to everyone.

According to this (vv. 1-7), the local church has a global, lifesaving mission. According to verse 1, the church is to pray for all people. According to verse 7, it is to proclaim the gospel to all people. The universal concern of the church arises from the universal concern of God. As John Stott says so well:

> It is because there is one God and one mediator that all people must be included in the church's prayers and proclamation. It is the unity of God and the uniqueness of Christ which demand the universality of the gospel. God's desire and Christ's death concern all people; therefore the church's duty concerns all people too, reaching out to them both in earnest prayer and in urgent witness.[7]

We are to be God's people, joyfully declaring Christ's glory among the nations!

A CALL TO A SAVING LIFESTYLE (vv. 8-10)

Paul concludes by saying nearly the same thing he had already said regarding praying and living when he introduced this section.

Praying. "I want men everywhere to lift up holy hands in prayer, without anger or disputing" (v. 8). He assumes they will pray with upraised hands, but his concern is not about body posture but about the attitude with which they will pray. He wants them to be free from anger and quarrels. He wants to see unified petitions go up for everyone — for the whole world! What grace this would produce in mission!

Living. He also wants the church to give careful attention to lifestyle — "I also want women to dress modestly, with decency and propriety, not with braided hair or gold or pearls or expensive clothes" (v. 9). Paul is not categorically forbidding women to style their hair or wear jewelry or nice clothing. Rather, he was forbidding the imitation of the elaborate new hairstyles and extravagant dress of the Roman court as depicted on the Roman coins in circulation at that time, as S. M. Baugh has shown in his definitive study of Ephesus in the first century. These styles connoted the excessive luxury and licentiousness of the Roman court. "Today," Baugh says, "it is the equivalent of warning Christians away from imitation of styles set by promiscuous pop singers or actresses."[8] Paul's overriding concern was that the way Christians deported themselves would not detract from but enhance their gospel mission, so that they adorn the message "with good deeds, appropriate for women who profess to worship God" (v. 10).

Everything in life is meant to enhance our carrying out God's desire for "all men to be saved and to come to a knowledge of the truth" — down to the attitudes with which we pray and the way we dress.

Today thousands of lifesaving stations have turned into social clubs. Their architecture with crossed masts pointing to heaven and pulpits at the bow tell us what they were once meant for. Ships still founder on their shores, but no soul has been saved for years. There are no prayers for the perishing. There is no outstretched hand. No one wants to risk their present comforts.

How wonderful, then, are the lifesaving stations where prayers are offered for the lost, where lives are ordered so as to reach the lost, and where people long for "all men to be saved and to come to a knowledge of the truth."

7

Living out God's Order

1 TIMOTHY 2:11-15

A woman should learn in quietness and full submission. I do not permit a woman to teach or to have authority over a man; she must be silent. For Adam was formed first, then Eve. And Adam was not the one deceived; it was the woman who was deceived and became a sinner. But women will be saved through childbearing — if they continue in faith, love and holiness with propriety.

This is a controversial text, upon which an immense amount of scholarship has been focused in recent years. Virtually no one in the liberal theological camp holds to the traditional, historic interpretation of this text. On the other hand, many, if not most, in the evangelical tradition do subscribe to the historic interpretation, but they have trouble articulating it. There are also many evangelicals who reject the historic interpretation, preferring what is called the "progressive" interpretation — even arguing for the ordination of women. I want to say at the outset that I adhere to the traditional, historic interpretation of this text, a view that today's secular culture finds shocking. Because the traditional interpretation understands that there is a divinely given order for the home and, here in 1 Timothy, for the church, it is dismissed by some as "sexist." However, nothing could be farther from the truth Biblically or personally.

I was raised by a community of gloriously strong women who had to make their way in a male-dominated, sexist world. Aside from my young brothers, there were no men in my life until I was a junior high student, when I became involved in church. Otherwise, my world was populated with wonderful women.

My mother was widowed at age twenty-three and sometimes worked two jobs to make ends *almost* meet. My maternal grandmother, Laura Anna Melissa McClurkin Bray, also a widow, gave herself to her "boys." Her death was the most traumatic event in our lives. My two adopted, unmarried aunts,

Beulah and Helen, are still alive at the time of this writing, ages ninety-seven and ninety-eight.

For a while we all lived in adjacent homes, and then across town. But we spent most weekends together, and for two long-anticipated weeks every summer all those women and we boys camped together at Big Sur in California.

My mother had a hard life. I recall men trying to "hit" on my attractive young mother — and her suffering professionally for keeping her virtues.

I say all this to emphasize that there is to my knowledge not an ounce of male superiority or sexism in my soul! I believe in the radical equality of men and women. My life is committed to seeing men and women develop in every area of life.

It is also crucial that we understand that the historic interpretation of 1 Timothy 2:11-15 has been the majority view of the church at large for most of the last 2,000 years. Bob Yarbrough, Professor of New Testament at Trinity Evangelical Divinity School, surveyed the scholarly articles in the standard bibliographical reference tool *New Testament Abstracts* and noted that it was only in 1969 that the progressive, revisionist view began to appear in the literature of the academy. But then in the period between 1969 and now a flood of articles appeared. He concludes that the rise in the progressive interpretation's promotion following the women's movement of the 1960s is "indebted significantly, and at times probably culpably, to the prevailing social climate rather than to the Biblical text."[1] Similarly, Harold O. J. Brown observes, "When opinions and convictions suddenly undergo dramatic alteration, although nothing new has been discovered and the only thing that has dramatically changed is the spirit of the age, it is difficult to avoid the conclusion that that spirit has had an important role to play in the shift."[2]

Understanding then that the popularity of the progressive interpretation of the last thirty years found its impetus in secular culture, and that the interpretation runs contrary to the prevailing interpretation of the preceding 1,970 years (some sixty-odd generations), the burden of proof certainly rests upon the progressive revisionists!

My concern is this: If we do not invite the Biblical text to define church order, the intrusive culture will. The *Zeitgeist*, the spirit of the age, is a tyrant to be resisted, not embraced.

Furthermore, we must never determine our theology by polling dead theologians. We must go to the living Biblical text.

APOSTOLIC PROHIBITION (vv. 11, 12)

The text simply states: "A woman should learn in quietness and full submission. I do not permit a woman to teach or to have authority over a man;

she must be silent" (vv. 11, 12). Simple it may sound, but simple it is not! While this passage is perfectly intelligible, it is nuanced by its context and its unique arrangement of words, as we shall see.

Creative "interpretations." Before we delve into this, we must note the ways in which some attempt to dodge its apparent meaning.

First, some simply argue that Paul is wrong. No one claiming to be evangelical ever put this view in print until 1975, when professor Paul K. Jewett ventured that Paul's teaching here was in error because it echoed a rabbinical misinterpretation of the second creation account of Genesis 2, which, he argued, did not give enough weight to the first creation account of Genesis 1.[3] Dr. Jewett understood what Paul was saying but believed Paul was wrong. Picking and choosing what to accept from Paul is not an acceptable evangelical custom. Jewett's writings caused quite a stir even in his own institution.[4]

A second way to do away with Paul's teaching is to argue that "Ephesus stood as a bastion of feminist supremacy of religion,"[5] and thus Paul's prohibitions against women teaching and exercising authority over men were aimed at the excesses, not against normal teaching and exercise of authority. The problem here is that a "feminist Ephesus" never existed, as S. M. Baugh has shown in his devastating essay and critique "A Foreign World: Ephesus in the First Century."[6] Ephesus was a very conventional Roman provincial city with no women magistrates and with a pagan cult hierarchy controlled by men.[7]

A third attempt at blunting Paul's teaching is to give the Greek word translated here "to have authority" a negative meaning such as "to domineer"[8] or "to control." Thus Paul would be prohibiting a patently negative activity — "I do not permit a woman to teach or to domineer a man." This would allow women to teach and exercise authority over men as long as it is not done in a controlling, domineering way. Though the word could mean domineer in some contexts, it cannot mean this here. The reason is that the word "or" (*oude*), which connects "to teach" and "to have authority," always requires that both words be either positive or negative. If they were negative, the phrase could read, "I do not permit a woman to teach error or to domineer over a man." But this cannot be the translation here because "to teach" is always viewed positively in the New Testament and in its many uses in 1 and 2 Timothy.[9] The *New International Version* renders the Greek phrase in question correctly, "to have authority," as do the *Revised Standard Version* and the *New Living Translation*. And the *New American Standard Bible* is similar — "exercise authority."

A fourth attempt to set aside what Paul says here is to argue that when Paul says, "I do not permit," it is in the present indicative and not the imperative, and that he is therefore speaking personally about a temporary arrangement.[10] But this ignores the fact that Paul often used present indicatives to give universal and authoritative instruction (cf. especially Romans 12:1 and 1 Timothy 2:8).[11] Also, to argue that Paul's instruction is temporary ignores the context because in the next verse he immediately rests his prohibition against women teaching and exercising authority on the unchanging order of creation. Paul's prohibition here is universal and enduring.

A fifth way to deflect Paul's prohibition is to hold that references to "woman" and "women" in this passage refer to wives because of the way this passage parallels 1 Peter 3:1-7. Thus the teaching is domestic, applying only to the home. But the differences in the passages are too distinct to import the "wives" designation from 1 Peter to 1 Timothy.[12] Very few feminist interpreters seriously use this argument to deflect Paul's prohibition because the argument is so weak.[13]

Lastly, a widely used way to discount Paul's prohibition is to misinterpret Galatians 3:28 and then to use that to erase what Paul says here. Galatians 3:28 reads, "There is neither Jew nor Greek, slave nor free, male nor female, for you are all one in Christ Jesus." That is a massive statement of our spiritual status in Christ. Every believer, every male and female who is "in Christ," fully inherits the Abrahamic promises by grace apart from works. This is a statement of our radical spiritual equality *coram Deo* (before God) whatever our status in life. But it does not do away with gender distinctions. None of the major teachers of church history thought so, much less taught it.

Yet, that is precisely what feminist hermeneutics does! Then it goes on to argue that the Galatians passage is a breakthrough text to which all others must bow. Those who think this way are following the very liberal lead of Krister Stendahl, one-time dean of Harvard Divinity School.[14] Paul Jewett did this when he declared that the Apostle Paul was in error in 1 Timothy.[15]

Correct interpretation. So we see that many creative ways are employed to muzzle Paul. But the question still remains: What did Paul mean when he said, "A woman should learn in quietness and full submission. I do not permit a woman to teach or to have authority over a man; she must be silent" (vv. 11, 12)? We need to back up a bit before moving on.

As we saw in the previous study of verses 1-10, Paul's desire was that when the Ephesian churches met, their prayer and deportment would promote God's desire for "all men to be saved and to come to a knowledge of the truth" (v. 4). This section begins in verses 1, 2 with Paul urging just such prayer and deportment, and it peaks in verses 8-10 with an admonishment regarding prayer and conduct: "I want men everywhere to lift up holy hands in prayer, without anger or disputing. I also want women to dress modestly, with decency and propriety, not with braided hair or gold or pearls or expensive clothes, but with good deeds, appropriate for women who profess to worship God." The way we pray and conduct ourselves has everything to do with the cause of the gospel. Evidently some men were contentious while offering public prayers, and some women were imitating the coiffures and lavish clothing of the Roman court, known for its licentiousness.

Now in verses 11-15, having mentioned women's deportment, Paul expands his discussion in respect to teaching and authority in the church. It must be noted that these instructions have nothing directly to say about teaching and authority in the marketplace or the academy or the public square. They are about order in the church. Neither do these directives allow any man within the church, by virtue of his gender, to exercise authority over women in the church. Such more generally explicit authority only exists within the sacred covenant of marriage and family, and then it is only to be exercised with the self-giving spirit of Christ (cf. Ephesians 5:22-32).

Lastly, Paul's instructions have nothing to say about male and female equality. Such equality had been established from the beginning (see Genesis 1:27) by virtue of man and woman being created in the *imago Dei*. And the mutual spiritual equality and status of men and women "in Christ" were given spectacular expression by Paul himself *earlier* in Galatians 3:28.

So how is Paul's prohibition of women from teaching and exercising authority over a man to be understood, especially since the words "to teach" and "have authority" contain no negative connotation such as "dominate" or "domineer"? The answer is that the word "to teach" (*didaskein*) and its noun forms "teaching" (*didaskalia*) and "teacher" (*didaskalos*) are used in the New Testament to describe the careful and authoritative transmission of Biblical truth. And in the Pastorals, "teaching" always has the sense of *authoritative* public doctrinal instruction[16] (cf. 1 Timothy 4:11-16; 2 Timothy 3:16; 4:2).

So what is prohibited is *preaching*, such as is enjoined in Paul's charge to Timothy: "Preach the Word; be prepared in season and out of season; correct, rebuke and encourage — with great patience and careful instruction" (2 Timothy 4:2). Also prohibited is the *teaching-elder* role of authoritatively defining and expositing the apostolic deposit. This is the realm of male elders who are "able to teach" (1 Timothy 3:2). The text is also very clear that attitude is of paramount importance — namely, submissiveness to leadership: "A woman should learn in quietness and full submission" (v. 11). Thus, a hectoring, argumentative attitude is excluded.

This, however, does not forbid men and women from instructing one another in regular discourse. Indeed, it is expected. Paul directed the Colossians, "Let the word of Christ dwell in you richly as you teach and admonish one another with all wisdom, and as you sing psalms, hymns and spiritual songs with gratitude in your hearts to God" (Colossians 3:16). To the Corinthians he likewise told the whole congregation, "When you come together, everyone has a hymn, or a word of instruction, a revelation, a tongue or an interpretation. All of these must be done for the strengthening of the church" (1 Corinthians 14:26). We ought to be teaching one another. Priscilla and Aquila taught Apollos in their home. Apollos learned his theology from both of them (Acts 18:26).

Within the divinely given order of the church, women are expected to develop into teachers. The writer of Hebrews chided his congregation in this respect, saying, ". . . by this time you ought to be teachers" (Hebrews 5:12). Our task, as a church, is to equip men and women for ministry.

Understanding that Scripture does not permit a woman to preach or exercise elder-like responsibility for the definition and exposition of the apostolic deposit, where then must we draw the line for women's ministry?

Personally, I am comfortable with a woman teaching an adult Sunday School class provided that the teaching is periodic and under the authority of the elders. I would not be comfortable with a woman having her own permanent class because such permanence would tend to foster an elder-like authoritativeness. The reason for this will become clearer as we examine the divine rationale behind Paul's teaching.

APOSTOLIC REASONING (vv. 13, 14)

The apostle goes straight to the point in his next words: "For Adam was formed first, then Eve. And Adam was not the one deceived; it was the woman who was deceived and became a sinner" (vv. 13, 14). Notice first that he has grounded the ordering of authority in the church upon the order of creation before the Fall — Adam came before Eve. John Stott says of this appeal to creation order:

> All attempts to get rid of Paul's teaching on headship (on grounds
> that it is mistaken, confusing, culture-bound or culture-specific)
> must be pronounced unsuccessful. It remains stubbornly there. It
> is rooted in divine revelation, not human opinion, and in divine
> creation, not human culture. In essence, therefore, it must be pre-
> served as having permanent and universal authority.[17]

In a later wide-ranging interview with *Christianity Today*, he strongly restated his position:

> But then I can't dismiss masculine headship in the cavalier way in
> which some evangelical feminists do. There is something in the
> Pauline teaching about headship that cannot be ignored as a purely
> cultural phenomenon, because he roots it in Creation. We may find
> his exegesis of Genesis 2 difficult — that women were made after
> men, out of men, and for men — but he does root his argument in

Creation. I have a very high view of apostolic authority. I don't feel able to reject Paul's exegesis.[18]

The creation order that gave men headship and authority over women consistently grounded Paul's teaching on church order. In the famous passage in 1 Corinthians 11 where Paul argued that a woman should cover her head while praying, and that a man should not (in effect prohibiting cross-dressing while praying), Paul referenced the creation order as his authority: "For man did not come from woman, but woman from man; neither was man created for woman, but woman for man" (vv. 8, 9). Again in 1 Corinthians 14, where he argues that the interpretation of prophecy must be done by men, he roots it in the creation order — "as the Law says" (v. 34).[19]

Firstness connotes authority throughout the Scriptures. Being the first-born conveys the privilege of being heir and ruler (cf. Colossians 1:15ff.). God could have created Adam and Eve at the same time, but he did not. He created Eve *for* Adam. She was created to be his "helper." The unchanging fact is that God desires that the order of creation be reflected in his church, the Body of Christ.

We miss the point of verse 14 entirely if we think that Eve was more gullible than Adam, and that is why she "was deceived and became a sinner." Eve's sin was not naivete but a willful attempt to overthrow the creation order. She hoped, in eating from the tree, that her eyes would be opened and she would be like God (cf. Genesis 3:5).

Here is the irony: God had given Adam and Eve awesome authority. The creation order issued like this: God made Adam, then made Eve to be Adam's helper, and both of them were to rule over all of creation. But due to her rebellion, a creature (part of creation), a snake, began to rule her because she obeyed it. Then Eve exercised woeful authority over her husband by leading him to do the same thing. And Adam? It appears from Genesis 3:6 that Adam was with Eve when she partook but did nothing, then "listened to [his] wife and ate from the tree" (cf. Genesis 3:17). As Phillip Jensen explains: "Eve's sin involved overturning the order of creation and teaching her husband. Similarly, Adam's sin came from 'listening' to his wife, in the sense of heeding and following her instruction. He was taught by her, thereby putting himself under her authority and reversing God's good ordering of creation."[20]

Significantly, when God pronounced judgment, the capsizing of the creation order was emphasized in the way the Lord first cursed the serpent, then the woman, then the man. The essence of Adam and Eve's sin was the overturning of the creation order. Yet despite Adam's sinful abdication, his headship was still recognized by God in that their eyes were opened after he ate (cf. Genesis 3:7), but then Adam alone was told that he would die (cf. Genesis 3:19). As goes the head, so go the members.

APOSTOLIC ADVICE (v. 15)

Paul closes this section in Timothy with some advice to women that on the surface is not particularly clear: "But women will be saved through childbearing — if they continue in faith, love and holiness with propriety" (v. 15). We know he cannot mean that women will be saved physically whenever they have children. Countless godly Christian mothers have died at childbirth. Some have detected a reference here to the Incarnation, believing that "saved through childbearing" refers to the birth of Christ and his ultimate atoning work. But this would be an obscure, unlikely way for the apostle to make his point.

Most likely Paul references childbearing because it is a universal example of the God-given difference in the roles of men and women (men do not give birth to children, and most women in every culture do have children).[21] So when Paul says "women will be saved through childbearing," he means that by not seeking a man's role they will more likely remain in the heart attitude that invites salvation and its attendant blessings. Moreover, as Duane Litfin has pointed out, "Whatever one understands the first part of the verse to be affirming, it is contingent on a woman's willingness to abide in these four virtues — 'faith, love and holiness with propriety.'"[22]

This passage is not about male or female superiority. Any honest male knows that the grading curve was always messed up by the girls in his class. What man has not been out-thought, out-talked, and outdone by his female counterparts? Your experiences need be no larger than your family to know women who are superior to their fathers, brothers, and husbands.

This is not about suitability for leadership either. It is a statistical fact that American women read more Christian books than men and attend church in greater numbers.[23] They are more relationally oriented and more naturally empathetic. They are more intuitive about where people are. They are more verbal and are natural communicators.

Furthermore, church leadership is not about power — it is about dying. That's how Paul defined the new-covenant ministry: "We always carry around in our body the death of Jesus, so that the life of Jesus may also be revealed in our body. For we who are alive are always being given over to death for Jesus' sake, so that his life may be revealed in our mortal body. So then, death is at work in us, but life is at work in you" (2 Corinthians 4:10-12).

This is about fidelity to God's Word. This is about inviting God's Word to shape the life of the church, rather than the intrusive winds of culture. And make no mistake — if we do not let the Bible do it, culture will!

This is about living out the creation order that comes from the character of God, God's goodness. We must exult with Paul, "What, then, shall we say in response to this? If God is for us, who can be against us? He who did not spare his own Son, but gave him up for us all — how will he not also, along with him, graciously give us all things?" (Romans 8:31, 32). When we live out our salvation, we can expect to receive everything we need. When we live out his creation order, it is a joyous venture. Paul lived it out, and to him, his colleagues were an invaluable treasure. Romans 16 is filled with names of both men and women who loved and laughed with and suffered with Paul in ministry.

This is about gospel and mission. Paul's concern that the church pray and deport itself so "all men [would] be saved and come to a knowledge of the truth" was one with the concern that godly men, not women, exercise authority in the church. Paul believed that if the church joyfully lived out the creation order in God's household, the gospel would continue to go out with power.

After all, Paul's stated purpose in writing was that the church "will know how people ought to conduct themselves in God's household, which is the church of the living God, the pillar and foundation of the truth" (1 Timothy 3:15).

8

The Good Elders

1 TIMOTHY 3:1-7

Here is a trustworthy saying: If anyone sets his heart on being an overseer, he desires a noble task. Now the overseer must be above reproach, the husband of but one wife, temperate, self-controlled, respectable, hospitable, able to teach, not given to drunkenness, not violent but gentle, not quarrelsome, not a lover of money. He must manage his own family well and see that his children obey him with proper respect. (If anyone does not know how to manage his own family, how can he take care of God's church?) He must not be a recent convert, or he may become conceited and fall under the same judgment as the devil. He must also have a good reputation with outsiders, so that he will not fall into disgrace and into the devil's trap.

I learned early in ministry, and with some pain, to be very careful in respect to the character of those appointed to church leadership. By my midthirties, after a little more than a decade in the ministry, I had "seen it all" as to the duplicity and hypocrisy and immense evil that can exist in church leaders. I knew a man who was prominent in his denomination and community, a married man with a family, who was discovered to be a practicing homosexual and regularly consorted with several of his male employees. In another instance the church treasurer appeared in the church narthex on a Sunday morning dead drunk, glass in hand, wildly whispering that he was leaving his wife and family — was departing that day on a private jet for the Middle East! I have known pious, Bible-quoting, "soul-winning" murderers. And over the years, while speaking at pastors' conferences, my wife and I have had pastors' trembling wives seek us out and reveal abuse and perversion by their publicly straight-laced husbands — tales that sound as if they were scripted by Flannery O'Connor!

I have said in times of despair that you have never been "had" until you have been "had" by a fellow born-again Christian who calls you "brother." Am I too cynical? I do not think so. I am a realist who also believes in the power of the gospel to deliver believing, humble, repentant sinners from their sins and instill a nobility of character that the angels admire.

Church leadership can attract people with mixed and sometimes outrightly sinful motives. The seeming prestige of spiritual leadership attracts some. The lure of power draws others. The spiritual directing of others' lives can be heady stuff. Some, I think, like the idea of having access to the supposed mysterious inner workings of the church. All these motives are empty pursuits, but that does not reduce the lure for some.

I say all this to emphasize that Christian ministry and leadership is without question a matter of character. One's authentic spirituality and Christian character is everything in church leadership. It is a sober fact that as goes the leadership, so goes the church. With some commonsense qualifications, it is an axiom that what we are as leaders in microcosm, the congregation will become in macrocosm as the years go by. Of course, there are always individual exceptions. But it is generally true that if the leadership is Word-centered, the church will be Word-centered. If the leadership is mission-minded, the church will be mission-minded. If the leadership is sincere, the people will be sincere. If the leadership is kind, the church will be kind. This is also true negatively — exponentially! Unloving, narrow, stingy leaders beget an unloving, narrow, stingy church.

This concern for one's character and the resultant lifestyle looms large in 1 Timothy and peaks here in the third chapter. Paul's stated purpose in writing, as he explained it to Timothy, was that "you will know how people ought to conduct themselves in God's household, which is the church of the living God, the pillar and foundation of the truth" (3:15). First Timothy is about church order and conduct. But there was also a deeper purpose — namely, world evangelization and mission as stated at the beginning of chapter 2 where Paul describes God as "our Savior, who wants all men to be saved and to come to a knowledge of the truth" (vv. 3, 4).

It was this divine saving desire that informed and energized Paul's instruction about lifestyle in verses 1-10 — that believers must lead quiet lives and pray without disputing, and that women dress modestly. And in verses 11-15 that desire likewise informed his teaching about women's roles in living out the creation order. And now in 3:1-7 it animates his directives about the necessary character and characteristics of Christian leaders.

All of this has to do with gospel and mission, because if the church is what it ought to be, it will pursue God's desire for "all men to be saved and to come to a knowledge of the truth" (2:4). As J. A. Hort, the celebrated Greek scholar, said: "To St. Paul the representative character of those who had oversight in the Ecclesia, their conspicuous embodiment of what the Ecclesia itself was meant to show, was more important than any acts or teachings by which their oversight could be exercised."[1]

Paul wanted the church to have leaders whose lives would grace the church and adorn the gospel before a needy world. As followers of Christ we cannot settle for anything less.

A NOBLE ASPIRATION (v. 1)

Paul begins by first affirming leadership as a noble aspiration: "Here is a trustworthy saying: If anyone sets his heart on being an overseer, he desires a noble task." The apostle hopes that certain men will aspire to leadership. The literal sense of oversight being a "beautiful task" may convey even more of Paul's feeling. Such aspiration in a man is a lovely thing. How beautiful it is when a man sets his heart on the virtues essential to spiritual leadership.

> *He who would play a leader's part*
> *On a noble task has set his heart.*

I hope some young men who read this study will set their hearts on spiritual leadership. It is an excellent pursuit.

At the same time, an overweening desire for position is reason for automatic disqualification. Such ambition indicates that a man does not understand either the job or what will be required personally and professionally.

NOBLE QUALIFICATIONS (vv. 2-7)

This said, Paul now lists the noble qualifications for spiritual leaders — here called "overseers" (*episkopoi*, from which we get the word *bishop*). The word is interchangeable with another Greek word, *presbyteroi* ("elders") — Acts 20:17, 28 and Titus 1:5 indicate they are synonymous. Thus the *episkopoi* here are church elders.[2] The following characteristics are not exhaustive but represent the bare minimum for elders if they are to grace both the church and the world.

His reputation. Paul begins with a general charge as to the elder's reputation — "Now the overseer must be above reproach" (v. 2). This refers to his *observable conduct*.[3] This apparently summarizes all the following qualifications, for we see that the final qualification is also about reputation: "He must also have a good reputation with outsiders, so that he will not fall into disgrace and into the devil's trap" (v. 7). Such should be his reputation that if the elder's name were posted for comment, no one would be able to bring a substantiated charge against him in respect to *anything* in the following list. High qualifications indeed!

His marriage. First place is given to the elder's marriage — "The husband of but one wife" (v. 2) — literally, a "one-woman/wife man." Winston Churchill once attended a formal banquet in London, where the dignitaries were asked the question, "If you could not be who you are, who would you like to be?" Naturally everyone was curious as to what Churchill, who was seated next to his beloved Clemmie, would say. When it was finally his turn, the old man, the last respondent to the question, rose and gave his answer. "If I could not be who I am, I would most like to be" — and here he paused to take his wife's hand — "Lady Churchill's second husband."[4] Churchill was a very clever man. He was also a most devoted man — a "one-woman man" — despite his other proclivities.

The standard here for elders is extraordinarily high. But not in the way it is so often misinterpreted. The common misinterpretation is *quantitative* — that he can have had only one wife. Thus, if he had been divorced or widowed and remarried he could not be an elder. The moral loophole in this quantitative interpretation is that a man can be married to only one woman his whole life and not be a one-woman man. It allows moral rationalization — such as we see on the nightly news, even from the highest office in our nation.

The correct sense here is not quantitative but *qualitative*. The man is truly a one-woman man.[5] There are no other women in his life. He is totally faithful. He does not flirt. There are no dalliances. As George Knight says, he is "a man who having contracted a monogamous marriage is faithful to his wedding vows."[6] As the *New Living Translation* has it, "He must be faithful to his wife." So the bar is set high. And no cleverness, no ancient or postmodern verbal sleight of hand can get around it!

His self-mastery.[7] The next three qualities, "temperate, self-controlled, respectable" (v. 2), group well under the heading of self-mastery. King David, who had sinned so grievously in respect to marital fidelity, ironically became an example of self-mastery amidst the misery and rebellion that followed his sin and repentance. His remarkable self-control occurred during Absalom's rebellion when, as David fled from Jerusalem, one of Saul's descendants, Shimei, followed alongside David pelting him with stones and tossing dirt on him as he shouted curses. Only a word and one of David's soldiers would have dispatched him.

But with immense self-mastery David saw that Shimei's cursings were not unexpected for the situation and left vengeance to God. The episode concludes, "So David and his men continued along the road while Shimei was going along the hillside opposite him, cursing as he went and throwing stones at him and showering him with dirt. The king and all the people with him arrived at their destination exhausted. And there he refreshed himself" (2 Samuel 16:13, 14).

Here in 1 Timothy's triad of self-mastery, "temperate" means "clearheaded," and David was that. "Self-controlled" means exactly what it says, and David was that too. "Respectable" refers to how people saw David. In this situation David was at his greatest! "Better . . . a man who controls his temper than one who takes a city" (Proverbs 16:32).

This "temperate, self-controlled" respectability is a must for every leader. Titus too says it is a necessity for leadership (Titus 1:8). And it is possible, with God's help: "But the fruit of the Spirit is love, joy, peace, patience, kindness, goodness, faithfulness, gentleness and self-control" (Galatians 5:22, 23). It is a self-mastery that comes from God.[8] The elder must be mastered by God.

His ministry. Then there is the matter of his ministry, which is given a twofold description — "hospitable, able to teach" (v. 2). As a young man the missionary statesman-to-be E. Stanley Jones experienced the ultimate in hospitality when he was preaching his first evangelistic service among the poor mountaineers of Kentucky. The meetings were held in the school-house. Says Dr. Jones:

> At the schoolhouse I was invited to stay with a man and his wife, and when I arrived I saw there was one bed. The husband said, "You take the far side." Then he got in, and then his wife. In the morning we reversed the process. I turned my face to the wall as they dressed, and they stepped out while I dressed. That was real hospitality! I have slept in palaces, but the hospitality of that one-bed-home is the most memorable and the most appreciated.[9]

Hospitality (*philazenos*, "love of strangers") is a telltale virtue of the people of God. Paul told the Roman church to "Share with God's people who are in need. Practice hospitality" (Romans 12:13). "Practice" means "pursue" or "chase" and sometimes means "strenuous pursuit." Christians, and especially leaders, are not simply to wait for opportunities for hospitality but are to pursue them. They are to do it "without grumbling," as Peter says (1 Peter 4:9).

Today's elder must be a joyous host. He must invite people to his table. His home must be open. Hospitality is all over the New Testament. And the writer of Hebrews offers an enchanting motivation: "Do not forget to entertain strangers, for by so doing some people have entertained angels without knowing it" (13:2). These are God's thoughts on hospitality!

Hospitality is paired with "able to teach" as the other elder ministry distinctive. Paul gives it fuller expression in Titus: "He must hold firmly to the trustworthy message as it has been taught, so that he can encourage others by sound doctrine and refute those who oppose it" (Titus 1:9). This demands that the elder be a student of the Word, a man who compares Scripture with Scripture and can communicate it and, when necessary, defend the faith.

His temperance. Next there is the demand for the elder's temperance

— "not given to drunkenness" (v. 3) — literally, "not lingering beside wine."
Anyone who longs for the halcyon days of the apostolic church longs for
an illusion. It was rough and tumble. Drunkenness was an ancient blight. In
Corinth some Christians were even in the habit of getting drunk at the Lord's
Supper (cf. 1 Corinthians 11:21)! Paul repeats this warning to deacons in
verse 8 ("not indulging in much wine") and again to elders in Titus 1:7
("not given to drunkenness").

This must be taken to heart today by church leaders in a culture that
romanticizes drinking — *In vino veritas* ("there is truth in wine"). That
may provide a convenient conceit for a play like *Who's Afraid of Virginia
Woolf?* But the real truth is, alcohol is a destroyer of truth, and its abuse is a
spiritual flamethrower.

His temperament. Temperance is logically followed by a prescription for
a particular temperament in the elder — "not violent but gentle, not quarrelsome" (v. 3). Churchgoers in Fyaras, Sweden, dragged furious choir director Sven-Aake Fagerkrantz away from sour-singing Erica Bengtsson as he
whacked her back and legs with his cane. His explanation? "I just went
wild because she kept singing off-key. . . . She was tone deaf and I begged
her for years not to sing so loud!" Whatever could be said about Mr.
Fagerkrantz, he definitely was not elder material!

The Greek translated "not violent" is literally "not a giver of blows"[10]
and is metaphorical for a pugnaciousness that corresponds to quarrelsomeness. These are elder no-no's. Gentleness is the elder's approved style. This
was Jesus' style as well — he was "gentle and humble in heart" (Matthew
11:29). It is also a fruit of the Spirit (cf. Galatians 5:22, 23). Paul describes
this requirement fully in his second letter to Timothy: "And the Lord's servant must not quarrel; instead, he must be kind to everyone, able to teach, not
resentful. Those who oppose him he must gently instruct, in the hope that
God will grant them repentance leading them to a knowledge of the truth"
(2 Timothy 2:24, 25).

His money. Money — specifically, one's attitude toward it — plays a big
role in elders' qualifications — "not a lover of money" (v. 3). In the last
century Orestes Brownson spoke of ministers who pay more attention to "the
fleece than to the flock,"[11] and that is true enough. But Os Guinness was more
to the point: "If a man is drunk on wine, you'll throw him out. But if he is
drunk on money, you'll make him a deacon."[12]

It is all so American! If a man has lots of money, that means God has
blessed him (never mind what the Bible says about the situation); it means
he's smart (well, maybe); it means he's a good manager, a practical man; that
he has power; it means he can lead. Oh really? Paul speaks so explicitly to
the contrary in the Pastorals. "People who want to get rich fall into temptation and a trap and into many foolish and harmful desires that plunge men
into ruin and destruction. For the love of money is a root of all kinds of

evil. Some people, eager for money, have wandered from the faith and pierced themselves with many griefs" (6:9, 10). And again in Titus 1:7, "Since an overseer is entrusted with God's work, he must be blameless — not overbearing, not quick-tempered, not given to drunkenness, not violent, not pursuing dishonest gain."

The point is not whether one is rich or poor. The disqualification, out of hand, for church leadership is to be "a lover of money." Some of the richest men I know are not lovers of money. But the truth is, it is hard to have a lot of money and not love it. It is also hard to be poor and not love money. Whatever the case, one cannot love money and be qualified for church leadership.

His family. As Paul details the last three qualifications, he becomes more descriptive. Regarding the elder's home he says, "He must manage his own family well and see that his children obey him with proper respect. (If anyone does not know how to manage his own family, how can he take care of God's church?)" (vv. 4, 5). This principle was especially cited because churches in those days met in homes — and very often the elders' homes. Also the word translated "family" here is *oikos* (literally, "house") and is the same word used in verse 15 as a metaphor for the church. Thus, the man who fails at the family *oikos* is thereby disqualified from the other *oikos*, the *church*.[13] The commonsense application is straightforward, and its disregard has brought great trouble to God's people over the centuries — beginning with Eli of old (cf. 1 Samuel 3:13).

His maturity. The logic of the next qualification is evident: "He must not be a recent convert, or he may become conceited and fall under the same judgment as the devil" (v. 6). The language here is so expressive — "become conceited" means "filled with smoke," full of hot air, we might say — a la-la-land of self-centered fantasy that would leave them open to the same judgment passed on the errant elders for their pride, mentioned earlier in the letter.[14] Humility seasoned by experience is an indispensable qualification for eldership.

His reputation again! The final qualification takes us full circle back to the matter of one's reputation, which is where we began — "He must also have a good reputation with outsiders, so that he will not fall into disgrace and into the devil's trap" (v. 7). "A good reputation" is literally a "beautiful witness" — "He must have a beautiful witness with outsiders." And indeed he will if *his reputation* is "above reproach," if *his self-mastery* is evidenced by his being "temperate, self-controlled, respectable," if in *his ministry* he is "hospitable, able to teach," if *his temperance* is evidenced by his "not [being] given to drunkenness," if *his temperament* is "not violent but gentle, not quarrelsome," if in respect to *his money* he is "not a lover of money," if *his family* is in order, if *his maturity* is established. Such a life will have a beautiful symmetry that adorns the gospel.

So much is at stake. What our leadership is in microcosm, the church will become in macrocosm, and what the church is has everything to do with gospel and mission.

Years ago the liberals set aside the Pastoral Epistles as too bourgeois and conventional. As a result some evangelicals lost confidence in the relevancy of the Pastorals. Today those epistles are radically bracing amidst postmodern confusion. We need to take their message to heart for the sake of the gospel. We need to raise the bar and hold it there. We need to see leadership as a calling. Church leadership is not a political position to be sought for oneself. It is a burden that some must accept. Leaders are not determined by popularity. They must be the kind of men profiled here by Paul to Timothy. And the church must recognize who they are.

We must see leadership as a calling.

We must determine to prepare and equip such leaders.

9

The Good Deacons

1 TIMOTHY 3:8-13

Deacons, likewise, are to be men worthy of respect, sincere, not indulging in much wine, and not pursuing dishonest gain. They must keep hold of the deep truths of the faith with a clear conscience. They must first be tested; and then if there is nothing against them, let them serve as deacons. In the same way, their wives are to be women worthy of respect, not malicious talkers but temperate and trustworthy in everything. A deacon must be the husband of but one wife and must manage his children and his household well. Those who have served well gain an excellent standing and great assurance in their faith in Christ Jesus.

The word *deacon* (Greek, *diakonos*) in the New Testament means "servant" or "attendant," one who ministers to and cares for others. This word is generally translated "servant," except in the few places where it specifically refers to the office of deacon as in 1 Timothy 3:8, 12, Philippians 1:1, and possibly Romans 16:1. It primarily refers to menial service such as waiting tables, as when Martha served Jesus (cf. John 12:2; also Luke 17:8; 22:26-27).

Jesus used the word to convey his radical ideal of human relationships as mutual service involving self-sacrifice. The famous text in Mark's Gospel that provides both the theme of that Gospel and the purpose of Jesus' life reads: "Whoever wants to become great among you must be your servant [deacon], and whoever wants to be first must be slave of all. For even the Son of Man did not come to be served [deaconed], but to serve [to deacon], and to give his life as a ransom for many" (10:43-45). Later, in the upper room in Jerusalem, on the night when he washed the feet of his disciples, Jesus said, "For who is greater, the one who is at the table or the one who serves [deacons]? Is it not the one who is at the table? But I am among you as one who serves [deacons]" (Luke 22:27).

It was natural, therefore, that the word came to represent all kinds of service in the cause of the gospel. An examination of the Greek New

Testament indicates that an apostle was designated a "deacon of Christ" (literal translation) (cf. 2 Corinthians 11:23; 4:1; Romans 11:13). Paul calls himself a "deacon" (literal translation) of the church (Colossians 1:25), and here in 1 Timothy, Timothy is described as a "good minister [literally, "deacon"] of Christ Jesus" (4:6).[1] There is certainly nothing officious, self-conscious, or self-promoting in the word *deacon*. The Lord's followers are to be humble servants.

How ironic then that the very act that Jesus used to dramatize the call to deacon-service — foot-washing — was made a ceremonial act. According to Canon 3 of the 17th Synod of Toledo (A.D. 694), foot-washing was made obligatory throughout the churches of Spain and Gaul. Over the years the postured humility of washing the feet of the poor became a public performance by leaders of church and state. For example, in 1530 Cardinal Wolsey "washed, wiped and kissed the feet of 59 poor men at Peterborough."[2] The English Royals did this with typical panache. In 1213 King John washed the feet of the poor, giving thirteen pence to each of the thirteen fortunate washees, an event that became known as the Royal Maundy. An entry some 400 years later in the Chapels Royal Register records that "on Maundy Thursday, April 1685, our gracious King James ye 2nd was'd, wip'd and kiss'd the feet of 52 poor men with wonderful humility." Right!

To the present Royals' credit, Royal Maundy continues today but without the foot-washing and affected hypocrisy of earlier centuries, as elderly people who have served others are honored with financial gifts for their years of service. The officials still wear towels as aprons, and the queen and her attendants still carry bouquets of fragrant herbs and flowers, as the sovereigns did in the days of the plague to guard against the risk of infection.[3]

Nevertheless, the range of ecclesiastical history demonstrates how prone the church has been to miss the point. Not only has the example of the foot-washing Lord been treated as a parody, but also, in some instances, the office of deacon has become a seat of power and even abuse. In some traditions it is even pursued as a political office.

How far this is from the spirit of Christ! How far from the heart of his followers, and how far from the profile of servants/deacons in 1 Timothy! The following list of credentials has everything to do with the gospel.

DEACONS' QUALIFICATIONS (vv. 8-12)

Elder-like. Although the deacon does not hold a teaching office, his position does require an elder-like bearing. "Deacons, likewise are to be men worthy of respect, sincere, not indulging in much wine, and not pursuing dishonest gain" (v. 8). Respectability is the operative word here, and in the original language it is defined by terms all beginning with "not." First, they are to be "sincere" (literally, "not double-talkers"). He is not the kind of man who says one thing to one man and a different thing to the next.[4] He is the kind of man whom Will Rogers described as "not afraid to sell the family parrot to the town gossip!" One could trust this man. He was respectable because he was credible, and he was credible because he was truthful. Second and third, he was also "not indulging in much wine, and not pursuing dishonest gain." To reference Os Guinness again, he was not drunk on wine or money. A man drunk on either does not deserve respect. To be a deacon is to embrace a position of character from first to last.

Informed belief. Though the deacons are not required to be "able to teach" as are elders, "They must keep hold of the deep truths of the faith with a clear conscience" (v. 9). More exactly, they must hold to "*the mystery of the faith.*" *Mystery* is a term commonly used by Paul to describe something that was once hidden but is now revealed to those who have spiritual discernment. Here it means the good news of the gospel. It is called "the mystery of the gospel" in Ephesians 6:19.

The Old Testament mystery was, how can God forgive sins? It was answered by Jesus' death as the Father's incarnate and sinless Son suffered the wrath we deserved, thus making forgiveness possible (cf. 1 John 2:1, 2; Romans 3:9-26). The mystery was made clear by Christ, and thus it is often called "the mystery of Christ" (cf. Ephesians 3:4; Colossians 4:3). This is what deacons must understand and hold on to: Christ Jesus died on the cross for their sins (indeed he became sin for them), and if they believe, trusting in his atoning work alone, they will be saved. In a word they must understand the mystery of the cross.

Living belief. But there is more — a deacon must hold on to the mystery of the faith "with a clear conscience." That is, what he understands must not only inform his life, but he must also live by it "with a clear conscience." A man's faith is in great shape when his conscience does not reproach the way he lives.

As we saw earlier, this matter of conscience is dominant in 1 Timothy. At the beginning of the letter Paul emphasized the necessity of a good conscience when he told Timothy to command the false teachers to stop spreading their errors, explaining that "The goal of this command is love, which comes from a pure heart and *a good conscience* and a sincere faith" (1:5, italics added). Next he told Timothy that essential to fighting the good fight is "holding on to faith and a *good conscience*" (1:19, italics added). Thus when a deacon holds on to the mysteries of the faith (the cross-centered gospel) "with a clear conscience," he is in great shape! His belief has penetrated his soul and is informing his life.

But we must also remember that conscience alone is not enough, because our conscience can deceive us. Jiminy Cricket's advice to Pinocchio, "let your conscience be your guide," is generally good advice. But if your conscience is seared by sin, it is of little help. Jonathan Edwards likened conscience to a sundial and God's Word to the sun. Only the light of the sun will give the correct reading. Moonlight cannot work. Candlelight is folly. Both will mislead you. The sunlight of Scripture will always tell the truth. And when we live by the truth "with a clear conscience," we are in great shape.

Tested. Next there is the matter of testing — "They must first be tested; and then if there is nothing against them, let them serve as deacons" (v. 10). The reason testing is required of deacons, and not in the preceding qualifications for elders, is that everyone was already aware of the testing required for eldership. Testing for such leaders is alluded to in 5:22, "Do not be hasty in the laying on of hands," and also in verse 24 of that chapter, "The sins of some men are obvious . . . the sins of others trail behind them." The testing here in 1 Timothy 3 does not refer to an official deacons' test or even a probationary period, but a testing as to reputation — the positive and negative evidences in a candidate's life.

The reality is that these men may in time become elders. So early in the process the church is charged to be very careful. Pressures will inevitably come as these deacons exercise their ministries, and their inner lives will become evident. We are like saturated sponges. If we apply pressure to a sponge, we immediately see what fills it. The pressures of their ministry would reveal what they were made of.

Help-mated. Some argue that the next sentence describes the qualifications of deaconesses, translating "wives" as "women," so that verse 11 would read, "In the same way, women [deaconesses] are to be women worthy of respect, not malicious talkers but temperate and trustworthy in everything." This is unlikely, though there is evidence that an order of deaconesses developed in the early church. Romans 16:1 reads, "I commend to you our sister Phoebe, a servant [*diakonon*] of the church in Cenchrea." And Pliny's famous letter to the Roman emperor Trajan, written in A.D. 112, mentions "two slave-women whom they call deaconesses."[5] Early on, there was an emerging order of deaconesses, the prototypes of deaconesses down through church history.

But despite some good arguments, it is a stretch to read in deaconesses here because deacons are the focus mentioned on both sides of verse 11. Also, the Greek word that can be translated "wife" or "woman" has to be translated "wife" in verse 12 ("the husband of but one wife").

Paul is simply telling Timothy that a deacon must have a wife who has a respectability that matches his own, that his wife's qualifications are part and parcel of his qualifications for the office of deacon.[6] Indeed, she will be expected to help him fulfill his duties. There is immense common sense here not only as to the nature of marriage in which two become one, but in the strength that a godly couple will bring to a deacon's ministry. The character qualifications of deacons in verse 8 and of the parallel qualifications for their wives in verse 11 insure that they will not only be mutually respectable but will have the same heart for ministry.[7]

Domesticated. Next, qualifications similar to the domestic qualifications for elders are demanded of deacons: "A deacon must be the husband of but one wife and must manage his children and his household well" (v. 12). He must be a one-wife man. No other woman can have his affections maritally, mentally, or emotionally. His wife ought to occupy his full horizon. He must love her as he loves himself. "He must pursue his own joy in the holy joy of his wife" (John Piper).[8] He rejects as treachery anything that would alter his loving focus. A one-wife man places his wife at the center of his heart.

> *"For she is wise, if I can judge of her,*
> *And fair she is, if that mine eyes be true,*
> *And true she is, as she hath prov'd herself;*
> *And therefore, like herself, wise, fair, and true,*
> *Shall she be placed in my constant soul."*
> The Merchant of Venice, II. vI, 52-57

Alongside this, the domestic qualification of a well-run household — "and must manage his children and his household well," a necessity if one is to minister to "God's household" (v. 15) — is understood and embraced. The logic is impeccable, and the outcome is predictable, whether the church heeds this advice or rejects it.

DEACONS' REWARD (v. 13)

The deacons "who have served well" will get a twofold reward — before men and before God. As to the first, "Those who have served well gain an excellent standing" before the people they serve. They will have the respect of and influence with the congregation. Though the office of deacon is not primarily a teaching position, it has its own eloquence.[9] Bishop Quail asks a rhetorical question: "Preaching is the art of making a sermon and delivering it? . . . Why no . . . preaching is the art of making a preacher and delivering that."[10] Similarly, the deacon's life speaks. Because of his *elder-like* respectability, his *informed belief* as he holds to the mystery of faith, his *living belief* that issues in "a clear conscience," his *tested* life oozes with character. His *help-mate* is his best qualification, and he is graciously *domesticated* in relation to his wife and children. All of this provides him an excellent standing with his people. His authority goes far beyond words.

As to the second aspect of the deacons' reward, they have "great assurance in their faith in Christ Jesus" (v. 13). They have confidence, even boldness, in their own faith in Christ.[11] There is an ever-deepening confidence in drawing close to God in Christ.

If it is true that what the leadership is in microcosm, the congregation will become in macrocosm (and it *is* true!), then the character of those who fill the office of deacon as well as that of elder is of utmost importance. We must pray for such leadership. We must seek such leadership. As is the leadership, so is the church.

The trajectories of our lives are of paramount importance. If we are off a bit, it may not show much at first. But it will be perceptible in a decade. And many years down the road our wrong example will lead many far astray and leave our churches in ruins.

Let us follow the advice of Scripture to God's glory. There is no better way!

10

The Church's Conduct and Confession

1 TIMOTHY 3:14-16

Although I hope to come to you soon, I am writing you these instructions so that, if I am delayed, you will know how people ought to conduct themselves in God's household, which is the church of the living God, the pillar and foundation of the truth. Beyond all question, the mystery of godliness is great: He appeared in a body, was vindicated by the Spirit, was seen by angels, was preached among the nations, was believed on in the world, was taken up in glory.

Timothy Dwight was Yale University's greatest president, and he was regarded as one of the great educators in American history. Dwight reformed both Yale's curriculum and administration and tripled the school's enrollment. Both Princeton (then the College of New Jersey) and Harvard conferred doctorates on him. But his greatest achievement took place under his preaching in 1802, when a third of his students were converted!

President Dwight was first of all a preacher of the Word and a lover of the church. His great hymn "I Love Thy Kingdom, Lord," authored in 1800, says it all. Its lines reveal a heart for the church that was apostolic — Pauline. In fact, if Paul were alive today, I am sure it would be one of his favorites because Paul taught and lived out every line of this hymn for the church, especially the third verse:

> *For her my tears shall fall;*
> *For her my prayers ascend;*
> *To her my cares and toils be giv'n,*
> *Till toils and cares shall end.*

That is how Paul lived and died. And it represents his passion for the church, which animates his pastoral texts such as 1 Timothy 3:14-16, where he calls the church to proper *conduct* and *confession*.

GOD'S HOUSEHOLD (v. 15b)

Before we take up the matter of the church's conduct and confession, we must take a good look at Paul's description of the church nestled in the last half of verse 15 where he employs three graphic phrases: 1) "God's household," 2) "which is the church of the living God," 3) "the pillar and foundation of the truth."

God's household. "Household" here is undoubtedly metaphorical language for "family" because that is what it means in verses 4, 5, 12 where the word is variously translated "family" or "household" (cf. also Galatians 6:10; Ephesians 2:19). So the church is a family — with God as the Father, believers as his children and therefore brothers and sisters, and elders and deacons as leaders to help the family carry out the Father's purposes.

The fact that we are family has profound implications. For starters, it means we are in eternal relationship — we will always be brothers and sisters. If you are not getting along with your brothers and sisters, the "eternal" aspect may not seem so inviting. But the happy fact is, in Heaven it will be the redeemed, perfected family with whom we will dwell.

> *To live above with the saints we love,*
> *Oh, that will be glory.*
> *To live below with the saints we know,*
> *Well, that's another story!*

Actually, living below with the saints we know is meant to be and can be glorious — if we draw close to the Father. The Apostle John alludes to this in 1 John 1:3 — "We proclaim to you what we have seen and heard, so that you also may have fellowship with us. And our fellowship is with the Father and with his Son, Jesus Christ." There is an implicit relational triangle here, with God (Father and Son) at the pinnacle and believers at the bottom angles. So the closer our relationship to him, the closer we become to one another.

A. W. Tozer gave this truth unforgettable expression when he wrote:

> Has it ever occurred to you that one hundred pianos all tuned to the same fork are automatically tuned to each other? They are of one accord by being tuned, not to each other, but to another standard to which each one must individually bow. So one hundred worshipers met together, each one looking away to Christ, are in heart nearer to each other than they could possibly be were they to become

"unity" conscious and turn their eyes away from God to strive for closer fellowship.[1]

The church of the living God. In the Old Testament God is called "the living God" to emphasize the deadness of idols. It is also a favorite designation for God in the New Testament, being used some fifteen times. It emphasizes that he is "eternal" and "immortal" (cf. 1 Timothy 1:17; 6:16). It stresses that he is the source of life and the One who communicates life to believers in Christ (cf. 1 Timothy 1:16). "What agreement is there between the temple of God and idols? For we are the temple of the living God. As God has said: 'I will live with them and walk among them, and I will be their God, and they will be my people'" (2 Corinthians 6:16). "And in him you too are being built together to become a dwelling in which God lives by his Spirit" (Ephesians 2:22).

Because God dwells in us, when we come together we come as "the church [the congregation] of the living God." This is the great glory of assembling together on the Lord's Day. All of us, indwelt, make up the dynamic assembly of the living God, and this induces vast spiritual encouragement among us.

Here's how this works: Listening to the Word of God alone is a good thing, and singing to God alone is also a good thing. But singing to God together and hearing his Word preached together is better! Our hearing and singing intensify when we are with brothers and sisters in whom God also dwells. "At home," says Martin Luther, "in my own house there is no warmth or vigor in me, but in the church when the multitude is gathered together, a fire is kindled in my heart and it breaks its way through."[2]

This is why God's Word is adamant that we believers meet together. "Let us not give up meeting together, as some are in the habit of doing, but let us encourage one another — and all the more as you see the Day approaching" (Hebrews 10:25). TV church won't do! Neither will cyber-church. People indwelt by the living God need the real thing — they need to regularly assemble with fellow temples of the living God. The Sunday gathering is an assembly of the living God!

The pillar and foundation of the truth. This is an awesome and descriptive phrase. John Calvin wrote: "It is no ordinary dignity that is ascribed to the church when it is called *the pillar and ground of the truth.* For what higher terms could he have used to describe it?"[3]

"Pillar" and "foundation" are graphic architectural metaphors. A foundation is essential to the building; a building is only as good as its foundation. The church provides the solid bedrock of truth. Pillars stand upright on the foundation as columns and give the building its structure and beauty. The church as a pillar upholds the truth. Of course, the truth comes from God. God is the source of truth and not the church. But whenever the church is faithful to God's Word, it is the foundation and pillar of God's truths in this world!

This awesome reality lays equally awesome responsibilities on the church. Just as a foundation undergirds a building or a pillar supports the roof, the assembly of believers has been appointed to uphold and undergird, in this world, the truth that God has revealed through Christ. This is a divine call to allow the Word of God to saturate all of life. Jesus himself prayed for the church, "Sanctify them by the truth; your word is truth" (John 17:17). The truth of the Bible is to form and inform the foundation and the pillars.

God's Word is to be everything to us in the church. As the preface to the Geneva Bible in the seventeenth century summarized, the Bible is "the light to our paths, the key of the kingdom of heaven, our comfort in affliction, our shield and sword against Satan, the school of all wisdom, the glass wherein we behold God's face, the testimony of his favor, and the only food and nourishment of our souls."[4] The Bible is light, key, comfort, shield, sword, school, mirror, testimony, food, nourishment, foundation, and pillar — everything!

These three descriptive phrases together make a compelling picture. As the church, we are family ("household"). And together we are to love as brothers and sisters who share the same heredity. We are "the church [congregation] of the living God." We come together as multiple temples of the living God, alive in dynamic, quickened community. As the church, we are "the pillar and foundation of the truth." The truth of God's Word is the bedrock, mortar, and bricks of our lives.

HOUSEHOLD CONDUCT (vv. 14, 15)

The verse in which this beautiful description of the church is embedded is the key verse in understanding what 1 Timothy is all about — namely, that there be proper conduct in the church. Verses 14, 15 read together make this very clear: "Although I hope to come to you soon, I am writing you these instructions so that, if I am delayed, you will know how people ought to conduct themselves in God's household, which is the church of the living God, the pillar and foundation of the truth."

Conduct in the church was such a concern to Paul that virtually all of chapters 2 and 3 are a call to exemplary conduct — to holy behavior and uncontentious prayer (2:1-8), modest dress (2:9, 10), Biblical church order (2:11-15), and godly elders and deacons (3:1-13).

The motivation for this exemplary conduct was openly evangelistic, as mentioned in 2:3, 4: "This is good, and pleases God our Savior, who wants all men to be saved and to come to a knowledge of the truth." And here in the key verse of 1 Timothy, the call to proper conduct in the church is made even more compelling by understanding that we are family, a gathering of people indwelt by the living God, the repository and heralds of truth.

When the people of God live out what they are in Christ, God is pleased to enhance the preaching of the truth of the gospel. I experienced a remarkable example of this after leading a young man to Christ and seeing his life radically changed. He was so changed that his overbearing, intimidating father paid me an unannounced visit in my home where he looked over everything from our furniture to our children, then left me with a challenge and a threat that "this had better be real" and "I will be watching you."

After months of hostile observation of his son, me, and the church, the son urged me to meet with his father. I well remember the terror I felt when I pressed the doorbell. The evening began with a curse — as that hard man cursed his own wickedness and began to weep. He sought Christ's forgiveness that night and found it, then lived the remainder of his life for Christ and his church.

HOUSEHOLD CONFESSION (v. 16)

Paul's two main concerns, as expressed in this text, are about the church's *conduct* and then the church's *confession* in respect to what they believed about Christ. Having stated that the church is "the pillar and foundation of the truth" at the end of verse 15, Paul naturally moves on to the subject of the truth of Christ. He does so by quoting six lines from a creedal hymn about the person of Christ, which he introduces by saying, "Beyond all question, the mystery of godliness is great" (v. 16). Whenever Paul uses the word *mystery*, he uses it to reference Christ as the revelation of the heretofore hidden plan of salvation. So in saying here that the "mystery of godliness is great," he is presenting the person and work of Christ as the key to godly conduct.[5] Jesus makes godliness possible. Then comes the Christ-saturated hymn:

> *He appeared in a body,*
> *was vindicated by the Spirit,*
> *was seen by angels,*
> *was preached among the nations,*
> *was believed on in the world,*
> *was taken up in glory. (v. 16)*

The six lines of the hymn fall into three pairs of contrasting couplets.[6]

The Revelation of Christ. The first couplet describes how Christ was revealed:

> *He appeared in a body,*
> *was vindicated by the Spirit.*

Jesus' appearance "in a body" is a reference to his birth and incarnation. The eternal Son, the architect and judge of the universe, who is without beginning and without end, spoke to the Father before he became a man:

> *"Sacrifice and offering you did not desire,*
> *but a body you prepared for me;*
> *with burnt offerings and sin offerings*
> *you were not pleased.*
> *Then I said, 'Here I am — it is written*
> *about me in the scroll —*
> *I have come to do your will, O God.'"*
> *(Hebrews 10:5-7; cf. Psalm 40:6-8)*

Then, so to speak, he stood at the rim of the universe and dove headlong past a billion stars, through the Milky Way, and into the womb of the Virgin Mary, where he swam and grew until his birth that cold winter's night. "He appeared in a body," sang the early church. This was the initial revelation of Christ. "For in Christ all the fullness of the Deity lives in bodily form" (Colossians 2:9).

The second half of the couplet — "was vindicated by the Spirit" — refers to the corresponding bookend of his earthly life — his resurrection. Romans 1:4 explains that Christ "through the Spirit of holiness was declared with power to be the Son of God by his resurrection from the dead." Likewise Romans 8:11 speaks of "the Spirit of him who raised Jesus from the dead." So the first couplet sings of the supernatural *incarnation* and *resurrection* of Christ that revealed him as the Messiah. This is the Jesus that the church must confess. Anything less is blasphemous.

The witnesses of Christ. The second couplet sings of the witnesses of Christ:

> *was seen by angels,*
> *was preached among the nations.*

This couplet contrasts the witnesses — heavenly angels and earthly nations. One is supernatural, the other natural. One is superhuman, the other human.

The angels saw everything. Angels foretold the birth of Christ to Mary and then to Joseph (cf. Luke 1:26-38; Matthew 1:18-24). At his birth, as my mind sees it, the sky was filled with angelic witnesses who sang:

> *"Glory to God in the highest,*
> *and on earth peace to men*
> *on whom his favor rests."*
> *(Luke 2:14)*

After Christ's temptation, "the devil left him, and angels came and attended him" (Matthew 4:11). In Gethsemane as he sweat as it were great drops of blood, "An angel from heaven appeared to him and strengthened him" (Luke 22:43). Angels witnessed the Resurrection and sat by his empty tomb (cf. Luke 24:4, 23). Angels comforted the disciples as he ascended to Heaven (cf. Acts 1:10, 11). And presently Jesus is adored in glory by vast angelic hosts who sing, "Worthy is the Lamb, who was slain, to receive power and wealth and wisdom and strength and honor and glory and praise!" (Revelation 5:12). And this same Jesus will return with his angels as our King and deliverer (cf. 1 Thessalonians 4:16). He was indeed "seen by angels." They could not get enough of him, and never will!

The angels were the least removed from him, and the Gentiles were farthest removed. And he "was preached among the nations." The whole realm of intelligent creation saw him. There was cosmic witness to Christ on earth and in Heaven.

The reception of Christ. The third couplet sings of the reception given to Christ:

> *was believed on in the world,*
> *was taken up in glory.*

Here we see his reception in two separate geographies — earth and Heaven. He "was believed on in the world." Regarding this the Apostle John wrote, "He was in the world, and though the world was made through him, the world did not recognize him. He came to that which was his own, but his own did not receive him. Yet to all who received him, to those who believed in his name, he gave the right to become children of God" (John 1:10-12). And again, "For God so loved the world that he gave his one and only Son, that whoever believes in him shall not perish but have eternal life" (John 3:16).

We have believed on him in the world! Because of this, Paul's triumphant shout is ours!

Here is a trustworthy saying that deserves full acceptance: Christ Jesus came into the world to save sinners — of whom I am the worst. But for that very reason I was shown mercy so that in me, the worst of sinners, Christ Jesus might display his unlimited patience as an example for those who would believe on him and receive eternal life. Now to the King eternal, immortal, invisible, the only God, be honor and glory for ever and ever. Amen. (1 Timothy 1:15-17)

At the end, his earthly reception was crowned with his heavenly reception — "was taken up in glory." This, of course, refers to Christ's ascension. If the angels sang in wonder at the birth of Christ when he came down to earth, how they must have sung when he returned to Heaven! What a shout must have gone up when the everlasting gates lifted for the King of glory! They were all there to meet him — the angels who raised their flaming swords at the gates of Eden, the angel of the Apocalypse who stood with one foot on the sea and the other on the land, the archangels Michael and Gabriel.[7]

Here is the point: The magnificent Christ of this grand confession makes possible the godly conduct that Paul so earnestly desires.

We are the church. We are family — "God's household." God is our Father, and we are brothers and sisters. We are "the church of the living God." He lives in each of us. We together are "the pillar and foundation of the truth."

And because of this, what we believe and confess about Christ is everything. We confess that he was *revealed* by his incarnation and resurrection.

> *He appeared in a body,*
> *was vindicated by the Spirit.*

We confess that he was witnessed by heaven and earth.

> *was seen by angels,*
> *was preached among the nations.*

We confess that he was received in earth and in Heaven.

> *was believed on in the world,*
> *was taken up in glory.*

Because we are the church, and because we confess such a Christ, we can and must conduct ourselves in a way that brings glory to him. As the apostle told another church, "So whether you eat or drink or whatever you do, do it all for the glory of God" (1 Corinthians 10:31).

11

Bless God's Good Creation

1 TIMOTHY 4:1-5

The Spirit clearly says that in later times some will abandon the faith and follow deceiving spirits and things taught by demons. Such teachings come through hypocritical liars, whose consciences have been seared as with a hot iron. They forbid people to marry and order them to abstain from certain foods, which God created to be received with thanksgiving by those who believe and who know the truth. For everything God created is good, and nothing is to be rejected if it is received with thanksgiving, because it is consecrated by the word of God and prayer.

Imagine yourself in a room with walls that are papered bright green. You walk to an adjoining room where the walls are green, but the shade is imperceptibly bluer. You enter a third room, bluer than the second. Again the difference is too small to be noticeable. After passing through fifty rooms, each slightly bluer than the last, someone hands you a sample of the wallpaper in the room where you started. You are astonished by how green it is. Suddenly you realize that the room you are now in is not green at all! It is blue.[1]

Something like this often happens when people move away from Christ. Subtle influences gradually edge one away from pure belief to that which is ultimately not belief at all. This has happened to thousands who have succumbed to siren songs of legalism, mysticism, or asceticism. The tragedy is that their departure was so imperceptible that they did not know their belief had changed.

This was evidently the case with some of the elders in the Ephesian church who, having begun so well in the gospel, were now hawking a "Christian" asceticism as the path to spirituality. Instead of looking to Christ's work on their behalf as their only hope of salvation and godliness, they now set their hopes on the ascetic denial of fleshly appetites through rules, which Paul elsewhere categorized as "Do not handle! Do not taste! Do not touch!" (Colossians 2:21).

Now, Paul was never opposed to spiritual discipline for the purpose of godliness. In the immediately following context we have his famous injunctions, "train yourself to be godly" and "godliness has value for all things" (vv. 7, 8). We also know that spiritual discipline sometimes involves restraint, and even some no-nos. But asceticism is altogether different because it involves the intentional denial of things that God has declared to be good. It declares that abstinence from these things is essential to spirituality. And ultimately it lays the ax to the life of the gospel.

Paul considered asceticism a heinous doctrine and emphasized its terribleness in the context of 1 Timothy by attacking it immediately after quoting the creedal hymn that sets forth Christ as "the mystery of godliness" — the source and origin of true godliness. Asceticism not only slams the Creator, but also the sufficiency of the Son's work.

ASCETICISM — ITS ORIGIN (vv. 1, 2)

Paul begins his exposé of the folly of the ascetic pursuit of godliness by showing that it was no surprise: "The Spirit clearly says that in later times some will abandon the faith and follow deceiving spirits and things taught by demons" (v. 1). The expression "The Spirit says" is a Biblical way of referring to a past prophetic message, much like saying "the Scripture says" (cf. 1 Timothy 5:18). Here the phrase "The Spirit clearly says" seems to be referring to what Jesus had earlier said, because in the book of Revelation the numerous occurrences of "the Spirit says" refer to Jesus' words. Additionally, the Gospels reveal that Jesus made earlier statements very much like what we have here in 1 Timothy 4:1 (cf. Matthew 24:10 and Mark 13:22).[2] And, of course, the Holy Spirit is sometimes titled "the Spirit of Christ" (Romans 8:9). Either way, Paul here claims explicit divine authority for his withering denunciation of asceticism. Those who feel that Paul is being too hard on asceticism will have to deal with God himself, for he has prophesied of its evils in the clearest terms.

Timothy also understood that the Spirit was talking about present Ephesus because the Ephesian believers were conscious of living in "the last days" (cf. 2 Timothy 3:1) — the days that began with the first advent of Christ and will close with the second advent.[3] The Spirit's explicit message here is that "in later times" (which extends from the first century and includes today) "some will abandon the faith" due to the lures of asceticism, forbidding themselves what God has allowed and making those self-deprivations the sum of their religion, thus displacing Christ.

Demonic origin. The Spirit of Christ leaves no doubt as to the ultimate origin of asceticism — "some will abandon the faith and follow deceiving spirits and things taught by demons" (v. 1b). Asceticism is demonic in origin and diabolical in its intent. I use this strong wording purposely, because it is natural for us to think, "What's so bad about self-denial, even abstaining from good things? After all, we live in an age that insists on being denied nothing." But the reality is, those who introduce a contrived holiness are acting at the instigation of the devil. God is never properly worshiped by a denial of his gifts. And self-denying asceticism, especially in its external, public display, moves one away from worshiping God "in spirit and in truth" (cf. John 4:24).

Human origin. While asceticism has its ultimate origin with demons, it is also rooted in wicked humanity — "Such teachings come through hypocritical liars, whose consciences have been seared as with a hot iron" (v. 2). There is blatant hypocrisy here like that of Benjamin Jowett, the Oxford classicist and theologian who abandoned orthodoxy while still a churchman. Jowett would recite the Apostles' Creed in chapel by saying "I" in a loud voice. Then he'd whisper "used to" to himself, followed by "believe" in a loud voice. High-handed hypocrisy!

Paul's characterization of the ascetic purveyors as "hypocritical liars" is scathing. Their sin was doubly deliberate. As John Stott notes, hypocrisy is a deliberate pretense, and a lie is a deliberate falsehood[4] — double liars! They did not believe their own teaching!

Such teachers have cauterized their consciences. They have allowed them to be so burnt that they have no feeling, no guilt, no remorse. Chrysostom described them as actors: "They utter not their falsehoods through ignorance and unknowingly, but as acting a part, knowing the truth, but 'having their conscience seared.'"[5] We must remember this when dealing with such teachers. However self-effacing and humble and "at your service" they may appear, the Bible says they are *conscious* liars!

ASCETICISM — ITS PARTICULARS (v. 3)

Ephesian asceticism focused its denial on two great gifts from God — namely, *marriage* and *food*: "They forbid people to marry and order them to abstain from certain foods, which God created to be received with thanksgiving by those who believe and who know the truth" (v. 3).

Unfortunately, ascetic teaching fell on fertile ground in the apostolic church. Though the Jews were not generally receptive to ascetic teaching, the Essenes of Qumran were reported by Josephus to "reject pleasure as evil, but esteem continence as a virtue" and to "neglect marriage."[6] Along with this contemporary sectarian tendency, the Greek culture of Ephesus had the seeds of second-century, gnostic dualism that regarded the human body and its functions as evil and taught that the godly must live above the physical. These ideas led both converted Jews and Gentiles to be open to asceticism.[7]

These ascetic tendencies were further fueled by the teaching of some false teachers in Ephesus that the resurrection of believers had already occurred. Second Timothy 2:17, 18 indicates that Hymenaeus and Philetus had believed this and as a result wandered away from the true faith. Philip Towner, in his recent commentary, summarizes:

> The false teachers in Ephesus evidently favored asceticism. It is possible that both marriage and the eating of certain foods were considered part of the old order (the order of things that they believed had passed away with the resurrection of Christ and the outpouring of the Holy Spirit) and therefore to be avoided. The asceticism alluded to in Colossians 2:16-23 bears a striking resemblance, especially where foods are concerned. But it is also possible that this behavior reflected the attempt to enact the life of resurrection paradise by following the model given in Genesis 1 and 2, before the fall into sin — after all, Jesus taught that there would be no marriage in the resurrection (Mt. 22:30), and vegetarianism seems to have been the rule in Eden/paradise (see discussion at 2:11-15). The negative view of marriage seems quite similar to sentiments held by some in Corinth (1 Cor 7:1-7). In any case, whether to cope with the evil material world or to implement the new theology, the heretics enforced a regimen of denial.[8]

Indeed, the Ephesian church was "plowed soil" for a virulent asceticism that Paul and Timothy viewed as toxic to a healthy faith. Most believe that Paul's warning given here in 1 Timothy held the day in Ephesus in the first century.

Asceticism prevails. However, over the following centuries asceticism has had its day and even prevailed at times against the church. Leland Ryken, in his book *Worldly Saints*, notes: "The dominant attitude of the Catholic church throughout the Middle Ages was that sexual love itself was evil and did not cease to be so if its object were one's spouse."[9]

The early church fathers Tertullian and Ambrose believed that the extinction of the human race was to be preferred to the sexual relationship within marriage. Ambrose wrote that "married people ought to blush at the state in which they are living." Augustine argued that the sexual relationship was innocent in marriage, but the passion that accompanies it is always sinful. He frequently counseled married couples to abstain. Albertus and Aquinas objected to marital intimacy because it subordinates the reason to the passions.

The church fathers are virtually unanimous in praising virginity as superior to marriage. This culminated in the Council of Trent in the sixteenth century, which denounced those who denied that virginity was superior to the married state. The Roman church kept adding days in which marital intimacy was prohibited until more than half the days in the year were excluded. No wonder there was a Reformation!

Puritans to the rescue! Seriously, the change did come through the Reformation with its return to the Bible and a focus on what it taught. And the great heroes here were the Puritans — yes, the Puritans! — as they took on the Roman church in straight-on debate. Portions of 1 Timothy 3, 4 were key texts in the argument.

Dr. Ryken concludes: "The Puritan doctrine of sex was a watershed on the cultural history of the West. The Puritans devalued celibacy, glorified companionate marriage, affirmed married sex as both necessary and pure, established the ideal of wedded romantic love, and exalted the role of the wife."[10] Puritan literature is filled with stunning expressions of marital love, such as the anonymous Puritan who offered that when two are made one by marriage they "may joyfully give due benevolence one to the other; as two musical instruments rightly fitted do make a most pleasant and sweet harmony in a well tuned consort [concert]."[11]

But it was John Milton, the great poet and a Puritan, who gave the most elegant expression of the Biblical perspective in his description of Adam and Eve.

> *Straight side by side were laid, nor turned I ween [imagine]*
> *Adam from his fair spouse, nor Eve the rites*
> *Mysterious of connubial love refused:*
> *Whatever hypocrites austerely talk*
> *Of purity and place and innocence,*
> *Defaming as impure what God declares*
> *Pure, and commands to some, leaves free to all.*
> *Our Maker bids increase, who bids abstain*
> *But our Destroyer, foe to God and man?*[12]

Puritanical a synonym for repression and grim asceticism? Not so. I'm with C. S. Lewis, who portrayed the devil Screwtape as boasting to his understudy Wormwood regarding the redefining of puritanism, "And may I remark in passing that the value we have given to that word is really one of the solid triumphs of the last hundred years?"[13]

Why the folly? What folly asceticism is! What fools Christians are who trade in their standing in Christ for ascetic pursuits. There are of course people who, according to both Jesus and Paul, are called to remain single. We also know that fasting is sometimes appropriate. This understood, the Scriptures are clear that celibacy and vegetarianism are not God's general will for his people. Those who forbid marriage and certain foods are guilty of grievous error.

Why would anyone find asceticism attractive, much less embrace it? One possible reason is to assuage one's conscience. It is the nature of all hypocrites and false prophets to create a guilty conscience in matters where there is no offense. The creation of an ascetic conscience that you can soothe by a fleshly abstention can anesthetize you to the inner demands of the Spirit. The trick is to hide your inner wickedness by outward observance — ascetic denials!

Another possible reason for ascetic folly is to create a compensatory righteousness. When you find you cannot abstain from selfishness or greed or cruelty or gossip, you attempt to acquire righteousness by abstaining from those things that God has left you free to do.[14]

One other possibility is what John Stott has called our "lingering evangelical asceticism"[15] — the perverse feeling that the material world with its pleasures such as marriage and food really is tainted. Therefore, if we will renounce these things we will further open ourselves to the spiritual and holy. This is a false claim.

ASCETICISM — ITS ANSWER (vv. 4, 5)

Paul joyfully expresses the answer for and antidote to ascetic folly in verses 4, 5 — "For everything God created is good, and nothing is to be rejected if its is received with thanksgiving, because it is consecrated by the Word of God and prayer."

Creation's goodness. The answer rests on our understanding and affirmation of the intrinsic goodness of everything created by God. We must embrace God's own verdict as stated at the end of Genesis 1: "God saw all that he had made, and it was very good" (v. 31). In reference to food, Jesus himself declared that all foods are clean (cf. Mark 7:19, 20). This fact was pounded into Peter's stubborn awareness through a vision in which a sheet containing earth's fauna was lowered three times before him and a heavenly voice thrice declared, "Do not call anything impure that God has made clean" (cf. Acts 10:9-16).

We are to celebrate creation's goodness in Heaven and earth — the stars and flowers and vegetables and animals and seas and rivers and fish and forest and gender and marriage and sex and family and friends and food.

Christian thanksgiving. Next, having understood creation's goodness, we are to receive it with thanksgiving — "and nothing is to be rejected if it is received with thanksgiving, because it is consecrated by the word of God and prayer" (vv. 4b, 5). Foods are to be received with a prayer of thanksgiving. The answer to asceticism is not mere reception but reception with thankful prayer to God as the giver of good gifts. Jesus consistently blessed God before his meals and offered thanks afterward (cf. Mark 6:41; 8:6; 14:22, 23; Luke 24:30). Paul likewise offered thanks, even for a ship's meals amidst a storm in the Adriatic (cf. Acts 27:35; Romans 14:6; 1 Corinthians 10:30).

Of course just saying a prayer ("grace") does not "consecrate" (literally, "sanctify") our food. What giving thanks does is set our food in its true perspective as God's good creation. Here the phrase "word of God and prayer" expresses a single idea. The word *prayer* references excerpts from Holy Scripture that were customarily used in giving thanks for food.

The implications of giving thanks go beyond eating to all of life. Here G. K. Chesterton helps us:

> *You say grace before meals.*
> *All right.*
> *But I say grace before the play and the opera,*
> *And grace before I open a book,*
> *And grace before sketching, painting,*
> *Swimming, fencing, boxing, walking,*
> *   playing, dancing;*
> *And grace before I dip the pen in the ink.*[16]

This is the way we should approach all of life. Certainly there are times for self-denial and discipline. There are things we do not do because we are Christians. But asceticism is anathema. To regard what God created as somehow unclean is sinful. To teach that abstention from marriage and certain foods is the high road to closeness with God is blasphemous. To require such abstinence from those who want to be good Christians is treacherous. Asceticism can begin the imperceptible drift from pure belief to that which is ultimately not belief at all.

C. S. Lewis wisely warned of the siren dangers of a subtle drift from authentic faith:

> As a matter of fact, if you examined a hundred people who had lost their faith in Christianity, I wonder how many of them would turn out to have been reasoned out of it by honest argument? Do not most people simply drift away?[17]

The Christian life is not meant to be lived in the negative but in the positive — as Jesus showed us by example. We are to be "saying grace" every minute of our lives. This gives glory to God!

12

Pursuing Godliness

1 TIMOTHY 4:6-10

If you point these things out to the brothers, you will be a good minister of Christ Jesus, brought up in the truths of the faith and of the good teaching that you have followed. Have nothing to do with godless myths and old wives' tales; rather, train yourself to be godly. For physical training is of some value, but godliness has value for all things, holding promise for both the present life and the life to come. This is a trustworthy saying that deserves full acceptance (and for this we labor and strive), that we have put our hope in the living God, who is the Savior of all men, and especially of those who believe.

It is clear that when the Apostle Paul focused on the practical life of the church, the godliness of the people was of intense concern. Of the fifteen occurrences of *godliness* in the New Testament, thirteen are in the brief span of the Pastoral Letters (1 and 2 Timothy and Titus), with a whopping nine in 1 Timothy alone. Since the Pastorals are the last of the old apostle's letters, the matter of godliness is naturally charged with final urgency.

For Paul *godliness* is no static, stained-glass word. It is active — kinetic obedience that springs from a reverent awe of God.[1] It is the Isaiah-like action that has a man, awestruck by God, rise from his face saying, "Here am I. Send me!" (Isaiah 6:8). Awe — then action! Godliness is not piety as we generally think of it — upturned eyes and folded hands. Godliness cannot be cloistered. The godly among us are those people whose reverent worship of God flows into obedience throughout the week. Only God-struck doers of the Word can rightly be termed godly.

Furthermore, true godliness is rooted in the mystery of Christ. The last verse of 1 Timothy 3 sings about this:

Beyond all question, the mystery of
   godliness is great:
He appeared in a body,
was vindicated by the Spirit,
was seen by angels,
was preached among the nations,
was believed on in the world,
was taken up in glory. (3:16)

Jesus is the essence and wellspring of godliness. He lived in godliness, and now as ascended Lord he gives us godliness. Godliness is not external but is the inner power to live a godly life (cf. 2 Timothy 3:5; 2 Peter 1:3).[2] The mystery of Christ makes godliness possible. Jesus strikes us with awe and then enables active obedience.

That is why Paul delivers a scathing attack on those who were promoting asceticism as *the* path to godliness through abstinence from marriage and certain foods. Outraged, Paul calls these ideas "things taught by demons" (4:1) and assails the teachers as "hypocritical liars, whose consciences have been seared as with a hot iron" (v. 2). What blasphemy it is to teach that things that God has declared good must be rejected in order to become godly. What a slam on the work of the exalted Christ!

Confronted with the force of such a fearsome denunciation of asceticism, we might conclude that we must steer clear of all bodily disciplines that claim to promote godliness. Not so. In the following paragraphs (vv. 6-10) Paul lays out the correct approach to godliness — which, ironically, he describes as coming through *diet* and *discipline*.

DIET FOR GODLINESS (vv. 6, 7a)

Paul first addresses the matter of a good spiritual diet: "If you point these things out to the brothers, you will be a good minister of Christ Jesus, brought up in the truths of the faith and of the good teaching that you have followed. Have nothing to do with godless myths and old wives' tales" (vv. 6, 7a.).

Reject bad doctrine. Essential to a health-giving spiritual diet is rejection of junk food, here described as "godless myths and old wives' tales." The trash that was coming from the false teachers was "godless" in that it was radically opposite to what is sacred.[3] In calling it "old wives' tales," Paul issued a sarcastic insult, seen frequently in Greek philosophical polemics, meaning "limitless credulity"[4] — they would believe anything. What a concoction it was! The primitive history of the Old Testament was overlaid with ridiculous legends, its genealogies were given absurd symbolism, and then it was sugarcoated with demon-inspired asceticism that promised spiritual superiority through sexual and dietary abstinence. Junk teaching! Reject it, says Paul.

Dine on good teaching. Positively, Paul encourages Timothy to "point these things out to the brothers." In doing so, he tells Timothy, "you will be a good minister of Christ Jesus, brought up in [literally, "nourishing yourself in"][5] the truths of the faith and of the good teaching that you have followed" (v. 6).

Timothy is to be continually feeding himself with the content of the gospel and apostolic teaching. Significantly, this nourishment in the Word was essential to Timothy's being "a good minister." A good diet makes a good minister. The most effective ministers have been those who persevered as students of the Word. Paul is repeatedly adamant about this to Timothy. "Do your best to present yourself to God as one approved, a workman who does not need to be ashamed and who correctly handles the word of truth" (2 Timothy 2:15). "Preach the Word; be prepared in season and out of season; correct, rebuke and encourage — with great patience and careful instruction" (2 Timothy 4:2).

This note needs to be heralded again today from the top of steeples because surveys reveal that the burdens of ministry have led some pastors and missionaries to neglect prayer and the study of God's Word. And that neglect exacts a tragic toll. John Stott, quoting Bishop Cyril Garbett, observed that when an evangelical minister does not study, he will by midlife become sentimentalist in his preaching[6] — depending primarily on a repertoire of clichés and sappy stories that tug at the heartstrings. I have myself witnessed the effects of a lack of study of the Word and an overdeveloped style of repetition, where the minister repeats himself in doublets and triplets because he has so little to say:

> We must go down the road. The road leads to Calvary, the Calvary road. Ah yes the road, the blessed road, the winding road.
> Calvary, you remember, is the high hill where Christ died. Christ died on Calvary to set us free. Sweet Calvary.
> See we are free, free indeed. Free to be free. Free, free, free. . . .[7]

The tragedy is that in such a message there is nothing fresh from the Word, no engagement with the Word's demands. As a result there is little to stir our souls to awestruck worship and active godliness. A Bible diet is essential to godliness.

EXERCISE FOR GODLINESS (vv. 7b-10)

The famous command to exercise abruptly follows the command to reject the diet of false teaching: "Rather, train yourself to be godly. For physical training of is some value, but godliness has value for all things, holding promise for both the present life and the life to come. This is a trustworthy saying that deserves full acceptance" (vv. 7b-9).

Called to exercise! The call to "train yourself to be godly" is highly expressive. The word *train* is a translation of the Greek word *gumnos*, which means "naked" and is the word from which we derive the English word *gymnasium*. In traditional Greek athletic contests, the participants competed without clothing, so their movements would not be hindered. So the word *train* originally carried the literal meaning, "to exercise naked."[8] By New Testament times it referred to exercise and training in general. But even then it was, and still is, a word with the smell of the gym in it — the sweat of a good workout. "Gymnasticize (exercise, work out, train) yourself for the purpose of godliness" conveys the feel of what Paul is saying. Run until your feet are like lead, and then choose to sprint. Pump iron until your muscles burn, until another rep is impossible, then do more.

This call comes to us all, and we can see its wisdom throughout all of life. The discipline of training 10,000 hours enables some of us mortals to run 100 meters in 10 seconds. Years of memorization and study of German may free us to speak Deutsch with the best. Hours watching game films can free a defensive back to play with utter abandon.

But when it comes to spiritual matters, we hesitate. *Discipline* sounds so much like legalism. But such thinking is mistaken. Legalism is self-centered, but discipline is God-centered. The legalistic heart says, "I will do this thing to gain merit with God." The disciplined heart says, "I will do this thing because I love God and want to please him." Paul knew this difference well, and he never gave an inch to legalists, even while challenging Christians to "train yourself to be godly."

Paul brought legendary disciplined energy to his service of God and yet viewed his labor as a product of free grace, reasoning, "But by the grace of God I am what I am, and his grace to me was not without effect. No, I worked harder than all of them — yet not I, but the grace of God that was with me" (1 Corinthians 15:10). Grace is the red blood of a disciplined life.

What is so important to note here is that "train yourself to be godly" in its context primarily refers to training ourselves *in and by the Scriptures* for the purpose of godliness. Our *diet* is to be the Scriptures, and we are to *exercise* ourselves in them. We will become godly only through the most godly Book ever written — God's own Word.[9]

This call is for all of us who know Christ — regardless of how busy we are or how demanding our occupation. Billy Graham has shared that his medical missionary father-in-law Nelson Bell (who ran a 400-bed hospital in China, often on his own) made it a point "to rise every morning at four-thirty and spend two to three hours in Bible reading. He didn't do his correspondence or any of his other work. He just read the Scriptures every morning, and he was a walking Bible encyclopedia. People wondered at the holiness and the greatness in his life." I asked a personal friend, Dr. Ken Gieser, who worked with Dr. Bell about this, and he affirmed every word.[10]

Consider the example of Lt. General William K. Harrison who was the most decorated soldier in the 30th Infantry Division, rated by General Eisenhower as the number one infantry division in World War II. General Harrison was the first American to enter Belgium during that war, which he did at the head of the Allied forces. He received every decoration for valor except the Congressional Medal of Honor — being honored with the Distinguished Service Cross, the Silver Star, the Bronze Star for Valor, and the Purple Heart (he was one of the few generals to be wounded in action). When the Korean War began, he served as Chief of Staff in the United Nations Command and because of his character and calm self-control was ultimately President Eisenhower's choice to head the long and tedious negotiations to end the war.

General Harrison was a soldier's soldier who led a busy, ultra-kinetic life, but he was also an amazing man of the Word. When he was a twenty-year-old West Point cadet, he began reading the Old Testament through once and the New Testament four times annually. General Harrison did this until the end of his life. Even in the thick of war he maintained his commitment by catching up during the two- and three-day respites for replacement and refitting that followed battles, so that when the war ended he was right on schedule. When at the age of ninety his failing eyesight no longer permitted this discipline, he had read the Old Testament seventy times and the New Testament 280 times! No wonder his godliness and wisdom were proverbial. It is no surprise that the Lord used him for eighteen fruitful years to lead Officers Christian Fellowship (OCF).[11]

General Harrison's story tells us that it is possible, even for the busiest of us, to systematically train ourselves in God's Word. His life also remains a demonstration of the benefits of a godly mind's programming itself with Scripture. His closest associates say that every area of his life (domestic, spiritual, and professional) and each of the great problems he faced was informed by the Scriptures. People marveled at his godliness and his ability to bring the Word's light to every area of life.

The call to discipline ourselves in the Word for the purpose of godliness is not a call to engage in legalism. We will not in this way gain standing before God. But we must for the right reasons train ourselves in God's Word — train ourselves to listen to its preaching, take notes, check cross-references, read the Bible regularly (the *One Year Bible* is an immense help), exercise the discipline of purchasing tapes of the Old and New Testaments and listening while commuting or exercising, and so on.

The benefits of exercise. The benefits of proper diet and exercise in the Word are extraordinary, "for physical training is of some value, but godliness has value for all things, holding promise for both the present life and the life to come. This is a trustworthy saying that deserves full acceptance" (vv. 8, 9).

Physical exercise does have "some value." It pays off health-wise. For this reason I jog and lift weights and minimize my intake of doughnuts and Twinkies. But the value of physical exercise is limited. Arnold Schwarzenegger will not take his massive biceps or cannonball deltoids into eternity — or probably even to the grave. But there is no doubt that physical exercise has profited him.

But training for godliness has *unlimited* benefits both in this world and in the coming world ("holding promise for both the present life and the life to come") — because the Christian life is one life. The godliness that comes from training in God's Word has unlimited value for every environment.

The superb lives of Nelson Bell and William K. Harrison declare this to us. Their Word-born godliness multiplied their effectiveness as physician and soldier. Their families received untold benefit. Consider the lives of two of Nelson Bell's children. Ruth Bell Graham became the extraordinary wife of the greatest evangelist of the twentieth century, and her brother Clayton Bell became an eminent Presbyterian preacher. By the way, a woman who was Ruth Graham's roommate during a semester at Wheaton College told me that Ruth regularly got up at 4:30 A.M. to read her Bible and pray! A great heritage was passed on!

The church universal and her institutions have received an untold boon from the lives of these two godly men. True godliness will make us better employees and employers, better spouses, and better members of Christ's Body.

Furthermore, the fact that "godliness has value for all things" applies to our own lives in this temporal environment and in our coming eternal environment — the soul's true climate. When godly lives move into the new climate, their godliness will bloom like an ever-unfolding flower for all eternity. Godliness will continue its occupation begun on earth — that of serving God to his glory. And who knows what reward the fruits of godliness, spoken of metaphorically by Paul as "gold, silver, costly stones" (1 Corinthians 3:12), will receive from God?

So godliness has unlimited value right now as we live out our lives, and will for all eternity. The *New International Version* should not have begun a new paragraph with verse 9 but should have stuck with the paragraphing of the UBS Greek text[12] — because Paul adds the clincher to verse 8 in verse 9: "This is a trustworthy saying that deserves full acceptance." All Christians ought to take Paul's words to heart. They ought to make this truth a part of their wisdom — "For physical training is of some value, but godliness has value for all things, holding promise for both the present life and the life to come" (v. 8). You can trust this to be true — now and eternally. Trust it! Live it!

As he wraps up his thoughts in this section, Paul raises high the hope that comes from the pursuit of godliness: "(and for this we labor and strive), that we have put our hope in the living God, who is the Savior of all men, and especially of those who believe" (v. 10). Paul is not suggesting that all people will be saved, because his other writings make it clear that this is not the case (cf. 2 Thessalonians 1:7b-10; 1 Thessalonians 1:10). The final phrase — "and especially of those who believe" — simply describes those who are saved. Confidence in salvation is the possession of believers alone. Paul's purpose here is not to plumb the question of the wideness of God's grace but to make it clear that those Christians who have placed their hope in the living God and pursue godliness will not be disappointed.

We certainly will not be disappointed if we have believed in Christ who is "the mystery of godliness" because he lived out all godliness and imparts to and inspires godliness in those who are in him. And this hope will grow ever larger if we avoid the lures of thinking that our godliness will increase if we employ fleshly denial of things that God has declared good for all. We can all grow in godliness if we cultivate the life within us by feeding and training ourselves on God's Word. It is all a matter of diet and discipline.

Step into God's gym and "train yourself to be godly. For physical training is of some value, but godliness has value for all things, holding promise for both the present life and the life to come. This is a trustworthy saying that deserves full acceptance" (vv. 7b-9).

13

Succeeding in Ministry

1 TIMOTHY 4:11-16

Command and teach these things. Don't let anyone look down on you because you are young, but set an example for the believers in speech, in life, in love, in faith and in purity. Until I come, devote yourself to the public reading of Scripture, to preaching and to teaching. Do not neglect your gift, which was given you through a prophetic message when the body of elders laid their hands on you. Be diligent in these matters; give yourself wholly to them, so that everyone may see your progress. Watch your life and doctrine closely. Persevere in them, because if you do, you will save both yourself and your hearers.

The transition to a new pastorate is difficult, even when the congregation has given you a solid call and you sense that the call is from God. And when you are young, the change to a new pastorate is especially difficult. The insecure feelings at such a time are universal. Standing in front of a sea of pleasantly inscrutable faces you do not know, you wonder what they are really like. Will they accept you? Will you "click"? Will they take to your style of preaching? Will you be able to lead them? Will you last six months?

I felt all this and more in my mid-thirties when I came to the church I now pastor, College Church (in Wheaton, Illinois). But I hid it by looking "pastoral" — like the benign face on the Quaker Oats box. My first winter I often woke to the snowplow's grinding blade and flashing yellow lights and thought, "What am I doing here? Will I make it?"

This helps me understand young Timothy, the newly appointed leader of the church of Ephesus. But his new situation was much less secure than mine was. The Ephesian church was troubled by false teachers, some of whom were actually in leadership. No congregational "call" had been extended to Timothy. Rather, the Apostle Paul had picked him up by the scruff of the neck and dropped him there like a player on his apostolic chessboard. There is no indication that anyone in Ephesus had asked for him to come, much less appointed or elected him to leadership. We sense from the opening chapter of this letter that Timothy would rather be somewhere else (cf. 1:3).

Timothy was timid by nature, certainly in part because he was young. He was not a "take charge" kind of guy (cf. 1 Corinthians 16:10, 11). The consensus is that he was in his mid-thirties[1] — which may not seem so young to us. But in a culture where one's elders were highly regarded, and in a church where the elders would have been older than he, his relatively young age was a handicap.[2] Second Timothy 1:7 records Paul's apostolic nudge for Timothy to assert himself: "For God did not give us a spirit of timidity, but a spirit of power. . . ."

The combination of Timothy's retiring nature and relative youth made him a natural target for critics. "Who is this pipsqueak to tell us what to do? We need a man with experience!" I am sure there were times when Timothy awoke in the Ephesian night with a pain in his sensitive stomach and murmured, "What am I doing here? Help me, Lord."

Paul was not unaware of Timothy's inner feelings. Notwithstanding his own apostolic boldness, Paul had "been there" himself. He knew the pressures and gut-wrenching concerns of pastoral responsibility (cf. 2 Corinthians 1:8, 9; 7:5-7; 11:28, 29). So Paul addresses Timothy in very personal, intimate terms in these final thoughts of chapter 4 as he urges Timothy to "Command and teach these things" (v. 11) — that is, to oppose the false teachers' asceticism as "things taught by demons" (4:1) and to instruct the church as to the proper diet and discipline in the Word, so necessary for godliness. The old apostle's advice to his young charge has become classic wisdom for all, young and old, who desire to thrive in ministry.

SUCCEEDING THROUGH PERSONAL GODLINESS (v. 12)

Paul's initial advice has to do with godly character: "Don't let anyone look down on you because you are young, but set an example for the believers in speech, in life, in love, in faith and in purity" (v. 12) — an exemplary, fivefold godliness.

The natural inclination when our leadership is challenged is not godliness but the opposite — to become defensive and respond with sarcasm or a put-down or to pull rank and become "presidential" ("I'm the chief here!" "Ever hear of the cloth"?) or to become coldly above it all, aloof, or grieved ("How could you ever question me?"). Any young believer (and some old ones too) can easily succumb to such responses. But ministry is thus diminished.

Paul's advice is to be an example of a lovely fivefold godliness that begins with the tongue — "speech." If a minister gets himself in trouble, it is usually with his mouth. Some of us just plain talk too much. People are always waiting for the pastor to pause, so they can say something. Along with too much talk goes the inability to listen — making it easier for us to say dumb things. Some Christian leaders are ecclesiastical gossips. No confidence or secret is safe with them. They are always prying, hoping for choice morsels to pass on. Rumors are ingested with nodding piety — "It's good that you told me this. I'll pray about it." Some clerics indulge in worldly-wise, double-leveled humor. Hip ecclesiastics — Jay Leno in a clerical collar! Some have problems with sticking to the truth, preferring pastoral prevarication.

So Paul commands Timothy to "set an example . . . in speech." Show people what a self-controlled tongue is. That is of first importance for the preacher. "When words are many, sin is not absent" (Proverbs 10:19). "He who answers before listening — that is his folly and his shame" (18:13). "The mouth of a fool feeds on folly" (15:14). "The heart of the righteous weighs its answers, but the mouth of the wicked gushes evil" (15:28). "The lips of the righteous know what is fitting" (10:32). "He who guards his lips guards his life" (13:3).

Along with this, Timothy is to be an example "in life." "Speech" and "life" go together because they are both observable conduct. "Life" here means "manner of life." In the day-in, day-out humdrum of existence — at the gas station, in the grocery line, at the soccer game, washing the car — we must be an example to all who believe.

In addition to his observable "speech" and "life," Timothy's godly character was to shine in the more abstract, inner qualities — "in love, in faith and in purity." Timothy was to be loving in every circumstance and to all persons, exhibiting his faith through faithfulness, and to be pure not only sexually but in matters of the heart.

So we see that Paul is telling Timothy that Christian leadership is a matter of godly character from beginning to end. The ministry is a character profession. Godly character creates moral authority. Ultimately, godly character wins over those who would naturally look down on one's youth. The first thing, second thing, and third thing for a young pastor is the cultivation of character! Not to do so is to despise his youth by neglecting to grow in godliness when he is most flexible.

SUCCEEDING THROUGH THE WORD (v. 13)

This charge to godly character is followed by Paul's command that Timothy ground his ministry on God's Word: "Until I come, devote yourself to the public reading of Scripture, to preaching and to teaching" (v. 13). This simple sentence is a landmark text in defining the major work of the pastor and the worship of the church. The "public reading of Scripture" was not new. It was already a part of Christian worship that had been adopted from the

Jewish synagogue (cf. Luke 4:16, 17; 2 Corinthians 3:14). The roots of this are found in the Old Testament, in Nehemiah where we read of the men and women of Israel standing from "daybreak till noon" as Ezra read the law (cf. Nehemiah 8:2-8). This is one of the reasons many congregations stand for the reading of God's Word in our worship services.

Not only did Christian churches adopt the custom of the reading of the Old Testament from the synagogues — they added to it readings from the apostles' letters and the Gospels (cf. Colossians 4:16; 1 Thessalonians 5:27). This meant that the apostolic church put the apostles' writings on the same level as the Old Testament. The early church had two public readings — one from a portion of the Old Testament, and then from the apostolic writings. Justin Martyr wrote just after the close of the first century: "On the day called Sunday, all who live in cities or in the country gather together to one place, and the memoirs of the apostles and the writings of the prophets are read, as long as time permits; then, when the reader has finished, the president speaks, instructing and exhorting the people to imitate these good things."[3]

The overall effect of this regular reading of the Old and New Testaments at worship was twofold: 1) It emphasized the radical continuity between the Old and New Testaments. 2) It meant that the authority of the preaching that followed was secondary to and derived from the reading of Scripture. It is an awesome thing when we reverently stand for the reading of God's Word. That is why the church has traditionally sung the *Gloria Patri* afterward.

According to Paul's directives, the reading of Scripture was to be followed by Timothy's attention "to preaching" (i.e., exhortation) "and to teaching" (doctrinal instruction). This is the defining point. As John Stott, the acknowledged master of Biblical exposition in the English-speaking world, has said: "It was taken for granted from the beginning that Christian preaching would be expository preaching, that is, that all Christian instruction and exhortation would be drawn out of the passage which had been read."[4] Biblical exposition was the apostolic norm. Therefore, any preaching that does not guide the listener through the Scriptures is an aberration from apostolic practice.

This sounds the alarm in regard to the "disexposition" that is issuing from so many evangelical pulpits today. The congregation hears the text read and waits in anticipation for its exposition — only to be disappointed when the text is never alluded to in the next thirty minutes. Or, more commonly, the text is handled superficially with no serious engagement of its meaning. The preacher mouths its words, but there is no substance. "Disexposition" takes many forms. Sometimes the text is so encrusted with stories and jokes that it is unseen and unheard. Other times it is distorted because it is preached through a therapeutic, political, or social lens.

Paul calls young Timothy to be radically Biblical in his preaching — expositional. He was to be the very opposite of the false teachers and their "godless myths and wives' tales" (4:7) and "endless genealogies" (1:4). The truth is, without the centrality of the Word and its exposition, there is no proper worship. Paul cites Word-centeredness as the key to young, timid Timothy's success.

SUCCEEDING THROUGH GIFTEDNESS (v. 14)

As young, reticent Timothy suffers under the glare of those who look down on him, the question that keeps running through his head is, "Do I have the right stuff?" So Paul affirms that he does indeed have it but also adds a bracing command: "Do not neglect your gift, which was given you through a prophetic message when the body of elders laid their hands on you" (v. 14).

Paul charges Timothy to remember that electric moment in the past, somewhere with Paul in his travels, when the young man knelt, and Paul and the local elders fixed their hands on him, intoning prophecies and prayers about his giftedness and future ministry. Paul has alluded to this in 1:18 — "Timothy, my son, I give you this instruction in keeping with the prophecies once made about you, so that by following them you may fight the good fight." And Paul will do so again in 2 Timothy 1:6 — "For this reason I remind you to fan into flame the gift of God, which is in you through the laying on of my hands."

This almost certainly had to do with his calling and gifting for ministry as a preacher of the Word. This is apparent from the repeated charges Paul gives to Timothy to minister the Word in 2 Timothy (2:15, 24-26; 3:14 — 4:5).[5] Timothy had heard with his own ears that God would enable and bless his preaching. There is wisdom here for everyone who has been called. If God has called you to ministry, he has gifted you. Personally, this staying conviction got me through the early transitions in my own ministry. And the conviction is still necessary many years later.

Underlying Paul's command is the unspoken maxim, "Use it or lose it." That is why he told his young disciple, "Fan into flame the gift of God." Timothy's gift here is not a once-and-for-all, unchanging endowment from God. It has to be used and cultivated.[6] As we know, shy Timothy did use his gift and was counted as a key player in the apostolic church. What practical wisdom we see here for ministry. *Use it or lose it!* This is true for anyone in ministry. And it is doubly true for those younger believers who are gifted for ministry.

SUCCEEDING THROUGH DILIGENCE (v. 15)

As we have surveyed Paul's advice to Timothy, we have seen that young Timothy will succeed, first, if he pursues *godliness*, second, if he bases his ministry on the *Word*, and thirdly, if he utilizes his *gift*. Now Paul links

Timothy's success to his *diligence*: "Be diligent in these matters; give yourself wholly to them, so that everyone may see your progress" (v. 15).

The diligence commanded here echoes the athletic metaphor of verses 7-10, where Christians are urged to train themselves for godliness. So it is a call to diligent sweat. But the sense is intensified by "give yourself wholly to them" (literally, "be in these things so as to be absorbed in them"). As Philip Towner said it, "Live and breathe these things."[7] Timothy is to give all he has — all his life — to being godly, to the ministry of the Word, and to exercising his gift of preaching.

There is simply no success in ministry apart from hard work. I know that workaholism is a sin, and I guard myself and warn my colleagues against it. But as I travel around the country to speak at ministers' conferences, I find that the greatest problem is sloth, and especially in regard to the pulpit. Many do not spend enough time to prepare and teach a good Sunday school lesson, much less preach effectively. In fact, the fare is often better in Sunday school! One lazy preacher prepared his sermon on Saturday night while watching television. Presumably the Bible was not enough to occupy his mind. The predictable corollary is that his preaching did not occupy his congregation's thoughts or hearts. That is scandalous, given the force of Paul's advice here and in the rest of the Pastorals (cf. 2 Timothy 2:15; 3:16, 17; 4:2).

SUCCEEDING THROUGH BALANCE (v. 16)

Paul's ending advice to Timothy has given the church a famous, and on the surface enigmatic, saying: "Watch your life and doctrine closely. Persevere in them, because if you do, you will save both yourself and your hearers" (v. 16). The opening line is an exquisite summary. "Watch your life" refers to the fivefold example of godliness commanded in verse 12: "in speech, in life, in love, in faith and in purity." "Watch your . . . doctrine" references his preaching and teaching (v. 13), which are to be exercised since he has been gifted for ministry (v. 14).

The balance of life and doctrine is the key to spiritual success. Doctrine has everything to do with life, because what we believe about God determines how we live. The more we know about God and his workings, the more we will love him, and the better we will serve him. Do you love him now? Will you love him less if you learn more of him and his Word? The great need of people today is to know more of God — to know more doctrine. Doctrine is the most practical thing in life!

On the other hand, godly lifestyle has everything to do with maintaining doctrine because if we do not live according to what we know of God and his Word, we will either disbelieve or will attempt to change his Word. This is exactly what has happened with so many who have departed from the faith.

So we need to "watch [our] life and doctrine." What am I like? Am I consistent? How is my "speech"? How is my "life"? How is my "love," my "faith," my "purity"? How is my "doctrine"? Is it truly Biblical? Or is it secularized or syncretized? Do I really believe what I say I believe? And am I believing it more as time goes on?

This is all so important for your ministry because if you "persevere in them . . . you will save both yourself and your hearers" (v. 16). Paul is being instructively enigmatic here because he taught again and again that salvation comes only through God's sovereign mercy and grace. He left no doubt — we do not and cannot save ourselves. His point is that those who persevere in life and doctrine will persevere in salvation.

Timid Timothy was in a tough spot — pastoring a church that had not called him — ministering to a people who despised his youth and inexperience. But he succeeded 1) because he was godly in character, 2) because he focused on the Word, 3) because he exercised his gift, 4) because he worked hard, and 5) because he carefully watched his life and doctrine.

Such lives work out their own salvation (Philippians 2:12). They save themselves and then save their hearers. How is your "life"? How is your "doctrine"?

14

Relating and Leading

1 TIMOTHY 5:1-16

Do not rebuke an older man harshly, but exhort him as if he were your father. Treat younger men as brothers, older women as mothers, and younger women as sisters, with absolute purity. Give proper recognition to those widows who are really in need. But if a widow has children or grandchildren, these should learn first of all to put their religion into practice by caring for their own family and so repaying their parents and grandparents, for this is pleasing to God. The widow who is really in need and left all alone puts her hope in God and continues night and day to pray and to ask God for help. But the widow who lives for pleasure is dead even while she lives. Give the people these instructions, too, so that no one may be open to blame. If anyone does not provide for his relatives, and especially for his immediate family, he has denied the faith and is worse than an unbeliever. No widow may be put on the list of widows unless she is over sixty, has been faithful to her husband, and is well known for her good deeds, such as bringing up children, showing hospitality, washing the feet of the saints, helping those in trouble and devoting herself to all kinds of good deeds. As for younger widows, do not put them on such a list. For when their sensual desires overcome their dedication to Christ, they want to marry. Thus they bring judgment on themselves, because they have broken their first pledge. Besides, they get into the habit of being idle and going about from house to house. And not only do they become idlers, but also gossips and busybodies, saying things they ought not to. So I counsel younger widows to marry, to have children, to manage their homes and to give the enemy no opportunity for slander. Some have in fact already turned away to follow Satan. If any woman who is a believer has widows in her family, she should help them and not let the church be burdened with them, so that the church can help those widows who are really in need

A chessboard come to life, as in *Alice in Wonderland*, is a scary thought. Robed bishops in towering miters dealing diagonal death. Armored knights on their clanking steeds charging at wild angles all over the board to dispatch surprised enemies. Mobile castles rushing the lanes like mountains of death.

Seemingly omnipotent kings and queens regally posed to terminate those who venture too near. And you — you are just a lowly pawn, an inevitable crimson smear on the checkered battlefield. Chess a la Lewis Carroll is only for brave hearts.

Young Timothy was a faint heart at this point in his life, certainly not someone who would by nature lead the charge into battle. Time would reveal that he indeed had a steadfast heart, but conflict was not his cup of tea. However, there he was on the checkered field of Ephesus with daunting figures swirling about him. Elders looked down on the young, inexperienced lightweight. Some of these elders had sinned against their consciences and shipwrecked their faith — men like Hymenaeus, who preached that the resurrection had already taken place, effectively tossing out the gospel (cf. 1 Timothy 1:19, 20; 2 Timothy 2:17, 18). "Godless myths" and "genealogies" and "old wives' tales" and "controversies" had become the main fare of these false teachers. Their "gospel" was a deadly, life-denying asceticism (cf. 1 Timothy 1:3, 4; 4:1-7).

Adding to the confusion, their female devotees, whom Paul terms "weak-willed women, who are loaded down with sins and are swayed by all kinds of evil desires, always learning but never able to acknowledge the truth" (2 Timothy 3:6, 7), had been involved in subverting church order (cf. 1 Timothy 2:8-15). The effect was a whirling chessboard of theological and relational confusion.

The ministry had become increasingly misshapen due to weak management. It was losing its center. The main things, gospel and mission, were becoming increasingly marginalized. Good things like the care of widows were becoming the main things. Timothy was being called to say some hard things. Rebukes were required.

Because uneasy and unwelcome Timothy was feeling the withering glare of the Ephesian leadership, Paul had given him the essentials of ministerial survival, namely: 1) godliness, 2) the Word, 3) giftedness, 4) diligence, and 5) balance in life and doctrine (cf. 4:11-16). Now Paul goes on to instruct Timothy on how to relate to the people while saying hard things and further dealing with the delicate issue of the care of widows.

RELATING TO EVERYONE (vv. 1, 2)

The apostle's relational advice is classic: "Do not rebuke an older man harshly, but exhort him as if he were your father. Treat younger men as brothers, older women as mothers, and younger women as sisters, with absolute purity" (vv. 1, 2).

Older men. Given Timothy's timidity and his natural distaste for confrontation, it was very possible that he might first rehearse his rebuke so that he could articulate it, then, with his adrenaline pumping, screw up his courage, approach the erring elder, and spit it out like an Old Testament prophet, leaving the impression that he neither respected the man's age nor cared for him personally. But Paul indicates that Timothy must not rebuke the elder from a posture of superiority or even of equality but of loving respect — "as if he were your father." Rather than an officious tongue lashing out, there must be a filial discomfort in rebuking an older man. Imagine yourself having to rebuke your father and the natural humility and trepidation that would engulf you, and you have the idea. Tone is so important in ministry, and with older people it must be that of affection and respect.

Younger men. Timothy is to exhort younger men "as brothers," as equals. His God-given pastoral leadership role is not to lead him to imagine that his flock are somehow "his people." Rather, they are his brothers and sisters. This eternal theological fact fuels and informs the proper manner of pastoral oversight and the occasional personal exhortations that are necessary.

Older women. Young Timothy is to admonish older women "as mothers." This is how a church leader ought to relate to older women in general. I heard R .C. Lucas, the unmarried, retired pastor of St. Helen's Bishopgate in London, say that "the life of a single pastor would be bleak without them" and then relate how the older women had been such an encouragement to him when he was a young pastor.[1] Paul seems to have enjoyed similar relationships. "Greet Rufus," he said, "chosen in the Lord, and his mother, who has been a mother to me, too" (Romans 16:13). If a rebuke was ever in order, he did it as a loving son to his mother.

Younger women. Younger women were to be ministered to "as sisters, with absolute purity" — literally "chastity."[2] Barbara and I raised two girls and two boys, and believe me, our grade-school boys were not into kissing their sisters! But at the same time, they would have died to protect them.

Pastoral warmth can easily be misinterpreted and also exploited, and there is reason to think this was happening in Ephesus (cf. 5:11 and 2 Timothy 3:6, 7). Timothy was to treat women with the same chaste manner and protectiveness that he would afford his own flesh-and-blood sister. How much grief the modern church could have been spared had this one dictum been taken to heart by its leaders!

What a rich store of relational wisdom Paul gives the church with its full span of age and gender. How beautiful is the church that has people who know who they are, then treat one another as fathers, mothers, brothers, and sisters. Such a graced family knows "how people ought to conduct themselves in God's household, which is the church of the living God, the pillar and foundation of the truth" (3:15). Such graced conduct means that the gospel will go forth unhindered. And this "pleases God our Savior, who wants all men to be saved and to come to a knowledge of the truth" (2:3, 4).

CARING FOR WIDOWS (vv. 3-16)

The provision regarding the care of widows was deeply rooted in the Jewish-Christian tradition. In the Old Testament, widows are accorded extraordinary care and honor. This came right out of the fifth commandment to "Honor your father and your mother" (Exodus 20:12). Honor was understood to include providing financial support, as Jesus made so clear when he scolded the Pharisees and teachers of the law for dodging their responsibility through the use of the "Corban" exemption (cf. Mark 7:8-13).

God himself was understood to defend widows. Soon after the giving of the fifth commandment we read, "Do not take advantage of a widow or an orphan. If you do and they cry out to me, I will certainly hear their cry" (Exodus 22:22, 23). Deuteronomy also attests that "He defends the cause of the fatherless and the widow" (10:18). So all Jewish culture understood its duty to care for widows (cf. Deuteronomy 14:28, 29; 24:17; 24:19ff.; 26:12, 13).

Jesus' heart was with the widows also — raising the son of the widow of Nain (Luke 7:11-14) and lauding the widow's two mites (Luke 21:1-3) and, as we already mentioned, excoriating those who ducked their family responsibility.

So under the force of Old Testament teaching and Jesus' example and words, the early church excelled in the care of widows. Acts 6 records how seven godly men were appointed to carry out the daily distribution of food to Grecian widows (Acts 6:1-6). And the apostle James made it ever so clear that "Religion that God our Father accepts as pure and faultless is this: to look after orphans and widows in their distress and to keep oneself from being polluted by the world" (1:27).

The apostolic church did so well in caring for widows that it overapplied the divine instructions, so that too many widows were on church welfare. And some may not even have been believers, as verse 6 may imply.

So Paul instructs Timothy to perform an intervention with some tough directives. And the advice he had just given to recognize age and gender in admonishing the church — to treat believers as fathers, brothers, mothers, and sisters — will prove crucial here.

Real widows only. His opening line cuts to the quick: "Give proper recognition to those widows who are really in need" (v. 3). The term "proper recognition" means care and financial support.[3] The descriptive phrase "widows who are really in need" appears three times in Paul's instructions (here and in verses 5 and 16) and literally reads, "widows who are real widows" (RSV).

The additional description in verse 5 ("and left all alone") means that she has no family to support her. So we see that simply being a widow did not qualify a woman for support. A widow was to be supported by the church only if she was destitute — without resources, without the customary dowry, with no family to help her.

Godly widows only. Paired with destitution, there was a second qualification for welfare for widows — *godliness*: "The widow who is really in need and left all alone puts her hope in God and continues night and day to pray and to ask God for help. But the widow who lives for pleasure is dead even while she lives. Give the people these instructions, too, so that no one may be open to blame" (vv. 5-7). Those who heed these instructions will not wrongly discern who qualifies and who does not qualify for the church's help. The widow who qualifies is like the elderly prophetess Anna, who was in the temple praying night and day at the time Mary and Joseph presented Jesus and "gave thanks to God and spoke about the child to all who were looking forward to the redemption of Jerusalem" (Luke 2:38).

So the only widows who qualified for church support were those who *financially* qualified through destitution and *spiritually* qualified through godliness.

Family responsibility. What about the widows who do not qualify for help? What would happen to them? They were to be taken care of by their families, as is *positively* stated in verse 4: "But if a widow has children or grandchildren, these should learn first of all to put their religion into practice by caring for their own family and so repaying their parents and grandparents, for this is pleasing to God." The inevitable fact is, with the rhythm of generations a dramatic reversal comes to us all. We who once held our helpless children in our arms and nursed them and provided for their every need will one day be held in their arms as they nurse us at the end of our lives. This responsibility will come to us all. And when we sons and daughters do this, we are only "repaying [our] parents and grandparents." We will be living out the fifth commandment. We will be putting our "religion [literally, "godliness"] into practice." We will not have God's approval without such loving family care — "for this is pleasing to God."

The *negative* expression of our filial responsibility is meant to shock us: "If anyone does not provide for his relatives, and especially for his immediate family, he has denied the faith and is worse than an unbeliever" (v. 8). This is a scathing judgment— almost all pagans in Roman times *did* take care of their parents. To do less than an unbeliever denies the faith because it is an act worse than a person who makes no profession of faith.

Applying these instructions for the first-century church in Ephesus to the church in the twenty-first century, we find the principles to be clear and demanding. Christian sons and daughters are responsible for the care of widows and, as the text expands it, of their helpless parents and grandparents. Today, despite the cultural nets of Social Security, retirement benefits, and interest on investments, Christian children are to care for their parents. If financial provision is unneeded, there is still a Christian obligation for hands-on, loving care. Nurses may be employed, but there must be more — the care cannot be done by proxy. Emotional neglect and abandonment is not an option, for such conduct "is worse than an unbeliever." The conduct of Christians in these areas should help unbelievers see that God's household is "the church of the living God, the pillar and foundation of the truth" (3:15).

And after the Christian family takes care of its own, the church must take care of the real widows — those without family who have no means and who put their hope in God. Such real widows are found in every congregation, and they are our sacred obligation. This comes very close to home for me. My own mother was widowed at the age of twenty-three and was left with three boys to raise. Her own family consisted of a widowed mother and a widowed sister and her daughter, who all did their best to help each other during the difficulties of the subsequent years. Sadly, their church, though it was evangelical, never did anything to help.

Today I believe the application of this passage should be wider, because modern American culture has produced a category of women virtually unknown in the first century — Christian women and children who have been abandoned by their spouses and left without family support. Godly single mothers are a new class of "widow." And those without family and resources are the church's sacred responsibility. Those believers who are involved in fleshing out our obligation are doing the work of God — true religion.

PROVIDING FOR THEIR MINISTRY (vv. 9-15)

Customarily, the following paragraphs (verses 9-15) have been read as listing further qualifications for widows who wish to be on the list to receive financial aid. But such a reading makes it virtually impossible for a widow to qualify for help unless she has been saintly for some years. This would leave many destitute and godly Christian sisters out in the cold.

There is another way to read this passage that makes more sense, and that is to understand that "the list" is a registry of widows capable of offering service. The stringent qualifications to get on "the list" are necessary for spiritual service.[4] The list was not a formal order of widows that came to exist at the end of the second century but an Ephesian list of special widows.

Older widows. First, there are three qualifications for the older widows, and they specify age, faithfulness, and good works: "No widow may be put on the list of widows unless she is over sixty, has been faithful to her husband, and is well known for her good deeds, such as bringing up children, showing hospitality, washing the feet of the saints, helping those in trouble and devoting herself to all kinds of good deeds" (vv. 9, 10). Sixty was culturally recognized as the age of retirement, as well as the age when remarriage was unlikely. It was an ideal age for a widow to commit herself to singleness and ministry. "Faithful to her husband" literally reads, "a one-man woman."[5] Such had been the faithful character of her married life. Here "good deeds" are described in beautiful fivefold practicality: 1) "bringing up children," 2) "showing hospitality," 3) "washing the feet of the saints," 4) "helping those in trouble," and 5) "devoting herself to all kinds of good deeds."

Younger widows. Paul's advice about younger widows excludes them from the registry for ministry out of hand:

> *As for younger widows, do not put them on such a list. For when their sensual desires overcome their dedication to Christ, they want to marry. Thus they bring judgment on themselves, because they have broken their first pledge. Besides, they get into the habit of being idle and going about from house to house. And not only do they become idlers, but also gossips and busybodies, saying things they ought not to. So I counsel younger widows to marry, to have children, to manage their homes and to give the enemy no opportunity for slander. Some have in fact already turned away to follow Satan. (vv. 11-15)*

Evidently, inclusion on "the list" of ministering widows involved a pledge not to marry. This would prove too much for many young widows. Besides, if they were fully supported by the church for ministry, they would have too much time on their hands and get into trouble. And in fact some had. According to Gordon Fee, the word *gossips* means "to talk nonsense or foolishness" and is used most often in a context of speaking something foolish or absurd in comparison with truth. This word suggests talk that is like that of the false teachers. They were likely purveyors of false teaching.[6] Thus Paul advised the young widows to marry.

The playing field in Ephesus was checkered indeed. Assaults could come from all angles on young Timothy as he delivered the apostolic directives. But Paul had wisely advised him to deliver his exhortations with proper deference to gender and age. And we can be sure that Timothy did.

And the advice regarding the problem of needy widows was brilliant. The number of widows receiving church support was reduced to those who qualified *financially* and *spiritually*. And some Christian families re-shouldered their sacred responsibilities, and thus the Ephesian testimony brightened before the pagan world.

But there was more. Many of those godly widows were given an avenue to serve. They not only received according to their need, but they were allowed to give according to their ability. These widows were given dignity and position. And the younger widows were encouraged to embrace life to the glory of God.

Brave-hearted Timothy stood and delivered the message amidst the swirling forces of Ephesus. And that message still resounds today!

15

Regarding Leaders

1 TIMOTHY 5:17-25

The elders who direct the affairs of the church well are worthy of double honor, especially those whose work is preaching and teaching. For the Scripture says, "Do not muzzle the ox while it is treading out the grain," and "The worker deserves his wages." Do not entertain an accusation against an elder unless it is brought by two or three witnesses. Those who sin are to be rebuked publicly, so that the others may take warning. I charge you, in the sight of God and Christ Jesus and the elect angels, to keep these instructions without partiality, and to do nothing out of favoritism. Do not be hasty in the laying on of hands, and do not share in the sins of others. Keep yourself pure. Stop drinking only water, and use a little wine because of your stomach and your frequent illnesses. The sins of some men are obvious, reaching the place of judgment ahead of them; the sins of others trail behind them. In the same way, good deeds are obvious, and even those that are not cannot be hidden.

I had the honor of giving the 1998 Mullins Lectures on Preaching at Southern Baptist Seminary in Louisville, Kentucky, one of the oldest endowed lectureships in the country. My initial lecture was given in Southern's Heritage Hall, a beautiful Georgian room with walls covered with portraits of the school's presidents, among them such luminaries as John Broadus and A. T. Robertson, the greatest Koine Greek scholar of his time.

After the final lecture, Southern's president, Albert Mohler, drove me to the Old Cave Hill National Cemetery and the graves of the seminary's leaders, among them its founder James Pitigru Boyce and E. Y. Mullins, for whom the lectures were named. At the graves of John Broadus and A. T. Robertson, Dr. Mohler reflected on the leadership of Southern over the years — both the mistakes and triumphs of his predecessors — and then his own dreams.

I will never forget that day because of the dramatic setting, including Broadus's imposing granite tombstone and Robertson's flat grave marker lying behind it "because," as President Mohler explained, "Robertson wanted to be buried in Broadus's shadow" — though A. T. Robertson was himself the towering genius of Southern Seminary. But what I will remember more than the juxtaposition of the tombstones is how crucial leadership is to the Christian enterprise. A careful examination of any Christian institution and any church will bear this out, regardless of its size or prominence.

The Apostle Paul, the greatest of the apostolic leaders, understood this in his own day — hence his letter to Timothy and especially the third chapter's famous list of qualifications for church leadership. Both the scarcity and fragility of church leadership dogged Paul's missionary heart. He knew that as the leadership goes, so goes the church! So here again in 5:17-25, Paul discourses on leadership, specifically in the matter of *maintaining the church's leadership* — everything from pay and discipline to the selection of leaders.

HONORING CHURCH LEADERS (vv. 17, 18)

The term "elders" (*presbuteroi*, "presbyters") as it is used here must be understood as equivalent to what is today called pastors. We know this because the designation "elders" includes the "overseers" (*episcopoi*) of chapter 3, as seen from a comparison of the parallel passage in Titus (cf. Titus 1:5-7 and Acts 20:17, 28). Also, the title *elder* originally came from the Jewish synagogue where it meant those who supervised the synagogue (cf. Acts 5:21; 25:15). Along with this, the size of their job as here described is analogous to the range of the duties of a full-time pastor — they were to "direct the affairs of the church" and work at "preaching and teaching." Such demanding duties would not allow time to work other jobs. Thus New Testament commentator Philip Towner concludes: "In modern terms, Paul has in mind the pastoral staff, whose members, in obedience to God's call, have devoted their lives to the service of the church."[1]

These elder-pastors, says Paul, were to be given double honor: "The elders who direct the affairs of the church well are worthy of double honor, especially those whose work is preaching and teaching" (v. 17). As a pastor, it is tempting to interpret "double honor" to mean double pay! But actually it means "twofold honor," honor shown in two ways: 1) respect and 2) remuneration.[2] This is not only correct — it is an ancient interpretation. St. Chrysostom said this called for reverence and support.[3]

Remuneration. Paul quotes two unquestioned authorities to bolster his insistence for pastoral remuneration — Moses and Jesus. First, he quotes Moses from Deuteronomy 25:4, "For the Scripture says, 'Do not muzzle the ox while it is treading out the grain'" (v. 18a). The quotation is used as an *a fortiori* argument (from the lesser to the greater), which he fully spelled out in 1 Corinthians 9:7-12a:

*Who serves as a soldier at his own expense? Who plants a vineyard
and does not eat of its grapes? Who tends a flock and does not drink
of the milk? Do I say this merely from a human point of view? Doesn't
the Law say the same thing? For it is written in the Law of Moses:
"Do not muzzle an ox while it is treading out the grain." Is it about
oxen that God is concerned? Surely he says this for us, doesn't he?
Yes, this was written for us, because when the plowman plows and
the thresher threshes, they ought to do so in the hope of sharing in the
harvest. If we have sown spiritual seed among you, is it too much if
we reap a material harvest from you? If others have this right of
support from you, shouldn't we have it all the more?*

Paul did not claim this for himself (cf. 1 Corinthians 9:12b) but nevertheless commended such remuneration as the norm for the established
church. In case this was not sufficiently convincing, his second quotation was
directly from Jesus: "The worker deserves his wages" (v. 18b), a word-for-
word duplication of Luke 10:7 (cf. Matthew 10:10). It is beautiful to find
Paul introducing both an Old Testament and a New Testament quotation
with, "The Scripture says." It is possible that Luke's Gospel, or an early draft
of it, had come to Paul's attention before he wrote 1 Timothy.[4] After all, Luke
and Paul were apostolic sidekicks.

So we have it from Paul (via Moses and Jesus) that churches are to honor
their pastors with appropriate remuneration. In my travels to pastors' conferences I have sometimes heard otherwise. At a conference that I will not
name, a pastor told me that a couple of families took it on themselves to
supply his family with eggs and milk. He was understandably heartened by
their generosity — until he learned that the cost of the gifts was deducted
from his salary!

So what is an honoring stipend, a fair wage? As a rule of thumb, pastors ought to be paid on the same scale as others in the congregation of the
same age, education, level of experience, and responsibilities. They should
not live above or below their congregation. And it is generally better for the
church to err on the plus side!

Respect. The other side of the "double honor" that Paul commends is
respect. Certainly there must be respect for the pastoral position. But not in
the way it has been pursued by the clergy with its accumulation of miters,
scepters, and vestments that would rival the high priest of Quezalquatal. And
certainly not in the proliferation of titles that some hunger for — "Reverend"
— "very reverend" — "the most very reverend" — "the reverend Dr.,
prebendary." A dependence upon professional titles for pastoral leadership is
an indication of evacuated authority.

So what is this respect? There is intrinsic respect in the pastoral position,
but it is established and authenticated by work. The word *work* in the phrase

"whose work is preaching and teaching" is literally "toil" or "work hard." As George Knight observes, "With this verb he is self-consciously designating the work of these elders as a vigorous and laborious work."[5] Honor properly goes to those who "work" hard in "direct[ing[the affairs of the church" and at "preaching and teaching." Sloth is anathema! It is the bane of the church and the modern pulpit. It deserves no honor, either in respect or in stipend. But double honor goes to those who are called by God and do their job.

DISCIPLINING CHURCH LEADERS (vv. 19-21)

There were leaders in Ephesus who were worthy of twofold honor because they did their jobs with integrity. Sadly, there were others who were failing. And so Paul addresses the matter of disciplining such leaders:

> *Do not entertain an accusation against an elder unless it is brought by two or three witnesses. Those who sin are to be rebuked publicly, so that the others may take warning. I charge you, in the sight of God and Christ Jesus and the elect angels, to keep these instructions without partiality, and to do nothing out of favoritism. (vv. 19-21)*

Caution, courage, and fairness are enjoined in exercising discipline.

Caution. Paul begins with a cautionary note: "Do not entertain an accusation against an elder unless it is brought by two or three witnesses" (v. 19). A high degree of caution is in order because pastoral leadership is a profession that depends on character. If you do not maintain character, you can lose everything except salvation. Next to your life in Christ, your character is your most valuable possession.

Also, church leaders are highly visible and are tragically vulnerable to the adverse actions of the disorderly, the malevolent, and the ill-willed — and to whispering gossip. The human proclivity to believe the worst sadly persists, even in the church. John Calvin, reflecting on his pastoral experience in Geneva, mused:

> . . . as soon as any charge is made against ministers of the Word, it is believed as surely and firmly as if it had been already proved. This happens not only because a higher standard of integrity is required from them, but because Satan makes most people, in fact nearly everyone, overcredulous so that without investigation, they eagerly condemn their pastors whose good name they ought to be defending.[6]

Perhaps Calvin was a bit defensive. But such has been the experience of many today as well.

When I was first in ministry, a woman who had recently spent some time in the state mental hospital began attending my college group. She looked deranged. Her hair was disheveled, her eyes disengaged, and the poor woman was in ill health. Other than a group greeting I never had a personal conversation with her. But she began to stalk our home, driving slowly by at all hours. And she began to tell others that "Pastor Hughes is going to leave his wife and marry me." Worse, some people actually believed her. How insulting! How wicked! How sub-Christian to entertain, much less give credence to, such slander! I was shocked that anyone could entertain such a thought about me. "The words of the wicked lie in wait for blood, but the speech of the upright rescues them" (Proverbs 12:6).

The remedy? Give your leaders the same protection that everyone else has. Never listen to gossip about leaders, or even to a serious accusation, if it only comes from one person. All charges must be substantiated by two or three responsible people if it is to be considered. How much grief would have been avoided in the church if this ancient Biblical pattern were followed (cf. Deuteronomy 19:15; 2 Corinthians 13:1).

Courage. Though we must be cautious in accusing, if the charge is substantiated, we must have the courage to rebuke: "Those who sin are to be rebuked publicly, so that the others may take warning" (v. 20). This may sound cold and unloving, but it must be done, for the sake of the church — "so that the others may take warning" — both minister and congregation. This is where today's church has lost its nerve. Leaders sin with impunity — and then move on to other churches to do the same thing. We must determine not to fall to such a loss of courage but rather to lovingly confront those who are doing wrong. A lack of fortitude is not loving but unloving — unloving of Christ, unloving of the church, and unloving of the offender.

Fairness. Lastly, in this matter of discipline there is the issue of fairness. Verse 21 is closely joined with verses 19, 20, and the NIV's beginning a new paragraph here is "a mystery," as Gordon Fee says. Its connection is urgent. "I charge you, in the sight of God and Christ Jesus and the elect angels, to keep these instructions without partiality, and to do nothing out of favoritism" (v. 21). Paul's force and passion here must be because there had been a scandalous exercise of favoritism shown in reference to some sinning church leaders.[7] The Ephesian "old boys" system had done its thing. Some guilty leader had gotten away with murder, so to speak.

This is a weighty matter! "God," "Christ Jesus," and "the elect angels" are called as witnesses. Timothy and his leaders are called to exercise fair, even-handed discipline in the sight of the very ones who will one day judge them. Calvin emphasizes the point: "And indeed the man who is not shaken out of his carelessness and laziness by the thought that the government of the church is conducted under the eye of God and His angels must be worse than stupid."[8] What does that say about us when we lose our nerve and defer

to a leader's prominence and reputation? Not only are we worse than stupid
— we are hard-hearted.

SELECTING CHURCH LEADERS (vv. 22-25)

Be careful. The distasteful task of disciplining church leaders called for
up-front wisdom and great care in their initial selection. So Paul advises,
"Do not be hasty in the laying on of hands, and do not share in the sins of
others" (v. 22). Earlier, in 3:6, Paul insisted that church leaders must not
be recent converts. Here he commands careful screening. Indifference
leaves the leaders culpable, partners in the sins of their appointees when
they fall short.

This is why in the church I pastor we ask new staff members the most
penetrating and personal questions in the hiring process. This is why we do
the same with ordinands. I think such care should be extended in the selection of all who are involved in church leadership. After all, the church is the
church of Christ!

A personal aside. Now comes verse 23: "Stop drinking only water, and
use a little wine because of your stomach and your frequent illnesses."
When James Moffatt penned his famous translation of the Bible, he left this
verse out because he did not think it was part of Paul's original since it is so
seemingly out of place. However, there is no doubt that it is in the original.
And J. N. D. Kelly has wisely noted that "the very banality of the verse
strikes a note of authenticity."[9]

It is really quite cogent and relevant here in its context because Paul's
charge in the preceding verse to "not share in the sins of others" prompted
him to admonish Timothy, "Keep yourself pure" (v. 22c) and then to address
Timothy's tendency to fleshly asceticism, as evidenced by his commitment
to drink only water. According to 4:3, 4 the false teachers "forbid people to
marry and order them to abstain from certain foods, which God created to
be received with thanksgiving by those who believe and who know the
truth. For everything God created is good, and nothing is to be rejected if it
is received with thanksgiving."

Timothy was not to participate in such asceticism in his pursuit of
purity.[10] Rather, he was to "use a little wine" to promote his good health. Paul
concurred with the ancient world's use of wine for medicinal purposes, especially in respect to stomach problems, as taught by Hippocrates (*Ancient
Medicine*, 13), the *Talmud* (*Berakoth, Baba Bathra*, 58b), Plutarch (*Advice
About Keeping Well*), and Pliny (*Natural History*, 217).[11] So the logic here is:
"'Keep yourself pure.' But in doing so, do not adopt the errant asceticism
of the false teachers."

Certainly Paul was not encouraging him to spend much time drinking
wine (cf. 3:3). That would disqualify him from leadership. The proper per-

spective comes to us from ancient commentaries, where wine is seen as an essential staple of everyday life. In the fourth century Chrysostom wrote, "He does not however allow him to indulge freely in wine, but as much as was for health."[12] And in the sixteenth century Calvin remarked: "He seems to be speaking of 'a little' wine to be guarding against intemperance."[13]

The perils of legalism and asceticism can entrap the most holy people, people like dear, godly Timothy! Certainly the Bible teaches temperance, but not self-righteous asceticism. There are a thousand reasons to abstain: 1) the rampant alcoholism that devours whole families; 2) alcohol's hazard to health as declared billions of times by the Surgeon General's warning — "(a) According to the Surgeon General, women should not drink alcoholic beverages during pregnancy because of the risk of birth defects. (b) Consumption of alcoholic beverages impairs your ability to drive a car or operate machinery, and may cause health problems"; 3) the social evils that occur from the lessening of inhibitions — sexual crimes, felonies, traffic deaths; 4) the alcohol industry's class exploitation that targets alcohol-blighted ghettos with niche advertising; 5) the presence within the church of "weaker brothers" whose spiritual development would be hindered by another's exercise of freedom (cf. Romans 14:1-18; 1 Corinthians 8:9-13). But these reasons aside, Timothy was abstaining for the wrong reason — asceticism, which could ensnare his soul.

Be discerning. In concluding his thoughts, Paul returns to the matter of choosing elders and urges discernment: "The sins of some men are obvious, reaching the place of judgment ahead of them; the sins of others trail behind them. In the same way, good deeds are obvious, and even those that are not cannot be hidden" (vv. 24, 25). The detection of sin and faulty character is easy with some people, but in others it is a very subtle task. So we must be prayerfully discerning. We are good at spotting gross sins, but the subtle, unseen sin may be even more damning because it resides silently in the depth of the spiritual being, close to the heart. Be careful!

Happily, good deeds are patently evident, and we ought to ready ourselves to see them — "In the same way, good deeds are obvious, and even those that are not cannot be hidden" (v. 25). We must not be fooled by showy lives and spectacular gifts, for an evil heart may lie beneath them. But watch closely and you will see beautiful things in the most humble lives.

We must honor our leaders. We must discipline our leaders. We must choose our leaders wisely. Perhaps by doing so we will someday bless our children and our children's children.

16

Regarding Servitude

1 TIMOTHY 6:1, 2

All who are under the yoke of slavery should consider their masters worthy of full respect, so that God's name and our teaching may not be slandered. Those who have believing masters are not to show less respect for them because they are brothers. Instead, they are to serve them even better, because those who benefit from their service are believers, and dear to them. These are the things you are to teach and urge on them.

It has been estimated that there were between fifty and sixty million slaves in the Roman Empire, and that as many as one third of the populations of large cities such as Rome, Corinth, and Ephesus were slaves.[1] Some in the Ephesian church were slave owners, as was Philemon in the Colossian church. Many in the church were either slaves or ex-slaves (called "freedmen"). And some in the Ephesian church were slaveless citizens who, because of their lack of servants, were often poor. So we must understand that the culture of slavery affected virtually every aspect of the Ephesian church.

At the same time, we must also understand that slavery was on the decline and that its exploitation of the masses was diminishing. True, Aristotle's teaching in the *Nichomachian Ethics* that "A slave is a living tool, just as a tool is an inanimate slave" had not been repudiated.[2] It is also true that under Roman law, according to Gaius, a slave was a thing to be bought and sold, and not a legal person.[3] It is also a fact that there had been major slave rebellions, such as that led by Spartacus. But those were pre-Christian (between the years 140-70 B.C.).[4]

By the time of the Christian era and the writing of 1 and 2 Timothy, sweeping changes had been introduced that radically improved the treatment of slaves. Slaves under first-century Roman law could generally count on eventually being set free. This was called manumission. Very few ever reached old age as slaves. Slave owners were releasing slaves at such a rate that Augustus Caesar introduced legal restrictions to curb the trend. Despite this, inscriptions indicate that almost 50 percent of slaves were freed before the age of thirty.[5]

Furthermore, while the slave remained his master's possession, he could own property — including other slaves! A slave completely controlled his own property and could invest and save to purchase his own freedom. In fact, the excesses of *nouveau riche* ex-slaves were scandalizing the "old money" Romans.[6]

We must also understand that being a slave did not indicate one's social class. Slaves were regularly accorded the social status of their owners. From outward appearance, it was usually impossible to distinguish a slave from free persons. Slavery was often preferred to freedom because of the security it offered.[7] A slave could be a custodian, a merchant, a C.E.O., and even a government official.[8] Many slaves lived separate from their owners. Finally, selling oneself into slavery was commonly used as a means of gaining Roman citizenship and gaining entrance into society.

Roman slavery in the first century was far more humane and civilized than American/African slavery practiced in this country during the seventeenth to nineteenth centuries. Whereas nineteenth-century slavery was tragically racist, theirs was rarely racist but rather reflected the economic and political realities of ancient culture. This does not suggest that ancient slavery was not evil. The buying and selling of people for one's economic well-being is sub-Christian. And Paul, though not openly advocating throwing off slavery, said, "Although if you can gain your freedom, do so" (1 Corinthians 7:21), for freedom was a preferable state.

Nevertheless, an understanding of slavery in New Testament times helps us discern why the apostolic writers did not attack slavery. This was: 1) because of the positive reforms then in effect in regard to Roman slavery; 2) because an assault on slavery would have wrongly labeled Christianity as subversive (besides, the immediate demise of slavery would have reduced both slaves and masters to poverty); 3) because the apostolic church was not greatly interested in social reform but it was looking forward to the immediate coming of the Lord; and 4) because the radical brotherhood and equality explicit in the gospel would sound the death knell for slavery, bringing its eventual demise (cf. Philemon 16; Galatians 3:28; and the entire book of Ephesians).

Now, in respect to the church in Ephesus, which Paul references in writing to Timothy, it is clear that slaves and freedmen comprised a large portion of the congregation. It is likely that slaves totaled more than the usual 30 percent. Indeed, the presence of a large percentage of Christian slaves in Ephesus is apparent because the earlier letter to the Ephesians contains an even longer passage on slaves, as does Colossians, which is in the same geographical area (cf. Ephesians 6:5-8; Colossians 3:22-25; Philemon 16).

This high slave-to-master ratio in the Ephesian church was a natural formula for tension. Many Christian slaves came from homes with non-Christian masters. Others had Christian masters, who would naturally be in the same house church. No doubt some of the elders were slave owners, as was Philemon in the church of Colosse. Add to this mix the gospel's great truth that in Christ all become brothers and sisters — that "There is neither . . . slave nor free . . . for you are all one in Christ Jesus" (Galatians 3:28) — and the possibility of relational stress heightens. Moreover, if some listened to the false teachers' emphasis that the end had already taken place, so that all earthly relationships were superseded, conflict was intensified.

This Paul could not have! Misconduct in the church would not only hurt the church but would harm its reputation with those outside and limit the spread of the gospel. In 1 Timothy 2:3, 4 he urges the Ephesians to live "peaceful and quiet," godly lives, saying "This is good, and pleases God our Savior, who wants all men to be saved and to come to a knowledge of the truth." If they lived exemplary lives, the knowledge of the gospel would spread. And in 3:7 he says of each elder, "He must also have a good reputation with outsiders, so that he will not fall into disgrace and into the devil's trap." To be spoken well of by outsiders is essential to the gospel. In 5:14 he counsels young widows "to marry, to have children, to manage their homes and to give the enemy no opportunity for slander." A slandered church loses gospel power.

And now, regarding slaves and masters, Paul gives explicit advice as to their conduct — for the sake of the gospel. The practical implications of these verses are important for us today too, because we all are subservient to someone.

SUBSERVIENCE TO NON-CHRISTIAN MASTERS (v. 1)

The opening verse provides specific advice to those who have non-Christian masters: "All who are under the yoke of slavery should consider their masters worthy of full respect, so that God's name and our teaching may not be slandered" (v. 1).

Sometimes Christians imagine that the new freedom Christ brings elevates us above the obligations that fall on others. A gnostic air of superiority invades our souls. Menial tasks are for others. Prayer and soul-winning take precedence, we argue. British New Testament scholar Philip Towner tells how this happened to him after becoming a Christian while serving in the military in England: "There were several of us who had just set out on the Christian adventure. In our enthusiasm to serve Christ we somehow concluded that we didn't need to concern ourselves with mundane rules about shined boots and clean, pressed uniforms." He concludes: "Our superiors quickly made the connection between our new faith and our sloppy appearance. And in that small corner of the world, Christianity was in danger of being linked with insubordination."⁹

I once had an employer tell me he had become skeptical about Christians because of his experience with two theological students who seemed to be always standing around talking about God during work hours. But what really did it was when the boss observed one go into the washroom for twenty minutes. When the employee emerged, he heard him whisper to his fellow-student, "I just had the most wonderful time. I read three chapters of the Gospel of John." Three chapters of John in the john (on the boss's time) pleases neither God nor man!

Something like this was going on in Ephesus. Non-Christian masters found that formerly profitable slaves had become brooding, disrespectful, and unprofitable. So their pagan masters blasphemed both the name of God and Paul's teaching of the gospel — "These Christians are a waste. Lazy, otherworldly, and in their pious way disrespectful. Mine doesn't hold a candle to the other slaves. Some teaching in that gospel! It takes a good man and makes him worthless."

A gathering smog of disrespect was dimming the glow of the Ephesian church, quenching the light of the gospel. Sadly, the Ephesians had already been warned about this, some four years before:

Slaves, obey your earthly masters with respect and fear, and with sincerity of heart, just as you would obey Christ. Obey them not only to win their favor when their eye is on you, but like slaves of Christ, doing the will of God from your heart. Serve wholeheartedly, as if you were serving the Lord, not men, because you know that the Lord will reward everyone for whatever good he does, whether he is slave or free. (Ephesians 6:5-8)

If you have ever observed a gym class doing push-ups, you will understand the sense of this verse. The coach orders everyone down and begins to intone "up, down, up, down." All are following his directions until he looks to the right, and in that moment those on the left go on hold. When his gaze begins to move back to the left, they begin to do proper push-ups again, and those on the right go on hold. Some employees are all action when the boss is around but otherwise loll around the watercooler. Away from his eye there is no energy, no enthusiasm, no heart — no respect.

The effect of such conduct was devastating to the gospel enterprise, and it still is today. The place where we work is, for most of us, our primary contact with a needy world. Most gospel sharing happens in the workplace. That is where people see what we are really made of because that is where the stress is and where most of our energy is expended.

Paul believed that the gospel and work were inseparable. "Teach slaves to be subject to their masters in everything, to try to please them, not to talk back to them, and not to steal from them, but to show that they can be fully trusted, so that in every way they will make the teaching about God our Savior attractive" (Titus 2:9, 10). That last phrase is literally, "adorn the doctrine of God" (KJV). Adorn him in your workplace. Make the teaching about God your Savior more attractive by how you work!

SUBSERVIENCE TO CHRISTIAN MASTERS (v. 2)

Paul is equally explicit about how those slaves who have Christian masters must perform their work: "Those who have believing masters are not to show less respect for them because they are brothers. Instead, they are to serve them even better, because those who benefit from their service are believers, and dear to them" (v. 2).

This seems to be where the real rub had developed in Ephesus. The mutual brotherhood of slave and master had led to an attitude of disrespect. As the *Revised Standard Version* puts it, "Those who have believing masters must not be disrespectful on the ground that they are brethren." They were "not to look down on them" (Knight). "You're a brother in Christ! So who are you to give me orders? What are you going to do — fire me?" They were not to succumb to such a mind-set.

It is this kind of attitude that is the scourge of Christian organizations and the mission field. Such a brooding, disrespectful, egalitarian lethargy brings disgrace to Christ. There is no place in the Christian employee's life for subtle insubordination toward his employer or for cleverly concealed contempt or mocking humor about his superiors.

Paul deftly turns the argument around: Slaves ought to serve all the better "because those who benefit from their service [their masters] are believers, and dear to them [the slaves]." God's love for both slave and master made them brothers, and thus they ought to regard one another in love.

Here again what is at stake is the spread of the gospel, our mission to a lost world. The enhancement and elevation of relationships in the church, the harmony of households with slaves and masters, would testify to the world about Christ's reality. The unity of purpose of both slave and master would enable whole houses and churches to reach out to the lost in dynamic accord.

The attitudes and ethics commanded in this passage make it clear that servitude is at the heart of the Christian calling.

Marriage is servitude. Being a husband is servanthood. A Christian man who commits to love his wife "as Christ loved the church and gave himself up for her" (Ephesians 5:25) commits his whole being to elevated servitude for perhaps fifty or sixty years. He is never so elevated as when he serves his wife. Being a wife is servanthood also. By loving the imperfect man that she is married to in a thousand day-in, day-out ways, she is serving God.

Family life is servitude. Parenting is servitude. It means giving all you have in order to see your children grow into spiritual maturity. It is giving, and giving, and giving — just like God our Father. Growing up is servitude — obeying one's parents and lovingly trying to please them.

The workplace is servitude. Being an employee is servanthood — giving the best hours of your day to an educational or corporate enterprise or government or business. Being an employer, rightly understood, is servitude too. You serve those under you with a heart for their success.

True servitude is Christ-centered, leads us to Christ, and makes us like Christ.

Listen to Jesus: "Now that I, your Lord and Teacher, have washed your feet, you also should wash one another's feet. I have set you an example that you should do as I have done for you" (John 13:14, 15). "Whoever wants to become great among you must be your servant, and whoever wants to be first must be slave of all. For even the Son of Man did not come to be served, but to serve" (Mark 10:43-45). The *a fortiori* force of this argument (from the greater to the lesser) is cosmic: If Christ the eternal Son of God and Creator of the universe (cf. Colossians 1:15-18) washed the feet of his children — serving his disciples — how much more ought we adopted sons and daughters do the same to one another? The power to live in exalted servitude comes from the fact that the ultimate servant is in us, and we are in him, as the New Testament repeatedly affirms.

Listen to Paul on this point as well: "Though I am free and belong to no man, I make myself a slave to everyone, to win as many as possible" (1 Corinthians 9:19) — *volitional* servitude. "You, my brothers, were called to be free. But do not use your freedom to indulge the sinful nature; rather, serve one another in love" (Galatians 5:13) — *loving* servitude. "Submit to one another out of reverence for Christ" (Ephesians 5:21) — *worshipful* servitude.

With all this in mind, listen again, with mind and heart, to the truth of the text we have been studying:

> *All who are under the yoke of slavery should consider their masters worthy of full respect, so that God's name and our teaching may not be slandered. Those who have believing masters are not to show less respect for them because they are brothers. Instead, they are to serve them even better, because those who benefit from their service are believers, and dear to them. These are the things you are to teach and urge on them. (1 Timothy 6:1, 2)*

17

Apostasy Analyzed: A Warning

1 TIMOTHY 6:3-10

If anyone teaches false doctrines and does not agree to the sound instruction of our Lord Jesus Christ and to godly teaching, he is conceited and understands nothing. He has an unhealthy interest in controversies and quarrels about words that result in envy, strife, malicious talk, evil suspicions and constant friction between men of corrupt mind, who have been robbed of the truth and who think that godliness is a means to financial gain. But godliness with contentment is great gain. For we brought nothing into the world, and we can take nothing out of it. But if we have food and clothing, we will be content with that. People who want to get rich fall into temptation and a trap and into many foolish and harmful desires that plunge men into ruin and destruction. For the love of money is a root of all kinds of evil. Some people, eager for money, have wandered from the faith and pierced themselves with many griefs.

Having ministered from the sixties on, I have seen many strange things take place under the broad title of Christianity. The sixties specialized in blasphemous events such as the pagan nature festival that took place in the Gothic splendor of San Francisco's Grace Cathedral, where it was reported that:

During one nature ceremony in the cathedral, a decidedly ecumenical audience watched reverently as the poet Allen Ginsberg, wearing a deer mask, joined others similarly garbed to ordain Senators Alan Cranston and John Tunney as godfathers of animals (Cranston of the Tule elk and Tunney of the California brown bear) . . . while movie projectors simultaneously cast images of buffalo herds and other endangered species on the walls and ceilings, to the accompaniment of rock music.[1]

On another occasion on the East Coast Harvey Cox, the famous radical theologian, staged his famous Easter celebration in a warehouse disco. As *Newsweek* magazine reported it, the ritual began at midnight one Saturday with "a projector [that] flashed images of Vietnam atrocities in an updated version of the Stations of the Cross. White-clad dancers from the Harvard Divinity School mimed agony, while harsh background music boomed a dissonant Passion of Christ. By 3:00 a.m., chains of dancers formed, swaying and lifting each other aloft. The crowd swelled to 1,500, and a rock band called The Apocrypha played 'I Can't Get No Satisfaction.'"

> Then Cox entered, dressed in white satin vestments trimmed in pink embroidery, followed by five other clerics costumed variously in Byzantine and psychedelic robes. Cox stepped forward to an altar laden with fruit, bread and wine to read the gospel account of Christ's Resurrection. And when he finished, the silence was suddenly burst by the deafening crash of Handel's "Hallelujah" chorus. Then using the highly politicized liturgy, Cox intoned the "Kyrie Eleison" (Lord, have mercy), to which the crowd responded: "Right on!" Bread and wine were passed around and the congregants reacted by feeding each other. Bright balloons wafted to the low warehouse ceiling and incense sweetened the air. At 5:45, someone pointed to the patch of morning visible through the skylight and the entire crowd rushed outside, chanting, "Sun, sun, sun."[2]

Far out, Harvey! Cool! Groovy! "There's no business like show business."

Much of what I have seen over these decades has been far more personal and distressing. I have had associates who became gnostic. That is, they purported to have entered a new level of understanding of the Scriptures because of their spirituality. They claimed that a "higher hermeneutic" (a transcending method of interpretation) had come to them through their scriptural meditation. When I tried to reason with them from the Scriptures, they called me rationalistic and "Greek." I have had friends succumb to asceticism, a religion of fleshly denial, in which life lost its color and faded to worn-out grays. Plainness became the trudging path to godliness. However, most of the departures from Christ have been less severe or obvious, though still costly. Many were profit-motivated as some sought to serve God and mammon. Fleshly sins have prevailed, consciences have been ruined, and ultimately beliefs have changed in order to accommodate ongoing sin.

These and similar apostasies swirled around Timothy and the Ephesian church in the A.D. 60s. There was incipient Gnosticism and teachers who were seen to "devote themselves to myths and endless genealogies" (1:4). There were ascetics — "They forbid people to marry and order them to abstain from certain foods, which God created to be received with thanksgiving by those who believe and who know the truth" (4:3). A desire for monetary gain took its toll on the likes of Hymenaeus and Alexander, who abandoned "faith and a good conscience" and became spiritual shipwrecks (cf. 1:19, 20; cf. 4:2). Religious hucksterism did not originate in the 1960s and 1970s but was rampant in the original sixties (the first century). Then, as today, many imagined that "godliness is a means to financial gain" (6:5b).

As Paul approaches the conclusion of his first letter to Timothy, he pens a final exposure and indictment of the apostate teachers. The situation was tragically poignant because they had begun well but had been ensnared by Satan. This is both an analysis and a warning about apostasy — and it is relevant for the church in every age.

AN ANALYSIS OF APOSTATES (vv. 3-5)

Paul provides his analysis in verses 3-5 in what is one long sentence in the Greek, profiling first their *teaching*, second, their *character*, and third, their *corruption*.

The apostates' teaching. The analysis begins with the conditional statement of verse 3: "If anyone teaches false doctrines and does not agree to the sound instruction of our Lord Jesus Christ and to godly teaching." This conditional description will be answered by Paul in verses 4 and 5. But the statement itself is a description of specific teachers Paul had in mind, because the Greek word translated "false doctrines" is only used earlier in 1:3, where Paul refers to certain men who teach "false doctrines."[3] Paul knew these false teachers.

The distinctive of these "false doctrines" is that they do not agree with "the sound instruction of our Lord Jesus Christ and to godly teaching." In simplest terms they were not in line with "the sound instruction" that originated with Christ, that which makes him the center of everything. We get this Christocentric sense because Jesus is spoken of here not as "our Lord Jesus" but "our Lord Jesus Christ" (the Messiah!), identifying him as the one who fulfilled the prophetic expectations of the Old Testament. Jesus, in fact, repeatedly identified himself as having this center and focus with phrases like "These are the Scriptures that testify about me" (John 5:39; cf. Luke 24:25-27, 44-46). The words "godly teaching" further center the phrase on Christ because he has been identified in 3:16 as "the mystery of godliness." According to that verse, his incarnation and ascension are what make godliness possible.

So we see that the false teachers were minimizing Christ and his teaching about himself as the center of the Scriptures and godliness. This is what asceticism does — it supplants Christ and his work with man-centered rigors. This is also what mysticism does with its mysteries. And this is what sensuality does as well.

The false teachers were marginalizing Christ with their "myths," "endless genealogies," and rigorous disciplines. Healthy Christianity focuses on Jesus Christ as the fulfillment of God's promises through his atoning death, resurrection, and ascension. It lifts up Jesus as the perfect second Adam. It lifts him up as the son of Abraham par excellence. It lifts him up as the true Israel. It lifts him up as the ultimate son of David. It lifts him up as the Lamb of God. It lifts him up as Redeemer and Savior. It lifts him up as the true Temple. It lifts him up as the Alpha and Omega. It glories in him as our only hope in life and death!

The apostates' character. Having described their false teaching, Paul details their character in two ways.

First, such a false teacher "is conceited and understands nothing" (v. 4). His conceit is not tongue-in-cheek like that of George Bernard Shaw ("I often quote myself. It adds spice to my conversation"[4]) or Disraeli ("When I want to read a great book, I write one"[5]). The conceit of such a false teacher was integral and unconscious, as indicated in 1:7 — "They want to be teachers of the law, but they do not know what they are talking about or what they so confidently affirm" (a marked contrast with Paul; see 1:15, 16). In his conceit, he thinks he knows something, but he "understands nothing." He has zero spiritual understanding because in rejecting sound, Christocentric instruction, he necessarily embraces opposing views of Christ's sufficiency, his own sinfulness, and the way of salvation. As the *New English Bible* puts it, he is a "pompous ignoramus."

Second, "He has an unhealthy [literally, "sick"] interest in controversies and quarrels about words" (v. 4). When you crave controversy and word battles, you are spiritually sick. Apostasy brings oppositional perversity. I have spent endless hours with such people, who cannot or will not grasp the plain meaning of a sentence or a paragraph in its context but rather fix on a word or sound bite and give it a definition that defies lexicons, history, and logic. Nothing dissuades them. Nothing informs them. They understand nothing — and they enjoy it!

The apostates' corruption. These men's false teaching, pompous ignorance, and sickly delights spawn corruption congregationally and personally. Congregationally, there are five results: "envy, strife, malicious talk, evil suspicions and constant friction" (vv. 4, 5). The first two, "envy" and "strife," are also found together in the catalogs of sin in Romans 1 and Galatians 5 (cf. Romans 1:29; Galatians 5:20, 21 ["dissensions"]). Envy in spiritual matters is exceedingly ugly. As St. John of the Cross put it: "As far as envy is concerned, many experience displeasure when they see others in possession of spiritual goods. They feel sensibly hurt because others surpass them on this road, and they resent it when others are praised."[6] Strife then follows, producing discord and divisiveness.

Among the clergy, envy manifests itself in jealousy over another leader's promotion and scarcely concealed glee when a supposed rival suffers reversals. It deeply resents others' receiving praise from those from whom they desire praise. Another's successful book becomes "The book I should have written," or a prized conference speaking engagement "should have been mine." These and similar attitudes corrode relationships between Christ's servants and within congregations, bringing strife, both subtle and direct, among God's people.

"Malicious talk" (literally, "blasphemy") follows as Christians blaspheme other Christians. Then come "evil suspicions" as people rush to think the worst of others. Paul's lovely words, "Love does not delight in evil but rejoices with the truth. It always protects, always trusts, always hopes, always perseveres" (1 Corinthians 13:6, 7), glance sadly off the hard-shelled souls of false teachers and their followers. The overall result is "constant friction" — "persistent collisions" as one commentator has it[7] — perpetual detonations, mini-A-bombs and now and then H-bombs! The symbol of the church becomes not the cross but a glowing mushroom cloud.

Personally, the corruption reaches its apex in the lives of the false teachers themselves. They become "men of corrupt mind, who have been robbed of the truth and who think that godliness is a means to financial gain" (v. 5b). "Men of corrupt mind" takes the sickness metaphor to its ultimate conclusion — settled decay.[8] Rotting minds.

"Who have been robbed of the truth" refers to being robbed of the content of Christianity as the absolute truth.[9] They are apostates who are "always learning but never able to acknowledge the truth. Just as Jannes and Jambres opposed Moses, so also these men oppose the truth — men of depraved minds, who, as far as the faith is concerned, are rejected" (2 Timothy 3:7, 8).

Then comes the ultimate degradation — "who think that godliness is a means to financial gain" (v. 5b). This is rock bottom. The ministry has become "a living." The fleece has become more important than the flock! Fleecing the flock is now a measure of professional competence.

A RESPONSE TO APOSTATES (vv. 6-10)

Paul now addresses the tragedy of pious greed, sharing principles for every Christian in every culture.

Godliness is gain. Those who thought that "godliness is a means to financial gain" (v. 5b) were partly right. There is great gain in godliness, with the proviso that it be coupled with contentment — "But godliness with contentment is great gain" (v. 6). Here the "gain" is spiritual, not financial. Paul implicitly separates financial gain from contentment. Paul would have nodded approvingly of the story of a king who was suffering from a persistent malady and was advised by his wise men that he would be cured if the shirt of a contented man were brought for him to wear. The search began for a contented man, but none could be found. So emissaries were sent to the edge of the realm, and after a long search a man was found who was truly content. But he had no shirt!

The pursuit of material riches is empty and futile. In Ecclesiastes the preacher informs us, "Whoever loves money never has money enough; whoever loves wealth is never satisfied with his income" (5:10).

> *Contentment is a constant feast,*
> *He's richest who requires the least.*
> *(Barnes)[10]*

Contentment is inextricably linked with godliness. And well it should be because for Paul, contentment is not self-sufficiency, as the Greeks understood it, but *Christ-sufficiency*, as he so memorably stated to the Philippians:

> *For I have learned to be content whatever the circumstances. I know what it is to be in need, and I know what it is to have plenty. I have learned the secret of being content in any and every situation, whether well fed or hungry, whether living in plenty or in want. I can do everything through him who gives me strength. (Philippians 4:11b-13)*

So it is in Christ that we possess both "godliness" and "contentment" — "great gain" beyond the dreams of avarice. We may become shirtless and shoeless and even homeless, but if we have Christ's life, his godliness, and his sufficiency, we will be rich.

> *Thou, O Christ, art all I want;*
> *More than all in Thee I find.*

Birth and death provide the bookends from which to appraise material wealth — "For we brought nothing into the world, and we can take nothing out of it" (v. 7). When John D. Rockefeller died, his aide was asked how much he left behind. The man wisely answered, "He left it *all* behind." That truth is as old as Biblical revelation. Job said it first: "Naked I came from my mother's womb, and naked shall I return" (1:21, RSV). "Naked a man comes from his mother's womb, and as he comes, so he departs. He takes nothing from his labor that he can carry in his hand" (Ecclesiastes 5:15) — a possessionless entrance and a possessionless exit. Greed for the Christian is irrational. It makes no sense at all.

Paul then offers the Biblical perspective: "But if we have food and clothing, we will be content with that" (v. 8). Whatever we have above this is to be enjoyed. Asceticism is no virtue. We are to enjoy the things God gives. "I know what it is to be in need, and I know what it is to have plenty. I have learned the secret of being content" (Philippians 4:12).

Listen to Jesus as well:

"Consider how the lilies grow. They do not labor or spin. Yet I tell you, not even Solomon in all his splendor was dressed like one of these. If that is how God clothes the grass of the field, which is here today, and tomorrow is thrown into the fire, how much more will he clothe you, O you of little faith! And do not set your heart on what you will eat or drink; do not worry about it. For the pagan world runs after all such things, and your Father knows that you need them." (Luke 12:27-30; cf. Matthew 6:25-34; Hebrews 13:5)

Real contentment and material prosperity have nothing to do with one another. Acquisitiveness has zip to do with godliness. It is so simple: Godliness is gain!

Greed is loss. Now comes a warning: "People who want to get rich fall into temptation and a trap and into many foolish and harmful desires that plunge men into ruin and destruction" (v. 9). Greed has a way of causing people to look in directions that they might never have looked otherwise.[11] Those pursuing riches push the edge of the envelope. They turn blind eyes away from ethical questions. They refuse to think things through. Many learn the price of everything only as they lose their values. And then if they become rich, they find themselves in circles where the rules are different and the peer pressure relentless. What was once unthinkable becomes natural.[12]

A famous proverb follows: "For the love of money is a root of all kinds of evil" (v. 10a). Note that it does not say, "Money is the root of all evil." And it does not mean that all evil has money at its root. The proverb simply means that greed is a trap, for the rich and the poor and everyone in between. To review verse 9, "People who want to get rich [the wanna-bes] fall into temptation." "If it be riches that slay you," wrote George MacDonald, "what matter if it be riches you have or riches you have not?"[13] You do not have to be rich to fall to greed. In fact, the danger may be even more intense for the ambitious poor. Some of the most greedy are those who once had or even now have so little.

This is apparently what had happened to the onetime spiritual leaders whom Paul references in his final line in this passage: "Some people, eager for money, have wandered from the faith and pierced themselves with many griefs" (v. 10b). The language here is gruesome (literally, "impaled with many griefs"). Certainly the griefs may be pangs of conscience, but more likely this refers to personal miseries that feel as though they have been driven like stakes through these persons' bodies. I have seen this repeatedly — once-eager Christians who were leaders in their churches who moved up and out of faith. Beautiful homes but cold hearts. They love money, but their children hate them. In some homes only their familial love for money keeps them together.

The tragedy in this passage is a Christian tragedy. Promising leader-teachers removed Christ from the center of their teaching to the periphery. He was in their theology, but he was not its focus. Their character also moved — downward. They became conceited ignoramuses. A moldering corruption ensued. Congregational life degenerated to "envy, strife, malicious talk, evil suspicions and constant friction" — persistent collisions. Their personal corruption peaked as they entered settled decay — "men of corrupt mind . . . robbed of the truth." Finally, they oozed corruption as they became religious hucksters who actually thought that "godliness is a means to financial gain." "There's no business like the religion business!"

But it is not all negative, for Paul adds, "But godliness with contentment is great gain" (v. 6). Here are riches — "godliness" made possible by the "mystery of godliness" himself (3:16) — and a "contentment" from his all-sufficiency (Philippians 4:11-13).

The Lord Jesus Christ is all we need! If we keep him at the center of the Bible, of history, of salvation, of our lives we have gained everything!

18

A Charge to the Man of God

1 TIMOTHY 6:11-16

But you, man of God, flee from all this, and pursue righteousness, godliness, faith, love, endurance and gentleness. Fight the good fight of the faith. Take hold of the eternal life to which you were called when you made your good confession in the presence of many witnesses. In the sight of God, who gives life to everything, and of Christ Jesus, who while testifying before Pontius Pilate made the good confession, I charge you to keep this command without spot or blame until the appearing of our Lord Jesus Christ, which God will bring about in his own time — God, the blessed and only Ruler, the King of kings and Lord of lords, who alone is immortal and who lives in unapproachable light, whom no one has seen or can see. To him be honor and might forever. Amen.

The abrupt personal designation "But you, man of God" that opens Paul's famous charge to Timothy reverses the focus of the apostle's remarks. He had just upbraided the false teachers of Ephesus for their corrupt doctrine and lifestyles, but now he instructs his godly understudy on how he ought to live.

The title "man of God" was intentionally motivating because it was the customary designation for the great leaders of Israel. "Moses the man of God" was a title for Israel's greatest leader (cf. Deuteronomy 33:1; Joshua 14:6). Likewise, we read of "David the man of God" (Nehemiah 12:24), and the prophet Samuel was similarly described (1 Samuel 9:6). When Elijah resuscitated the widow's son, she replied, "Now I know that you are a man of God and that the word of the LORD from your mouth is the truth" (1 Kings 17:24). Elisha was also understood to be "the man of God" (cf. 2 Kings 4:7, 9). The title *man of God* "connotes one who is in God's service, represents God and speaks in his name."[1]

When Paul addresses Timothy emphatically, "But you, man of God," he got Timothy's attention. The young disciple knew heavy instructions were to follow. And those injunctions remain the standard for all who are called to ministerial leadership today.

SUMMARY ADMONISHMENTS (vv. 11, 12)

Helpfully, Paul's opening admonishments come in four successive commands that can be remembered under four simple headings — *Flee, Follow, Fight*, and *Fasten onto*.

Flee. Paul begins, "But you, man of God, flee from all this" (v. 11a.) — that is, flee from the things that characterize false teachers, just described in verses 3-10. Flee the false teaching that marginalized Christ and his teaching (v. 3). Flee the petty "controversies and quarrels about words" (v. 4). Flee divisive talk (vv. 4, 5). And flee the religious delusion that imagines "godliness is a means to financial gain" (v. 5).

Flight as a spiritual strategy was crucial to Paul's philosophy of ministry. Later in 2 Timothy 2:22 Paul recommends flight as a defense from sensuality: "Flee the evil desires of youth." It was this wisdom that centuries before had saved the patriarch Joseph from Potiphar's wife when he left his cloak in her grasping hand and fled from the house (Genesis 39:12). Any attempt to stay and reason with Potiphar's seductive wife would have been too much for Joseph.

Likewise, Timothy is to flee "controversies and quarrels about words" lest he be sucked into the vortex of such decay. He is also to flee those who are promoting what is today called "the prosperity gospel," which equates godliness with gain. If we desire to be men and women of God, there are times we must show our back to evil and run as fast as our legs will take us in the other direction. Some who are reading this need to indulge in some sanctified flight!

Follow. But the Christian life does not consist only of flight. God's servants are also to follow hard after spiritual virtues — "and pursue righteousness, godliness, faith, love, endurance and gentleness" (v. 11b). The six pursuits here are a poetic summary (arranged in three pairs) of the balanced spirituality of the Christian leader.

He is to pursue "righteousness" and "godliness," terms that cover the horizontal and vertical dimensions of the Christian life.[2] Horizontally, there must be righteous conduct (uprightness) and fairness in dealings with other people. Vertically, a godly life is called for, which as Paul has said "has value for all things, holding promise for both the present life and the life to come" (4:8). Both "righteousness" and "godliness" reference observable conduct. They go together and enhance each other, producing a life well spoken of on earth and in Heaven.

Next Paul commends the ultimate Christian virtues of "faith" and "love"

(v. 11). *Faith* and *love* are a regular couplet in the Pastorals (cf. 1 Timothy 1:5; 2:15; 4:12; 2 Timothy 2:22; Titus 2:2). Here the emphasis is on faithfulness and love for others.

Last on the list is "endurance and gentleness." These are especially helpful ministry qualities. Endurance is "won't quit" determination in the face of opposition to the gospel (cf. 2 Timothy 3:10).[3] Gentleness is the quality of tender, patient self-control in dealing with people amidst the difficulties of ministry — strength under control.

So we see that Paul commands Timothy to pursue a balanced spirituality in his ministry persona — righteousness and godliness, then faith and love, and then endurance and gentleness.

But what stands out in all of this is the contrasting emphases on fleeing and pursuing. Negatively, we are to constantly flee from evil. But positively we are to keep on pursuing good. The irony is that we humans regularly pursue ends we know are disastrous, and we turn our backs on and flee those things that bring fullness and joy. The wisdom here is so elementary. As John Stott explains it: "We are simply to run from evil as we run from danger, and to run after goodness as we run after success. That is, we have to give our mind, time and energy to both flight and pursuit."[4]

Fight. Timothy is to, at one and the same time, flee and follow (pursue), but he is also to fight — "fight the good fight of the faith" (v. 12a). Notice: this is not just any fight, but a fight for the faith from which some have wandered (cf. vv. 10, 21), meaning that Timothy is to fight for the essential apostolic faith that is described variously in the Pastorals as "the truth" (cf. 2:4; 3:15; 4:3), "the teaching" or "the message" or "the doctrine" (cf. 4:6; 6:1; Titus 1:9; 2:1), and "what has been entrusted" or "the deposit" (6:20; 2 Timothy 1:12, 14).

Here in respect to the apostolic faith (the truth, the doctrine, the deposit) Timothy is commanded to "Fight the good fight." The language here is intense. Earlier in 1:18 ("Fight the good fight") Paul used language that elicited military metaphors. Here the language for "Fight the good fight" suggests voluntary athletic agony — the kind that takes place in a grueling race or boxing match (cf. 2 Timothy 4:7; 1 Corinthians 9:24-27). The Greek literally means, "agonize the good agony."

Anyone who has run competitively understands the intensity insinuated here. You run until you think you can run no more, but you keep on running, until your lungs burn and your feet feel like lead, and then you reach way down and agonizingly increase your speed as you approach the finish line. Those who have put on the gloves also know what it is like to give and receive blows until it takes all you have to keep your hands up. This is what it means to agonize the good agony.

Significantly Paul did this himself, and so he could say near the end of his second letter to Timothy, "For I am already being poured out like a drink offering, and the time has come for my departure. I have fought the good fight, I have finished the race, I have kept the faith" (4:6, 7). This call comes to every generation. During the Reformation, Luther "agonized the good agony" at Worms and amidst the constant agonies that followed. John Calvin, despite a pitiful multitude of physical maladies that he referred to as a "constant death struggle," despite the persistent intrigues within the church and without, fought a good agony. In our own century, Gresham Machen, the founder of Westminster Seminary, stood tall in the good fight.

Our generation must contend for the faith. We must not be contentious, but we must fight for the apostolic faith. Doctrine is all-important because it determines the course of our lives. The truth of the gospel is everything — it is the difference between life and death. We must withstand false teachers. We must think clearly as we define our theology. We must never compromise the truth.

Fasten onto. As Timothy fights "the good fight of the faith," Paul instructs him to "Take hold of the eternal life to which you were called when you made your good confession in the presence of many witnesses" (v. 12b). Timothy already had eternal life, as had been confirmed at his conversion and baptism when he made his good confession.[5]

Eternal life is, obviously, everlasting, but the emphasis here is on its quality. Eternal life is the life of the age to come, which is given only in Jesus Christ. As Jesus explained, "Now this is eternal life: that they may know you, the only true God, and Jesus Christ, whom you have sent" (John 17:3). Timothy, like all believers, has eternal life both as a present possession and as a future hope (1:16 and 2 Timothy 1:10 give the present sense; Titus 1:2; 3:7 give the future sense).[6]

Nevertheless, Paul tells Timothy (and by extension all of us) to grab — to fasten onto — eternal life. According to Bauer's lexicon, the word translated "take hold of" means "to take hold of, grasp . . . sometimes with violence" or to "take hold of, in order to make one's own." The "violence" in the word is seen when it is used to describe how Jesus "caught" Peter as he began to sink (Matthew 14:31) and for the crowd's "seizing" Paul and dragging him from the temple (Acts 21:30).[7] This is the idea: Timothy already had eternal life, but he is instructed to grab it for all he is worth, to live it to the full.

Best-selling author Annie Dillard heard of a man who, after shooting an eagle from the sky, examined it and found the dry skull of a weasel fixed by the jaws to the bird's throat. Evidently when the eagle pounced on the weasel, the animal bit onto the bird with determination. Though torn and eviscerated, the weasel refused to let go and became an airborne skull. Dillard reflects:

> I think it would be well, and proper, and obedient, and pure, to grasp your one necessity and not let it go, to dangle from it limp wher-

ever it takes you. . . . Seize it and let it seize you up aloft even till
your eyes burn out and drop; let your musky flesh fall off in shreds,
and let your very bones unhinge and scatter, loosened over fields,
over fields and woods, lightly, thoughtless, from any height at all,
from as high as eagles.[8]

Just so! We are to grab onto the eternal life that is already ours and ride
it for all it's worth through the ups and downs of following Christ. Eternal
life — the knowledge of God the Father and Christ his Son, the indwelling
of the Holy Spirit, the knowledge of sins forgiven, the peace of Christ, the
fruits of the Spirit, the joy of service, the love of God — these are things
we must grab onto and joyously hold until we arrive in Heaven.

There is such balanced wisdom for Timothy (and for all who would be
men and women of God) in these four imperatives. He is to *flee* sin. At the
same time he is to *follow* or pursue holiness. While doing these he also
fights the good fight of the faith, *fastened* with all he has to eternal life.

AN AWESOME CHARGE (vv. 13-16)

These four imperatives set the stage for Paul's solemn charge to Timothy in
verses 13-16.

Awesome witnesses. The apostle calls two ultimate witnesses for this
charge — namely, God the Father and God the Son: "In the sight of God, who
gives life to everything, and of Christ Jesus, who while testifying before
Pontius Pilate made the good confession" (v. 13). It was natural for Paul to
call such majestic witnesses because Paul himself consciously lived in their
presence.

By calling the Father and the Son as witnesses, Paul meant to encourage Timothy, not intimidate him. He wanted Timothy to be heartened
because God is the one "who gives life to everything." He preserves and
maintains life, and he would sustain Timothy for all his allotted days.
Timothy was likewise to be strengthened not only by Christ's presence but
by his example — "who while testifying before Pontius Pilate made the good
confession." Jesus was the witness par excellence (cf. Revelation 3:14).
Jesus had already done what Timothy would be asked to do!

An awesome charge. Braced by the presence of these two awesome
witnesses, Paul delivers his solemn charge: "I charge you to keep this command without spot or blame until the appearing of our Lord Jesus Christ,
which God will bring about in his own time" (vv. 13b-15a).

"Command" here references Timothy's ministerial calling to uphold
the faith — to accomplish what Paul did — "I have kept the faith" (2 Timothy
4:7). This involved the command to "watch your life and doctrine closely.
Persevere in them, because if you do, you will save both yourself and your

hearers" (1 Timothy 4:16). It also involved Paul's other admonitions: "Timothy, guard what has been entrusted to your care" (6:20a) and "Guard the good deposit that was entrusted to you — guard it with the help of the Holy Spirit who lives in us" (2 Timothy 1:14). Timothy was to cleave to his calling until the return of Christ ("the appearing of our Lord Jesus Christ"), which could happen at any time.[9]

Paul summons Timothy (and all spiritual leaders) to a dogged persistence in fulfilling the call to preach and to defend the apostolic faith — to run well to the end, as Robertson McQuilkin's poetry has so eloquently prayed:

> *The darkness of a spirit*
> *grown mean and small, fruit shriveled on the vine,*
> *bitter to the taste of my companions,*
> *burden to be borne by those brave few who love me still.*
> *No, Lord. Let the fruit grow lush and sweet,*
> *A joy to all who taste;*
> *Spirit-sign of God at work,*
> *stronger, fuller, brighter at the end.*
> *Lord, let me get home before dark.*
>
> *The darkness of tattered gifts,*
> *rust-locked, half-spent or ill-spent,*
> *A life that once was used of God*
> *now set aside.*
> *Grief for glories gone or*
> *Fretting for a task God never gave.*
> *Mourning in the hollow chambers of memory,*
> *Gazing on the faded banners of victories long gone.*
> *Cannot I run well unto the end?*
> *Lord, let me get home before dark.*[10]

Awesome benediction. Paul seals his grand charge with a majestic benediction that extols God's sovereignty: "God, the blessed and only Ruler, the King of kings and Lord of lords, who alone is immortal and who lives in unapproachable light, whom no one has seen or can see. To him be honor and might forever. Amen" (vv. 15b, 16).

• "God, the blessed and only Ruler, the King of kings and Lord of lords." This sings of his absolute sovereignty over all powers, human and divine.
• "Who alone is immortal" — literally, "who alone possesses immortality." This lifts God up as the bestower of life. We humans

are immortal because we will exist after death, whether in Heaven or Hell. But this is only because he who possesses life has created us so. He is the absolute sovereign of all life.

• "And who lives in unapproachable light, whom no one has seen or can see." This celebrates his holiness and purity as it is manifested in his glory. All anyone has even seen of this is the afterglow of his glory (cf. Exodus 33:17-23). He is sovereignly beyond all humanity. But he is the One who directs, equips, and uses Timothy in his ministry.

• "To him be honor and might forever. Amen." This is a natural doxology for Paul. But whereas normally Paul says "honor and glory" (cf. 1:17), here he prays "honor and might," emphasizing God's sovereign power.

The message to Timothy is clear: "Though your calling is immense, the God who calls you is far greater — and he will enable you to do it."

So "man of God" (all who are men and women of God); *flee* evil; *follow* hard after "righteousness, godliness, faith, love, endurance and gentleness"; "*fight* the good fight of the faith"; *fasten onto* and "Take hold of the eternal life to which you were called."

And having thus properly *fled*, *followed*, *fought*, and *fastened onto*, accept your charge before God the Father and God the Son "to keep this command [your ministerial call to preach the apostolic faith] without spot or blame until the appearing of our Lord Jesus Christ, which God will bring about in his own time."

Man of God, do it with an eye to and celebrating the awesome power of your sovereign God who will bring it to pass! This charge is for all of us!

> *Fight the good fight with all thy might!*
> *Christ is thy strength and Christ thy right;*
> *Lay hold on life and it shall be*
> *Thy joy and crown eternally.*
> (*William Boyd, 1864*)

19

Closing Words to the Rich and Their Leader

1 TIMOTHY 6:17-21

Command those who are rich in this present world not to be arrogant nor to put their hope in wealth, which is so uncertain, but to put their hope in God, who richly provides us with everything for our enjoyment. Command them to do good, to be rich in good deeds, and to be generous and willing to share. In this way they will lay up treasure for themselves as a firm foundation for the coming age, so that they may take hold of the life that is truly life. Timothy, guard what has been entrusted to your care. Turn away from godless chatter and the opposing ideas of what is falsely called knowledge, which some have professed and in so doing have wandered from the faith. Grace be with you.

The Puritan Cotton Mather, alarmed by the trend toward materialism in New England society, made this statement in his famous book *Magnalia Christi Americana*: "Religion begat prosperity and the daughter devoured the mother."[1] Mather was noting a common, though not inevitable, effect of Christianity. Authentic conversion to Christ so changes people's lives that bad habits fall away, and they become better workers and managers as they live out the Scriptures, resulting in economic prosperity. But tragically, in many cases the new prosperity and material wealth devour the same Christianity that gave them birth — especially in the second or third generations.

This cannibalism by prosperity, so to speak, has haunted God's people throughout history. The apostolic church itself was not exempt, especially in centers like Ephesus. When Christianity came to Ephesus, it was already a rich city, one of the wealthiest in the ancient world. Quite naturally some of the Ephesian converts were "rich in this present world" (v. 17). Some, in fact, were wealthy slave owners (cf. 6:2). And Christianity went on to make them even richer as they abandoned wasteful excesses, managed their households better, and profited from the hard work of converted slaves. As a result the jaws of prosperity opened wide, ready to devour a fresh harvest of the rich.

Just a few lines earlier in this chapter Paul had attacked the greed that seduced the false teachers in Ephesus, who thought "godliness is a means to financial gain" (6:5), characterizing them as "people who want to get rich" (6:9). Then he gave Timothy an extended charge that began, "But you, man of God, flee from all this" (v. 11) and ended with a resounding doxology.

Now Paul returns to the subject of riches in order to say a few words — not to those who want to get rich, but to those who are *already* rich. Here Paul does not condemn riches as such but delivers the plain truth about the dangers and responsibilities of wealth. His final words to a rich church have not lost their edge over the centuries. Prosperity is always ready to devour its Christian mother — and today's rich church must not forget it.

CLOSING WORDS FOR THE RICH (vv. 17-19)

About attitude. Paul's closing words to the rich cut right to the chase: "Command those who are rich in this present world not to be arrogant" (v. 17a). "Arrogant" here is a composite of two Greek words meaning "to think" and "exalted thoughts"[2] — to cherish high thoughts of yourself. Arrogance is self-conscious pride, and haughtiness is its telltale sign. And it breeds insolence and contempt.

Arrogance is accompanied by dark, telltale shadows. Wealth deludes people into imagining they are of superior value. The delusion goes like this: "I have more than other people — therefore I am superior. And certainly God sees my superiority — otherwise I would not be so *blessed*." Of course, a Mafia don could use the same reasoning. Nevertheless, that is the way our culture thinks, with its pathetic elevation of the rich — so that a vacuous millionaire prominent in the media or the entertainment industry or whatever is held in awe by the masses. Moral superiority is believed to be a matter of homes and cars and yachts and designer labels. Timex and Rolex both end in *ex*, but the wearer of one is seen as a universe of superiority above the other. The novelist Boris Pasternak touched on this when his Dr. Zhivago observed of the Russian aristocracy that wealth "could itself create an illusion of genuine character and originality."[3] The same can be said about the rich and famous in America. The materialistic illusion.

Of course, Christians are not to think in this crass way. It is sub-Christian. But the shadows can be found in the church. An air of distance develops between us and the poor. We do not really connect with those who struggle financially. A subterranean contempt roots in our hearts, then surfaces in insensitive slips of the tongue, revealing the shadows. There is also the dark inclination of the well-off to overestimate their own wisdom, to take themselves too seriously and throw their weight around. When such happens, generosity can become nothing more than part of the rich Christian's *noblesse oblige*. Arrogance too easily overshadows and darkens the Christian life.

This was a danger in the opulent homes and in the house churches in Ephesus. Similar shadows loom large over the middle-class church in America today — in my church, in your church. Prosperity can devour the church. The apostle's injunction calls to us today: "Command those who are rich in this present world not to be arrogant."

About hope. The other cannibalizing temptation for the rich is misplaced hope. Paul's injunction says it clearly: "Command those who are rich in this present world not to be arrogant nor to put their hope in wealth, which is so uncertain, but to put their hope in God, who richly provides us with everything for our enjoyment" (v. 17).

Negatively, we Christians are not to put our "hope in wealth, which is so uncertain." How hard this is if you have an abundance! If you have a comfortable, well-furnished home and a top-of-the-line car, it is hard not to rely upon your things to insulate you and carry you through life. In truth, the only thing *certain* about material riches is that they are passing away. In fact, your possession of them is so transitory that upon death, they will become like things unknown. This is the certainty of wealth.

The other certitude is that wealth does not satisfy. Christina Onassis, heiress of the Greek shipping tycoon and daughter of Jacqueline Kennedy Onassis, inherited an annual income of one million dollars a week. Once when she was out of Diet Coke, she dispatched her private jet on a $30,000 round-trip to America for a few cases. "I left my David Bowie tape in Switzerland, but the helicopter's on the way!" Your friends are too busy to spend time with you? Just pay them $20,000 or $30,000 a month to do so. That is what Christina did.

But all the money in the world didn't satisfy Christina during her short thirty-seven years. She died of heart failure brought on by dieting and barbiturates.[4] Riches may grow, but they do not bring happiness. In this life "wealth . . . is so uncertain."

> *Do not wear yourself out to get rich;*
> *have the wisdom to show restraint.*
> *Cast but a glance at riches, and they are gone,*
> *for they will surely sprout wings*
> *and fly off to the sky like an eagle.*
> (*Proverbs 23:4, 5*)

The reality is that today's gains are tomorrow's losses. And we all know it — like the Wall Street broker who sleeps with three telephones!

Positively, Paul urged Timothy to command the Ephesians (and us) "to put their hope in God, who richly provides us with everything for our enjoyment." Notice very carefully: Paul did not tell those rich in this world to divest themselves of their wealth, but not to place their hope in it. Paul does not call for the false self-denial that was being preached by the false teachers. The believers were not to exchange materialism for asceticism. Nevertheless, they had to divest themselves of hope in their possessions and invest all their hope in God, whose divine intention for his children is not asceticism but "everything for our enjoyment."

So the question that our text asks is: On what does our hope honestly depend? If Jesus (who knows all things and will call you to account for any lie) were to sit in your home today and ask you that question, how would you answer? Another good question is: Has the arrogance of wealth darkened your soul? Do you imagine you are somehow better than those who have little — say, for example, a homeless person? God knows. We must own up to the truth, however painful, because arrogance due to riches and misplaced hope in them will devour our faith.

About generosity. On the other hand, a conscious move away from arrogance toward humility, and from hoping in wealth to hoping in God alone, will liberate God's people to live out the command to be generous — "Command them to do good, to be rich in good deeds, and to be generous and willing to share" (v. 18). This is a "I'll help you get it" sentence because it repeats the same message three times, with each repetition being a bit more specific.

First, "Command them to do good." "Do good" is a single word in the Greek, a word used only one other place in the New Testament, where it speaks of God showering his good gifts on his hearers (Acts 14:17). We are not called to shapeless good but to substantive action.

Second, and more specifically, they (and we) are "to be rich in good deeds." Such richness, by contrast, suggests good deeds that involve giving. Get it, Ephesians?

Third, "to be generous and willing to share" nails the meaning down, emphasizing giving that is from the hand as well as from the heart ("willing to share" comes from the Greek word *koinonia*, meaning "fellowship"). As Frank Gaebelein says, "A kind heart as well as a generous hand is demanded of the rich."[5] One's whole being is to be involved in giving. The rich in Ephesus had to understand and heed this, and so do we.

We must remember that Paul wrote this to real churches in Ephesus and that Paul's letter was read aloud in the wealthy Ephesian homes — to the well-to-do host elders and to their mixed congregations of wealthy masters and poor slaves. We can imagine that in some of those wealthy homes there were those who took a long, painful look at themselves and repented. They turned away from the arrogance of wealth, became more humble, and apologized to their brothers and sisters. They likewise turned from hoping in their wealth and placed their hope in God. And they gave generously from both hand and heart toward the welfare of needy members of the Body of Christ.

The New Testament teaches that wealth is not a sin, but it is an immense responsibility. If it feeds pride and roots us deeper in this world, it will devour us. But wealth is also a vast opportunity because as Calvin wisely remarked, "A man's opportunities to do good to others increase with the abundance of his riches."[6] Awesome opportunity lies before our affluent generation as we enter a new millennium — "to do good, to be rich in good deeds, and to be generous and willing to share."

About incentives. Paul closed his final word to the rich with a dazzling incentive: "In this way they will lay up treasure for themselves as a firm foundation for the coming age, so that they may take hold of the life that is truly life" (v. 19). The amassing of treasure in heaven by generous giving is consistent with what Jesus repeatedly taught. We read in his Sermon on the Mount, "Do not store up for yourselves treasures on earth, where moth and rust destroy, and where thieves break in and steal. But store up for yourselves treasures in heaven, where moth and rust do not destroy, and where thieves do not break in and steal" (Matthew 6:19, 20). And later to the rich ruler he declared, "You still lack one thing. Sell everything you have and give to the poor, and you will have treasure in heaven" (Luke 18:22).

Of course, neither Jesus nor Paul taught that one could buy salvation or promoted moralism based on human merit. Far from buying shares in Heaven, Paul is emphasizing that true riches have nothing to do with earthly wealth, which is uncertain and for this age only. The only riches that will survive this world are those invested by God's people through generous giving. God reconciles us through his free grace, moves us to serve him, and then accepts our services, flawed as they are, and bestows on our services a reward they do not merit.[7] Those who give never suffer loss but get richer and richer and richer in the age to come. Incredible incentive! Listen to Augustine:

> From the goods which they distributed to others and so placed in greater safety, they derived more happiness than they incurred sorrow from the goods which they anxiously hoarded and so lost more easily. Nothing could be really lost on earth save what one would be ashamed to take to heaven.[8]

Such generous giving hangs on tightly to "the life that is truly life" (v. 19). Believers already have life, but a generous, giving Christian is one who has taken hold of eternal life now (cf. v. 12) and is riding life for all it is worth. Generous givers thrill in their salvation, rejoice in the fruit of the Spirit, and live the life of the coming age now.

What incentives — amassed treasure in Heaven and a hold now on "the life that is truly life"! A church with such people escapes Cotton Mather's dictum. They are not devoured by prosperity. The rewards are so high!

We must remember that Paul was so concerned about this church because it was the missionary lighthouse to Asia. His stated reason for writing was that "you will know how people ought to conduct themselves in God's household, which is the church of the living God, the pillar and foundation of the truth" (3:15). The way they used their money was crucial, and that is why the apostle's final words dealt with it. May they not be lost on us!

CLOSING WORDS TO THEIR LEADER (vv. 20, 21)

Paul also gave some closing words to Timothy, the church's leader, which by virtue of their final position in the letter carry the same urgency for him personally. As with the leaders, Paul goes again right to the chase: "Timothy, guard what has been entrusted to your care. Turn away from godless chatter and the opposing ideas of what is falsely called knowledge, which some have professed and in so doing have wandered from the faith. Grace be with you" (vv. 20, 21).

Guard! The opening command is simple and direct (literally, "Guard the deposit"; cf. 2 Timothy 1:14). The deposit is the pure faith of the gospel, the essential apostolic teaching, which became known as "the rule of faith" or "the canon of truth." This was not something Timothy was to work out for himself or was entitled to enlarge. It was divine revelation committed to his care.[9] In the fifth century St. Leo gave Timothy's charge classic expression:

> What is meant by *the deposit?* That which is committed to thee, not that which is invented by thee; that which thou hast received, not that which thou hast devised; a thing not of wit, but of learning; not of private assumption, but of public tradition; a thing brought to thee, not brought forth of thee; wherein thou must not be an author, but a keeper; not a leader but a follower. Keep the deposit.[10]

This defines the essential work of the church and its leadership today. It is not responsible to do new theology but to guard and exposit the apostolic deposit. As William Barclay has suggested, an elder and preacher does well to remember that his duty is not to himself but to the truth and to his children and his children's children. If in our day the church is weakened and enfeebled by inattention to the deposit, if in our day Christian ethics are more and more melded into the world because of neglect of the deposit, if in our day the Christian faith is distorted by attempts to make it culturally relevant, we would not be the only losers, but also our children and their children.[11] We must guard the deposit. The apostolic urgency has not diminished.

Avoid! Guarding the deposit requires avoidance: "Turn away from godless chatter and the opposing ideas of what is falsely called knowledge, which some have professed and in so doing have wandered from the faith" (vv. 20, 21).

In distinct contrast to simply guarding the deposit are godless empty sounds. The false teachers made great use of pseudo-theological rhetoric, as do many of today's revisionist theologians. Take, for example, the "God is Dead" theologian J. J. Altizer and his ridiculous "god talk" jargon: "Insofar as an eschatological epiphany of Christ can occur only in conjunction with a realization in total experience of the kenotic process of self-negation, we should expect that epiphany to occur in the heart of darkness, for only the universal triumph of the Antichrist can provide an arena for the total manifestation of Christ."[12] It makes no sense at all.

This "godless chatter" also involved "the opposing ideas [Greek, *antitheseis*] of what is falsely called knowledge." The false teachers had systematically developed antitheses to Christian truth that denied the gospel.[13] And they pretentiously called their system "knowledge," *gnosis* — a pseudo-science that would become full-blown Gnosticism by the second century.

Paul's advice here is: Do not engage these men on their terms. He does not want Timothy to fall to the seductive maze of their thinking. Such knowledge, says Paul, is "falsely called knowledge."

Leo the Great was right — the apostolic deposit is to be guarded, not embellished. And it is not best served by a foolish dialogue.

Final words carry great weight, and when they come from the great apostle, we must listen closely. "Those who are rich in this present world" must flee the besetting sins of arrogance and faith in wealth. They must do a difficult thing — place all their hope in God. And they must give. And we must remember that they are us! May it never be true of us that "Religion begat prosperity and the daughter devoured the mother."

Those who are leaders must guard the truth. We have received gold, and we must render gold!

2 Timothy

20

Ministry: Retrospect and Reality

2 TIMOTHY 1:1-7

*Paul, an apostle of Christ Jesus by the will of God, according to the prom-
ise of life that is in Christ Jesus, To Timothy, my dear son: Grace, mercy and
peace from God the Father and Christ Jesus our Lord. I thank God, whom
I serve, as my forefathers did, with a clear conscience, as night and day I
constantly remember you in my prayers. Recalling your tears, I long to
see you, so that I may be filled with joy. I have been reminded of your sincere faith, which first lived in your grandmother Lois and in your mother
Eunice and, I am persuaded, now lives in you also. For this reason I remind
you to fan into flame the gift of God, which is in you through the laying on
of my hands. For God did not give us a spirit of timidity, but a spirit of
power, of love and of self-discipline.*

INTRODUCTION (vv. 1, 2)

Paul and Timothy. Tough times had fallen on the Apostle Paul since the
writing of 1 Timothy. When he first wrote to Timothy he was on the road,
hoping to visit him in Ephesus (cf. 3:14, 15). Now he is chained in prison (his
second Roman imprisonment; cf. 1:16, 17; 2:9). Many think, as tradition suggests, it was the Mammertine prison in Rome. If so, it was a dismal under-
ground chamber with a single hole in the ceiling for light and air. Paul had
already had a court hearing (which he alludes to in 4:16-18), and he expects
that he will soon be executed (cf. 4:6-8). He was lonely. Luke was the only
one with him. Demas had abandoned him "because he loved this world"
(4:10). Crescens had gone to Galatia or, as some translate it, to Gallia (Gaul),
and Titus was off to Dalmatia (cf. 4:10, 11). At the same time, things had
deteriorated in Ephesus where Timothy was pastoring. Not only were there

desertions, but Hymenaeus, whom he had excommunicated, was still doing his evil work (cf. 1 Timothy 1:18-20; 2 Timothy 2:17, 18).

Cold and alone, Paul would conclude this letter by requesting that Timothy come quickly and that he bring John Mark and a warm cloak and the apostle's parchments (4:9-13). It is not known whether Timothy and Mark reached Paul before his execution.

As you would expect, these were also tough times for Timothy. However much the teachings of Paul's first letter had been applied by the young man, the church at Ephesus was still under siege from heretics. And now, apparently, even heavier burdens were about to fall on Timothy.

1 and 2 Timothy. So we can understand why there are such marked differences between Paul's first and second letter to Timothy. First Timothy focuses on the church and is a kind of church manual, as Paul explained in 3:14, 15: "I am writing you these instructions so that, if I am delayed, you will know how people ought to conduct themselves in God's household." Paul knew that a well-ordered church is a key to people being saved and coming to the knowledge of the truth.

On the other hand, while 2 Timothy also refers to the false teachers and urges sound doctrine, the focus is almost entirely on Timothy. Timothy is the man! Paul's writing here is intensely personal. It is his last will and testament, "written," as Calvin said, "not merely in ink but in Paul's life blood."[1] Passion and urgency ooze from Paul's pen as he addresses Timothy. The purpose of the letter is to charge Timothy to persevere in the ministry of the gospel — to fill the apostle's immense gospel sandals. Paul will urge Timothy in various verses to "fan into flame the gift of God" (1:6, 7), to "guard the good deposit" (1:14), and to "preach the Word" (4:2).[2]

Paul's greeting. As intensely personal as this letter is, Paul intended that his letter also be read by and to the church in Ephesus, and ultimately by the church universal. If his writing was for Timothy alone, he would never have begun with such a formal and lofty assertion of his apostleship: "Paul, an apostle of Christ Jesus by the will of God, according to the promise of life that is in Christ Jesus" (v. 1).

How had he been made an apostle? "By the will of God." Paul's authority came from God (cf. 1 Corinthians 1:1; 2 Corinthians 1:1; Ephesians 1:1; Colossians 1:1). Why had he been made an apostle? "According to the promise of life that is in Christ Jesus" — that is, the gospel, which has as its main purpose bringing people into new life.[3] The teaching in this personal letter is universally authoritative and is essential to the experience and perpetuation of "the promise of life that is in Christ Jesus."

From the lofty universal greeting, Paul switches in verse 2 to the intimate language of love: "To Timothy, my dear son" (literally, "my beloved child"). The cold and lonely old apostle was warmed by the thought of his beloved young disciple and penned this triple blessing, which is a promise and a prayer: "Grace, mercy and peace from God the Father and Christ Jesus our Lord." "Grace" to the undeserving, "mercy" to the helpless, and "peace" to the restless. How sweet it was — and how soothing to Timothy's soul!

After this, Paul immediately engages in a heartening personal retrospect about himself and then about Timothy, then gives a charge to Timothy based upon bracing spiritual realities.

RETROSPECT (vv. 3-5)

A Retrospect on Himself (v. 3)

> "I thank God, whom I serve, as my forefathers did, with a clear conscience, as night and day I constantly remember you in my prayers." (v. 3)

Paul possessed the happy retrospect and reality of "a clear conscience." That had not always been the case with Paul. Before coming to know Christ, his conscience repeatedly accused him and slew him, as Romans 7 dramatically chronicles. But when he met Christ, his heart was sprinkled with Jesus' blood, and he was cleansed from "a guilty conscience" (Hebrews 10:22).

So Paul had come to serve God with "a clear conscience." There were times, of course, when his conscience convicted him of sin, and he had to confess it. But overall as he looked at his life, he had "a clear conscience."

This was essential in Paul's having "fought the good fight" (cf. 4:7). In his first letter he had advised Timothy to "fight the good fight, holding on to faith and a good conscience. Some have rejected these and so have shipwrecked their faith. Among them are Hymenaeus and Alexander" (1 Timothy 1:18-20). Hymenaeus and Alexander had violated their consciences in respect to the faith they claimed to have, and so they became apostates. They ignored the flashing lights of conscience as they departed from the Word and shipwrecked their souls. But Paul kept "a clear conscience" in respect to the faith of his forefathers.

This is invaluably instructive! The old warrior is chained in a dripping, winter-cold dungeon awaiting the executioner's axe, and as he surveys his life — his conversion and then the kaleidoscope of sermons preached, shipwrecks, confrontations, deliverances, stonings, beatings, and victories — his conscience is absolutely clear. There is no guilt, no weight of unresolved sins, nothing to confess. He has been true to the gospel and his calling. He was not sinless, but he was blameless, and he was faithful.

Moreover, as he sits chained, he "constantly" remembers Timothy in his prayers (v. 3). One commentator, believing that such uninterrupted prayer was impossible, argues that this refers to Paul's periodic prayers. But we must take Paul at his word — he was continually engaged in prayer — not literally every minute of every day, but nevertheless continually. His whole waking being was in a spirit of intercession. He lived out his own dictum to "pray in the Spirit on all occasions" (Ephesians 6:18), and the Holy Spirit was constantly bringing fresh supplications to his mind. Whether the apostle was awake or asleep, the Spirit interceded for him "with groans that words cannot express" (Romans 8:26).

What a way to end life — thankful, with "a clear conscience," engaged in perpetual prayer! And what a motivating example to Timothy!

A Retrospect on Timothy (vv. 4, 5)

The apostle's retrospect on Timothy brims with emotion: "Recalling your tears, I long to see you, so that I may be filled with joy" (v. 4).

His tears. Acts 20 tells us that when Paul said farewell to the Ephesian elders at Miletus, the whole company shed tears (v. 37). But that event had taken place years before. Therefore, Timothy's "tears" here refers to something more recent. Perhaps it was tears shed over the beleaguered church. More likely, it was a tearful good-bye to Paul as the apostle was carried off to Rome.[4] The memory of Timothy's tearful love made the old apostle's heart ache for Timothy's presence — "I long to see you, so that I may be filled with joy." This makes Paul's later poignant plea, "Get here before winter" (4:21), even more haunting.

It must be noted here that Timothy was not at all like Paul, the great apostle. He was still young and to a large extent inexperienced. In 1 Timothy Paul told the young disciple to allow no one to look down on his youth (4:12). And here in this letter Timothy is told to "Flee the evil desires of youth" (2:22). He had a weak constitution. He had frequent ailments and a weak stomach (cf. 1 Timothy 5:23). He was timid by nature. He was naturally shy — what today we would call an introvert. On one occasion Paul wrote to the Corinthians, "If Timothy comes, see to it that he has nothing to fear while he is with you, for he is carrying on the work of the Lord, just as I am. No one, then, should refuse to accept him" (1 Corinthians 16:10, 11a).

Paul, by contrast, was mature and experienced, constitutionally tough, and lionhearted, not young, weak, and shy like Timothy. And yet, not only did Paul love Timothy — he believed in him. And he thanked God for Timothy! Why? Because God had made him who he was and because God was at work in Timothy to make him adequate for ministry.

If you sense that God is calling you to do something far beyond your natural capabilities, you can take heart from Timothy's life. In truth, God always calls us to minister beyond our natural endowments, no matter how great they are. You may be naturally eloquent, but your giftedness will never be sufficient to preach the Word. You may be merciful by nature, but that is not enough to be able to live out the full call of God to be merciful. Take heart! God's call is always too great for us to do in ourselves. But if he calls you, he will equip and enable you to do it.

His sincere faith. Paul's retrospect remembered not only Timothy's tears but his faith: "I have been reminded of your sincere faith, which first lived in your grandmother Lois and in your mother Eunice and, I am persuaded, now lives in you also" (v. 5). Timothy's father was an unbelieving Gentile, but his grandmother and mother were Jews who came to Christ in fulfillment of their Jewish heritage, experiencing the profound continuity of the old and new covenants. The result was a deep, living, "sincere faith."

Their faith was genuine. It penetrated their hearts and wills, so that everything was touched by it — their fears and hopes and loves and desires and joys and compassions and zeal. They were the genuine article. And such faith had come to characterize Timothy as well. This was not a case of eugenics (good breeding). Rather, he had seen faith in them, then he came to Christ, and then his life demonstrated the same genuineness.

There was no doubt about Timothy's "sincere faith." He might be young, he might be weak, he might be shy, but he and his faith were genuine. And he was totally sincere. His whole heart was in it. Paul had just argued that his own faith was in continuity with his forefathers (v. 3), and here he encourages Timothy that his is in continuity with his estimable "foremothers."

The transcending point is that Paul believed in Timothy's faith, and he believed in Timothy. This kind of confidence in another is heartening. The man who led me to Christ, Verl Lindley, and his belief in me and my calling had a huge impact on my life. He still exerts a vast effect on me. Though it has been many years, and he is now retired from ministry, he still believes in me. And his belief in me still braces me.

The effect of godly people who believe in us is beyond accounting. Timothy was called to stand tall by the heartening recollection of Eunice and Lois and Paul. He was their boy!

REALITY (vv. 6, 7)

The soil of Timothy's life, watered by such love and faith, was ready to be planted with Paul's appeal: "For this reason I remind you to fan into flame the gift of God, which is in you through the laying on of my hands. For God did not give us a spirit of timidity, but a spirit of power, of love and of self-discipline" (vv. 6, 7). At first reading it might appear that "the gift of God" that Timothy is to "fan into flame" is the giftedness for ministry that he received at his ordination (cf. 1 Timothy 4:14). And this is correct as far as it goes. But the following verse makes it clear that Paul wants Timothy to fan "the gift of God" by relying on the Holy Spirit, whom he received at his conversion.

Gordon Fee is right in establishing that "spirit" in verse 7 should have a capital *S* and is in fact referring to the Holy Spirit of God. Verse 7 is not speaking about the human spirit or an attitude that God has given us, but to the Holy Spirit. There are several reasons for concluding this, among which are: 1) The word "For" that begins verse 7 gives it the closest possible tie to verse 6. 2) The close tie between "gift" (v. 6) and "the Spirit" (v. 7) is characteristic of Paul (cf. 1 Corinthians 12, esp. v. 4). 3) The words "power" and "love" in verse 7 are used especially for the work of the Holy Spirit in Paul's writings. And 4) there are close ties between this text and 1 Timothy 4:14, where the gifting of Timothy is implicitly a work of the Holy Spirit. So for these and other reasons, Fee gives this paraphrase in verse 7: "For when God gave us his Spirit, it was not timidity that we received, but power, love, and self-discipline."[5] A number of translations convey a similar reading (for example, *Today's English Version* and the *Jerusalem Bible*).

This fits perfectly with verse 6 and explains it. In that verse Paul urges Timothy to "fan into flame the gift of God," his giftedness for ministry. The basis for this appeal goes back to his original gift of the Spirit, given at conversion.[6] He is therefore to exercise his Spirit-given gifts for ministry with the power, love, and self-discipline given him by the Holy Spirit from the very first. Martin Luther celebrated this reality in the hymn "A Mighty Fortress": "The Spirit and the gifts are ours."

Understanding that it is the work of the Holy Spirit that is in view in verse 7, we read, "For God did not give us [the] Spirit of timidity." The Holy Spirit simply does not give this fainting quality. Or as some renderings suggest, he did not give us "cowardice."[7] The Spirit does not give fear that makes us shrink from duty, as Timothy was tempted to do. Rather, the Spirit breathes "power" into the weak.

The marvelous fact is, the Timothies of this world make perfect receptacles for the Spirit's power when they turn to him. As quoted earlier, Oswald Chambers wrote:

> God can achieve his purpose either through the absence of human power and resources, or the abandonment of reliance on them. All through history God has chosen and used nobodies, because their unusual dependence on him made possible the unique display of his power and grace. He chose and used somebodies only when they renounced dependence on their natural abilities and resources.[8]

Feeling weak, timid, inadequate even though you want to serve God? Feeling like Timothy? If so, you are an inviting prospect for the Holy Spirit. And if you call upon him, he will fill you with "power."

Next, the Spirit gives "love." In the New Testament love is much more than a feeling, because it eventuates in service for others in the power of the Holy Spirit. The love that the Spirit gives stands tall and perseveres.

The graces of "power" and "love" are mutually complementary. Their qualities flow from one to the other and back again.

Finally, the Spirit gives "self-discipline," in the sense of self-mastery. This has been defined as "the sanity of saintliness."[9] Philip Towner explains:

> Paul has in mind a measure of control over one's thinking and actions that allows a balanced outlook on any situation. When everything is coming unglued, this quality of "levelheadedness" will keep the Christian focused calmly on the power and love that the Spirit provides, and so it makes perseverance in life and ministry possible.[10]

This concern will be expressed again in 4:5 when Paul commands Timothy, "But you, keep your head in all situations." The Spirit gives the self-mastery that enables us to lead because we have been mastered for Christ.

We have all been given gifts for ministry, and we all have been given the Spirit, and therefore we all (even those who are naturally timid) are endowed with power, love, and levelheadedness. We must be humble and wise enough to live in constant dependence upon him.

The specific command to Timothy is in verse 6: "For this reason I remind you to fan into flame the gift of God, which is in you through the laying on of my hands." The giftedness was there, but there was a need for more fire. Timothy was to fan his gift to full flame. He was young and weak and timid, but he was called to stand tall. And he could because Paul believed in him and the Spirit enabled him.

There was special application in this command for Timothy, but the principle applies to all Christians, because every Christian has received ministry gifts and the same Spirit.

We must exercise our gifts or we will lose them. An untended fire finally becomes ashes. But when we fan the fire and step out to serve (no matter how inadequate we feel), we can expect the Spirit's power and love and levelheaded self-control.

Perhaps you have been experiencing those strange and sometimes terrifying inner workings that come when God is calling you to step out to serve him. For some the call may be a dramatic change of direction, even a vocational change. For most, it will be a call to step up and use your gifts right where you are. Quite likely, it will be to assume further responsibility in your church — to work in Sunday school or with students or to teach or to visit shut-ins. The ministries to which God calls his people are myriad. So "fan into flame the gift" and do the work he asks of you, because he has given you through his Spirit the power and love and self-discipline to do it.

21

Stand Tall, Suffer, and Keep the Faith

2 TIMOTHY 1:8-14

So do not be ashamed to testify about our Lord, or ashamed of me his prisoner. But join with me in suffering for the gospel, by the power of God, who has saved us and called us to a holy life — not because of anything we have done but because of his own purpose and grace. This grace was given us in Christ Jesus before the beginning of time, but it has now been revealed through the appearing of our Savior, Christ Jesus, who has destroyed death and has brought life and immortality to light through the gospel. And of this gospel I was appointed a herald and an apostle and a teacher. That is why I am suffering as I am. Yet I am not ashamed, because I know whom I have believed, and am convinced that he is able to guard what I have entrusted to him for that day. What you heard from me, keep as the pattern of sound teaching, with faith and love in Christ Jesus. Guard the good deposit that was entrusted to you — guard it with the help of the Holy Spirit who lives in us.

Again, consider what Oswald Chambers wrote, "All through history God has chosen and used nobodies, because their unusual dependence on him made possible the unique display of his power and grace. He chose and used somebodies only when they renounced dependence on their natural abilities and resources."[1]

If this is true (and it is!), then Timothy was the right man for the job. He was not endowed with a powerful body and iron constitution — he was frail. He was not bold but reticent. And he was not a natural leader. If the job was to get done, he would have to rely upon God. Everything would have to be the result of Timothy's profound dependence upon God's power and grace.

Timothy was surely heartened by Paul's introductory remarks in which the apostle reminded him that he was in the apostle's constant prayers and of his longing affection for his young disciple and of his confidence in the sincerity of Timothy's faith. And Timothy undoubtedly took further heart from Paul's reminder of the giftedness for ministry that he was to "fan into flame" and of the Holy Spirit's gifts of "power" and "love" and "self-discipline" (levelheadedness) for ministry. These bracing realities primed Timothy for the solemn charges to stand tall, suffer, and keep the faith — heady exhortations that range through verses 8-14.

STAND TALL AND SUFFER (vv. 8-12)

The dual call to stand and suffer is immediately introduced: "So do not be ashamed to testify about our Lord, or ashamed of me his prisoner. But join with me in suffering for the gospel, by the power of God" (v. 8). Stronger men than Timothy had wilted when faced with shame and suffering. The iron-willed, sword-wielding Apostle Peter had loudly declared, "Lord, I am ready to go with you to prison and to death" (Luke 22:33) but soon was ashamed to admit he knew Jesus and denied him outright before the soldiers and a servant girl as Jesus watched (cf. vv. 56-62). In those storied and (thankfully) fleeting moments, Peter fled the shame and suffering of Christ.

Stand Tall

The temptation for Timothy to succumb to shame was not a figment of Paul's imagination. The cross of Christianity was a scandal. It may seem incredible that people would view Jesus as shameful. But both Jews and Gentiles viewed crucifixion (a penalty reserved only for the worst of criminals) as the ultimate emblem of disgrace and dishonor. Polite pagan company never mentioned the equivalent of the English word *cross*. The loathsome word was too obscene. And in the sophisticated Greek environment, the preaching of the cross was held to be absurd (cf. 1 Corinthians 1:23). The idea of a Jewish peasant becoming the substitutionary atonement for people's sins was laughable. Educated, urbane Greeks snickered at such crudeness.

There were also some in the Ephesian church (for example, Hymenaeus; cf. 2:17) who viewed Paul's sufferings and imprisonment as public proof that the Holy Spirit was not with Paul. Paul's enemies within the church believed that the resurrection (a spiritual resurrection) had already taken place and that those who had experienced it had been so endowed with the Spirit that their difficulties evaporated. Their theology was similar to today's "health and wealth" preachers. To them, Paul's sufferings and imprisonment in Rome were due to his shamefully unspiritual nature and the disapproval of the Holy Spirit.[2]

But Paul urged Timothy not to succumb to such ungrounded shame, whether over the scandal of the cross or the ignominious suffering of Christ's servants. Rather, he was to stand tall, as Paul himself did in that foul dungeon. Paul's unbowed, towering posture is detected here in his subtle use of words as he describes himself as "his prisoner" — that is, *the Lord's* prisoner![3] He is in Caesar's dungeon, but Nero is not his captor — Christ is. And the apostle is proud, not shamed. Thus Timothy also ought to stand tall. "Be the man you are meant to be, Timothy!"

Suffer

The parallel call to suffer is explicit: "But join with me in suffering for the gospel, by the power of God" (v. 8b). Rather than being ashamed of Paul's suffering, Timothy must stand tall and freely choose to suffer with the great apostle. Oswald Chambers was right when he wrote: "To choose to suffer means that there is something wrong; to choose God's will even if it means suffering is a very different thing. No healthy saint ever chooses suffering; he chooses God's will, as Paul did, whether it means suffering or not."[4]

This said, suffering, rather than being removed by the gospel (as the health and wealth gospelers would have it), is actually part of the gospel. Jesus made this clear from the beginning when he forewarned his followers in the Upper Room:

> "If the world hates you, keep in mind that it hated me first. If you belonged to the world, it would love you as its own. As it is, you do not belong to the world, but I have chosen you out of the world. That is why the world hates you. Remember the words I spoke to you: 'No servant is greater than his master.' If they persecuted me, they will persecute you also. If they obeyed my teaching, they will obey yours also." (John 15:18-20)

In the same way, Jesus crowned the Beatitudes with suffering, in essence saying that when you have attained the seven blessed qualities of poverty of spirit, mourning, meekness, spiritual hunger, mercy, purity of heart, and peacemaking, you will suffer! "Blessed are those who are persecuted because of righteousness, for theirs is the kingdom of heaven" (Matthew 5:10). Suffering is part of God's gospel blessing.

When Jesus called Paul on the road to Damascus, he immediately sent Ananias to him, saying, "Go! This man is my chosen instrument to carry my name before the Gentiles and their kings and before the people of Israel. I will show him how much he must suffer for my name" (Acts 9:15, 16). And as the years passed, Paul would describe his ministry like this:

> We are hard pressed on every side, but not crushed; perplexed, but not in despair; persecuted, but not abandoned; struck down, but not

*destroyed. We always carry around in our body the death of Jesus,
so that the life of Jesus may also be revealed in our body. For we
who are alive are always being given over to death for Jesus' sake,
so that his life may be revealed in our mortal body. So then, death is
at work in us, but life is at work in you. (2 Corinthians 4:8-12)*

Paul encouraged the Colossians by telling them that suffering is a privilege: "Now I rejoice in what was suffered for you, and I fill up in my flesh what is still lacking in regard to Christ's afflictions, for the sake of his body, which is the church" (Colossians 1:24). Likewise, he informed the Philippians about their privilege: "For it has been granted to you on behalf of Christ not only to believe on him, but also to suffer for him" (Philippians 1:29). Later in 2 Timothy he will say again to his young protégé, "In fact, everyone who wants to live a godly life in Christ Jesus will be persecuted" (3:12; cf. Romans 8:17; 1 Thessalonians 1:6; 2:14; 3:4). And Paul's words were sealed with his own blood.

This first-century theology needs to be central in our twenty-first century theology. Persecution is inevitable for serious Christians. It is a privilege — "It has been granted to you . . . to suffer for him." It is a blessing — "Blessed are those who are persecuted" (Matthew 5:10).

Suffering is never pleasurable. But it can be eased by the company of those undergoing the same thing. Timothy was called to join Paul in suffering for the gospel because what is so difficult alone is easier to endure (and even rejoice over) in the company of other believers. In the same way, "The apostles left the Sanhedrin, rejoicing because they had been counted worthy of suffering disgrace for the Name" (Acts 5:41). Suffering is not something any person or group chooses or endures in its own power, and that is why Paul calls Timothy to do it "by the power of God," which Timothy had been given, as verse 7 said.

Everything of God

The reason that Timothy (and Christians of any age) can rely on God's power is because it is inseparable from God's grace. Paul here sets forth the gospel in all its fullness by repeatedly holding high the gracious glories of the gospel in verses 9 and 10. William Barclay correctly declares of this section: "There are few passages in the New Testament which have in them and behind them such a sense of the sheer grandeur of the gospel of Jesus Christ."[5]

Sovereign grace. The power or ability to suffer in a godly way is rooted in God's sovereign grace. "But join with me in suffering for the gospel, by the power of God, who has saved us and called us to a holy life — not because of anything we have done but because of his own purpose and grace" (vv. 8b, 9a). The gospel originated in God, and the gospel is totally the good news of God's grace. It is not only the gospel of Jesus Christ but "the gospel of God," as Paul calls it in Romans 1:1. It is not based on anything we have done. It is all of grace — undeserved kindness from above.

As Paul puts it in Titus 3:5, "He saved us, not because of righteous things we had done, but because of his mercy." And most famously he says in Ephesians 2:8, 9, "By grace you have been saved, through faith — and this not from yourselves, it is the gift of God — not by works, so that no one can boast." If our salvation depended on anything in us, our position, based on any realistic estimate of ourselves, would be hopeless. All glory goes to God for his sovereign, omnipotent, sustaining grace!

Preexistent grace. The next phrase celebrates not only sovereign grace but preexistent grace: "This grace was given us in Christ Jesus before the beginning of time" (v. 9b) — literally, "before times eternal."[6] Thus we understand that Christ existed before the beginning of time and that grace preexisted in Christ. This thought is expanded in Ephesians 1:4-6 — "For he chose us in him before the creation of the world to be holy and blameless in his sight. In love he predestined us to be adopted as his sons through Jesus Christ, in accordance with his pleasure and will — to the praise of his glorious grace, which he has freely given us in the One he loves." And since God gave grace to us in Christ before history began, it is absolutely certain that salvation is not from our works. God the Father gave us grace in Christ before we did or could do any good works. Our salvation is due only to God's preexistent grace.

Visible grace. Ultimately, God's sovereign grace, preexistent in Christ, became visible and effective in the incarnation, death, and resurrection of Christ. "But it [grace] has now been revealed through the appearing of our Savior, Christ Jesus, who has destroyed death and has brought life and immortality to light through the gospel" (v. 10). The gospel is the good news "that Christ died for our sins according to the Scriptures, that he was buried, that he was raised on the third day according to the Scriptures" (1 Corinthians 15:3b, 4). This gospel is all-powerful. It can save anyone who believes, as Paul celebrates: "I am not ashamed of the gospel, because it is the power of God for the salvation of everyone who believes: first for the Jew; then for the Gentile" (Romans 1:16). The glory of the gospel is that everything is of God. It is a gospel of sovereign grace, preexistent grace, visible grace that begins and ends in him.

Standing and Suffering

At this last mention of the gospel, Paul exults in his privilege. His soul dances at the thought of his call: "And of this gospel I was appointed a herald and an apostle and a teacher" (v. 11). He was a *kerux*, one who sounds forth the evangel, the greatest news ever told. He was an *apostolos*, one sent with a specific commission from God. And he was a teacher, a *didoskolos* (his favorite word in the Pastorals), as he outlined the great doctrines of the faith, the apostolic deposit. And as he marvels at his privilege, he reflects on his suffering: "That is why I am suffering as I am" (v. 12a). "I am suffering because the gospel is so unutterably glorious. I am suffering because it is so powerful. I am suffering because it is the only hope of the lost."

As he stands tall, he further exults, "Yet I am not ashamed, because I know whom I have believed, and am convinced that he is able to guard what I have entrusted to him for that day" (v. 12b). Think of it! Though he is entombed below ground in a dark, dripping cell, awaiting execution, though he seems to be a forgotten cast-off to the world, and certainly to his enemies, he vows, "I am not ashamed."

Why? "Because I know whom I have believed." Certainly Paul knew *what* he believed as well as any Christian who has ever lived. He authored at least thirteen of the twenty-seven books of the New Testament. But he stresses *whom* he has believed in and continues to believe in (perfect tense). There is no wavering, no doubt — only the profound confidence of perpetual faith and a constant relationship with God. Thus he stands imperially tall, unashamed.

Why else is he not ashamed? "I . . . am convinced that he is able to guard what I have entrusted to him for that day" (v. 12). Paul lived with the certainty that God would guard his life's commitment to the gospel until the great day of Christ's return and final judgment (4:8). Paul was absolutely certain that his gospel deposit would be protected right up to and at the judgment, where God would assess everything to his glory. So Paul towered unashamed. God would vindicate him!

John Calvin remarked, "We should always remember that Paul was not philosophizing in the dark, but with the reality before his eyes."[7] This was real life. He stood tall because he intimately knew in whom he believed, and he remained unashamed because he knew that God would guard his life's investment until the judgment.

What Paul was doing here by letter was extending his apostolic hand out of his Roman prison, across the boot of Italy, across the Adriatic Sea, across Greece, across the Aegean to Ephesus and was beckoning Timothy to join him in standing unashamed while suffering for Christ. His hand still reaches out through the centuries to Christ's followers.

The glorious gospel never demands less. As a young preacher from Zimbabwe so memorably expressed it:

I'm part of the fellowship of the unashamed. I have the Holy Spirit's power. The die has been cast. I have stepped over the line. The decision has been made; I'm a disciple of *His!* I won't look back, let up, slow down, back away, or be still. . . . I won't give up, shut up, let up, until I have stayed up, stored up, prayed up, paid up, and preached up for the cause of Christ. I am a disciple of Jesus.[8]

It is a great day when by faith your heart says yes to whatever the gospel brings and you join hands with the apostle. Will you do so today?

KEEP THE FAITH (vv. 13, 14)

Paul concludes this section with his famous charge to Timothy to keep the faith by living out two parallel commands. First: "What you heard from me, keep as the pattern of sound teaching, with faith and love in Christ Jesus" (v. 13). Second: "Guard the good deposit that was entrusted to you — guard it with the help of the Holy Spirit who lives in us" (v. 14).

Keep it. By urging Timothy to keep his instruction as the pattern for sound teaching, Paul set the theological parameters for the preaching of the gospel. But Paul was especially concerned about how it was done — about Timothy's attitude — that it be "with faith and love in Christ Jesus." The attitude with which Timothy maintained his orthodoxy was almost as important as the orthodoxy itself.[9] How different church history would have been if the church in succeeding generations had taken this to heart. How different the church would be if this were true today.

Guard it. The second imperative — to "Guard the good deposit" — goes a step further.[10] It is the same note that was sounded at the end of 1 Timothy: "Timothy, guard what has been entrusted to your care. Turn away from godless chatter and the opposing ideas of what is falsely called knowledge, which some have professed and in so doing have wandered from the faith" (1 Timothy 6:20, 21). Timothy must always be loving. But at the same time he must be perpetually vigilant — like a soldier. Timothy must be tough!

But this is not the task of Timothy alone. He must do it with the help of the indwelling Holy Spirit. And here the appeal comes full circle. It began in verses 6, 7 with an appeal to Timothy to live out his ministry through the power of the Holy Spirit. Then followed four commands: 1) "Do not be ashamed." 2) "Join with me in suffering." 3) "Keep . . . the pattern." 4) "Guard the good deposit." Now again he returns to the Holy Spirit's enabling power: "Guard it with the help of the Holy Spirit who lives in us."

There was no doubt that Timothy could do this. He was a prime candidate because, in Oswald Chambers's words again, "All through history God has chosen and used nobodies, because their unusual dependence on him made possible the unique display of his power and grace. He chose and used somebodies only when they renounced dependence on their natural abilities and resources."

God is looking for a few good "nobodies" — people who know they cannot succeed in serving him in their own strength. These are the people who are able to stand tall and who will unashamedly testify about Jesus. Like Paul they are unashamed of the gospel because in their weaknesses they rely on the Holy Spirit. These are the people who join in suffering for the gospel, by the power of God. They are humble because they see gospel grace for what it is — sovereign grace, preexistent grace, visible grace in the Lord Jesus Christ — all of God and not ourselves. They are so overwhelmed by the gospel that they both suffer and stand tall. These are the people who keep the pattern of sound teaching and guard the gospel. Their weakness is the occasion for God's power, their reticence for his loving aggression, their need for the help of the Holy Spirit.

22

Mercy to the Merciful

2 TIMOTHY 1:15-18

You know that everyone in the province of Asia has deserted me, including Phygelus and Hermogenes. May the Lord show mercy to the household of Onesiphorus, because he often refreshed me and was not ashamed of my chains. On the contrary, when he was in Rome, he searched hard for me until he found me. May the Lord grant that he will find mercy from the Lord on that day! You know very well in how many ways he helped me in Ephesus.

The ancient fable of "The Two Travelers and the Bear" describes a fearsome encounter with a huge bear. One traveler, in great fear, shimmied high into a tree, giving no thought to his friend. The other, with no chance to go anywhere, remembered that bears often lose interest in the dead and so fell to the ground feigning death. The bear came alongside and nuzzled and sniffed at his face and ears. Thinking the man to be dead, the beast ambled away. When the bear was long gone, the man up in the tree climbed down and asked his friend what the bear had whispered to him, "because," he said, "I noticed that his mouth was long at your ear." The other said, as he stood dusting himself off, "It is no secret what he told me. What he said was that I should be careful about keeping company with those who, when danger arises, leave their friends in the lurch!"[1]

Such a fable would probably have evoked a knowing smile from the Apostle Paul because he had been abandoned by his fair-weather friends in Asia, among them Phygelus and Hermogenes. But at the same time he experienced the upside — the coming to him of Onesiphorus, who cared for him in his need.

The story, as he tells it in the brief span of verses 15-18, is one of *desertion* and *encouragement.* Paul relates this to further steel Timothy to stand tall and suffer with him for the gospel, as he had just charged him in verses 8-14. In essence he says, "Remember Phygelus and Hermogenes? Don't be like those tree-climbing deserters. Remember Onesiphorus who refreshed me? Be like him."

DESERTED (v. 15)

Paul's friends. Behind this text lies the fact that Paul was a lover of people and that he had an immense capacity for friendship. His vast circle of comrades included John Mark who had grown to be so helpful to Paul, Silas who accompanied him on his second journey, Onesimus, the fugitive Asian slave converted in Rome, Epaphroditus, the friend of the Philippian church who came to see Paul in Rome, Priscilla and Aquila who risked their lives to help him, Tychicus, a "dear brother" (Ephesians 6:21), Tertias, his secretary, Amplias, "whom I love in the Lord" (Romans 16:8), Luke, and of course Timothy, "my dear son" (1:2).

If you had no information about Paul, you would probably assume that the massive, magisterial theology of Romans must have come from an ivory-tower intellectual with several Ph.D.s who had no time for people. But in the final chapter of Romans (vv. 1-24) Paul's closing greetings mention thirty-three names, twenty-four of whom were in Rome. What makes this even more impressive is that Paul had never been to Rome! Most of the people he mentions there had met him on his journeys and had subsequently taken up residence in Rome. Paul's magnanimous heart knew where each friend was geographically and spiritually.

He prayed for his friends constantly, as he regularly reminded them in his letters. Their ups and downs were his ups and downs. "Who is weak, and I do not feel weak? Who is led into sin, and I do not inwardly burn?" (2 Corinthians 11:29). People, relationships, and friendships consumed Paul!

Paul's loneliness. As seen here, during his second Roman imprisonment Paul was lonely. The final chapter of the present letter reveals that only Luke was with him (4:11). Titus and Crescens had gone away (4:10), Demas had forsaken him (4:10), and Alexander had done him much harm (4:14).

Paul's situation here was much different from his first Roman imprisonment as he earlier described it in his letter to the Philippians. Granted, he had been abused and doubled-crossed at that time! "It is true," he wrote, "that some preach Christ out of envy and rivalry" (Philippians 1:15). That is, some were using his incarceration to promote their own ministries. Yet he did not feel abandoned. He was not alone, for the faithful surrounded him. But now in the dungeon he was isolated and lonely. Even if people wanted to see him, his cell was very hard to find.

Paul's desertion. In reality, Paul had been deserted by a substantial group of people as he reminds Timothy: "You know that everyone in the province of Asia has deserted me, including Phygelus and Hermogenes" (v. 15). Certainly "everyone" was not strictly literal (all Christians in Asia), because

Timothy, Onesiphorus and his household, and others like them were residents of Asia. But the defections were so staggering that it felt as if everyone had "deserted" him — an "exaggeration characteristic of depression."[2] This tragic defection encompassed the entire province of Asia Minor and its capital of Ephesus — and the majority of Paul's one-time supporters. Many Ephesians were prominent in this defection. We do not know whether Phygelus and Hermogenes were Ephesians or not. But they needed no identification to Timothy. He knew who they were!

This desertion evidently refers to a specific event, though we do not know for sure what it was.[3] Most think it was Paul's arrest. The Roman courts would never have prosecuted Paul on a purely religious accusation. He would have been held on a political charge, such as sedition or endangering the peace. Nothing less would have made him a prisoner of the state. Proverbs 17:17 says, "A friend loves at all times, and a brother is born for adversity." Adversity separates the chaff of surface friendship from the substance of real friendship. The truth had become apparent through Paul's difficulties.

As the Shadow once said to the Body: "Who is a friend like me? I follow you wherever you go. In sunlight or moonlight I never forsake you." "True," said the Body. "You go with me in sunlight and moonlight. But where are you when neither the sun nor the moon shines upon me?"[4]

Also, some of Paul's detractors may have seized on his arrest as *prima facie* evidence that God was not with him, claiming that if he had resurrection life and the blessing of the Spirit, he would be the picture of prosperity, not a Roman prisoner. In any event, Phygelus and Hermogenes had led the shameful and painful desertion.

Paul's pain. Paul, the great people-oriented person, a passionate lover of the church, was in pain. You have to be in a real relationship with people for them to really hurt you. People you do not know cannot hurt you. Hurt comes when you have known them, loved them, and invested in them. C. S. Lewis said, "To love at all is to be vulnerable. If you don't want to be hurt, give yourself to no one. Not even a cat. . . ."[5] But Paul had given them his heart, his whole life — everything.

John Calvin, who experienced similar hurts when he was expelled from Geneva and was abandoned by onetime friends, remarked that such deserters invariably became accusers and that many of his former colleagues wandered through the France of his day trying "to establish their own innocence by directing against us all the accusations they can."[6]

Paul, having such a great heart, had been deserted and slandered by people he loved. Consequently, he was heartbroken. His implicit message to Timothy was, "Don't be like Phygelus and Hermogenes. Stand with me.

Suffer with me. Keep the faith with me — in the dark of this dungeon where neither the sun nor the moon shines."

REFRESHED (vv. 16-18)

Onesiphorus's example. A universe removed from desertion by some is Onesiphorus's treatment of Paul. So Paul blesses him: "May the Lord show mercy to the household of Onesiphorus, because he often refreshed me and was not ashamed of my chains. On the contrary, when he was in Rome, he searched hard for me until he found me" (vv. 16, 17).

There are many reasons why it was difficult for the Asian Onesiphorus to locate Paul. He had never been in Rome and did not know his way around. Part of the city had been destroyed when Nero burned it. For some time the location of Paul's imprisonment had been kept from the Christians. Also, believers in Rome had been reduced in numbers due to persecution and flight, and not all were eager to reveal to a stranger that they had any doings with Paul.[7]

But Onesiphorus "searched hard," treading the serpentine passages of Rome, knocking at doors, asking in his provincial accent about Paul. Doors slammed shut, disapproving eyes watched as he continued his search, but he refused to desist. He was asking dangerous questions. The lesser devoted would have made no search at all. Others would have cooled their consciences with minimal effort — "He simply couldn't be found!" But not this man. Imagine the potent joy that jolted Paul when in came his old friend bearing supplies.

And once Onesiphorus found Paul, he kept returning. "He often refreshed me," says Paul. The refreshment was more than material. It was emphatically spiritual — soul refreshment — because the root of the Greek translated "refreshed" is the word for soul.[8] Whereas most had recoiled from Paul's chains, Onesiphorus apparently counted it an honor to return again and again to refresh Paul. It had been dangerous to ask where Paul was. It was dangerous to visit him. It was most dangerous to return again and again. But Onesiphorus was there for Paul, when neither the sun nor the moon shone on his friend. "A friend loves at all times, and a brother is born for adversity."

In Onesiphorus' visit to Paul in prison we see the living out of Christian mercy that Jesus said will be so grandly rewarded in the final judgment — because the mercy was actually done to him.

"Then the King will say to those on his right, 'Come, you who are blessed by my Father; take your inheritance, the kingdom prepared for you since the creation of the world. For I was hungry and you gave me something to eat, I was thirsty and you gave me some-

thing to drink, I was a stranger and you invited me in, I needed clothes and you clothed me, I was sick and you looked after me, I was in prison and you came to visit me.' Then the righteous will answer him, 'Lord, when did we see you hungry and feed you, or thirsty and give you something to drink? When did we see you a stranger and invite you in, or needing clothes and clothe you? When did we see you sick or in prison and go to visit you?' The King will reply, 'I tell you the truth, whatever you did for one of the least of these brothers of mine, you did for me.'" (Matthew 25:34-40)

The connection between Christ and genuine believers is like that of brother to brother and brother to sister. Because Christ is so intimately identified with Paul, when Onesiphorus "refreshed" Paul, *he refreshed Christ!* There in that subterranean dungeon Onesiphorus ministered to Christ. Someday Onesiphorus in utter self-forgetting humility may say something like "When did I see you in prison?" And Jesus will say, "I tell you the truth, whatever you did for one of the least of these brothers of mine (what you did for forsaken Paul in the dark of the dungeon), you did for me." "Timothy, don't be like the world — don't be like Phygelus and Hermogenes. Be like Onesiphorus."

Paul's wish. Paul was obviously moved as he retold this incident and therefore breaks off the account and voices his appreciation for Onesiphorus by expressing his wish for him: "May the Lord grant that he will find mercy from the Lord on that day! You know very well in how many ways he helped me in Ephesus" (v. 18). Some believe that this wish and a similar wish for mercy in verse 16 indicate that Onesiphorus was dead. Paul wishes that the Lord will show mercy to "the household of Onesiphorus" (v. 16) but does not mention the good man himself. And they conclude that in verse 18 Paul's wish that "he will find mercy from the Lord on that day" refers to the Second Advent and the final judgment that awaits departed Onesiphorus.[9]

If this is so, the wish is extremely poignant. If this view is correct, Onesiphorus perished during his journey and care for Paul. Perhaps it was due to the rigors of ancient travel or even possibly to foul play in the Roman labyrinth. Others argue that while this is possible, the wishes expressed for his household and then that Onesiphorus will find mercy at the judgment may be due to the fact that he and his household were separated. The evidence is inconclusive. That Onesiphorus was alive and separated from his family is as possible as that he was dead.[10]

What *is* conclusive is that this was not a prayer for the dead, as some have argued. Paul's wish was not directed as a prayer to God. Paul was merely expressing his good will regarding this excellent man — "May he find mercy."[11]

Notice how beautifully Paul expressed his wish. The first mention of

"Lord" refers to Christ, and the second mention of "Lord" to God the Father: "May the Lord *Christ* grant that Onesiphorus will find mercy from the Lord — *God the Father* — on that day!"[12]

Did Onesiphorus find mercy? We can be sure he did. Jesus had said in the Sermon on the Mount, "Blessed are the merciful, for they will be shown mercy" (Matthew 5:7). This spiritual axiom will forever be realized by Paul's good friend. And did he receive rewards? Onesiphorus actually refreshed the Lord Jesus Christ! Jesus' words were, and are, to that good man, "Come, you who are blessed by my Father; take your inheritance, the kingdom prepared for you since the creation of the world."[13] He actually refreshed Jesus Christ. Think of it. And think of his reward.

Paul, that lover of souls, that amazing lover of people, whose very heart rate rose and fell with the church — the man who always kept on "praying for all the saints" (Ephesians 6:18) — this man sat isolated and lonely in a Roman dungeon for the sake of the gospel. He would exit the cell only when he was led to his death.

And how did the church respond? Tragically, most of the believers in Asia Minor deserted him out of fear. Two of them we know by name.

Timothy must not be like them! Rather, he must stand tall, suffer, and keep the faith — like Onesiphorus who risked his life to find Paul, then refreshed him again and again. He was not ashamed of Paul's chains.

And what Onesiphorus did for Paul, he actually did to Jesus! What mercy he will see on the day of judgment!

"Timothy, be like him. Stand tall and unashamed."

23

On Guarding the Gospel

2 TIMOTHY 2:1-7

You then, my son, be strong in the grace that is in Christ Jesus. And the things you have heard me say in the presence of many witnesses entrust to reliable men who will also be qualified to teach others. Endure hardship with us like a good soldier of Christ Jesus. No one serving as a soldier gets involved in civilian affairs — he wants to please his commanding officer. Similarly, if anyone competes as an athlete, he does not receive the victor's crown unless he competes according to the rules. The hard-working farmer should be the first to receive a share of the crops. Reflect on what I am saying, for the Lord will give you insight into all this.

When Gideon assembled an army of 32,000 men to fight the allied armies of the Midianites numbering some 135,000, the odds did not look very good to Israel! The Midianites had a four to one advantage. Classic military wisdom today says that you need a one to four ratio to defend a position and that a one to four ratio when attacking is suicide. No wonder that most of the army of Israel trembled with fear.

God did not like the odds either (but for different reasons). So the Lord said to Gideon, "You have too many men for me to deliver Midian into their hands . . . announce now to the people, 'Anyone who trembles with fear may turn back.'" So 22,000 left, making the new ratio one Israelite to thirteen Midianites (Judges 7:2, 3). But God still did not like the odds. So he ordered a screening process in which all the remaining soldiers were observed as they drank from the Jordan. Only the 300 who cupped their hands and drank were retained. Now the odds were one Israelite to 450 Midianites! We know the end of the story — how God used those 300 to surround the Midianites in the night with blaring trumpets and flaming torches, causing the Midianites to fall into confusion, destroying each other. God does not do things the way we do.

But think for a moment about the brave hearts of those 300 men. They had come from among the 10,000 who did not tremble. They had been willing to go into battle despite a one to thirteen disadvantage. And when the ratio became one to 450 they still hung tough. They were *semper fidelis* (always faithful) all the way! The impossible odds steeled their hearts. They might die, but they would die with their sandals on, defending Israel. So in the middle of the night the 300 valiant men crept up to the edge of the Midianite camp (the size of some football stadiums) and issued their battle cry: "A sword for the LORD and for Gideon!" (7:20). *Semper fi!*

Men do not become battle-ready soldiers by hearing stories of easy victories and exotic lands, but by becoming men of gallantry and sacrifice. Fervent disciples are those who are energized by the challenge and rise to it.

Paul has been laying before Timothy, in an extended challenge, the hardships and hard work of the gospel. In 2 Timothy 1:1-7 he encouraged Timothy via a heartening retrospect about his and Timothy's past and some bracing realities about Timothy's giftedness for ministry. Then in verses 8-14 he challenged Timothy to stand tall and suffer and guard the gospel. Next in verses 15-18 Paul presented motivational examples, negative and positive: "Don't be like those deserters Phygelus and Hermogenes. Instead rise to the glittering example of Onesiphorus." Now in 2:1-7 the apostle enlarges on what Timothy must do to guard the gospel deposit as he was charged in 1:14. Later, in 2:8-14, he will conclude the long challenge by urging upon Timothy the essential memory of Jesus Christ himself.

GUARD THE GOSPEL BY BEING STRONG (v. 1)

Here Paul reasserts a highly personal tone: "You then, my son, be strong in the grace that is in Christ Jesus" (v. 1). Timid Timothy needed to be a strong man. He must not hide behind his retiring personality. He must be the man!

But, happily, the resource for his strength is not himself but comes from divine grace — a theme Paul had already enlarged upon in 1:9-11. Because grace is so awesome, there was immense enabling power in Paul's charge: "You then, my son, be strong in the *grace* that is in Christ Jesus." "Timothy, your power comes from grace."

Timothy, as is the case with every person in union with Christ, already had this grace. It was already in him. As the apostle John put it, "And from his fulness have we all received, grace upon grace" (John 1:16, RSV). Grace was heaped upon grace in Timothy's life. It could never be depleted. Grace is so much a part of those who are in Christ that the apostle James would remark, "But he gives us more grace" (James 4:6). More grace was always there for Timothy — like a poised pitcher, ready at the slightest nudge, to pour grace upon him. The same graced power to do God's work that Paul had was Timothy's. As Paul wrote elsewhere, "But by the grace of God I am what I am, and his grace to me was not without effect. No, I worked harder than all of them — yet not I, but the grace of God that was with me" (1 Corinthians 15:10). And this incredible power was equally Timothy's.

The application of the energy of Paul's command to Timothy to "be strong in the grace that is in Christ Jesus" is lodged in the Greek nuance because this command is a present passive. The sense is continuous: "Keep on being strong" — "understand that you are to do this through God who is actively strengthening you."[1] How was he to keep on being "strong in the grace that is in Christ Jesus"? By constantly calling to mind that he had this grace, Christ's grace — "grace upon grace." By humbly realizing that there is always more grace. The promise in James reads in its entirety, "But he gives us more grace. That is why Scripture says: 'God opposes the proud but gives grace to the humble'" (James 4:6). We remain strong by prayerfully asking for the grace that is in Christ Jesus.

Nothing would come Timothy's way as he guarded the gospel that he would not have the graced strength to handle — no person, no pain, no problem, no responsibility, no tragedy. There would be no time when he could not stand tall. And that is true for all who are in Christ and thus under his grace. If he calls you to do something, he will supply sufficient strength through his grace. If he calls you to step forward, he will give you the power. If he calls you to step up, he will give you the fortitude. If he calls you to endure, the strength you need will be found in "the grace that is in Christ Jesus."

Is he calling you? Then keep on being "strong in the grace that is in Christ Jesus."

GUARD IT BY DELEGATION (v. 2)

This charge to guard the gospel through graced strength is followed by a challenge to likewise protect it through careful delegation. Notice that in 1:14 Timothy had been delegated the gospel as a trust to guard: "Guard the good deposit that was *entrusted* to you — guard it with the help of the Holy Spirit who lives in us" (italics added). Here in chapter 2 Timothy is charged to further delegate the gospel deposit as a part of his ministerial responsibility: "And the things you have heard me say in the presence of many witnesses *entrust* to reliable men who will also be qualified to teach others" (v. 2, italics added).

Paul hopes for a living chain of truth that will extend through the centuries. In the early seventeenth century Dr. Richard Sibbes wrote a little book about Christ called *The Bruised Reed*. A copy of that book fell into the hands of a tin peddler, who gave it to a boy named Richard Baxter, who became the greatest of Puritan pastors. Baxter wrote, among other things, *A Call to the Unconverted*, which Philip Doddridge read in the early eighteenth century, and he in turn wrote *The Rise and Progress of Religion in the Soul*.

William Wilberforce read that book, and it so changed his life that he led the fight for the abolition of slavery. He was a tiny, stunted man but had such eloquence for Christ that James Boswell immortalized it by writing that during one of his speeches "the shrimp grew and grew and grew and became a whale." Indeed Wilberforce became a huge influence in nineteenth-century British culture and saw the abolition of slavery in Britain just three days before his death.[2] Significantly, Wilberforce has been an inspiration for Charles Colson and the organization he founded, Prison Ministries.[3]

Paul's directive was explicit: The gospel deposit was to be entrusted to "reliable men who will also be qualified to teach others." The Ephesian church was loaded with plenty of theological wild hares who were not only unsound but who opposed the truth (cf. 2 Timothy 3:8; 4:3, 4). We believe that Timothy did his best to entrust the deposit to faithful men, and this brought abundant blessing to the church, and this has been duplicated time and time again down through the centuries. However, the church has also spawned heresies that outdo even the superstitions of the Gentiles.

Today we cannot undo the past. But we can follow Paul's directives, which means first that we must understand, believe, and uphold the apostolic gospel deposit and then entrust it to "reliable" (faithful) men who are qualified to teach others. Preaching is not enough! If we are to fully obey the apostolic directives, we must carefully instruct those who are younger as to what the apostolic deposit is and must enable faithful believers to teach others.

The implications are far-reaching. It is our duty to guard the deposit, and guarding it involves carefully teaching and training our people, so they can do likewise. Entrusting the apostolic deposit to others is our God-given task and joy.

GUARD THE GOSPEL BY SUFFERING (vv. 3-7)

Paul has challenged Timothy to guard the deposit by being strong in the grace of Christ and by delegating the deposit to the faithful. Now he charges Timothy to guard it by suffering for Christ: "Endure hardship" (v. 3). The translation "endure hardship" does not really convey the sense of the original. The correct sense is, "Join with us in suffering," because the same word is used in 1:8 ("join with me in suffering") where it is correctly translated.[4] *Suffer together with us!*

The soldier. To remove all vagueness about what he means, Paul adds, "like a good soldier of Christ Jesus." The horrors of warfare have made some readers question the appropriateness of the metaphor to illustrate the life of the servants of the Prince of Peace. But Paul rightly has in mind the grand qualities seen in soldiers at war in their best light. Paul loved this metaphor. He told Timothy to "fight the good fight" (1 Timothy 1:18). He called Archippus, who hosted a church in his home, a "fellow soldier" (Philemon

2). He likewise called Epaphroditus, the gentle messenger to the church at Philippi, a "fellow soldier" (Philippians 2:25). In Ephesians 6 Paul used each article of the soldier's armament as an object lesson for spiritual warfare (vv. 10-18).

The image of soldiering suggested awesome qualities — for example, proverbial obedience or deep loyalty. Marshall Foch, a French general in World War I, commanded an officer, "You must not retire, you must hold at all costs." "Then," said the officer, "that means we must die." Foch answered "Precisely!"[5] Warfare means courage, commitment, sacrifice. "Timothy, join in suffering with us. Join us in obedience. Join us in unflagging loyalty. Join us in sacrifice."

Paul now extended the soldiering analogy further: "No one serving as a soldier gets involved in civilian affairs — he wants to please his commanding officer" (v. 4). Perhaps he was referring to the Roman code of Theodosius: "We forbid men engaged in military service to engage in civilian occupations."[6] Whether this is the case or not, his spiritual application is perfectly clear: "A good soldier of Christ Jesus" (v. 3) has single-minded devotion to Jesus Christ, the "captain of . . . salvation" (Hebrews 2:10, KJV). Single-mindedness, the ability to focus, to shut everything out when necessary, is the key to success in virtually every area of life. It is the essential ingredient of the manic virtue of basketball heroes Michael Jordan and Tim Duncan or of golf great Jack Nicklaus or the creative musical genius Wolfgang Amadeus Mozart.

But here the focus is not a basketball rim, a flag fluttering on a distant green, or a musical score — it is Christ himself and how to please him. The single-minded disciple is in the world, but he does not get "entangled" (literal translation) in the world. He avoids anything that will hinder single-minded dedication to his Master. Paul put it this way to the Philippians: "But one thing I do: Forgetting what is behind and straining toward what is ahead, I press on toward the goal to win the prize for which God has called me heavenward in Christ Jesus" (3:13, 14). Paul was fervent!

Single-minded devotion to a thing (a sport, a philosophy, or a cause) can turn you into a machine. But when it is given to Christ who is perfect God and perfect man, whose commands are consonant with perfect love and wisdom and our highest good, then we become what we ought to be and can stand tall even in suffering.

We must purposely focus on him and willingly join with his followers in suffering hardship like good soldiers of Jesus Christ. Charles Spurgeon expressed the point with such power:

Up, I pray you now. By him whose eyes are like a flame of fire, and yet were wet with tears, by him on whose head are many crowns, and who yet wore the crown of thorns, by him who is King of kings and Lord of lords, and yet bowed his head to death for you, resolve that to life's latest breath you will spend and be spent for his praise. The Lord grant that there may be many such in this church — good soldiers of Jesus Christ.[7]

The athlete. Paul now gives an illustration from athletics: "Similarly, if anyone competes as an athlete, he does not receive the victor's crown unless he competes according to the rules" (v. 5). The word "similarly" indicates that this analogy suggests a parallel truth, not unlike what has just been said. Ancient athletes who participated in the Olympiad first had to complete a required ten-month training period and then swear an oath that they had done it. Those were the rules. And very likely this is what "according to the rules" references.[8]

So Paul says again that there must be single-minded, wholehearted discipline. The truth is, none of us will get anywhere without this in any area of life. Disciplined training is very close to single-mindedness, though not exactly the same. In addition to focus, it suggests rigor and sweat. A person conditioned by such dedication will be able to willingly join in the suffering.

The farmer. The third analogy is from agriculture and takes a different but complementary direction: "The hardworking farmer should be the first to receive a share of the crops" (v. 6). Farming is hard work today, and it was especially hard in the first century. The farmer's life involved: 1) early and long hours because he could not afford to lose time; 2) constant toil (plowing, sowing, tending, weeding, reaping, storing); 3) regular disappointments — frosts, pests, and disease; 4) much patience — everything happened at less than slow motion; and 5) boredom.

Paul was speaking by analogy about the hard work of spiritual ministry. The Greek word translated "hardworking" is almost a technical term in Paul's vocabulary for ministerial labor.[9] The ministry of the gospel requires strain, struggle, and diligence — all of which are akin to suffering. Diligent people are better at suffering. But note: The hardworking will be first in line for the reward, and the reward will far outweigh the toil. Because of this, Paul would tell the Corinthians, "Therefore, my dear brothers, stand firm. Let nothing move you. Always give yourselves fully to the work of the Lord, because you know that your labor in the Lord is not in vain" (1 Corinthians 15:58).

Paul concludes, "Reflect on what I am saying, for the Lord will give you insight into all this" (v. 7). These analogies of the farmer, the athlete, and the soldier would help Timothy understand the call to join with him in suffering. All three have the element of suffering — the soldier's single-minded devotion, the athlete's rigorous exercise, the farmer's toil — and they all have their reward. As C. K. Barrett observes: "Beyond warfare is victory, beyond the athlete's effort is the prize, and beyond agricultural labor is the crop."[10]

All of this steeled Timothy to guard the apostolic deposit, as such challenges have often done to men and women throughout history. Hebrews 13:23 alludes to Timothy's "release," indicating that not long after Paul's death, young Timothy did in fact suffer imprisonment. Timid Timothy was a good soldier of the Lord Jesus Christ.

The apostolic gospel is everything. We must guard it by being *strong* — "be strong in the grace that is in Christ Jesus." Because we are "in Christ" we have "the grace" — "grace upon grace" — the inexhaustible goodness of God — free grace, saving grace, gifting grace, enabling grace, providing grace, abounding grace, strengthening grace. Nothing that we will encounter in guarding the gospel will exceed God's grace.

We must also guard the deposit by *delegating* it to the faithful. This delegation begins with our children but also involves entrusting the gospel to faithful believers who are qualified to teach it to others.

We must also guard the deposit by willingly *joining in suffering* for it "like a good soldier of Christ Jesus." We must be single-minded in our devotion to Christ like a soldier who wants only to please his commander. We must be disciplined like an athlete. We must labor like a hardworking farmer.

Such a life is not safe, but it is glorious.

Semper fidelis!

24

The Essential Memory

2 TIMOTHY 2:8-13

Remember Jesus Christ, raised from the dead, descended from David. This is my gospel, for which I am suffering even to the point of being chained like a criminal. But God's word is not chained. Therefore I endure everything for the sake of the elect, that they too may obtain the salvation that is in Christ Jesus, with eternal glory. Here is a trustworthy saying: If we died with him, we will also live with him; if we endure, we will also reign with him. If we disown him, he will also disown us; if we are faithless, he will remain faithful, for he cannot disown himself.

It is apparent from the Old Testament that remembering the great acts of God is essential to the spiritual well-being of God's children. In fact, God is very directive about this.

The Passover. On the night before the Exodus, when God instituted the Passover rite as a perpetual ceremony in Israel, he instructed Moses to say, "And when your children ask you, 'What does this ceremony mean to you?' then tell them, 'It is the Passover sacrifice to the LORD, who passed over the houses of the Israelites in Egypt and spared our homes when he struck down the Egyptians'" (Exodus 12:26, 27). Passover was meant to bring about heartening spiritual memory and reflection.

The Law. Later, after God thundered the Ten Commandments from Sinai and charged Israel with the *Shema* and specific instructions to "impress them on your children" (Deuteronomy 6:7ff.), Moses went on to say:

In the future, when your son asks you, "What is the meaning of the stipulations, decrees and laws the LORD our God has commanded you?" tell him: "We were slaves of Pharaoh in Egypt, but the LORD brought us out of Egypt with a mighty hand. Before our eyes the LORD sent miraculous signs and wonders — great and terrible — upon Egypt and Pharaoh and his whole household. But he brought

us out from there to bring us in and give us the land that he prom-
ised on oath to our forefathers." (Deuteronomy 6:20-23)

Again we see the value of memory and reflection.

Crossing the Jordan. The most notable example of God's concern for his people's memory was at the crossing of the Jordan, when he instructed the priests of Israel to take twelve stones from the Jordan and pile them in Gilgal in the Promised Land. His subsequent instructions were explicit: "In the future, when your children ask you, 'What do these stones mean?' tell them that the flow of the Jordan was cut off before the ark of the covenant of the LORD. When it crossed the Jordan, the waters of the Jordan were cut off. These stones are to be a memorial to the people of Israel forever" (Joshua 4:6, 7). The Israelites were to look on the stones and remember that they did not get across the Jordan through their own ability. It was all the work of God. And realizing this, they were to conduct all of life accordingly, whether warfare, business, or family life.

Why all this emphasis on remembering? Because God's children have always tended to forget the wonderful things he has done. The seventy-two verses of Psalm 78 mourn Israel's tendency to forget God's faithfulness. Verses 10, 11 sum it up.

> *They did not keep God's covenant*
> *and refused to live by his law.*
> *They forgot what he had done,*
> *the wonders he had shown them.*

We present-day children of God confirm our sad continuity with the children of old by our forgetfulness of things that were once so vivid and vital to our faith and way of life.

But the emphasis here in 2 Timothy 2 is altogether positive! Those who remember what God has done, those who cultivate the memory of God's great works on their behalf, will live to God's glory. The Apostle Peter did just this when he remembered how God preserved Noah and delivered Lot and concluded with a resounding statement of confidence: "if this is so, then the Lord knows how to rescue godly men from trials" (2 Peter 2:9). "If God did it for them, he will do it for us!" How important theological memory is.

This matter of remembering was on Paul's mind as he wrote his second letter to Timothy. Immediately after the greeting, he heartened Timothy by calling to memory the faith of their forefathers (1:3), his and Timothy's own deep friendship (1:4), Timothy's rich spiritual heritage (1:5), the day of Timothy's call and gifting for ministry (1:6, 7; cf. 3:14, 15), and lastly the pattern of sound teaching he had given Timothy (1:13). Remember, remember, remember, remember.

REMEMBER THE GOSPEL (v. 8a)

Beginning with verse 8, Paul again takes up the emphasis on godly memory by urging upon Timothy the grand essential memory — "Remember Jesus Christ, raised from the dead, descended from David. This is my gospel." This is the first and foremost of three successive memories essential to standing tall and suffering for Christ. They are: 1) the gospel (v. 8a); 2) the gospel's power (vv. 8b-10); and 3) a trustworthy saying (vv. 11-13) — all essential memories to being the man God wants him to be.

The command to "Remember Jesus Christ" calls for the remembrance of two things: First, he was "raised from the dead," and, second, he was "descended from David." These dual remembrances correspond to his two names "Jesus" and "Christ." "Jesus" (his human name given him at his birth) matches "raised from the dead." "Christ" (which means "Messiah") matches "descended from David." Interestingly, in the rest of 2 Timothy Paul uses the term "Christ Jesus," but here he says "Jesus Christ" to correspond to the order of his emphases.

Remember his resurrection. The initial emphasis is on Christ's resurrection, "Remember Jesus . . . raised from the dead." The tense of "raised from the dead" is the Greek perfect, which means he was raised and still is raised. The reason to remember the Resurrection is that Jesus' resurrection proved the gospel message. Paul had said, "And if Christ has not been raised, our preaching is useless and so is your faith" (1 Corinthians 15:14). But he *had* been raised, as Paul so vigorously argues in that same chapter (cf. vv. 3-8). This resurrection substantiated the gospel.

Jesus' resurrection demonstrated the gospel's power. The good news of the gospel itself brings about the power for resurrection — *spiritual* resurrection — as Paul proclaimed to the Romans: "We were therefore buried with him through baptism into death in order that, just as Christ was raised from the dead through the glory of the Father, we too may live a new life" (6:4). He later explained this to the Ephesians as well: "That power is like the working of his mighty strength, which he exerted in Christ when he raised him from the dead and seated him at his right hand in the heavenly realms" (Ephesians 1:19b, 20). All those who have been born again have experienced this resurrection power.

Furthermore, ultimately Jesus' resurrection means power for *bodily* resurrections — "But Christ has indeed been raised from the dead, the first-fruits of those who have fallen asleep. For since death came through a man, the resurrection of the dead comes also through a man. For as in Adam all die, so in Christ all will be made alive" (1 Corinthians 15:20-22). Memory of Jesus' resurrection therefore engenders a perpetual Easter season in the lives of his children. It invites spiritual resurrections when through the good news people believe and are born again. And it instills hope of a glorious bodily resurrection for all who believe — eternal Easter! "Remember Jesus . . . risen from the dead."

Remember his messiahship. The parallel emphasis is on remembering our Savior's messiahship. The title "Christ" always means "Messiah." So the sense here is, "Remember . . . Christ [Messiah] . . . descended from David." Jesus Christ fulfilled the Davidic covenant, the promise first made to King David in 2 Samuel 7:12ff. and repeatedly reiterated throughout the Old Testament: A descendant of David would reign forever.

Significantly it was after his resurrection, on the road to Emmaus, that Jesus explained, "'Did not the Christ [Messiah] have to suffer these things and then enter his glory?' And beginning with Moses and all the Prophets, he explained to them what was said in all the Scriptures concerning himself" (Luke 24:26, 27). Memory of Jesus' messiahship invites the believer to see Jesus as the culmination of God's plan of salvation and to bow before him as King.

"My gospel." It is important for us to realize that these two things — his resurrection and his messiahship — make up the essential gospel. Paul says, "Remember Jesus Christ, raised from the dead, descended from David. *This is my gospel*" (v. 8, italics added). Certainly there are other elements in the gospel (Christ's atoning death, imputed righteousness that comes by faith alone through Christ alone, forgiveness of sins, eternal life, and so on), but this is shorthand for the whole thing. "Remember Jesus Christ, raised from the dead, descended from David. This is my gospel."

Paul makes this essentiality clear in two other places in the New Testament. Notice the occurrences of the signature words and motifs (the gospel, Christ, descendant of David, resurrection) in Romans 1:1-4:

> *Paul, a servant of Christ Jesus, called to be an apostle and set apart for the gospel of God — the gospel he promised beforehand through his prophets in the Holy Scriptures regarding his Son, who as to his human nature was a descendant of David, and who through the Spirit of holiness was declared with power to be the Son of God by his resurrection from the dead: Jesus Christ our Lord.*

Note the similarities in 1 Corinthians 15:1-4:

> *Now, brothers, I want to remind you of the gospel I preached to you, which you received and on which you have taken your stand. By this gospel you are saved, if you hold firmly to the word I preached to you. Otherwise, you have believed in vain. For what I received I passed on to you as of first importance: that Christ [Messiah] died for our sins according to the Scriptures, that he was buried, that he was raised on the third day according to the Scriptures.*

This is the good news: Jesus Christ is the predicted, long-awaited Messiah, and he has been raised from the dead and ever lives. This is the gospel. Everything else in the gospel is implicit in and flows from these two supreme realities. As Messiah, he fulfills the cascade of Old Testament messianic prophecy and the gospel and is King of kings and Lord of lords. As resurrected Lord, all authority in heaven and earth is his (cf. Matthew 28:18). He is victor. He is all-powerful. It is this good news that Paul himself clings to as his death approaches. This is the theological reality from which he takes strength.

We must keep before us that Paul's command "Remember" is a continuous command. Timothy is to "remember [and keep on remembering] Jesus Christ, raised from the dead, descended from David." Other recollections are important, but this is *the* essential memory. This gospel memory, constantly replayed, will enable him to stand and suffer with Paul. Jesus Christ is the resurrected, living Messiah. He is everything we need for life and salvation.

This is the theological memory that we must constantly set before us in all of its Scriptural dimensions. Jesus Christ did not come out of nowhere. He is the fulfillment of everything the Scriptures pointed to concerning the Messiah. Jesus Christ was resurrected and remains so. He lives! He is all-powerful! Keep on remembering this.

REMEMBER THE GOSPEL'S POWER (vv. 8b-10)

The theological grounds for suffering were more than theory for Paul. His own present experience bore witness to the reality of the Resurrection and the availability of power to stand and suffer. So Paul had a right to affirm the gospel's power in suffering: "This is my gospel, for which I am suffering even to the point of being chained like a criminal. But God's word is not chained" (vv. 8b, 9). Paul's circumstances were humiliating and personally repugnant to him because he was considered to be a criminal. The word translated "criminal" is a strong one, a technical term used for violent people — murderers, thieves, traitors who were punished by torture.[1]

Nero had just burned Rome (A.D. 64) and blamed the Christians, of whom Paul was a leader.[2] Thus Paul was chained and treated like criminal scum. All this for the gospel.

But there was no hint of self-pity in Paul. Rather, there was confident power: "But God's word is not chained." A famous picture in the convent library in Erfurt, Germany, depicts young Martin Luther poring over a copy of Scripture in the morning light. The dawn steals through the open lattice, illuminating the Bible and his eager face. A broken chain hangs from the Bible.[3] Such has been the experience of the church, even in darkest times.

The unchained Word here in 2 Timothy is the gospel. God's Word ("my gospel") had not been and was not then chained.[4] Paul was speaking from experience. During his first Roman imprisonment, he wrote to the Philippians:

Now I want you to know, brothers, that what has happened to me has
really served to advance the gospel. As a result, it has become clear
throughout the whole palace guard and to everyone else that I am
in chains for Christ. Because of my chains, most of the brothers in
the Lord have been encouraged to speak the word of God more
courageously and fearlessly. (1:12-14)

In fact, in Paul's present imprisonment the Lord had stood by his side
and had given him the strength to proclaim the message before the Roman
court, as he reports in 2 Timothy 4:16, 17.

Paul was powerfully stating the absolute freedom of the Word of God.
And it is so today. In the 1930s Stalin ordered a purge of all Bibles and all
believers. In Stavropol, Russia, this order was carried out with a vengeance.
Thousands of Bibles were confiscated, and multitudes of believers were
sent to the gulags where many died for being "enemies of the state."

After the fall of Communism, the missionary organization CoMission
sent a team to Stavropol. (The city's history was not known to them at that
time.) When the team experienced difficulty getting Bibles shipped from
Moscow, someone mentioned a warehouse outside of town where confiscated Bibles had been stored since Stalin's day. After prayer, one member got
up the courage to go to the warehouse and ask the officials if the Bibles
were still there. They were! They then asked if the Bibles could be removed
and distributed again to the people of Stavropol. The answer was yes. A truck
was obtained, and several Russian people helped load the Bibles.

One of the helpers was a young man — a skeptical, hostile, agnostic col-
legian who had come only for the day's wages. As they were loading Bibles,
the young man disappeared. They found him in a corner of the warehouse,
weeping. He had slipped away, hoping to quietly take a Bible for himself.
What he found shook him to the core. The inside page of the Bible he picked
up had the handwritten signature of his own grandmother! It had been her
personal Bible. He had stolen the very Bible that had belonged to his grandmother — a woman persecuted for her faith all her life. His grandmother
had no doubt prayed for him and for her city.[5]

God's Word can no more be chained than God himself.

Thus Paul declares that God gives us the power to suffer: "Therefore I
endure everything for the sake of the elect, that they too may obtain the salvation that is in Christ Jesus, with eternal glory" (v. 10). The unutterable,
unstoppable power of the Word means that it will prevail with "the elect"
so that they will be saved and brought to eternal glory. The mighty, effectual Word gives us a reason to "endure" — and Paul does. And Timothy
will likewise stand tall as he wields the unchained Word.

REMEMBER THE TRUSTWORTHY SAYING (vv. 11-13)

Paul concludes this long admonishment to stand and suffer with him (which began in 1:4) with an easy-to-remember poem. Each stanza begins with an "if" that describes the believer's actions and is followed by a responding phrase that gives Christ's response.[6]

First stanza (conversion): "If we died with him, we will also live with him" (v. 11b). This is a poetic reference to the exalted teaching of Romans 6 where Paul uses baptismal imagery to describe conversion as dying and rising with Christ. Romans 6:8 is almost identical with this stanza: "Now if we died with Christ, we believe that we will also live with him." In both Romans and here "we will also live with him" has primarily to do with the present.[7] Jesus Christ's resurrection gives us resurrection life right now. And, of course, resurrection is also still coming!

Second stanza (perseverance): "If we endure, we will also reign with him" (v. 12a). This plainly addresses Paul's main concern. "Endure" is the word he uses to describe himself in verse 10: "Therefore I endure everything." It means to hold your ground, particularly during affliction, and it involves suffering.[8]

The reward for this amazes us — because it goes beyond being with him to *reigning* with him! This is not a "pie-in-the-sky" reward. Jesus was specific about this in the parable of the minas, where he has the master say, "Well done, my good servant! . . . Because you have been trustworthy in a very small matter, take charge of ten cities" (Luke 19:17). Co-regency speaks of privileged intimacy. Those who endure will be his co-reigning viceroys and confidants. What joy! The eternal reward goes beyond eternal rest to eternal responsibility as Christ's co-regents, teaming with him on vast new enterprises.[9]

Third stanza (apostasy): "If we disown him, he will also disown us" (v. 12b). Paul here references Jesus' well-known saying, "Whoever acknowledges me before men, I will also acknowledge him before my Father in heaven. But whoever disowns me before men, I will disown him before my Father in heaven" (Matthew 10:32, 33). To disown or deny has a wide range of meanings in the New Testament, from temporary disowning (like Peter did to Jesus) to full-blown apostasy. Here it represents apostasy 1) because Christ denies those who do it, 2) because of the close similarity with Jesus' saying, and 3) because the fourth stanza refers to temporary unfaithfulness.[10]

This is an ominous declaration for the likes of Hymenaeus and Philetus, who will be mentioned in verses 17, 18. The warning is in the future tense: "If we [will] disown him, he will also disown us." The terror that will unfold in final judgment is a reciprocal, eternal disownment. The stakes were high for Timothy, and they remain equally high today.

Fourth stanza (faithlessness). The final stanza comes as a surprise, a magnificent reversal: "If we are faithless, he will remain faithful, for he cannot disown himself " (v. 13). Whereas the preceding stanza was a warning, this is a *promise*, as are the first two stanzas. It departs from the future tense, returning to the present tense of the first two stanzas.[11] If we lapse into unfaithfulness, he remains faithful, as Jesus did during the temporary denial by Peter (cf. Peter's restoration in John 21:15-19). What comfort to Timothy (who probably wavered and fell into unfaithfulness at times). And what a balm to us who are often faithless Christians.

Why is God like this? The magnificent coda tells us — "for he cannot disown himself." His faithfulness is rooted deep within his graciousness as the covenantal God who always acts in conformity to his nature. What God is, he always is. No man is always himself, but God is always himself — he cannot be untrue to his own nature.

As the saintly Samuel Rutherford, who spent years in an Aberdeen prison, wrote, "Often and often, I have in my folly torn up my copy of God's covenant with me; but, blessed be His name, He keeps it in heaven safe; and He stands by it always."[12]

Timothy (and all of like flesh and aspiration) can find courage from these wonderful "hang in there" lines.

This is all so beautiful. These memories are essential for standing and suffering. The first is most essential. *Remember the gospel*: "Remember Jesus Christ, raised from the dead, descended from David. This is my gospel" (v. 8). Remember that he is the Messiah who fulfills all the promises of salvation. And remember that he is resurrected, that he is living today. This is the essential gospel. Hang on to it, and keep on remembering it.

Next, *remember the gospel's power* in Paul's life: "This is my gospel, for which I am suffering even to the point of being chained like a criminal. But God's Word is not chained" (vv. 8b, 9). As Luther said, "The body they may kill, God's truth abideth still: His kingdom is forever."

This gospel also gives us the power to suffer: "Therefore I endure everything for the sake of the elect, that they too may obtain the salvation that is in Christ Jesus, with eternal glory" (v. 10). Then comes a poem to seal this to our souls:

> *If we died with him,*
> *we will also live with him;*
> *if we endure,*
> *we will also reign with him.*
> *If we disown him,*
> *he will also disown us;*
> *if we are faithless,*
> *he will remain faithful,*
> *for he cannot disown himself.*
> *(vv. 11-13)*

25

Handling God's Word

2 TIMOTHY 2:14-19

Keep reminding them of these things. Warn them before God against quarreling about words; it is of no value, and only ruins those who listen. Do your best to present yourself to God as one approved, a workman who does not need to be ashamed and who correctly handles the word of truth. Avoid godless chatter, because those who indulge in it will become more and more ungodly. Their teaching will spread like gangrene. Among them are Hymenaeus and Philetus, who have wandered away from the truth. They say that the resurrection has already taken place, and they destroy the faith of some. Nevertheless, God's solid foundation stands firm, sealed with this inscription: "The Lord knows those who are his," and, "Everyone who confesses the name of the Lord must turn away from wickedness."

Memorization, and the cultivation of memory, was an essential pursuit in ancient culture right up to the invention of the printed page.

Daniel Boorstin tells us in his book *The Discoverers* that the elder Seneca (whose life was contemporary to that of our Lord, c. 55 B.C.-A.D. 37) was reportedly able to repeat long passages of speeches he had heard only once many years before. He would impress his large class of students of rhetoric by asking each of the 200 members to recite a line of poetry. Then he would repeat word for word all the lines they had quoted — in reverse order, from last to first![1]

St. Augustine, who had also been a teacher of rhetoric, told of his admiration for a friend who could recite the whole text of Virgil backwards![2]

The biographers of Thomas Aquinas boasted that he remembered everything his teachers had ever told him in school. The sayings of the church fathers that Thomas collected for Pope Urban IV, after his visits to the great monastic libraries, came not from notes (he needed no notes) but simply from what he had seen.[3]

Early Hebrew Biblical culture relied on memory, what we call oral tradition, when no one could possibly own a personal copy of the Torah and the developing canon. Of course, in the first century when Paul wrote Timothy it was much the same.

So we see that the trustworthy saying in verses 11-13 (rendered in easy-to-remember verse) was helpful for spiritual growth. The poem was easy to remember because it hung on four simple words —*died, endure, disown,* and *faithless.* The overall message of the poem was one of encouragement, with only one line given to warning. Its rhythm throbs with spiritual sustenance. We would do well to memorize it for ourselves.

Now in verse 14, as Paul leaves off his extended appeal to Timothy to stand tall and suffer (1:4 — 2:13) and turns to his overarching concern of countering false teachers who subvert the Word, he commands Timothy to "Keep reminding them of these things" (v. 14a) — that is, to keep reminding the Ephesian church of the faithful saying, of both its comfort to believers and its warning to apostates.[4] "Keep reminding the church of what is at stake."

ABOUT WORD FIGHTS (v. 14)

At the same time that Timothy was charged to "keep reminding" the Ephesians of the faithful saying, he was also to "Warn them before God against quarreling about words" (v. 14b)[5] — literally, "word fights." Word fights seem so intellectual. Such arguing can be so nuanced and ego-puffing with its tangled subtleties. It can foster a kind of "theological discussion which is in the end purely verbal, having nothing to do with the realities of the Christian religion" (Kelly).[6] Word fights are the feast of dilettantes.

Paul adds, "It ['quarreling about words'] is of no value, and only ruins those who listen" (v. 14c). Paul had described the ruin that comes from quarreling over words earlier, in his first letter to Timothy, when he said that the one who teaches false doctrine "has an unhealthy interest in controversies and arguments [same word — "word fights"] that result in envy, quarreling, malicious talk, evil suspicions and constant friction between men of corrupt mind" (1 Timothy 6:4, 5). Hassle follows hassle, producing perpetual ruinous conflict.

Later, when advising Titus about similar people, Paul ordered, "Warn a divisive person once, and then warn him a second time. After that, have nothing to do with him. You may be sure that such a man is warped and sinful; he is self-condemned" (Titus 3:10, 11). Notice in the present text that Timothy is told to "Warn them before God" (v. 14a). Quarreling over words is a very grave matter. God himself will call such "word-warriors"[7] into account. Remember this when you encounter people like this in the church or at your door.

ABOUT HANDLING THE WORD (v. 15)

Paul's warning to the word-warriors in Ephesus is closely followed by a very personal (and famous) command to Timothy: "Do your best to present yourself to God as one approved, a workman who does not need to be ashamed and who correctly handles the word of truth" (v. 15).

Give It Straight

Being one who "correctly handles" the Word requires getting it straight and giving it straight. "Correctly handles" has as its basis the Greek word *orthos* ("straight"), the same word from which we build words like *orthopedic* and *orthodoxy*. The exact charge to Timothy is to "impart the word of truth *without deviation, straight, undiluted*."[8] Here it refers to the straight, precise, careful communication of the word of truth, the gospel (cf. Ephesians 1:13; Colossians 1:5), which both have "the word of truth, the gospel"). This apostolic command to get it and give it straight has become a 2,000-year-old charge to all who are called to teach and preach the gospel.

Sadly, as discussed earlier, this flies directly in the face of so much that is happening today in our churches, where instead of faithful exposition there is "disexposition." The text is announced and read, and it is so rich and promising. You settle back, Bible open, for a good Sunday meal, only to find that the text is departed from, never to return. Disexposition! Sunday indigestion!

On other occasions you have experienced gospel disexposition where, no matter what the text, the preacher always encrusted it with the same string of gospel texts, so that all his sermons sounded the same. As a result, the hearers suffer a kind of gospel brain death. Some Christians may have sat under the same preacher for years, but they cannot recall anything specific they learned from his sermons! Some disexposition parades as exposition in which the text is referred to, but there is no rigor, no engagement with the text in its context, no attempt to convey what it really said then or says today — only well-traveled bromides. Disexposition invites multiple abuses of the text, some of which have been listed by Peter Adam in his book *Speaking God's Words*.[9]

De-contexted. Scripture is often wrenched from its context and mistakenly and obviously misapplied, like the preacher who used Revelation 11:10 (KJV) as a Christmas text: "And they that dwell upon the earth shall rejoice over them, and make merry, and shall send gifts one to another." The preacher neglected to include the final clause of the verse: "because these two prophets tormented them that dwell on the earth." "Have yourself a very merry Christmas."

Lensed. Sometimes the text is errantly viewed through a favorite lens — psychological, therapeutic, political, chauvinistic, social, or domestic —

so that no matter what text the preacher began with, the sermon always ends up on the home or the flag or wholeness. The psychologized lens is especially pernicious because the hearer may not recognize the psychological subtext that is being read into the passage.

Moralized. In this type of mistaken preaching, the text is subjected to moralizing. For example, Paul's words in Philippians 3:13 (KJV), "this one thing I do," are taken to teach the importance of having goals. Thus the pastor preaches on goal-setting without once referencing Paul's magnificent goal: "Forgetting what is behind and straining toward what is ahead, I press on toward the goal to win the prize for which God has called me heavenward in Christ Jesus" (3:13, 14).

Doctrinalized. Scripture is sometimes mistakenly organized into an array of proof-texts to promote the doctrinal preferences of the preacher.

Silenced. Some preach on Scripture's silences, the gaps in God's Word — "Now the Bible doesn't tell us how Mary felt about this. But we may be sure she felt . . . and therefore we ought to . . ." Sermons have actually been preached from the perspective of the "lowing oxen"!

How far all this is from the call to be one "who correctly handles the word of truth" — who gets it and gives it straight. How far Paul's exhortation is from so much of today's preaching, which, as William Willimon has said, reduces "salvation to self-esteem, sin to maladjustment, church to group therapy, and Jesus to Dear Abby."[10]

Work Hard

Much of the contemporary disexpositional disaster would find alleviation if Paul's command to Timothy here was obeyed: "Do your best to present yourself to God as one approved, a workman who does not need to be ashamed" (v. 15a).

The preacher must be given to hard, hard work. And that is what I think is the great problem with preaching today — homiletical sloth. Possibly this is because some believe that the homiletical payoff does not merit the added work. It is God before whom we all will stand; it is God before whom we must not be ashamed. This command draws the picture of a workman who has done his work well and therefore can submit it to his superior without hesitation or embarrassment. As my old seminary classmate John MacArthur eloquently states concerning preparation for preaching:

> Give him a chapter and order him to walk around it, camp on it, sup with it, and come at last to speak it backward and forward, until all he says about it rings with the truth of eternity. And when he's burned out by the flaming Word, when he's consumed at last by the fiery grace blazing through him, and when he's privileged to

translate the truth of God to man, finally transferred from earth to heaven, then bear him away gently and blow a muted trumpet and lay him down softly. Place a two-edged sword in his coffin.[11]

Do your best to present yourself to God as one approved, a workman who does not need to be ashamed and who correctly handles the word of truth. (v. 15)

ABOUT GODLESS CHATTER (vv. 16-18)

Having instructed Timothy to warn the Ephesians about mishandling God's Word in their word fights, and having instructed Timothy on how to correctly handle the Word of truth, Paul returns to the subject of mishandling it through too much talk: "Avoid godless chatter, because those who indulge in it will become more and more ungodly" (v. 16). What is so bad about such "chatter"?

It brings ungodliness. Paul is using cutting, slashing sarcasm because the assertion that they "will become" is literally "will advance" or "will make progress" (apparently a slogan the false teachers used to describe their teaching). But here the movement is *downward* — to ungodliness. Fee calls this "a fine piece of irony."[12] Because "godless chatter" is not godly talk, it is against God — it is godless, trivial chatterings. For such chatterers, words become substitutes for deeds. An abundance of theological chatter produces clever, speculative, intellectually reckless, and spiritually destructive talk. An unfailing test for what takes place in our Bible studies and small groups, and the times we characteristically call "fellowship," is: Has it moved us closer to God and elevated our conversation and conduct? "Godless chatter" comes from godless chatterboxes whose drivel leads to increasing ungodliness.[13]

It is gangrenous. Paul's biting sarcasm is followed by a repulsive metaphor: "Their teaching will spread like gangrene" (v. 17a). The metaphorical language is thoroughly unpleasant. "Their teaching will spread [literally, "have pasture"] like gangrene." The picture either is of gangrene spreading like a flock of sheep pouring into an open pasture or of sheep devouring new fodder.[14] Either way the image is meant to be repulsive.

Two of the principal purveyors of this infection ooze with heresy: "Among them are Hymenaeus and Philetus, who have wandered away from the truth. They say that the resurrection has already taken place, and they destroy the faith of some" (vv. 17b, 18). We have already met Hymenaeus in 1 Timothy 1:20, where Paul states he had excommunicated him and Alexander. Now Hymenaeus has a new sidekick, and they are working hard to spread a virulent infection. Times are still tough in Ephesus.

Their insistence that "the resurrection has already taken place" was not primarily about Christ's resurrection. Rather, their insistence was that the final resurrection, the great resurrection of the living and the dead, had taken place *spiritually* for all believers. It was over, they claimed, and all the promised end-time, eternal realizations were now theirs.

The damning thing about this teaching (apart from its plain untruthfulness) is that it attacked the reality of Jesus' *physical* resurrection. The physical resurrection of believers is so linked to Christ's that if Christians are not physically resurrected, that would prove Christ had not been bodily resurrected either. As Paul argued, "But if it is preached that Christ has been raised from the dead, how can some of you say that there is no resurrection of the dead? If there is no resurrection of the dead, then not even Christ has been raised. And if Christ has not been raised, our preaching is useless and so is your faith" (1 Corinthians 15:12-14).

This gangrenous teaching had been sugarcoated and wrapped in Hymenaeus' and Philetus' smiling declaration that they had the fullness of the resurrection *now* — all its health, all its wealth, all its privilege, all its power. This was the good news, they said. Paul's preaching? Why, his circumstances — he was in prison! — gave it the lie. If he had the authentic good news, he would be living like them! Of course, their so-called gospel was pure, unadulterated anthrax, and with it "they destroy[ed] the faith of some."

ABOUT JUDGMENT (v. 19)

How will it turn out for those who mishandle the Word with their word fights and "godless chatter," as opposed to the believer who "correctly handles the word of truth" — those who get it straight and give it straight?

In answer, Paul deftly references a famous event in Israel's history — the rebellion of Korah, as described in Numbers 16. There the Levites Korah and Dathan and Abiram and some 250 other leaders rose up against Moses' leadership in an effort to take over the priesthood. "They came as a group to oppose Moses and Aaron and said to them, 'You have gone too far! The whole community is holy, every one of them, and the LORD is with them. Why then do you set yourselves above the LORD's assembly?'" (Numbers 16:3).

At this Moses fell facedown before God. "Then he said to Korah and all his followers: 'In the morning the LORD will show who belongs to him and who is holy, and he will have that person come near him. The man he chooses he will cause to come near him" (v. 5). Then Moses set up a confrontation. Korah, Dathan, and Abiram and their families and the 250 leaders were to present themselves carrying priestly censers and stand before Aaron and his priests bearing their censers.

At the appointed moment the glory of the Lord appeared, and the Lord ordered Moses and the rest of the congregation to distance themselves from the rebels. So all moved away from the tents of Korah, Dathan, and Abiram. Moses mightily prophesied, and the earth split apart like a great mouth and swallowed their tents, livestock, and families — every trace of them. "At their cries, all the Israelites around them fled, shouting, 'The earth is going to swallow us too!'" (v. 34). Then fire roared down from Heaven on the 250 leaders, incinerating them. All that remained were their red-hot censers, which were gathered and hammered out to overlay the altar.

God had delivered Moses from the rebellious usurpers, vindicating Moses' words to Korah the day before: "In the morning the LORD will show who belongs to him" (Numbers 16:5; literally, in the Septuagint, "the LORD knows those who are his";[15] cf. 2 Timothy 2:19). How will it turn out for Paul and Timothy in relation to those who are rebelling against God's Word, men like Hymenaeus and Philetus? Paul gives the answer: "Nevertheless, God's solid foundation stands firm." That is, the true believers of the church of Ephesus, those not swayed by heresy, will stand firm.[16]

The "foundation" (the faithful Christians at Ephesus) is inscribed with a dual inscription — first about God's knowledge and then about mankind's duty.

First, regarding *God's knowledge*: "'The Lord knows those who are his.'" Paul quotes Moses' reproof to Korah, Dathan, and Abiram at their rebellion (and by application reproves Hymenaeus and Philetus). At the same time these words are a sovereign comfort to the church — "The Lord knows those who are his." When the ultimate fires of judgment fall, and the cosmos is but a cinder, the Lord will know who are his. Jesus had earlier said to his own, "I know my sheep and my sheep know me — just as the Father knows me and I know the Father" (John 10:14, 15). So deep is God's knowledge of his own that it is explained in the analogy of the mutual knowledge of the Holy Trinity. Some think that "The Lord knows those who are his" became a proverbial saying of comfort in the early church.[17] It still is today — "The Lord knows those who are his."

Second, regarding *man's duty*: "'Everyone who confesses the name of the Lord must turn away from wickedness'" (v. 19b). Those who would take comfort in the first inscription must take responsibility for the second. This is proverbial too, because that is the way it is with true believers — they "turn away from wickedness." Knowing the deep things about God demands deep things from us. There is no *election* (cf. v. 10) apart from *sanctification*. It is written on our souls.

So the handling of the Word is paramount. Whether preacher or layperson, we must not duck our privilege and responsibility to "Do your best to present yourself to God as one approved, a workman who does not need to be ashamed and who correctly handles the word of truth" (v. 15).

We must get it straight and give it straight. We must apply it straight to our souls, as it is. Forget the word-warring and the "godless chatter."

Do your best to "present yourself to God as one approved, a workman who does not need to be ashamed." Read it. Meditate on it. Memorize it.

"He will remain faithful, for he cannot disown himself" (v. 13). Do not forget. "The Lord knows those who are his." Paul remembered that. So should we.

26

For Noble Purposes

2 TIMOTHY 2:20-26

In a large house there are articles not only of gold and silver, but also of wood and clay; some are for noble purposes and some for ignoble. If a man cleanses himself from the latter, he will be an instrument for noble purposes, made holy, useful to the Master and prepared to do any good work. Flee the evil desires of youth, and pursue righteousness, faith, love and peace, along with those who call on the Lord out of a pure heart. Don't have anything to do with foolish and stupid arguments, because you know they produce quarrels. And the Lord's servant must not quarrel; instead, he must be kind to everyone, able to teach, not resentful. Those who oppose him he must gently instruct, in the hope that God will grant them repentance leading them to a knowledge of the truth, and that they will come to their senses and escape from the trap of the devil, who has taken them captive to do his will.

Today many loudly claim there is no connection between character and performance. The argument has been particularly heated in reference to those in political life — where the analogy is often made between the head of state and an airline pilot. "Who would you rather have at the control of the plane?" it is asked. "A competent pilot with moral weaknesses, or an incompetent pilot with moral character?"

The problem with the analogy is that it is apples and oranges. Skillfully landing a plane is not an intrinsically moral task, but piloting the state is. Even granting the analogy, suppose the plane crashed in the Pacific, and you and the other survivors are in a lifeboat captained by the competent (but immoral) pilot, and there are insufficient rations to maintain life until rescue. Would you want *him* to make the decisions about who gets rations and who does not?

Admittedly, however, there are some jobs where a lack of moral character can be a plus, like jobs where winning is everything. Many would argue that in some sports the absence of a moral compass is a definite advantage.

Similarly, there are segments of the financial world where a sensitive conscience is seen to be a detriment. Today the amoral entertainer will be more likely to rise to the top of the charts. So we have to understand that in many areas immorality has its professional advantage. It aids "competency," *if* winning is everything. And this is where general culture is. As *Chicago Sun Times* columnist Sydney J. Harris put it: "Since most of us would rather be admired for what we *do*, rather than for what we *are*, we are normally willing to sacrifice character for conduct, and integrity for achievement."

But when all is considered, the closer a job gets to the moral core of a person, the more important moral character becomes. Perhaps it does not make much difference to the performance of a pilot, or a surgeon, or an athlete, or a gardener (though this is all very debatable). But when it comes to the teaching profession, moral character comes to the fore. And more so in personal counseling.

And in matters of the heart, especially in regard to Christ and the church, it is everything. What we are is of utmost importance. A noble life must have for its core a noble heart. Honorable vessels are used for honorable purposes. This is what 2 Timothy 2:20-26 is all about. Paul here instructs Timothy on how to become an instrument for noble purposes, a vessel for honor.

THE MAKING OF A NOBLE INSTRUMENT (vv. 20, 21)

House vessels. To illustrate his point, Paul set before Timothy the image of a house and its vessels and containers: "In a large house there are articles not only of gold and silver, but also of wood and clay; some are for noble purposes and some for ignoble" (v. 20). A large house would have buckets, jars, and cups made of wood and clay that would be used for dishonorable purposes such as disposal of garbage and human waste. It would also have vessels of silver and gold that were used for noble functions such as dining and entertaining.[1]

"A large house" is Paul's metaphor for the church, the Christian community that Paul had earlier called "God's household" (1 Timothy 3:15). We are to understand that the Christian community contains both "noble" and "ignoble" vessels — that is, both believers and false teachers — just as Israel had at the time of the rebellion of Korah (cf. v. 19). Jesus taught exactly the same thing when he described the mixed nature of the church in the story of the wheat and the tares or weeds (Matthew 13:24-30).

The Christian community is, and has always been, a mixed bag. In fact, that is the answer to those who avoid church because it contains hypocrites. Of course it does! Church is for hypocrites because it is there that they may become vessels of honor. St. Chrysostom had it right early on: "Let it not disturb thee that there are corrupt and wicked men. For in a great house there are such vessels."[2]

Cleansing the vessels. Paul applies the picture in the next verse: "If a man cleanses himself from the latter, he will be an instrument for noble purposes, made holy, useful to the Master and prepared to do any good work" (v. 21). Cleansing your life will make you an honorable vessel with great usefulness. This is the exact opposite of the contemporary delusion that character is irrelevant! A holy inner life is essential to doing any good work in this life.

This calls for a conscious, willful cleansing — "If a man cleanses himself." But this is never, in Paul's thinking, something we do apart from grace (cf. Ephesians 2:8-10; Romans 11:6). Paul's advice elsewhere was, "Continue to work out your salvation with fear and trembling, for it is God who works in you to will and to act according to his good purpose" (Philippians 2:12, 13). God does it. And then by his grace we will do it.

The self-cleansing here is from false teachers and their erroneous doctrines — and a returning to the pure gospel of Jesus Christ, who is descended from David and risen from the dead (cf. v. 8). The cleansed thus become golden vessels — "made holy, useful to the Master and prepared to do any good work." They have been, as Paul told the Ephesians, "created in Christ Jesus to do good works, which God prepared in advance for us to do" (Ephesians 2:10). Such people became golden, and their works match. Instead of being wood, hay, and straw, they are gold, silver, and precious stones (cf. 1 Corinthians 3:12). Far from their character being irrelevant, it is everything. What they are inside determines what they do.

This teaching was for Timothy, but it is also for us. What we *are* is first, second, third, and fourth (first and last — everything). What we do will come from this — and it will be substantial.

THE MAINTAINING OF AN INSTRUMENT FOR NOBLE PURPOSES (v. 22)

Paul's advice now naturally moves from the making of an honorable vessel to a double command regarding the maintenance of it: "Flee the evil desires of youth, and pursue righteousness, faith, love, and peace, along with those who call on the Lord with a pure heart" (v. 22).

He flees. A noble vessel is maintained by flight — "Flee the evil desires of youth." Often this is interpreted to mean flee *sensual* desires and is then tied in with the example of young Joseph fleeing hot-blooded Mrs. Potiphar as she clutched his robe (Genesis 39:11-18). Yes, running from sensuality is an essential survival tactic. Flee or fall!

But that is not the emphasis here because 1) the Greek simply reads "and flee youthful desires,"[3] and 2) the following verses give no emphasis to sensuality but rather stress qualities that spring from a youthful temperament. Fee translates "the evil desires of youth" as "headstrong passions of youth"[4] — the desires characteristic of youth.

Both the following context and ministerial experience indicate what these youthful desires are. *Impatience* is a chronic sin of youth. It is incomprehensible to the young pastor that the situation cannot be changed right now! Today's impatience is fed by the media's quick fix. After all, on television everything gets resolved in the space of an hour (films take longer — two or three hours!). The problem is, real church isn't *Church, the Movie.*

What those in the ministry need to understand is that a church with any history at all is like a huge ship at sea — a freighter or ocean liner or battleship (an appropriate metaphor in some cases!). It takes seven miles to turn a great ship around. Young pastors who ignore this imperil themselves and their churches. Perfectly seaworthy churches have been swamped and sunk by impatient young leaders.

Harshness is another telltale sign of youthful desires. It may rarely show up in the pulpit or at board meetings. But it shows itself in conversations with confidants. It surfaces in figures of speech, nicknames for detractors, the cast of the eye, the set of the jaw, the tone of voice.

Likewise, *contentiousness* — the love of debate and winning — is a sin of youth. Here dogmatism flourishes, fed by an inability to comprehend or tolerate other points of view. The listening faculty is undeveloped. "Conversation" is punctuated with adversatives — "but . . . but . . . but." The headstrong young cleric has forgotten that God has given him one mouth and two ears because he ought to listen twice as much as he speaks.

So the youthful proclivities go. And Paul makes no bones about it — "Flee youthful desires!" (literal Greek translation). Run, and keep on running, Timothy. Do not get sucked into fruitless controversy by your detractors. Do not allow yourself to succumb to impatience and harshness. It is so important to remain a vessel for noble purposes.

He pursues. But the running isn't all in the negative. Timothy was also to chase after four virtues: "and pursue righteousness, faith, love and peace, along with those who call on the Lord out of a pure heart" (v. 22b).

He was to "pursue righteousness" — that is, "the right conduct of a man who pleases God and is pleasing to him."[5] He must personally pursue ethical conduct that glorifies God.

He was also to "pursue . . . faith." This faith is a combination of belief plus trust in God, and this simple trust must characterize his life. His congregation should see a man who trusts God implicitly and faithfully.

Timothy was also to "pursue . . . love" — namely, love for people. He was to love the saints, and when time and circumstances revealed that some of his "saints" were sinners, he was to go on loving them with all their faults and weaknesses.

He was also to "pursue . . . peace" — tranquillity and harmony with his people. This he was to do in the company of other believers[6] — "along with those who call on the Lord out of a pure heart."

The picture created by Paul's contrasting commands of "flee" and "follow" (KJV) is dynamic. Timothy was to flee as fast as his feet would carry him away from the headstrong desires of youth (impatience, harshness, the love of debate). At the same time he was to sprint, arms stretched out, after righteous conduct, faith (trust), love for others, and peace.

Such divinely ordered flight and pursuit would insure the maintenance of his life as a vessel for honor. Christ would be pleased to fill him with his grace and to serve it to the church through Timothy. Here is wisdom: Fleeing is as important as pursuing. Our no is as important as our yes. And when we say no to unprofitable desires, we can then say yes to the best things. What should you flee? And what should you be running after?

THE MINISTRY OF A NOBLE INSTRUMENT (vv. 23-26)

Paul has given instructions about the *making* of an honorable vessel (vv. 20, 21), then the *maintenance* of an honorable vessel (v. 22), and now he instructs about the *ministry* of an honorable vessel (cf. "an instrument for noble purposes," v. 21).

Not quarrelsome. God's instrument must not quarrel: "Don't have anything to do with foolish and stupid arguments, because you know they produce quarrels. And the Lord's servant must not quarrel" (vv. 23, 24a). The false teachers' arguments were literally moronic and ignorant, and it was tempting to use their foolishness against them because it was so thoroughly silly. Timothy could certainly show his stuff — his Biblical fidelity, his chic reasoned argument in contrast to their drivel. But Paul warned him to refrain "because you know they ["stupid arguments"] produce quarrels." I have been in such conversations, and I knew I was right, but I was sick of every word after I said it. But I kept on arguing anyway. My argumentative chic was totally uncool. The Lord's servant must not do this.

But pastoral. Rather than quarrel, God's vessel lives out four positive injunctions. First, "he must be kind to everyone" (v. 24). Yes, we must be firm or forceful, but we must also "be kind to everyone," even our enemies. In brief, we should be Christlike. Paul himself ministered like this, as he reminded the Thessalonians: "We were gentle among you, like a mother caring for her little children" (1 Thessalonians 2:7).

Second, Timothy was to be "able to teach" (v. 24) — skillful in teaching, fulfilling the major concern of the Pastoral Epistles (cf. 1 Timothy 3:2 and multiple other references). The fourth injunction complements this: "Those who oppose him he must gently instruct" (v. 25a). No clever put-downs of the false teachers were allowed, but only gentle correction — what Paul described in Ephesians 4:15 as "speaking the truth in love." The loud, foolish heretics got more than they deserved — "gentle instruction"! This is divine wisdom for all of Christ's servants.

Third, the Lord's instrument "must be . . . not resentful." William Barclay remarks, "There may be greater sins than touchiness, but there is none which does greater damage in the Christian church."[7] Many of us are quick to take offense and slow to forgive. The great Samuel Johnson once made a sarcastic remark about an acquaintance that was repeated by a hearer to the man, but without the accompanying remark that "he was a very good man." His biographer Boswell writes that the man

> could never forgive this hasty contemptuous expression. It rankled in his mind; and though I informed him of all that Johnson said, and that he would be very glad to meet him amicably, he positively declined repeated offers which I made, and once went off abruptly from a house where he and I were engaged to dine, because he was told that Dr. Johnson was to be there. I have no sympathetic feeling with such persevering resentment.[8]

Indeed God's Word has no such sympathy either, because God's honored servants must bear evil without being resentful.[9] There are few things more beautiful than a forbearing spirit in God's servants, and this is so good for the church.

There is power in a life that refuses to quarrel and is gentle with detractors — the power of Christlikeness. This is why Paul would sometimes say, "By the meekness and gentleness of Christ, I appeal to you" (2 Corinthians 10:1).

The final sentence expresses the noble hope of a noble instrument for his enemies: "Those who oppose him he must gently instruct, in the hope that God will grant them repentance leading them to a knowledge of the truth, and that they will come to their senses and escape from the trap of the devil, who has taken them captive to do his will" (vv. 25, 26). This is the noblest hope that could ever be.

Christians, the character of your pilot or your surgeon or your mechanic may be irrelevant to his or her occupational competency. But in spiritual matters, the character of God's servant is everything. The *making* of his vessel requires a radical cleansing, so it can be used for honorable purposes. The *maintenance* of his instrument involves intense flight and intense following — flight from youthful desires, impatience, quarrelsomeness, and harshness and the pursuit of profound virtues. The *ministry* of his vessel must not be quarrelsome but pastoral — kind to all, teaching, free of resentment, gently instructing. The hope of such a servant is the eternal blessing of his enemies.

Glorious has been the train of such servants. May this be the standard for all who would aspire to lead Christ's church.

27

Hearts of Darkness

2 TIMOTHY 3:1-9

But mark this: There will be terrible times in the last days. People will be lovers of themselves, lovers of money, boastful, proud, abusive, disobedient to their parents, ungrateful, unholy, without love, unforgiving, slanderous, without self-control, brutal, not lovers of the good, treacherous, rash, conceited, lovers of pleasure rather than lovers of God — having a form of godliness but denying its power. Have nothing to do with them. They are the kind who worm their way into homes and gain control over weak-willed women, who are loaded down with sins and are swayed by all kinds of evil desires, always learning but never able to acknowledge the truth. Just as Jannes and Jambres opposed Moses, so also these men oppose the truth —men of depraved minds, who, as far as the faith is concerned, are rejected. But they will not get very far because, as in the case of those men, their folly will be clear to everyone.

*U*nbelievable! I thought to myself as I listened to members of a newly founded church describe its beginning. It started when several members of a church sensed the need for increased Bible knowledge and began attending a community Bible study, where they learned that their pastor's denials of Christ's virgin birth and resurrection were at variance with what the Bible actually taught. They came to see that, though their church weekly said the Apostles' Creed, their pastors had personally redefined the terms so they could repeat the words without actually believing them. Their leaders viewed the incarnation and resurrection of Christ as metaphors for God's presence and a life-giving source, not actual historical events. When parishioners protested, they were told they were bringing dishonor to the Body of Christ by their divisiveness. The intimidation worked, and they quieted down. After all, they were only laypeople.

But the situation reheated when one of the pastors was discovered to be an active pedophile, and it was further learned that the local church authorities knew it and had been covering it up! This time their parishioners would not be put off. They demanded changes.

Again the response was that they were dividing Christ's Body and must no longer meet for Bible study or else. So it was that Bible-believing, creed-confessing, Biblically-orthodox Christians (whose great offenses were believing in the incarnation, death, and resurrection of Christ and in his ethical teachings) were kicked out of their church. Unbelievable! Sadly, "having a form of godliness but denying its power" (v. 5) is nothing new.

Indeed, Paul warned Timothy, "But mark this: There will be terrible times in the last days" (v. 1) — referring to the time period that had begun with the coming of Christ, continued in Timothy's day, and continues in our day as we await Christ's return. The "last days" and the "terrible times" have been in effect for 2,000 years. This is clear from the context because in verse 5, where Timothy is commanded in the *present tense* to "[h]ave nothing to do with them," the "them" is the false leaders of "the last days" whom Paul so scathingly describes in verses 2-4.[1]

THE FALSE TEACHERS — THEIR LIVES (vv. 1-5)

Verses 1-5 are an explicit description of the teachers who were abusing the Ephesian church with their false teaching. But at the same time they realistically portend today's errant church leadership, reminding us that we too are in "the last days."

Their inverse love. Paul's brutal description springs from the inversion that had taken place in the false teachers' hearts, where love of God had been replaced by love of self. You can see this by reading the opening and closing characteristics together: "People will be lovers of themselves . . . rather than lovers of God" (vv. 2a, 4b). Christ's Great Commandment to "'Love the Lord your God with all your heart and with all your soul and with all your mind'" and to "'Love your neighbor as yourself'" (Matthew 22:37, 39) had been turned upside-down in the hearts of the false teachers in Ephesus. Self-love reigned. Notice that love suffers six tragic perversions in Paul's description: 1) "People will be lovers of themselves," 2) "lovers of money," 3) "without love," 4) "not lovers of the good," 5) "lovers of pleasure," 6) "rather than lovers of God." When love of God is replaced with love of self, all sorts of vices inevitably follow.

Paul's description of the inversion divides for the most part into brutal couplets. As we briefly look at them, we must remember that they are an inspired description of the false teachers and their converts as they "ministered" amidst the intimacy of the house churches in Ephesus. What an interpersonal mess this had become. Paul paints a tragic picture from a lurid palette.

"People will be *lovers of themselves, lovers of money*" (v. 2, italics added). The false teachers were a narcissistic lot. Having switched their souls' gravity from God to themselves, they in effect wrapped their arms around themselves in loving embrace. Their passion for self was matched with a love for money, which Paul had already described as "a root of all kinds of evil" (1 Timothy 6:10). Love of money is a spiritual corollary to self-love. Both serve self.

They were *"boastful, proud"* (v. 2, italics added) — that is, given to boastful *words* and proud *thoughts*.[2] The psalmist's cry, "My soul will boast in the LORD" (Psalm 34:2) was as far from their hearts and lips as the moon is from the earth.

They were also *"abusive, disobedient to their parents"* (v. 2, italics added). Beavis and Butthead, the cartoon caricatures of insolence, would have found their soul mates in these false teachers.

They were also *"ungrateful, unholy"* (v. 2, italics added), both of which naturally flow from abuse and disobedience to parents. Ingratitude and disregard of the fundamental decencies of life are natural twins to the former.[3]

The false teachers were *"without love, unforgiving"* (v. 3, italics added). They violated their most intimate relationships. They lacked family affection.[4] Their natural domestic affections were smothered. They were unforgiving because they were implacable when offended.[5]

They were *"slanderous, without self-control"* (v. 3, italics added). Their slandering tongues resided in bodies that could not govern themselves. They were "set on fire by hell" (cf. James 3:6).

They were *"brutal, not lovers of the good"* (v. 3, italics added). Their brutality was like that of savage, untamed beasts.[6] They loathed authentic goodness.

Verse 4 brings the description of the false teachers to a blistering conclusion: They were *"treacherous, rash"* (italics added). The first word is a Judas adjective. In fact, the same Greek word was used to describe that supposed disciple as a traitor (Luke 6:16). The second adjective, "rash," fits well, for false teachers will stop at nothing to get what they want.[7]

They were *"conceited"* (v. 4, italics added) — that is, swollen with conceit, like Oscar Wilde who once told a customs officer as he returned to England, "I have nothing to declare but my genius."

Lastly, they were *"lovers of pleasure rather than lovers of God"* (v. 4, italics added). "Lovers of pleasure" is the translation of two Greek words *philos* (love) and *hedonai* (pleasure — compare our English word *hedonism*). They were controlled by pleasure, as are many in today's brave new world.

What a devastating critique of these false teachers! There is not a redemptive syllable in the entire paragraph. How claustrophobic those house churches must have become where the false teachers had done their work. Self-love dominated and suffocated the most sacred relationships between

God's children. Remember, this brutal critique was not the product of Paul's morbid musings from his dungeon or the skewed perspective of someone who needed a breath of fresh air. This is the Holy Spirit's description of spiritual reality in many of the house fellowships of the early church. These were real people whom Paul knew very well.

Their bogus godliness. Paul's searing summation states the stark spiritual reality within the false teachers — "having a form of godliness but denying its power" (v. 5a). They had "a form of godliness" in that they had the externals of religion in place. They were experts on the externals. They were masters of asceticism, as Paul had earlier said: "They forbid people to marry and order them to abstain from certain foods, which God created to be received with thanksgiving by those who believe and who know the truth" (1 Timothy 4:3). Legalism was their forte. They had carefully metered everything out for their followers — they had a rule for *everything*.

Arcane "myths and endless genealogies" rolled from their lips, mixed with the most delicious Hebrew fables (cf. 1 Timothy 1:4). But tragically, everything was form — empty form — because they denied the power of the gospel, as we see from Paul's critique of their lives. They were absolute phonies, forms without substance.

This was the "last days" reality for Timothy and the Ephesian church, and it still pertains in these last days in the contemporary church. J. C. Ryle, the great evangelical leader of 100 years ago, understood the reality as few have. Ryle wrote:

> Look in another direction at those hundreds of people whose whole religion seems to consist in talk and high profession. They know the theory of the gospel intellectually and profess to delight in evangelical doctrine. They can say much about the "soundness" of their own views, and the "darkness" of all who disagree with them, but they never get any further! When you examine their inner lives, you find that they know nothing of practical godliness. They are neither truthful, nor charitable, nor humble, nor honest, nor kind-tempered, nor gentle, nor unselfish, nor honorable. What shall we say of these people? They are Christians, no doubt, in name and yet there is neither substance nor fruit in their Christianity. There is but one thing to be said — they are formal Christians. Their religion is an empty *form*.[8] (italics added)

Just as it was possible to be a member and even a teacher in the church of Ephesus and be lost, it is possible to be lost in today's church. Unregenerate evangelicals are a growing reality in both clergy and congregations. It is so easy to acquire "a form of godliness," to subscribe to all the right subcultural expressions and customs and yet be "denying its power" by the quality of our lives.

What does Paul say to Timothy? Flee those leaders whose lives contradict the gospel — "Have nothing to do with them" (v. 4). That is Paul's sole advice in this context. The lives of leaders must demonstrate the power of the gospel. If they do not, "have nothing to do with them."

THE FALSE TEACHERS — THEIR "MINISTRIES" (vv. 6-9)

The first paragraph profiled the lives of false teachers, and this paragraph describes their "ministries." Paul continues derisively, "They are the kind who worm their way into homes" (v. 6a). These homes were apparently well-known because the original Greek says "*the* homes." They were probably the spacious homes of the wealthy, where house churches often met. The verb literally suggests "creeping in" under false pretenses. The idea is stealth.[9] They were religious sneaks.

Their disciples. Their disciples are described as "weak-willed women, who are loaded down with sins and are swayed by all kinds of evil desires, always learning but never able to acknowledge the truth" (vv. 6, 7). The epithet "weak-willed women" is purposely derisive, literally reading "little women." The diminutive is not intended for women in general but describes a situation involving particular women and suggests immature, childish women.[10]

These immature women were "loaded down with sins and . . . swayed by all kinds of evil desires." Their consciences were burdened, and thus they gave ready ears to impostors who promised to ease their guilt. Their unconfessed sin stood between them and God and made their reasoning faulty. Their sins, like an especially virulent flu, left them vulnerable to worse diseases.

Their guilt and oppressive desires had turned them into "religious dilettantes,"[11] women who were "always learning but never able to acknowledge the truth" (v. 7). Here in the Pastorals knowledge of the truth means faith, repentance, and salvation. The terrible reality was that they were learning and learning and learning but never coming to know Christ (cf. 1 Timothy 6:3-10). This "last days" quest goes on today. Some devote their lives to the rediscovery of the mysteries of the heart, or the discovery of the numerical key to prophecy as in the spurious bestseller *The Bible Code*. But they are put off by the simple gospel because they find it too guilt-inducing. So in all their learning, they never become free.

Their futility. Paul frames the monumental futility of the false teachers' enterprise with a telling allusion to the Egyptian sorcerers who opposed Moses before Pharaoh: "Just as Jannes and Jambres opposed Moses, so also these men oppose the truth — men of depraved minds, who, as far as the faith is concerned, are rejected" (v. 8). Though Jannes and Jambres are not mentioned in the Exodus account (or anywhere else in Scripture), the Jewish Targums and even some pagan writers mention their names.[12] They were the magicians in Pharaoh's court who, when Moses threw down Aaron's rod and it became a snake, cast their rods down and they likewise became snakes. But Aaron's rod (snake) swallowed their snakes (Exodus 7:12). At every turn these sorcerers opposed Moses, sometimes performing ostensible miracles.

The false teachers in Ephesus were much the same. They opposed the truth, just as the sorcerers opposed the truth of Moses' message. The magicians' rods looked just like Aaron's. And by analogy, today the same language of the gospel is used by false teachers, but with different meanings. Their commands may sound like God's commands. Their religious paraphernalia may look the same — the same clothing, the same Bible, the same creeds. They may use the same meter in their prayers, just like authentic prayers. But they enslave people.[13] They remain "men of depraved minds, who, as far as the faith is concerned, are rejected" (v. 8).

This has all been so dark, but Paul closes his thought in this section with an encouraging word to Timothy: "But they will not get very far because, as in the case of those men, their folly will be clear to everyone" (v. 9). The folly of Jannes and Jambres became evident when they could not match the power of Moses and duplicate all his miracles (cf. Exodus 8:18, 19; 9:11). All then saw that what they taught was false and that they must not be followed. The same will happen to the false teachers who oppose Timothy.

This was an important word to Timothy, who could only see the false teachers' growing success. He was to understand that those men could compete only for so long, and then their folly would become evident to all. So it is today. There are places where lies seem to be winning, where preachers deny Christ's incarnation and resurrection and preach another gospel, where charlatans promise a new age. But they will not last, and their folly will be clear to everyone!

What we must especially watch for in our own lives is the inversion of love — where we become lovers of self "rather than lovers of God — having a form of godliness but denying its power." Whenever this happens, the Great Commandment has been turned on its head. When we become lovers of self rather than of God, the whole withering paragraph slides through our souls.

These truths are crucial in these "last days" because many evangelicals have imperceptibly become lovers of themselves. James Davison Hunter, in his landmark book *Evangelicalism, The Coming Generation,* published in the late 1980s, wrote: "The fascination with the self and human subjectivity has then become a well-established cultural feature of Evangelicalism generally in the latter part of the twentieth century, not simply an ephemeral fashion among the younger generation."[14]

This shift of gravity to self must be resisted with all we have. The Great Commandment will never change: "'Love the Lord your God with all your heart and with all your soul and with all your mind. . . . Love your neighbor as yourself'" (Matthew 22:37, 39). Significantly, some thirty years later when the Apostle John penned the book of Revelation, he recorded these words to the same Ephesian church that Timothy had served: "Yet I [the Lord] hold this against you: You have forsaken your first love" (Revelation 2:4).

Love, fresh love for God, must be the true north of our lives.

28

Remembrance and Continuance

2 TIMOTHY 3:10-13

You, however, know all about my teaching, my way of life, my purpose, faith, patience, love, endurance, persecutions, sufferings — what kinds of things happened to me in Antioch, Iconium and Lystra, the persecutions I endured. Yet the Lord rescued me from all of them. In fact, everyone who wants to live a godly life in Christ Jesus will be persecuted, while evil men and impostors will go from bad to worse, deceiving and being deceived.

As I look back on my life, I can clearly see that Christian training and experiences and exposures to certain people during my teenage years decisively set my attitudes toward the gospel and Christian ministry. Shortly after I came to Christ, I became deeply involved in Los Angeles Youth for Christ, which existed for one defining purpose — evangelism. I became president of my local high school's Youth for Christ club and attended huge Saturday night rallies in downtown Los Angeles, where the spotlight was literally on people who did evangelism, from Roy Rogers and Dale Evans to recent Rose Bowl heroes. I carried my Bible on top of my high school textbooks, hoping that other students would ask me why. This was definitely not cool in the fifties, but I did not care. So influential was YFC and its leaders upon me that after high school I led several junior high clubs in East Los Angeles.

Following my YFC involvement came Open Air Campaigners, through which I handed out tracts and often preached on the streets in downtown Los Angeles.

But the biggest evangelistic influence in my life was Robert Seelye, a young petroleum salesman and a member of my church. Robert lived missions and evangelism (and still does!), and he occasionally invited me along.

I learned by watching him engage his customers about the gospel. To this day he is the most effective personal evangelist I have ever known.

It was also Robert Seelye who gave me a love and trust for God's Word. Robert always had a hundred plus collegians in his Sunday school class where he taught only one book, the book of Romans. Romans was his text for exploring the rest of the Bible. He took two years to teach through Romans, and then he would begin again. I owe my life's conviction about the absolute infallibility, total sufficiency, and massive potency of Scripture to this man.

I learned what *church* means through my pastor, Verl Lindley, a master pastor. His benign face looms large in my life — like an inset on a television screen. There were others also — men like Ray Stedman of Peninsula Bible Church in Palo Alto and Ray Ortlund, Sr., of Lake Avenue Congregational Church in Pasadena, which I would visit just to hear him preach.

There are several reasons why these experiences and people, and their beliefs and commitments, their battles and triumphs and disappointments, have played such a major role in my life. One was my age. Their influence began when I was a preadolescent. Everything is big when you are small. Everything is new when you know nothing. So they rose huge in my limited world.

Another factor, of course, was that I was impressionable. Who is not during those years? And my impressionability was heightened by having truly come to Christ and wanting him and his will in my life. At the bottom of this, I can see in retrospect, was God's guiding hand in bringing these wonderful people and influences into my life.

Over the years these remembrances have fueled my continuance in the gospel. There is a powerful link between remembrance and continuance. Such connections are part of God's way of working in our lives. Many older Christians are informed and sustained by similar remembrances, some of which extend back many years. Certain names and events from their spiritually formative years regularly surface in their conversations. Similarly, the memories of youth pastors and their staffs will stand disproportionately tall in many lives for the next fifty to sixty years — beckoning continuance in the gospel.

Timothy's continuance in the apostolic ministry was a vital concern of Paul in the Pastoral Letters. And it is the main concern of 2 Timothy 3:10-17, which has as its central imperative the word *continue* in verse 14 — "But as for you, continue in what you have learned. . . ."[1] Paul grounds this call to continuance on two things — first, remembering the past (vv. 10-13) and, second, focusing on the Scriptures (vv. 14-17). In this chapter we will take up the first part, which exhorts Timothy to continue in his calling to remember how Paul himself lived.

REMEMBER MY LIFE (v. 10)

In contrast to the phony lives and "ministries" of the false teachers, Paul issued an emphatic call to Timothy to remember his apostolic lifestyle and virtues: "You, however, know all about my teaching, my way of life, my purpose, faith, patience, love, endurance" (v. 10). The language behind the opening phrase, "You, however, know all about . . ." suggests deep intimacy. The literal meaning is "to follow alongside, to accompany" — "You have followed alongside me." According to J. N. D. Kelly, "It is also a technical term defining the relation of a disciple to his master and can be paraphrased 'study at close quarters,' 'follow in spirit,' 'carefully note with a view to reproducing,' and so 'take as an example.'"[2]

Paul was challenging Timothy to recall the deep master-disciple intimacy that had begun with Timothy's conversion as a teenager during Paul's first missionary journey in Asia Minor. Paul had been present and very likely was instrumental in Timothy's conversion. Certainly Paul had become large in Timothy's world at this time. Since that time the young man had walked alongside Paul, studying him in varied circumstances in diverse cultures. He had seen Paul challenged and heard his responses. Paul's repeated sermons comprised Timothy's theology. And he had observed that Paul's life matched his doctrine.

My lifestyle. So Paul confidently affirmed that Timothy was intimately acquainted with his lifestyle — as Paul termed it, "my teaching, my way of life, my purpose" (v. 10). Unlike the false teachers, Paul's "way of life" confirmed his teaching. Indeed, in his first letter to Timothy, he had commanded Timothy to be sure that his teaching and way of life matched: "Watch your life and doctrine [teaching] closely. Persevere in them, because if you do, you will save both yourself and your hearers" (4:16). That command had a bite to it, because Timothy saw that Paul walked his talk.

In addition, Paul's consistent lifestyle was infused with purpose. One of Charles Schulz's *Peanuts* cartoons memorably pictures Snoopy coming to terms with purposelessness. Linus had just thrown a stick for Snoopy to retrieve. His first instinct was to do what he was accustomed to doing — chase the stick. But he paused for a few moments and decided against it, thinking, "I want people to have more to say about me after I'm gone than 'He was a nice guy . . . He chased sticks.'" Paul never merely chased sticks. He was single-minded about the most important things — the gospel and Christ's glory. As the remembrances of Paul's way of life, teaching, and purpose rose on Timothy's horizon, he would be elevated in his continuance.

My virtues. Alongside his lifestyle, Paul raised the memory of his virtues — his "faith, patience, love, endurance" (v. 10b). There was no ego in this. He was at the end of his life, and he desired with all his heart that Timothy carry on. These virtues were simple fact.

"Faith . . . love, endurance" are the cardinal Christian virtues — faith, love, and hope. (Endurance stands for hope in this list because it leads to the next subject — persecution.)[3] The unusual virtue inserted here is "patience," thus giving it special emphasis. "Timothy, remember my faith, love and endurance, and especially my patience." Several years ago I took some of my grandchildren fishing. Among them was then three-year-old Joshua who was, shall we say, very active. So I was constantly telling him, "Now, Joshua, you have to sit and be patient." Every few minutes Joshua would say, "I'm being patient, huh, Grandpa?" When strangers walked by, Josh would tell them, "I'm being patient!" It all came to an end when his uncle Wil dropped by, and Joshua handed him his pole saying, "Here, Uncle Wil, you be patient!"

Paul was patient because he was fishing for much bigger game, the souls of men. The word here means patience with people. These four virtues — faith (toward God), love (toward all), patience (toward others), and endurance (to the end)[4] — were showcased in Paul's life. These remembrances loomed large and beautiful before Timothy, and they would draw him upward.

REMEMBER MY PERSECUTIONS (v. 11)

My persecutions. With Timothy's memory activated, Paul recalls their shared history — "persecutions, sufferings — what kinds of things happened to me in Antioch, Iconium and Lystra, the persecutions I endured" (v. 11a). Paul could have recalled other instances that Timothy had observed — say, in Philippi (Acts 16:19-34) or Ephesus (2 Corinthians 1:1-11) or Rome (Philippians 1:12-18). But he chose to appeal to sufferings that surrounded Timothy's origins.[5] Apparently Paul's purpose was to concentrate on sufferings that had left an indelible impression on the young man.[6]

Paul had been driven by persecution from Pisidian Antioch (Acts 13:50), he had to flee from Iconium when a plot to lynch him was uncovered (Acts 14:5, 6), and Timothy was in Lystra when Paul was stoned. Rocks crashed against Paul's skull, and he fell blood-spattered and broken beneath the rubble. He was dead, they all thought, and his murderers departed, leaving his body to his followers. How the believers mourned. What would they do without him? Suddenly Paul popped one eye open, then the other. "It's all right, brothers! No funeral today! Let's get out of here!" And "he got up and went back into the city" (Acts 14:20). What a memory for Timothy! How that must have played and replayed in the young man's heart. Remembrance of these things steeled him for faithful continuance.

As a youth I never saw anything as dramatic as this. But I did see men and women stand up for the truth when it cost them. I saw a pastor who kept on despite intense opposition, with gentleness and good cheer. I saw Christians put their faith before their vocation and material well-being. How big do you think this shared history — "Antioch, Iconium and Lystra" — was in Timothy's sky? It was like a rising planet!

My rescue. There was positive recollection to boot — "Yet the Lord rescued me from them all of them" (v. 11b). This is a near quotation of Psalm 34:19, where King David celebrated his deliverance. The only way Paul was going to get released from his dungeon was by going to his death, and he was at peace with that. But God had rescued him time and time again, which meant that he would do it for Timothy again and again if he willed to do so. Actually God always rescues his people — either in this life or by taking them to Heaven! And God's final rescue of Paul was the best of all.

REMEMBER THE AXIOM (vv. 12, 13)

For the true teacher. Fittingly, Paul gave Timothy a spiritual axiom to remember. The first part was specifically for him: "In fact, everyone who wants to live a godly life in Christ Jesus will be persecuted" (v. 12). Jesus, the very "mystery of godliness" himself (1 Timothy 3:16), gave this truth classic expression: "'No servant is greater than his master.' If they persecuted me, they will persecute you also" (John 15:20). Jesus (both God and the godliest of men) was the persecuted man par excellence! "He was oppressed and afflicted, yet he did not open his mouth; he was led like a lamb to the slaughter" (Isaiah 53:7).

Paul himself had been made to understand the persecution axiom — from the very first. Immediately after Paul's Damascus Road conversion, the Lord said to Ananias, "Go! This man is my chosen instrument to carry my name before the Gentiles and their kings and before the people of Israel. I will show him how much he must suffer for my name" (Acts 9:15, 16). After Paul's stoning in Lystra, Luke reports, "They preached the good news in that city and won a large number of disciples. Then they returned to Lystra, Iconium and Antioch, strengthening the disciples and encouraging them to remain true to the faith. 'We must go through many hardships to enter the kingdom of God,' they said" (Acts 14:21, 22).

Paul strengthened the Thessalonians with these words about the inevitability of their suffering: "We sent Timothy, who is our brother and God's fellow worker in spreading the gospel of Christ, to strengthen and encourage you in your faith, so that no one would be unsettled by these trials. You know quite well that we were destined for them" (1 Thessalonians 3:2, 3). Paul was also straight up with the Philippians about suffering: "For it has been granted to you on behalf of Christ not only to believe on him, but also to suffer for him" (Philippians 1:29). He also shared his own personal prayer with the Philippians: "I want to know Christ and the power of his resurrection and the fellowship of sharing in his sufferings, becoming like him in his death, and so, somehow, to attain to the resurrection from the dead" (Philippians 3:10, 11).

So there is no doubt about the axiom, "Everyone who wants to live a godly life in Christ Jesus will be persecuted" (v. 12). If those without Christ are "God's enemies" (Romans 5:10), then those who know Christ become the opponents of the devil. If anyone accepts a set of standards that are different from the world's standards, he is bound to have trouble. And if, as Barclay says, "Anyone proposes to introduce into his life a loyalty which surpasses all earthly loyalties, then there are bound to be clashes and collisions."[7] Some form of opposition will come if we attempt to witness to a world that hates to be told the truth and loves darkness.

This may come in subtle forms of rejection — being ignored, being patronized, a mocking look, condescension. It will hurt, as St. Augustine explained, "even when no one molests or vexes their body; for they suffer this persecution, not in their bodies, but in their hearts."[8]

Timothy knew all this. But to hear it from Paul again in the period just before his death was bracing. This was reality, and the acceptance of it placed Timothy on solid ground for what was to come. Such reality will stand us well in today's battles. Our culture flees suffering, seeing nothing noble in it or beyond it. But Christians must expect it in the regular course of serving God. And those who do will stand strong.

For false teachers. There was another, final part of the axiom: "while evil men and impostors will go from bad to worse, deceiving and being deceived" (v. 13). Impostors like Jannes and Jambres (cf. vv. 6-9) will progress downward to a fate far worse than persecution.

Paul's call to remembrance as a key to continuance was a substantial gift to Timothy, and Timothy took it to heart, finishing well.

He remembered Paul's *lifestyle* — his teaching, his way of life, and the way Paul lived validated what he taught. This gave Timothy an eternal purpose.

He remembered Paul's *virtues* — his "faith, patience, love and endurance" — and held them high as his standards.

He remembered Paul's *persecutions* in Antioch, Iconium, and Lystra and how the Lord rescued him from them all — and he took heart.

He remembered the *axiom* — "In fact, everyone who wants to live a godly life in Christ Jesus will be persecuted, while evil men and impostors will go from bad to worse, deceiving and being deceived" (vv. 12, 13). He embraced it, and its reality steeled him.

What wisdom there is for today's church in Timothy's elevated memories of Paul. The church's Timothies (its recent converts, its young impressionable Christians) need Pauls and Paulines whose lifestyles, virtues, and deportment even during persecutions summon them to embrace the axiom that "everyone who wants to live a godly life in Christ Jesus will be persecuted." We need to be the kind of men and women whose remembrance encourages continuance.

29

Continue in the Word

2 TIMOTHY 3:14-17

But as for you, continue in what you have learned and have become con-
vinced of, because you know those from whom you learned it, and how from
infancy you have known the holy Scriptures, which are able to make you
wise for salvation through faith in Christ Jesus. All Scripture is God-
breathed and is useful for teaching, rebuking, correcting and training in
righteousness, so that the man of God may be thoroughly equipped for
every good work.

Dr. William Evans, who pastored College Church from 1906-1909, was
an unusually accomplished man. He had the entire *King James Version* of the
Bible memorized as well as the New Testament of the *American Standard
Version*. Dr. Evans also authored over fifty books. His son, Louis, became
one of the best-known preachers in America and for many years pastored
the eminent First Presbyterian Church of Hollywood. When Dr. William
Evans retired, he moved to Hollywood to be near his son, and when Louis
was away he would substitute for him.

One unforgettable Sunday Dr. William, as he was affectionately called,
spoke on the virgin birth. All were amazed when he raised his Bible and tore
out the pages that narrate the birth of the Lord. As the tattered scraps floated
down toward the congregation, he shouted, "If we can't believe in the virgin
birth, let's tear it out of the Bible!" And then as he drove home his point, he
tore out the resurrection chapters, then the miracle narratives, then anything
conveying the supernatural. The floor was littered with mutilated pages.

Finally, with immense drama he held up the only remaining portion
and said, "And this is all we have left — the Sermon on the Mount. And
that has no authority for me if a divine Christ didn't preach it." After a few
more words, he asked his listeners to bow for the benediction. But before
he could pray, a man in that vast and sedate congregation stood and cried,

"No, no! Go on! We want more!" Several others joined in. So Dr. Evans preached for another fifty minutes.[1]

Dr. Evans was right. You cannot pick and choose from the Bible what you want to believe is inspired. The Bible does not present itself that way. Even more, the Bible will have no sustaining power for life if you make yourself the arbiter of what you will and will not believe about it.

Significantly, the text before us, containing the Bible's most famous statement of the inspiration of Scripture, is set in the context of continuance — going on, remaining in the gospel. What Christians believe about the Scriptures has everything to do with their continuance and service in the faith.

CONTINUE IN THE GOSPEL BECAUSE OF YOUR GODLY INFORMANTS (v. 14)

In verses 10-13, which immediately precede the text we will consider in this chapter, Paul encouraged Timothy to remain steadfast by recalling the apostle's character, his conduct during persecutions, and the axiom that "everyone who wants to live a godly life in Christ Jesus will be persecuted, while evil men and impostors will go from bad to worse, deceiving and being deceived" (vv. 12, 13).

Now Paul urges Timothy to continue in the gospel: "But as for you, continue in what you have learned and have become convinced of, because you know those from whom you learned it" (v. 14). Timothy had become convinced of the gospel through the instruction of three people — his beloved mother Lois, his grandmother Eunice, and his closest friend, the Apostle Paul. Evidently though Timothy's father was a Gentile (which accounts for Timothy's not being circumcised), his Hebrew mother and grandmother had educated him in the Old Testament Scriptures. When Paul came preaching the gospel from the Old Testament, they believed in Christ and, with Paul's aid, then instructed Timothy, so that he too believed.

Therefore Timothy had the enviable privilege of learning the gospel from both the lips and lives of these three people. Such a powerful combination! Earlier Paul had advised Timothy to "Watch your life and doctrine closely. Persevere in them, because if you do, you will save both yourself and your hearers" (1 Timothy 4:16). From the lips of his mother, grandmother, and Paul, Timothy heard the doctrine of the gospel message, and from their impeccable lives he saw it lived out. And that had a saving effect on him.

Think what it would mean if we could say to all our children, "But as for you, continue in what you have learned and have become convinced of, because you know those from whom you learned it" (v. 14). "You know your pastors, you know your Sunday school teachers, you know your fathers and mothers and grandparents. You know what they have taught you, and you know that their lives match the teaching of their lips. So continue in the gospel because you know from whom you learned it." Fellow Christians, this kind of challenge will bring continuance. This is what the church needs.

CONTINUE IN THE GOSPEL BECAUSE YOU HAVE HAD THE SCRIPTURES (v. 15)

Paul further grounds his appeal for Timothy to continue steadfast upon that young man's early knowledge of the Scriptures, from childhood — "and how from infancy you have known the holy Scriptures, which are able to make you wise for salvation through faith in Christ Jesus" (v. 15).

Lois and Eunice began to teach Timothy from the earliest possible age the substance of the Old Testament. His first stories were Bible stories. There were no picture books, but Timothy was blessed by the beautiful oral tellings and retellings by those godly women. From them he learned of the great events and grand passages of the Old Testament. And building on that, they taught him the Bible's precepts and principles.

Very possibly they had sought special instruction for Timothy. The Mishnah records a rabbi who dates from the end of the first century A.D. as saying, "At five years old [one is fit] for the Scripture, and ten years old the Mishnah, at thirteen for [the fulfilling of] the commandments . . ." (*Pirke Aboth* 5.21).[2] Whether Timothy had formal instruction or not, we understand that these godly women filled his head and heart with God's Word, which made him fertile ground for the gospel.

The phrase "the holy Scriptures, which are able to make you wise for salvation through faith in Christ Jesus" echoes Jesus' postresurrection declaration that the Old Testament Scriptures point to him (cf. Luke 24:25-27, 44-47). As Timothy came to faith, he understood that Jesus fulfilled the sacrificial system, the Passover lamb, the Tabernacle, and all the array of messianic prophesies. Timothy also saw that the "by faith" principle seen first with Abram's salvation found its fulfillment in Christ (cf. Genesis 15:6; 22:15-18; Romans 1:17; 3:22, 28; 4:1-25; Galatians 2:15, 16; 3:8-14, 22, 24; 5:5, 6). Indeed, Timothy had been made "wise for salvation" through the holy writings and their gospel counterparts.[3]

Timothy's knowledge of the Scriptures from infancy on formed a substantial ground and reason to continue in the gospel. He could see how it all fit together, how everything culminated in Christ, and that salvation through Christ alone was the answer.

CONTINUE IN THE GOSPEL BECAUSE OF WHAT SCRIPTURE IS (vv. 16, 17)

The mention of the holy writings occasioned Paul's classic statement about the nature and sufficiency of the Bible: "All Scripture is God-breathed and is useful for teaching, rebuking, correcting and training in righteousness, so that the man of God may be thoroughly equipped for every good work" (vv. 16, 17).

Scripture is inspired. Paul affirmed with elegant finality that "All Scripture is God-breathed." You can hear the meaning in the transliteration of the Greek word *Theopneustos* (God-breathed — *Theo* = "God" and *pneustos* = "breath"). More literally, "All Scripture is breathed into by God."[4] When you speak, your word is "you-breathed" — your breath, conditioned by your mind, pours forth in speech. You breathe out your words. This belief that Scripture was "breathed into by God" perfectly expresses the view of the first-century Jews about the Old Testament writings.[5]

The early church believed exactly the same thing. As Peter declared, "Above all, you must understand that no prophecy of Scripture came about by the prophet's own interpretation. For prophecy never had its origin in the will of man, but men spoke from God as they were carried along by the Holy Spirit" (2 Peter 1:20, 21). The Old Testament Scriptures were God's breath, God's words.

Beautifully, we see that this is also how the early church regarded the Gospels and the epistles. In 1 Timothy 5:18 Paul uses the same word for Scripture (*graphe*) that he uses here in 3:16 to refer to quotations from both the Old Testament and New Testament: "For the Scripture says, 'Do not muzzle the ox while it is treading out the grain' [Deuteronomy 25:4] and 'The worker deserves his wages' [Luke 10:7]."

Similarly, the Apostle Peter includes Paul's writings in the category of Scripture (*graphe*): "His [i.e., Paul's] letters contain some things that are hard to understand, which ignorant and unstable people distort, as they do the other Scriptures" (2 Peter 3:16). It is clear that Peter regarded Paul's writings to be Scripture!

Add to this Paul's insistence that his own writings be read (1 Thessalonians 5:27), exchanged and shared (Colossians 4:16), and obeyed (1 Corinthians 14:37; 2 Thessalonians 2:15), and his claim that the very words of his message were "words taught by the Spirit" (1 Corinthians 2:13). It is evident that he regarded his own writings as Scripture.[6]

Therefore, when he says, "All Scripture is God-breathed," he is including the apostolic writings. This is certainly what the early church came to believe and died for! For Timothy, this awesome view of Scripture is meant to make firm the ground of his continuance. And this is what Paul affirms as he goes on to describe Scripture's usefulness and sufficiency.

Scripture is useful. The apostle uses two pairs of words to flesh out Scripture's usefulness — "and is useful for teaching, rebuking, correcting and training in righteousness" (v. 16b). The first pair — "teaching, rebuking" — have to do with *doctrine.* Positively, all Scripture is "useful for teaching." That is why the whole of both Testaments must be studied — not just

Romans, not just the narratives of the Old Testament, not just the Gospels. All the didactic, poetic, narrative, apocalyptic, proverbial, and epical sections together are to make up the tapestry of our teaching. "All Scripture is God-breathed and is useful for teaching."

And of course when this is done, there will also be "rebuking." Those true to the Scriptures cannot escape this duty. Together the "teaching" and the "rebuking" produce the boon of sound doctrine. It is for want of both that the church has so often fallen into error.

The second pair — "correcting and training in righteousness" — have to do with *conduct*. "Correcting" comes from the Greek word for "straight," which the *New Living Translation* helpfully renders, "It straightens us out." God's Word is useful in a practical way. Those who accept its reproof will begin to find their lives straightening out. Then they will be ready for the Word's positive effect of "training in righteousness." The righteousness that has come to the believer by faith is actualized by the training of God's Word. In sum, the God-breathed Word is "useful" for all of life, all doctrine and all duty, all creed and all conduct — everything!

Scripture equips. Paul ends this section on the sufficiency of Scripture by saying, "so that the man of God may be thoroughly equipped for every good work" (v. 17). Though we cannot see it in English, Paul here uses two forms of the Greek word for *equip* (an adjective and a participle) to make his point. The man of God is super-equipped by the Word of God. The man of God is before all else a man of the Bible.

History records that John Calvin took the logic of this to heart. He believed that the Scripture was God-breathed and useful and thoroughly equipping. According to the recent Calvin translator and biographer T. H. L. Parker, commenting on the content of Calvin's preaching, "On Sunday he took always the New Testament, except for a few Psalms on Sunday afternoon. During the week . . . it was always the Old Testament."[7] He took five years to complete the book of Acts. He preached forty-six sermons on Thessalonians, 186 on Corinthians, eighty-six on the Pastorals, forty-three on Galatians, forty-eight on Ephesians. He spent five years on his harmony of the Gospels. That was just his Sunday work! During the weekdays in those five years he preached 159 sermons on Job, 200 on Deuteronomy, 353 on Isaiah, and 123 on Genesis.[8]

All this because of what Calvin believed about the Bible. He believed that the whole of Scripture was the Word of God and must be mined by exposition. "We must not pick and cull the Scriptures to please our own fancy, but must receive the whole without exception," wrote Calvin.[9]

In retrospect, we can see what Paul was doing here to encourage Timothy to endure. As Timothy recalled Lois and Eunice and Paul and how their lives matched the teaching of their lips, he would be strengthened to continue. As Timothy recalled his immersion from infancy in the sacred writings that had made him wise and a recipient of salvation through faith in Christ, he would be further heartened to continue on. And then as Timothy reflected on the Scriptures as the very breath of God and thus useful for everything and equipping him for ministry, he would continue to stand up for the gospel.

When William Evans, well into his eighties, stood amidst the strewn pages of his Bible on a Sunday more than fifty years ago, surrounded by the elegant mahogany of the nave of First Presbyterian Church of Hollywood, he made his point. Either all Scripture is God-breathed or it is not. Either it is useful or it is not. It either equips or it does not.

The testimony of God's Holy Word is that it is his breath and that it is everything to believers. The book of Deuteronomy records that when Moses had finished writing the words of the law and had given it to the Levites to place beside the ark and had sung his song, the Song of Moses, he said, "Take to heart all the words I have solemnly declared to you this day, so that you may command your children to obey carefully all the words of this law. They are not just idle words for you — they are your life" (Deuteronomy 32:46, 47; cf. 31:9-13; 32:1-43).

This set the standard for the proper regard for the Scriptures of the old covenant. This is why the psalmist devoted the 176 verses of Psalm 119 to the celebration of Scripture, using the twenty-two letters of the Hebrew alphabet as a structure. In effect, he said God's Word is everything from A to Z. The Scriptures are life!

When Jesus began his ministry and was tempted by Satan, his encyclopedic knowledge of the Word enabled him to defeat the tempter with three deft quotations from Deuteronomy (see Luke 4:1-13; cf. Deuteronomy 8:3; 6:13, 16). *Jesus Christ, God incarnate, leaned on the sufficiency of Scripture in his hour of need.* Indeed, his summary response to the tempter was like a bookend to Moses' declaration that the Scriptures are "your life," for Jesus insisted that they are the soul's essential food — "It is written, 'Man does not live on bread alone, but on every word that comes from the mouth of God'" (Matthew 4:4; cf. Luke 4:4; Deuteronomy 8:3).

The Scriptures were *life* to Moses and *food* to Jesus. They cannot and must not be anything less to us. They are the very breath of God. They are our *breath*, our *life*, our *food*.

Because Scripture is all of this, we too can continue on in the gospel.

30

Preach the Word

2 TIMOTHY 4:1-5

In the presence of God and of Christ Jesus, who will judge the living and the dead, and in view of his appearing and his kingdom, I give you this charge: Preach the Word; be prepared in season and out of season; correct, rebuke and encourage — with great patience and careful instruction. For the time will come when men will not put up with sound doctrine. Instead, to suit their own desires, they will gather around them a great number of teachers to say what their itching ears want to hear. They will turn their ears away from the truth and turn aside to myths. But you, keep your head in all situations, endure hardship, do the work of an evangelist, discharge all the duties of your ministry.

Author's Note: *This exposition has been purposely edited to preserve its unusually personal nature because I wanted to convey its original application and piquancy.*

When I realized that this text (which is by far the most preached upon at ordinations and installations) would fall on the final Sunday that my son would attend the church I pastor (and the church he grew up in) before assuming his own pastoral duties at a church on the West Coast, I saw that circumstance as remarkable providence. Considering the variables —that this was my thirtieth consecutive sermon on the Pastorals, punctuated by holiday messages and vacation days away, and that my son and his family's departure date had been only recently determined, and also that Peter Jensen, the principal of Moore College in Sydney, Australia, the school from which my son took his theological degree, happened to be visiting us with his wife, Christine — the coincidence of this special text can only be a work of sovereign providence. I will always regard it as a *sweet* providence as well, an unnecessary but gracious bounty from God. So as I preached this text, it was with an eye not only to my hearers but to my own son, William Carey Hughes, on the eve of assuming his own divine call.

Paul's focus, of course, was on his retiring, sometimes reticent protégé, Timothy. And the heat of the apostle's focus was intensified by the burning realization that he himself was in truth a dying man — "For I am already being poured out like a drink offering, and the time has come for my departure" (v. 6). The charge in verses 1-5 initiates the final thoughts of what is the old apostle's ministerial last will and testament.

THE CHARGE — ITS SOLEMNITY (v. 1)

Paul's words resound with passion: "In the presence of God and of Christ Jesus, who will judge the living and the dead, and in view of his appearing and his kingdom, I give you this charge" (v. 1). The charge could not be more solemn. Paul has invoked here what is in fact an eternal, unchangeable reality — the actual presence of God the Father and his Son Christ Jesus. They were present. They saw Paul write the words to Timothy. They saw Timothy read them for the first time. They read Timothy's heart.

The solemn charge was electrified by three realities about Jesus, which Timothy would see in full voltage.

Jesus' judgment. Paul makes it clear that it is Jesus (not God the Father) "who will judge the living and the dead." Early in his ministry Jesus warned his detractors, "Moreover, the Father judges no one, but has entrusted all judgment to the Son, that all may honor the Son just as they honor the Father" (John 5:22, 23). All judgment is committed to Jesus. And later in the same discussion, Jesus informed them that God had "given him authority to judge because he is the Son of Man" (v. 27). Thus Jesus claimed that he is the awesome Son of Man of Daniel's vision, whom Daniel saw coming in the clouds of Heaven to the Ancient of Days, where, as Daniel records, "He was given authority, glory and sovereign power; all peoples, nations and men of every language worshiped him. His dominion is an everlasting dominion that will not pass away, and his kingdom is one that will never be destroyed" (Daniel 7:14).

This awesome Son of Man who came in the flesh as Jesus and lived before the Father on earth as the one appointed to serve him and did so perfectly will be the judge of Timothy's service (cf. 2 Corinthians 5:10). This was meant to energize Timothy — to add some voltage to Paul's charge.

John Calvin said of this, "He makes special mention of the judgment of Christ because He will require of us, who are his representatives, a stricter account of our failures in His ministry."[1] This echoes James's caution: "Not many of you should presume to be teachers, my brothers, because you know that we who teach will be judged more strictly" (James 3:1). Similarly the writer of Hebrews observes about leaders, "They keep watch over you as men who must give an account" (13:17). The realization that our service will be judged by the Servant of all servants is jolting. This is not negative for the faithful servant but is rather a source of added electricity.

Jesus' appearing. There is also here the approaching reality of Jesus' brilliant "appearing," his epiphany, which Scripture describes as the rising of the sun, and Paul calls in the third of the Pastoral Letters "the blessed hope — the glorious appearing of our great God and Savior, Jesus Christ, who gave himself for us to redeem us from all wickedness and to purify for himself a people that are his very own, eager to do what is good" (Titus 2:13, 14). This awaits Timothy and all like him. What a charged day that will be!

Jesus' kingdom. This dazzling reality will be followed by "his kingdom," when

> *The kingdom of this world is become*
> *the kingdom of our Lord and of his Christ.*
> *(G. F. Handel,* Messiah;
> *cf. Revelation 11:15)*

And Timothy and those in his train will rule with him forever and ever.

Paul's charge — so solemn in the presence of God, so jolting, so charged — certainly activated the current of Timothy's soul, as it must ours because Jesus is also present with us, and his judgment and appearing and kingdom are coming.

My son, William Carey Hughes, may the solemn grandeur of the realities surrounding the great pastoral charge ravish your soul. Remember it always in its divine setting.

THE CHARGE DELIVERED (v. 2)

The charge is contained in a single statement made up of five terse imperatives: "Preach the Word; be prepared in season and out of season; correct, rebuke and encourage — with great patience and careful instruction" (v. 2). The abruptness of these commands convey urgency — terminal urgency. Timothy must waste no time. He must get to it. It is clear that some of the commands are directed at Timothy's reticence, at the things he did not naturally like to do. In truth, no preacher likes to do certain of these things, especially if he is the least bit shy or retiring. But Paul is insistent.

First, Paul demands that Timothy "preach the Word." Most preachers can recite this command in Greek: *keryxon ton logon* — that is, "proclaim aloud or herald the Word." It was foreshadowed in this letter in 2:9 when Paul proclaimed, "But God's word is not chained," and then in 2:15 when he said, "Do your best to present yourself to God as one approved, a workman who does not need to be ashamed and who correctly handles the word of truth" — one who, as we already noted, gets it straight and gives it straight!

By placing the command to "preach the Word" first, and then enlarging it in the following imperatives, Paul makes it the signature of Christian ministry. The message to Timothy is, "Though you may be shy, though you may prefer to remain in the background, you must give yourself to the public preaching of the Word of God."

I have an intimate understanding of this because though I was called to preach at an early age, I remained painfully shy into young adulthood. Because of my call I volunteered to be a leader in my church youth group, but I would blush if called upon to make announcements. Even after marriage, if I was asked to preside at a meeting or service I would script every remark. Often my cheek would twitch uncontrollably in front of a large group. On occasions when I gave a devotional or taught adult Sunday school, my wife would sit on the periphery so as not to catch my eye and distract me. Today most people probably think I preach because I am "a natural." Little do they know.

My son, understand that the call to preach is not a matter of preference or our natural giftedness as we understand it. It is simply a matter of obedience. If God has called you to preach, that must be the signature of your soul and life.

It is a matter of historical fact that John Calvin's own inclinations were to closet himself and give his great mind to private studies. And early on that is what he decided to do. However, when he visited the city of Geneva, William Farel, the fiery leader of Geneva, discovered he was there and sought him out. It was a meeting that changed the course of history. Calvin relates what happened in his preface to his commentary on the Psalms:

> Farel, who burned with an extraordinary zeal to advance the gospel, immediately learned that my heart was set upon devoting myself to private studies, for which I wished to keep myself free from other pursuits, and finding that he gained nothing by entreaties, he proceeded to utter an imprecation that God would curse my retirement, and the tranquility of the studies which I sought, if I should withdraw and refuse to give assistance, when the necessity was so urgent. By this imprecation I was so stricken with terror, that I desisted from the journey which I had undertaken.[2]

Calvin's biographer John Dillenberger writes of this encounter:

> The course of his life was irrevocably changed. Not just geographically, but vocationally. Never again would Calvin work in what he called the "tranquility of studies." From now on every page of the forty-eight volumes of books and tracts and sermons and commen-

taries and letters that he wrote would be hammered out on the anvil of pastoral responsibility.[3]

It is precisely because Calvin, despite his inclinations, gave himself to the public proclamation and ministry of the Word that his writings have such pungency and practicality. He did it all in Geneva! He preached the Word on every occasion — correcting, rebuking, encouraging with patience and careful instruction.

Again, my son, it is not a matter of personality type or even inclination. It is a matter of divine call and obedience to that call.

And here we must not gloss over the obvious, as so many preachers do today. It is the Word that is to be preached! As the imminent theologian and patristic scholar Tom Oden says:

> There is no hint here that preaching is thought of primarily as self-expression of subjective experience or feeling-disclosure or auto-biography or "telling one's story" so as to neglect Scripture. . . . The whole counsel of God is to be preached, without fanciful, idio-syncratic amendment or individualistic addition.[4]

Son, don't preach yourself (cf. 2 Corinthians 4:5). Like Paul, preach the whole counsel of God (cf. Acts 20:27, NASB). Let the Word do the work.

The second imperative expands the thought: "be prepared in season and out of season" — that is, whether it is convenient or inconvenient.[5] You must not reserve preaching only to when you feel like it, or when you are psychologically ready, or when the time seems good. My own experience is that very often when I feel least like preaching or I don't feel good about my preaching — those are the times that God especially uses.

Frankly, there have been times when I mounted the pulpit thinking I had a "silver bullet" — only to discover that it was a rubber bullet that fell harmlessly into the center aisle — ignominiously impotent.

The call here is for radical availability. Calvin came to understand for himself that it even called for "aggressiveness" in overcoming hindrances and even a "ruthless persistence"[6] — "in season and out of season."

Two days before the death of Clarence Edward Macartney, the great Presbyterian preacher and upholder of orthodoxy in this country, he was visited by his brother Robertson who was on his way to preach at a nearby church. As Robertson left, he heard his famous brother say: "Put all the Bible you can into it."

As Dr. Oswald T. Allis remarked, "It was the counsel of one who had spent fifty years in the gospel ministry, occupied three historic pulpits, preached to thousands, written many books, read and traveled extensively, and played a prominent role in the life of the Christian church. And with these simple words this famous preacher summed it all up: 'Put all the Bible you can into it.'"[7]

Be a man of the Word! Study it. Learn the themes and outlines of all the books. Memorize the great passages. Immerse yourself in its narratives. Know its great souls. Walk in and with them. Make your blood "bibline" (Spurgeon's term). And when you preach, put all the Bible you can into it. Let the Word do the work.

The final three imperatives form a neat group — a triple ministry: "correct, rebuke and encourage — with great patience and careful instruction" (v. 2). If you enjoy correcting and rebuking, you are likely not fit for the ministry. But if you do not do it, you are a shirker.

John Stott, who has so much to do with the rebirth of Biblical exposition in the English-speaking world, came to Christ as a boy through the ministry of a remarkable Church of England clergyman, E. J. H. Nash. Nash, or "Bash" as he is affectionately called, was used of God to point a number of preachers to Christ — men such as R. C. Lucas, Michael Green, John Pollock, and a number of prominent presidents of Cambridge Union. Part of Nash's genius was that he was aggressive in his correction of his disciples. Stott writes: "His letters to me often contained rebuke, for I was a wayward young Christian and needed to be disciplined. In fact, so frequent were his admonitions at one period, that whenever I saw his familiar writing on an envelope, I needed to pray and prepare myself for half an hour before I felt ready to open it."[8]

Correction (showing your people where they are wrong) and rebuke (telling them to stop)[9] require that you not be a people pleaser or popularity seeker — and certainly not a flatterer.

It also requires that you have no interior joy in setting others straight. But most of all, it requires the third imperative of the triple ministry — that you "encourage — with great patience and careful instruction." You must come alongside your people with encouraging words — "That's right. You are doing fine. You're making progress. That was beautiful." And in doing this, you are called to immense "patience" because you will rarely see quick results to your ministry. Correction and rebuke must be teamed with careful teaching, or they will be unprofitable.

What a massive charge this is: "Preach the Word; be prepared in season and out of season; correct, rebuke and encourage — with great patience and careful instruction." No one is capable for the task. The call itself is an invitation to let God possess you — to live a life of profound dependence on him.

THE CHARGE — ITS REASON (vv. 3, 4)

Paul is precise in giving Timothy the reason why he must preach the Word. It is because people naturally move away from the truth. "For the time will come when men will not put up with sound doctrine. Instead, to suit their own desires, they will gather around them a great number of teachers to say what their itching ears want to hear. They will turn their ears away from the truth and turn aside to myths" (vv. 3, 4).

This prophetic word covers the whole of Biblical history, both in retrospect and prospect. Jeremiah lamented, "The prophets prophesy lies . . . and my people love it this way" (Jeremiah 5:31). God later explained to Ezekiel, "Indeed, to them you are nothing more than one who sings love songs with a beautiful voice and plays an instrument well, for they hear your words but do not put them into practice" (Ezekiel 33:32).

Jesus explained in the parable of the four soils that many ostensible believers are really unbelievers. Indeed it is only the fourth soil, the fruit-bearing soil, that has real faith (cf. Matthew 13:1-23; Luke 8:1-15). People love to hear something different and sensational ("what their itching ears want to hear" is literally "tickled in their hearing"[10]). So they seek teachers who will confirm their illusions. In the fourth century Gregory of Nazianzus wrote concerning "itching ears," "When this syndrome is in place, people who call themselves Christian will find the truth in Christ Jesus intolerable and will seek to stamp it out."[11]

Today preachers fill sports arenas by telling people what they want to hear about their money or politics, by entertaining them, and by proclaiming bizarre doctrines that appeal to the curiosity. Whole intellectual careers are made and spent on "demythologizing" the Bible and reducing the words of Jesus to a few moralizing sound bites. The masses prefer myth to truth.

That is why you must preach the Word in its historical setting and in the context of the whole Bible, making the appropriate Biblical connections and discerning all the ways it is a revelation of Jesus Christ. That is why you must sweat in the study and sweat in the pulpit.

THE CHARGE — ITS NECESSITIES (v. 5)

Paul sums up the necessities of the charge as he finishes his thought: "But you, keep your head in all situations, endure hardship, do the work of an evangelist, discharge all the duties of your ministry" (v. 5). In keeping his head, Timothy was to literally be sober and cool in all circumstances, just as a commercial pilot must in an emergency when the passengers are crying out with fear. Stability must characterize the preacher in an upside-down world. Enduring hardship is a recurrent theme in the Pastorals (cf. 2 Timothy 1:8; 2:3, 9; 3:12).

The gospel was to be Timothy's lifework — "do the work of an evangelist." The good news was to be constantly on his lips — the message that Jesus Christ is descended from David and raised from the dead (cf. 2:8).

Timothy was to shun no area of ministry: "Discharge all the duties of your ministry." Do all the imperatives, for they will always be imperative.

Late one afternoon Alistair Begg was meeting with a number of pastors, including myself. He wistfully quoted this very verse, then said, "I increasingly find that verse to be the anchor point for all of my days. I wake up on a Monday, and say, 'well, what will I do now?' Then I say, 'Well, I think I'll try to keep my head, endure hardship, do the work of an evangelist, and discharge all the duties of my ministry.' And when I am lifted up by a little encouragement, which sometimes comes, I say to myself, 'Well, what shall I do?' The answer is keep your head, endure hardship, and so on."

He paused, then went on, "And when the waves beat on me and I feel just like running away to the hills somewhere, what should I do? 'Well, Alistair, just keep your head, endure hardship, do the work of an evangelist, and discharge all the duties of your ministry.'"

Then he concluded, "So, that's a word in season for us to take away and think of."

And so it is. The years will fly by like the fence posts on a farm road in Illinois as you drive along — years quickly become decades. You and I will change with those years. But God's call will never change. Jesus — your judge, your Savior, your king — will always be present, charging your call with divine voltage. And his charge will always be, "Preach the Word; be prepared in season and out of season; correct, rebuke and encourage — with great patience and careful instruction. . . . But you, keep your head in all situations, endure hardship, do the work of an evangelist, discharge all the duties of your ministry" (vv. 2, 5).

31

Paul's Terminal Perspectives

2 TIMOTHY 4:6-8

For I am already being poured out like a drink offering, and the time has come for my departure. I have fought the good fight, I have finished the race, I have kept the faith. Now there is in store for me the crown of right-eousness, which the Lord, the righteous Judge, will award to me on that day — and not only to me, but also to all who have longed for his appearing.

A memorable line by Frederick Langbridge pictures two men who are both in prison but are a universe apart in their thoughts.

> *Two men looked through the bars.*
> *One saw the mud, the other, the stars.*[1]

As Paul languished in Rome's cold, dripping, subterranean Mamartine prison, mud and dust coated his existence and seemed an appropriate symbol for his life. He was now a nobody, having lost his highborn status by following Jesus. He was a poor man, shivering in inadequate clothing. And apart from Luke he was bereft of the presence of friends and was forsaken by his one-time followers. Charged with sedition, he suffered contempt and abuse from his jailers. Paul had become a joke among his enemies. They reasoned that his final miseries were proof that God was not with him. And as he languished in his dungeon cell, his work in Ephesus was being torn by religious wolves like Hymenaeus and Philetus, who taught that the future resurrection of believers was past and that all the prosperities of Heaven were present now.

> *Name it and claim it, that's what faith's about!*
> *You can have what you want if you just have no doubt.*[2]

Therefore, Paul's plight and imminent death were due to his own errant theology and sin, they said. "Shame on Paul."

So there was plenty of mud around — enough to fill anyone's horizons. But amazingly, the old apostle looked up and saw the stars! The brief paragraph that is comprised of verses 6-8 is in fact a glorious declaration of personal triumph. In verse 6 he looks at the *present* and sees the stars, in verse 7 he looks back on the *past* and sees the stars, and in verse 8 he looks at the *future* and sees the stars.

Paul's perspectives at the end of his life, his dying perspectives, covering every conceivable span of Paul's existence, are awesome. They tell us how to live and how to die.

STARS IN THE PRESENT (v. 6)

The present reality for Paul was that he was dying and departing: "For I am already being poured out like a drink offering, and the time has come for my departure" (v. 6).

Dying. Paul borrowed the vivid image of "being poured out like a drink offering" from the Jewish custom of pouring out wine at the base of the altar as part of the ritual sacrifice of a lamb (cf. Exodus 29:40, 41; Leviticus 23:13; Numbers 15:1-12; 28:7, 24).

The image of red wine splashing down upon the altar became an operative metaphor for how Paul regarded his life. Some five years earlier Paul had written to the Philippians about the possibility of his death, describing it as "being poured out like a drink offering on the sacrifice and service" of their faith (2:17). There it was hypothetical. Now as he writes to Timothy it is actual. He uses the present tense in its progressive sense to indicate the certainty of the event, as if it were actually taking place.[3] Though there would be some more time before the event (he will ask for his books and a warm coat, v. 13), the last drops of Paul's blood were in a sense beginning to fall.

Yet Paul was triumphant. It is clear that Paul did not think of himself as about to be executed but rather as offering himself to God. From the time of his conversion on the Damascus Road, everything he had was given to God — his wealth, his body, his brilliant mind, his passions, his position, his reputation, his relationships, his dreams. For years the red blood of his life had been spilling onto the altar. Now all that remained was his life's breath, and he triumphantly gave that.

Departing. By calling death a "departure" — "and the time has come for my departure" (v. 6b), Paul indicated the certitude that his life would not end and that he had no fear of death. The word translated "departure" is used in Greek literature to describe the loosing of a ship from its moorings or a soldier loosing the stakes of his tent. It pictures a ship lifting anchor, tossing off the ropes, and rising on the tide so the winds can carry her to sea. The word radiates sweet, triumphant continuance. Lewis had it right in *The Last Battle* where it is explained to the deceased children that "they were beginning Chapter One of the Great Story which no one on earth has read: which goes on for ever: in which every chapter is better than the one before."[4]

Final "departure" was the culmination of Paul's long-held dream that he had earlier expressed to the Philippians saying, "I desire to depart [to cast off the ropes] and be with Christ, which is better by far" (1:23). He believed with all his heart that it was "better by far." Those who have departed to be with Christ are far better off. Though you have lived seventy-five years, it is better to be with Christ. Though you are the richest man in town, life in Heaven with Christ is far better. Though you are brilliant, it is far better. If you have lived only five years, it is better to be above with Christ. Though you have the greatest gifts for ministry, it is far better. The "far better" dominated Paul's thoughts, as it should ours.

Here was a man who looked imminent death in the face and saw the stars.

STARS IN THE PAST (v. 7)

The present held no fears for Paul. It was a triumph. And as he looked back to the past, he was equally triumphant: "I have fought the good fight, I have finished the race, I have kept the faith" (v. 7).

The fight. I once imaginatively pictured the Apostle Paul at the end of his career dressed in the armor that he described in Ephesians 6. Here is how I saw him: He has worn his war belt so long that it is sweaty through and through and salt-stained and comfortable like an old horse's bridle, and it holds everything perfectly in place. The "belt of truth," God's truth, has girded him tight for years, so that it has permeated his life and reigns within. He is armed with the clear eyes of a clean conscience. He can face anything. His torso is sheathed with a battle-tarnished breastplate. It is crisscrossed with great lateral grooves from slicing sword blows and dented from enemy artillery. The "breastplate of righteousness" has preserved his vitals intact. His holy life has rendered his heart impervious to the spiritual assaults of Satan.

His gnarled legs are comfortable in his ancient war boots. He has stood his ground on several continents. The boots are the "gospel of peace," the peace *with* God that comes through faith in him and the resultant peace *of* God — the sense of well-being and wholeness — *shalom*. He stands in peace, and being rooted in peace he cannot be moved.

Paul's great shield terrifies the eyes, for the broken shafts and the many charred holes reveal him to be the victor of many fierce battles. The "shield of faith," held up as he has repeatedly believed God's Word, has caught and extinguished every fiery dart of doubt and sensuality and materialism. None have touched him.

On his old gray head he wears a helmet that has seen better days. Great dents mar its symmetry, reminders of furtive blows dealt him by the enemy. Because the "helmet of salvation," the confidence of knowing that he *is* saved and *will be* saved, has allowed him to stand tall against the most vicious assaults, his imperial confidence gives him a regal bearing.

Then there is his sword. He was equal to a hundred when his sword flashed. The "sword of the Spirit, which is the Word of God," the ultimate offensive weapon, cut through everything — armor, flesh, glistening bone, marrow — and even the soul.

What an awesome figure the apostle was. He had stood before Felix and Agrippa, the legates and officials of Rome — and had not given an inch. He was the consummate warrior.[5]

So when he says here, "I have fought the good fight," every nuance is true. He had begun on the Damascus Road thirty years earlier, and after his time in the Arabian desert he traveled the ancient world in three missionary journeys. The fourth, I believe, ended in Rome as he sought to take the Word to Spain's "spires away on the world's rim."[6]

Brave Paul contended not only with the false teachers and false brethren among his own people and with the sovereigns of imperial Rome but also "against the rulers, against the authorities, against the powers of this dark world and against the spiritual forces of evil in the heavenly realms" (Ephesians 6:12). He suffered an amazing litany of dangers and indignities (cf. 2 Corinthians 11:23-33) but shouted in the midst of the battle, "In all these things we are more than conquerors through him who loved us" (Romans 8:37).

So now, with the day fading, he could look back on his life and say, "I have fought the good fight" (Greek perfect tense, "I have fought it; it is complete — forever done"). This was good. This was noble.

What a triumph to look back over the mud and dust of the years, over your mistakes and losses and victories and faintings, and say, "I have fought the good fight — I see the stars!"

The race. The second of Paul's declarations, "I have finished the race," means "I have finished the race course."[7] God had set a specific course before Paul, some of which had been revealed to him at the beginning when Ananias informed him of the things he would suffer (Acts 9:15, 16). Now Paul had completed the course.

It is significant that Paul made no boast as to having won the race but simply stated he had finished it. There was no ego here, only satisfaction in having completed the race. Everything God had set before him had been done.

The writer of Hebrews noted that each believer has a course marked out for him or her: "and let us run with perseverance the race marked out for us" (Hebrews 12:1). The course for each of us is unique. You do not have to run my course, and I do not have to run yours. Some courses are relatively straight, some are all turns. Some seem all uphill, some are as flat as Illinois. All seem long, but some are longer.

The glory is that each of us can finish the race "marked out for us" because the course laid out for us by our sovereign, omniscient God is perfect for us. Those with only a few years left and those who are just beginning (high school students, college freshmen, whatever) can all finish the course with distinction. There is no way you will not be able to complete yours, unless you willfully run your own race rather than God's.

Paul completed his race because he set his heart to do so, as he earlier had expressed to the Ephesian elders — "if only I may finish the race and complete the task the Lord Jesus has given me" (Acts 20:24). What satisfaction was Paul's (despite his circumstances, despite the judgments of his detractors, despite his execution) — to look back on his life and say, "I have finished the race." He saw the stars!

The faith. Paul's third retrospect — "I have kept the faith" — refers to having maintained the apostolic deposit of doctrine, the gospel, which he had in various places charged Timothy to keep: "Timothy, guard what has been entrusted to your care" (1 Timothy 6:20). "Guard the good deposit that was entrusted to you — guard it with the help of the Holy Spirit who lives in us" (2 Timothy 1:14). "Preach the Word" (4:2). All this Paul had done himself with distinction. And he had done it with deepest belief. *Paul persevered in what he preserved!*[8]

What triumph it was for Paul to raise his eyes from the mud of his surroundings (the prison's close atmosphere of failure and death), look back across the embattled years, and proclaim with utter confidence and finality, "*I have fought the good fight.* I was noble in the struggle. I did not back away — ever. I weathered all that came my way. I took up the sword of the Word and fought until it was one with my arm."

What victory to declare, "*I have finished the race.* I kept the course you laid out for me from the beginning of time. My boast, if there is any, is that I finished the marathon. I am done. I rest in that."

What satisfaction to aver, "*I have kept the faith.* I kept it pure. I preached it. I lived it. My life has been and is a gospel life. It has not diminished one bit."

What supreme closure to say, "These three things have been done, and they will always remain done."

The stars fill the sky over Paul — and he shines in their light.

STARS IN THE FUTURE (v. 8)

Paul has looked at the present and the past. Now, to complete his thought, he looks to the future: "Now there is in store for me the crown of righteousness, which the Lord, the righteous Judge, will award to me on that day — and not only to me, but also to all who have longed for his appearing" (v. 8).

Paul's crown. Notice that the crown that awaits Paul is not a crown of glory or a crown of peace or a crown of joy, but "*the* crown of righteousness." The righteous judge is Jesus himself (2 Corinthians 5:10, italics added; cf. 1 Corinthians 1:30). He had already given Paul his righteousness when Paul believed (cf. Romans 3:21, 22; Philippians 3:9). And now he gives him the ultimate "crown of righteousness," the ultimate permanent state of righteousness.[9] As Gordon Fee aptly remarks, "One receives the final crown of righteousness precisely because one has already received the righteousness of Christ."[10]

Why a "crown of righteousness" instead of, say, a crown of glory? Because righteousness is the greatest need we sinful humans have. It is *the* singular thing we cannot do for ourselves. And it is from "the crown of righteousness" that all other crowns will come.

Paul looked up through the bars to the future and saw the Morning Star, Jesus Christ, bearing in his hand Paul's future "crown of righteousness."

Our crown. Wonder of wonders, the ultimate crown is not reserved only for great ones like Paul, "but also to all who have longed for his [Christ's] appearing" (v. 8b.). Christians are people who love Jesus Christ. And because they love him, they long for his appearing. Their true country is Heaven, and they characteristically look forward to "the blessed hope" of Christ's return (cf. Titus 2:13). They pray Maranatha! — "Come, O Lord!" (1 Corinthians 16:22; cf. Revelation 22:20).

Do you love his appearing? That is the question the text literally suggests. Do you? Do you truly? If so, "the crown of righteousness" is reserved for you on that day.

Paul's brilliant paragraph no doubt burst like the white light of fireworks on Timothy's soul — and it still shines bright on us.

The way a period of history interprets death is a valuable key to understanding the spirit of that age. An era like ours, which has made death into the final obscenity — and apparently the only obscenity — tells us a great deal about itself. The dread of death surrounds us. But, oh, how we are refreshed by the perspectives of this great Christian!

Deep in the mud of the earth, Paul looked at his *present* death as a triumphant sacrifice and as a loosing of the moorings at the beginning of a great voyage. The bars of death became a grid for the stars.

And as he looked *back* on his life he voiced a trio of unshakable satisfactions: "I have fought the good fight." That fact could not be denied. "I have finished the race." Nothing was left undone. "I have kept the faith." He was true to the gospel in every way. He never slackened. From the mud he saw it all. And the stars shone brightly.

And as he looked *forward*, he saw the Lord Jesus himself, the bright Morning Star, bringing "the crown of righteousness" to place on his servant's waiting brow. There was light at midnight.

The end awaits us all, and for some it will be sooner than we think. At that final moment, may we have lived in such a way that as we see our approaching death we see the stars, and as we look back on our life we see the stars, and as we look forward we see the Star.

32

Tough Friends for Tough Times

2 TIMOTHY 4:9-15

Do your best to come to me quickly, for Demas, because he loved this world, has deserted me and has gone to Thessalonica. Crescens has gone to Galatia, and Titus to Dalmatia. Only Luke is with me. Get Mark and bring him with you, because he is helpful to me in my ministry. I sent Tychicus to Ephesus. When you come, bring the cloak that I left with Carpus at Troas, and my scrolls, especially the parchments. Alexander the metalworker did me a great deal of harm. The Lord will repay him for what he has done. You too should be on your guard against him, because he strongly opposed our message.

The Apostle Paul understood the importance of friends — and especially the importance of friends during tough times. Years earlier while he was ministering in Macedonia, he became so exhausted by external conflicts and inner fears about the work and about the relentless fact that his body had no rest that he became "downcast" (2 Corinthians 7:6; "depressed," as the *New American Standard Bible* translates it). Times were tough, and his discouragement was substantial. "But God . . . comforted us by the coming of Titus." It was not things that brought him comfort. It was the touch of Titus, the loving encouragement of a trusted friend. And the effect was priceless, indeed golden. Titus relayed the affirmations of other friends, and so Paul said, "My joy was greater than ever" (v. 7). Titus modeled a ministry that God's people so need today. It would do the church great good to meditate on those beautiful verses in 2 Corinthians 7:5-7.

Here in his second letter to Timothy, Paul has already praised the Titus-like ministry done for him by Onesiphorus (1:16-18). After Paul's arrest, most believers in the province of Asia, where Ephesus was located, deserted him, including leaders like Phygelus and Hermogenes (1:15). But excellent

Onesiphorus traveled to Rome and "searched hard" for Paul — treading the back alleys of Rome, knocking on doors, asking suspicious questions. And once he found Paul, "He often refreshed me." Despite the danger, Onesiphorus returned again and again to Paul's dungeon and ministered to him. Onesiphorus was there for Paul when neither the sun nor the moon shone on his friend.

Now, in the mud of the dungeon, there was no evidence that Paul was depressed. On the contrary, the preceding paragraph is a triumphant declaration that as he looked through the bars, he saw not the mud but the stars. Nevertheless this was a tough time for Paul, perhaps his toughest. And Paul knew the importance of "Tough Friends for Tough Times" — the importance of Christian relationships to Christian continuance. So the old apostle took charge of his relationships at the end. He became intensely directive and called the shots from his death cell with four explicit orders.

COME QUICKLY (vv. 9-11a)

The first directive was that Timothy drop everything in Ephesus and come immediately to Rome: "Do your best to come to me quickly, for Demas, because he loved this world, has deserted me and has gone to Thessalonica. Crescens has gone to Galatia, and Titus to Dalmatia. Only Luke is with me" (vv. 9-11a). Paul's motivations were several.

Beloved Timothy. Overarching was his father-son love for Timothy. Paul began this letter by calling him "my dear son" (1:2), followed by an emotional retrospect: "Recalling your tears, I long to see you, so that I may be filled with joy" (1:4). The memory of Timothy's tearful love made the dying apostle's heart ache for his presence. Timothy was the son Paul never had. He was his soul-son.

Paul's insistence that Timothy come "quickly" was demanding, to say the least. The journey would take Timothy four to six months over land and sea — mostly land — by way of Troas (cf. v. 13), Philippi, the great Egnatian road to Dyrrachium, and then across to Brundisium and on to Rome.[1] Paul was counting on the slow, grinding pace of Roman justice to allow Timothy to beat the apostle's appointment with death. The journey would have to be made as quickly as possible despite its inherent dangers.

Some have criticized Paul for this, saying he was selfishly putting his own needs above that of the church, especially the troubled Ephesian church that Timothy was attempting to help. Obviously they neither understand the depth of relationship between the two men, nor the fact that Paul had important truths and strategies to impart to Timothy — which could only be communicated in the give-and-take of extended personal exchange.

Paul's armchair critics fail to understand that this event marks the end of the initial era of Christian mission, and that what Paul would impart would be essential to the future health of the church universal. They also fail to note that trusted Tychicus was being sent by Paul to Ephesus (probably with this letter in hand), where he would serve as Timothy's replacement.

Disappointing Demas. The critics also do not give enough weight to the depth of the apostle's isolation and the need of tough friends for tough times, which is embedded right here in his own words — "for Demas, because he loved this world, has deserted me and has gone to Thessalonica" (v. 10a).

Demas had splendid potential. In Paul's earlier prison letter to Philemon, Paul honored Demas by referring to him as a "fellow worker" along with the likes of Mark and Luke (v. 24). He was part of the inner circle, in close communion with these other greats. Demas was a spiritual man of substance. Accordingly, in Paul's letter to the Colossians, he is included as one who sends greetings — "Our dear friend Luke, the doctor, and Demas send greetings" (4:14). Demas wasn't a lightweight, and he had been with Paul in many ups and downs. But this time the situation in Rome was apparently too much for him. Paul was not under house arrest as before but was in the infamous Mamartine prison, on his way to a sure death for sedition. So Demas packed his bags and took off to Thessalonica.

There is no suggestion here that Demas became a heretic or apostate. Calvin writes:

> But we are not to suppose that he completely denied Christ and gave himself over again to ungodliness or the allurements of the world, but only that he cared more for his own convenience and safety than for the life of Paul. He could not stay with Paul without involving himself in many troubles and vexations and a real risk to his life; he was exposed to many reproaches, he was laid open to many insults, he was forced to give up caring for his own concerns, and in the circumstances he was overcome by his dislike for the cross and decided to look to his own interests.[2]

Demas had no intention of quitting his Christianity. In fact, there was a healthy body of believers in Thessalonica, and that is where he went.

Paul's assessment that it was "because he loved this world" does not make Demas a villain, but merely a man, so much like us, who came into disgrace by a well-worn path. Demas did not want to lose his Christianity, but it hurt to keep it.[3] Love for "this world," or "this present age" as the Greek literally reads, takes many shapes, depending on who and where we are. It could be shaped as comfort or take on the form of wealth or come in the contours of fame or advantage or the love of specific things.

Perhaps Demas never truly counted the cost. It may be he did not understand that when we come to Christ, we will face troubles because we will always collide with the world. Or it may be, as William Barclay has suggested, that "the years have a way of taking our ideals away, of making us satisfied with less and less, of lowering our standards. . . . There is no threat so dangerous and so insidious, as the threat of years to a man's ideals."[4] There is not a single soul that is not swayed by the lure of comfort. And the older we get, the more alluring the siren songs are. This is the short-sighted temptation to love the present world instead of Christ's appearing (cf. v. 8).

Demas' departure devastated Paul. Your deepest hurts can only come from people you love, your deepest disappointments from the destruction of your deepest hopes. What a bitter pill this was for Paul. I can testify that over years of ministry the greatest heartaches have not come from enemies but from those who began so well, who raised my hopes high, only to become lovers of this world rather than lovers of Christ.

The mention of Demas reminded Paul of two other departures that no doubt had Paul's blessing — "Crescens has gone to Galatia, and Titus to Dalmatia" (v. 10b.). Both of these had likely gone out on missions. Dalmatia was across the Adriatic Sea, and Galatia across the Aegean. Titus was the one who had given Paul the healing touch in Macedonia and whom Paul came to call "my true son" (Titus 1:4). It was right and good that these two men had gone out. But their absence heightened the apostle's need for Timothy.

Dependable Luke. Some might read "Only Luke is with me" (v. 11a) as a disparaging aside. But that was not so because Luke was the antithesis of Demas. He too had been with Demas during Paul's first imprisonment (cf. Philemon 24). He too was included in the greeting to the Colossians and was given the beautiful description, "the beloved physician" (cf. Colossians 4:14, RSV). But Luke was a tough friend for tough times. He was with Paul in prison from the first time to the last. He was Paul's biographer, and the "we" passages in Acts indicate that he was with the apostle during some of the most difficult times. Acts 27, for example, which records Paul's being taken to Rome for the last time, is a "we" passage. Luke was there!

Luke was not only Paul's Boswell — he was his traveling physician. He tended Paul's ailing bones and doctored the "thorn in [his] flesh" (2 Corinthians 12:7). His cultured Greek style has not only given us the book of Acts but the most theological of all the Gospels. Perhaps as Paul wrote his final epistle, he was concerned for Luke who had to shoulder not only care for Paul but many other details while in Rome. Likely, Luke was Paul's secretary for the writing of 2 Timothy and penned the personal, self-effacing "Only Luke" with a wry smile.

Paul is so intensely directive here. Timothy must come running from Asia — an intercontinental sprint. His arrival will form the heart of a tough team for the apostle's final days on earth. Paul knows what he needs and is not afraid to voice it.

BRING MARK (vv. 11b, 12)

Paul's second directive to Timothy was to "Get Mark and bring him with you, because he is helpful to me in my ministry" (v. 11). Mark had been a remarkably advantaged young man. His mother's home had been one of the centers of the Jerusalem church, the home to which Peter came when the angel delivered him from prison (Acts 12:12). John Mark had known all the apostles since boyhood. So when Paul embarked on his first missionary trip John Mark accompanied him as a helper on the campaign through Cyprus. But for some unknown reason he left Paul in Pamphylia and went home (Acts 13:5, 13).

Paul considered this nothing less than a desertion. And later when Barnabas wanted to let John Mark accompany them on a subsequent journey, Paul would have none of it. The argument between Paul and Barnabas was so sharp that Paul took Silas and went one way, and Barnabas took John Mark the other (Acts 15:36-40).

We have no record of exactly what happened to Mark afterward, but evidently the time with Barnabas was a time of healing because we find that Mark was again with Paul during his first Roman imprisonment: "My fellow prisoner Aristarchus sends you his greetings, as does Mark, the cousin of Barnabas" (Colossians 4:10). Paul also called him a "fellow worker" (Philemon 24). Significantly, Mark also became a veritable son to the apostle Peter (1 Peter 5:13).

And now Paul, in his time of greatest need, called for John Mark — "Bring him with you because he is helpful to me in my ministry" — meaning the ministry of the gospel, though there is probably also the idea of "personally helpful to me."[5] Mark had rocketed from uselessness to usefulness!

There is also this beautiful fact: John Mark, the missionary dropout, became St. Mark, the writer of the great action Gospel that emphasizes the servanthood of our Lord. And Mark was just the right man to write it.

What profound encouragement we find in the life of John Mark. Past failure, even rejection, does not prevent present usability. You can come back from disgrace. Not only that, you can become immensely useful to Christ. Even a shirker can become a major worker in the gospel enterprise — the kind of man or woman that the apostle would call for.

In a few months Luke, Mark, and Timothy are all going to be gathered together for Paul's departure. *That* is a tough team for tough times!

BRING MY NECESSITIES (v. 13)

Paul requested certain items he considered necessities: "When you come, bring the cloak that I left with Carpus at Troas, and my scrolls, especially the parchments" (v. 13). Paul had probably been forced to part with his cloak in Troas after his arrest. Since it is cold in Rome and getting colder, he asked for this necessity, later adding, "Do your best to get here before winter" (v. 21).

In asking for his "scrolls, especially the parchments," Paul was emphasizing that it is "the parchments," the animal-skin, precious vellum codices, that he especially wanted. Certainly this was a reference to a copy of the Old Testament Scriptures, and possibly some books containing his own personal notes.[6] Some scholars speculate that the parchments may have contained copies of the Lord's words or early narratives of his life.[7] Drew University's Thomas Oden asks some intriguing questions:

> Could they have been early Christian documents, perhaps collections of sayings of Jesus or early versions of Christian preaching or Old Testament exegesis? Could these have been the materials Luke and Mark used later to put together their Gospel accounts? . . . We do not know, but it is not a completely implausible hypothesis, in my view, that they contained early Christian literature — either of Paul's own manuscripts or of sayings of Jesus or fragments or primitive accounts of the Lord's life antedating the four Gospel writers. . . . Was Paul deliberately interested in a written record of Christ's life? Would not this be consistent with the central theme of the Pastorals — to guard the deposit of the gospel?[8]

Intriguing speculations!

WATCH OUT (vv. 14, 15)

But we do know that three important commodities were coming to Rome in the next few months, all set to arrive on the same day — Timothy, Mark, and the Scriptures! Each of these involved dangers of one kind or another. Thus the final directive: "Alexander the metalworker did me a great deal of harm. The Lord will repay him for what he has done. You too should be on your guard against him, because he strongly opposed our message" (vv. 14, 15). The harm likely came from Alexander's informing on Paul because that is what the Greek suggests. Alexander, in fact, may have been the direct cause of his arrest.[9] So Timothy and Mark must be on their guard against him.

It is clear what Paul was up to in giving such explicit directives for his final days on earth. If Timothy and Mark arrived before his execution, this may be what happened.

Strengthening. They first gave themselves to strengthening Paul. What a group of encouragers they would have been: "The beloved physician," Luke, who had always been there from the beginning and was absolutely devoted to Paul, knew the apostle better than anyone in the world. And he loved him as he loved himself. Timothy, whose early tears for Paul had so refreshed him, was Paul's spiritual son, so full of filial love, so sensitive and kind. Then there was Mark, the successful failure with such a Spirit-developed humility and a desire to serve. Oh, how Paul was strengthened for death! But it was also a two-way street because if they were there to the end, Paul would have shown them how to die. His "departure" (v. 6), his final pouring out (v. 6), went beyond words in steeling them for the future.

Theologizing. Can you imagine the theologizing that went on as these four heavyweights pored over the parchments? Together they sought out Christ in all the Scriptures (cf. Luke 24:25, 26, 44-46). They were amazed at and meditated on Jesus' use of the Word. They learned and rejoiced together.

Strategizing. Paul was the missionary general of the apostolic church, and they were his colonels. "Luke, after my death, you go to such and such a place. And, Timothy, here's what to do in Ephesus. Mark, stay close to Peter."

Perhaps they even strategized about writing. After all, the three of them wrote more than half of the New Testament! Did they discuss the Gospels that Luke and Mark later wrote? If so, what advice did Paul provide?

Tough friends for tough times! That is what we need. And that is what we must be.

33

Final Confidence

2 TIMOTHY 4:16-22

At my first defense, no one came to my support, but everyone deserted me.
May it not be held against them. But the Lord stood at my side and gave
me strength, so that through me the message might be fully proclaimed
and all the Gentiles might hear it. And I was delivered from the lion's mouth.
The Lord will rescue me from every evil attack and will bring me safely to
his heavenly kingdom. To him be glory for ever and ever. Amen. Greet
Priscilla and Aquila and the household of Onesiphorus. Erastus stayed in
Corinth, and I left Trophimus sick in Miletus. Do your best to get here before
winter. Eubulus greets you, and so do Pudens, Linus, Claudia and all the
brothers. The Lord be with your spirit. Grace be with you.

Some five years earlier Paul had returned to Jerusalem with high hopes that
his preaching would at last receive a positive hearing among his own people. In taking care to make no offense, he underwent the traditional seven
days of purification rites with several others and paid for all the expenses. But
Paul's hopes unraveled when near the end of the seven days some visiting
Jews from Asia saw Paul in the temple and grabbed him, shouting, "Men of
Israel, help us! This is the man who teaches all men everywhere against our
people and our law and this place" (Acts 21:28). Because they had seen
Trophimus the Ephesian with Paul in Jerusalem, they also wrongly accused
him of bringing Greeks into the temple. The effect was catastrophic.

The whole city was aroused, and the people came running from all
directions. Seizing Paul, they dragged him from the temple, and
immediately the gates were shut. While they were trying to kill him,
news reached the commander of the Roman troops that the whole city
of Jerusalem was in an uproar. He at once took some officers and sol-
diers and ran down to the crowd. When the rioters saw the com-
mander and his soldiers, they stopped beating Paul. (vv. 30-32)

The mob momentarily desisted as the soldiers chained the torn and bloodied prisoner. But when the soldiers attempted to take Paul up the steps to their barracks in the tower of Antonia, the violence resumed, becoming so great that the soldiers had to carry Paul through the crowd.

Here the Apostle Paul amazes us! Above the crowd at the mouth of the barracks, he began to hold forth on how he had come to preach the gospel. Hearing his flawless Aramaic, the mob quieted and listened to his epic testimony. But when he mentioned his mission to the Gentiles, they went berserk (22:21-23). Paul escaped flogging by his Roman captors only when they learned that he was a natural-born Roman citizen.

The next day, in an attempt to get to the bottom of the matter, the Roman commander arranged for Paul to speak to the Sanhedrin. Through his swollen features, "Paul looked straight at the Sanhedrin and said, 'My brothers, I have fulfilled my duty to God in all good conscience to this day'" (23:1). At this the high priest had him struck on the mouth. Again there was an uproar as Paul asserted his belief in the resurrection. The dispute became so violent that the commander was afraid Paul would be torn to pieces. So he had his troops take him by force into their barracks.

This was one of the darkest times in Paul's life. His high hopes of convincing the leadership of his people of the truth of the gospel had gone up in smoke. He also feared that his vision to take the gospel to Rome would become ashes. As he sat aching in the tower of Antonia, bloodied, black-and-blue, rejected, he needed assurance.

And Paul got it, as few mortals ever have: "The following night the Lord stood near Paul and said, 'Take courage! As you have testified about me in Jerusalem, so you must also testify in Rome'" (23:11). Christ stood by Paul not through a *vision* as had happened in Corinth (18:9) or through a *trance* as in the Jerusalem temple (22:17) but *physically* — Jesus was standing right there!

The Lord greeted Paul with one word (in the original Greek): "Courage!" (though our English Bible renders it with two — "Take courage"). How that word must have jump-started Paul's soul! Every faculty of the apostle was engaged with Jesus and was energized. Only Jesus uses this word in the New Testament, and all five instances brought wonderful comfort. He called to the bedridden paralytic, "Take heart [courage], son; your sins are forgiven" (Matthew 9:2). To the woman with the twelve-year hemorrhage he said, "Take heart [courage], daughter, your faith has healed you" (Matthew 9:22). To his frightened disciples as he came to them across the storm-tossed Sea of Galilee he said, "Take courage! It is I. Don't be afraid" (Matthew 14:27). In the Upper Room, on the night of his crucifixion, he said, "Take heart [courage]! I have overcome the world" (John 16:33). This is Christ's unique word for all who are trying to serve him, however feebly, however difficult their circumstances. To the missionary deep in the heart of suffocating pagan darkness, "Courage!" To the executive amidst the cyber-wastes of his corporate culture, "Courage!" To the young mother who is surrounded with hardened women cynical about Christianity, "Courage!"

Paul did take courage, and Paul did go to Rome as a prisoner. And during his first imprisonment, he called out, "Now I want you to know, brothers, that what has happened to me has really served to advance the gospel. Because of my chains, most of the brothers in the Lord have been encouraged to speak the word of God more courageously and fearlessly" (Philippians 1:12, 14). It was there in Rome that he first saw not the mud through the bars but the stars!

Christ's presence with him and his Savior's singular charge — "Courage" — became the refrain of Paul's incredible life. And here at the very end, it is his coda. The refrain echoes in this passage in Paul's supreme courage and confidence in death.

THE BUILDING OF PAUL'S CONFIDENCE (vv. 16, 17)

Deserted by all. Curiously, Paul relates that during his present captivity he found himself abandoned: "At my first defense, no one came to my support, but everyone deserted me" (v. 16a). The Roman judicial process initially involved what was called a "first action" (*prima actio*), a preliminary defense hearing before the emperor or a magistrate roughly equivalent in purpose to a grand jury hearing.[1] Unaccountably, this defense was a solo event for Paul. There was no witness or advocate standing forward in Paul's behalf, as the phrase "no one came to my support" clearly indicates.[2] No one was there at all! We surmise that Luke and Tychicus (who were now with Paul) were on missions or perhaps had not arrived, because otherwise they would certainly have been there. But it is a complete mystery why no members of the church in Rome, with whom he was so close, were there. Not one! Perhaps it was because of fear of the Roman authorities.

Whatever the reasons, the situation was pathetic — scandalous! Here was the great missionary general, who had weathered the storms of several continents for the gospel, standing at the end alone before the Roman court. It seems impossible, but it was a fact.

Perhaps equally remarkable was Paul's attitude — "May it not be held against them" (v. 16b). No bitterness here — only a prayer for forgiveness. How like Jesus he was.

Attended by Jesus. Paul had been abandoned by his friends but not by Jesus: "But the Lord stood at my side and gave me strength, so that through me the message might be fully proclaimed and all the Gentiles might hear it. And I was delivered from the lion's mouth" (v. 17).

As to whether Jesus again stood with Paul physically as he had in the tower of Antonia in Jerusalem, we do not know. The language certainly can be read that way (though this took place in the public Roman court). On the other hand this was not necessarily literal. Paul still had the magnificent memory of Jesus' physical visitation on that earlier occasion. The Lord's greeting — "Courage!" — still rang as loudly as it had in that tower, as did the Savior's subsequent prophecy ("As you have testified about me in Jerusalem, so you must also testify in Rome," Acts 23:11). And now he was in Rome just as Jesus had said!

Paul knew his Old Testament well. He knew Psalm 139:

> *If I go up to the heavens, you are there;*
> *if I make my bed in the depths, you are there.*
> *If I rise on the wings of the dawn,*
> *if I settle on the far side of the sea,*
> *even there your hand will guide me,*
> *your right hand will hold me fast.*
>
> *(vv. 8-10)*

Paul never thought of God as spatially near or remote. He knew that God is "not here or there but carried here or there in his heart" (A. W. Tozer).[3]

That visit to Paul in Antonia by Jesus was a reprise of what had happened some 600 years before to Shadrach, Meshach, and Abednego in their captivity. Remember their response to Nebuchadnezzar's threat to throw them into the fiery furnace? "The God we serve is able to save us from it, and he will rescue us from your hand, O king. But even if he does not, we want you to know, O king, that we will not serve your gods or worship the image of gold you have set up" (Daniel 3:17, 18). And do you remember what Nebuchadnezzar saw? "Look! I see four men walking around in the fire, unbound and unharmed, and the fourth looks like a son of the gods" (3:25). I am sure Paul connected with this. The same Son was with him in *his* distress!

Moreover, Christ was in him, and he was in Christ. For Paul, being aware of Christ's presence was as natural as breathing. The wondrous reality was that the Lord was at Paul's side as he stood before imperial Rome at his first hearing and that, in Paul's words, he "gave me strength" — or as A. T. Robertson renders it, "poured power into me"[4] (cf. Philippians 4:13). It was as if a pair of jumper cables were attached to Christ and then to Paul, so that Jesus' voltage poured into Paul.

Paul's spirit filled and expanded with God's power, "so that," Paul says, "through me the message might be fully proclaimed [literally, "completed or fulfilled"[5]] and all the Gentiles might hear it" (v. 17b). Paul saw this opportunity of preaching the gospel in the official center of Rome, the mistress of the nations, as the fulfilling of his call.[6] So he gave the court both barrels! His message was probably something like what he delivered before Felix in Acts 24, and then to Agrippa in Acts 26, to which Agrippa responded, "'Do you think that in such a short time you can persuade me to be a Christian?' Paul replied, 'Short time or long — I pray God that not only you but all who are listening to me today may become what I am, except for these chains'" (vv. 28, 29). Paul was awesome as he preached with Christ at his side — for the Savior poured power into him!

The result was, says Paul, "And I was delivered from the lion's mouth" (v. 17c) — that is, from death. While preaching before the court, his head had been in the proverbial lion's mouth. The court's jaws could easily have snapped shut. Instead, the court held that there must be a subsequent hearing, and Paul thus had a temporary reprieve.

There is something else remarkable here, in that Paul's reference to the lion's mouth is substantial evidence that as he faced death on this occasion he was meditating on Psalm 22, the same Psalm that occupied Jesus at his death. The text here resounds with allusions to Psalm 22: 1) Verse 16, "everyone deserted me," alludes to Psalm 22:1, "why have you forsaken me?" 2) Verse 16, "no one came to my support," references Psalm 22:11, "there is no one to help." 3) Verse 17, "I was delivered from the lion's mouth," alludes to Psalm 22:21, "Rescue me from the mouth of the lions." 4) Verse 17, "and all the Gentiles might hear it," is similar to Psalm 22:27, "All the ends of the earth will remember and turn to the LORD." 5) Verse 18, "and will bring me safely to his heavenly kingdom," echoes Psalm 22:28, "dominion belongs to the LORD."[7] The old apostle was filled with the Word so that he was like a lion — confident and regal.

THE DECLARATION OF PAUL'S CONFIDENCE (v. 18)

Paul did not expect acquittal — he was certain of death (cf. v. 6). But he looked death straight in the face and roared with confidence: "The Lord will rescue me from every evil attack and will bring me safely to his heavenly kingdom. To him be glory for ever and ever. Amen" (v. 18).

Confident of rescue. His confidence — "the Lord will rescue me from every evil attack" — was not an expectation of deliverance from death but rather that no evil attack would undermine his faith or his courage or cause him to lapse into disastrous sin. Furthermore, this death would deliver him once and for all from all evil. It appears that Paul had been praying the sixth petition of the Lord's Prayer — "but deliver us from evil" (KJV) — and was confident that would happen in his life and at his martyrdom.

Confident of Heaven. Death held in one of its hands his deliverance, but in the other hand his destination — Heaven — "and will bring me safely to his heavenly kingdom" (literally, "and will save me into his heavenly kingdom" [8]). Paul calls it a "heavenly kingdom" because he was already in Christ's kingdom, but this would be the heavenly aspect.

Such soaring, roaring confidence came primarily from Paul's belief in God's Word. God's holy Word was both his life and his food (cf. Deuteronomy 32:45-47; Matthew 4:4). His confidence in the Word was like that of Jesus himself. His confidence was also shored by his long experience in following God. Paul's yesterdays were prophecies of his tomorrows! And his tomorrows with Christ would be like his todays with Christ.

Everyone expects the sun to rise tomorrow and for millions of years to come. Yet there will come a day when it will not rise. There will be a last time, the very last.[9] But Christ and his Word will not change. They will remain the same forever. Paul had terminal and yet unending confidence!

His doxology. Paul's heart was such that nearly every time he discoursed on God's power and goodness, he burst into a doxology, just as he did here: "To him be glory for ever and ever. Amen" (v. 18b). "To him" refers back to "the Lord," a title for Christ, which makes this and Romans 9:5 the only doxologies offered to Christ.[10] As Paul looked at his imminent death, Christ filled his horizon. Christ would give him "the crown of righteousness" (v. 8). He would be with Christ, "which is better by far" (Philippians 1:23). It was Christ who held his citizenship and who would transform his lowly body so that it "will be like his glorious body" (Philippians 3:20, 21). To Christ be glory for ever and ever. Amen! Let it be, Lord, let it be!

FINAL GRACES (vv. 19-22)

Names were important to Paul, and he knew that the mention of names assured his friends of their significance. He greeted the extraordinary "Priscilla and Aquila," who had served with him in Corinth, Ephesus, and Rome and were now back in Ephesus. Significantly he greeted not "Onesiphorus" but his "household" (cf. 1:16). Had that man died on his way home after refreshing Paul? We do not know. Paul then conveyed personal knowledge about "Erastus" and "Trophimus" to Timothy. Timothy would know what to do.

"Do your best to get here before winter" was not a primary reference to Paul's discomfort from the cold but to the ancient shipping lanes, which were considered closed to traffic from November 10 to March 10. Paul had once been shipwrecked when his ship tried to beat the season.[11] It was now or never!

Timothy surely took the now and was there with Luke and John Mark when (if Clement of Rome is correct) Paul was taken outside the city and beheaded at the Ostian Gate.

> *But looking upward, full of grace*
> *He prayed, and from a happy place*
> *God's glory smote him on the face.*
>   *(Tennyson)*

Paul conveyed greetings from some members of the Roman church. Only one is known, and that is "Linus" who almost certainly succeeded Peter as leader of the Roman church, according to Irenaeus in *Against Heresies* 3:3.[12]

Now come the very final written words of the Apostle Paul — a benediction and an expression of grace.

The benediction — "The Lord be with your spirit" — is in the singular, being for Timothy alone. "Timothy, may the Lord Christ Jesus be with your human spirit." Timothy would carry that blessing to the end.

The expression of grace — "Grace be with you" — is in the plural, being for the Christian community. Every one of Paul's benedictions contains the word *grace*.[13] So Paul's terminal word and wish was that God's unmerited favor, forgiveness, and enabling power would be showered upon his children.

"Grace be with you."

Soli Deo gloria!

Titus

34

A Greeting of Grace

TITUS 1:1-4

Paul, a servant of God and an apostle of Jesus Christ for the faith of God's elect and the knowledge of the truth that leads to godliness — a faith and knowledge resting on the hope of eternal life, which God, who does not lie, promised before the beginning of time, and at his appointed season he brought his word to light through the preaching entrusted to me by the command of God our Savior, to Titus, my true son in our common faith: Grace and peace from God the Father and Christ Jesus our Savior.

I took a deep breath and plunged into the conversation. My sons were in their early teens and thus facing all the angst, trials, and temptations of adolescence — and they were in trouble. We were having this talk because there had been a problem and we needed to address it. After the conversation my wife and I discussed what had happened. Kathy said, "I feel so terrible that even in our family we have to deal with such things." I well understood her feelings, but I also felt strangely exhilarated. I said to her, "I feel as though I have been preparing for years to have that conversation with my sons." As a result of the disciplining talk, I got to tell my sons that I love them, and because I love them I must teach them to steer clear of things that can damage their lives. At the same time I told them I understood what they had experienced since I am a man who is subject to similar challenges and temptations. I shared with them experiences — both positive and negative — in my life in order to caution them about dangerous paths and to remind them of the beauty of God's plan when we honor his commands.

"My sons," I said, "let's consider this situation an opportunity to confess to each other that because we are all men, such things appeal to us even though they can damage us, and let's keep challenging one another to grow in godliness in order to experience the goodness God wants for us. Most of all, though, I want you to know that even when you have failed the Lord, you can ask his forgiveness because he loves you even more than I do."

Dealing with adolescent problems gave me an opportunity to pull back the curtain that can exist between parents and children and to show my sons my parental plan for their lives. I want them to know God's grace, to grow in godliness, and to respect the relationships that can help them know his goodness now and in the future.

My goal for my sons in this conversation was similar to Paul's in his letter to Titus, whom the apostle calls, "my true son in our common faith" (v. 4). Much as I was seeking to prepare my children for adulthood, the apostle writes to this young pastor on the island of Crete to prepare him for mature ministry that will include its own challenges, fears, and temptations. Through the apostle's words we gain an understanding of what God requires of those who would provide leadership in the local church. In essence, Paul pulls back the curtain between Heaven and earth to show us God's plan for mature ministry. Even the opening verses that contain the apostle's greeting indicate priorities that should characterize those who serve God by leading others: embrace grace, love godliness, and share Christ.

EMBRACE GRACE

The dimensions of grace that Christian leaders must embrace are spelled out as the apostle describes his own person, purpose, and message. Each description highlights an aspect of the grace of God.

Grace's Measure (v. 1a)

Though the opening salutation is longer than in most of Paul's letters, it still almost goes by too quickly for us to catch its full implications. Paul identifies himself as "a servant of God and an apostle of Jesus Christ" (v. 1). This zealous Jewish leader had always seen himself as a servant of God, but the service he had offered earlier in life was designed to establish his own status and station before God. In arrogant pursuit of his own righteousness, Paul had become an enemy of Jesus Christ—denying the necessity of the Savior's sacrifice, breathing out threats against his church, and participating in the murder of his people (see Acts 7:58; 9:1-4; 22:4, 5; 26:9-11). Now this same persecutor calls himself "an apostle [i.e., a chosen messenger] of Jesus Christ." That the Savior would and could use Paul reminds us of *the measure of God's grace: very great*. God will pardon the worst sinners and will grant useful service to those whose sin is monstrous, though there is no human reason for such divine love.

Grace's Means (v. 1b)

Paul furthers the message of unconditional care by explaining the purpose of his apostleship. He is an apostle of Jesus Christ "for the faith of God's elect and the knowledge of the truth that leads to godliness" (v. 1b). This extremely compact language explicitly reminds us of the means of grace. Paul does not tell others what they must *do* to qualify as God's elect but rather speaks of the "faith" that characterizes those who are God's. Those who believe are "God's elect," meaning their eternal status is determined by the love of a heavenly heart and not by the work of human hands.

The term *elect* here and elsewhere (e.g., Romans 8:33; 16:13; Colossians 3:12; 1 Timothy 5:21; 2 Timothy 2:10) reminds us that God chooses his people to be his own out of his mercy rather than because they have achieved some mysterious level of holiness. To emphasize the point, Paul says that "the knowledge of the truth" (words in Scripture that are more about being in a convinced and committed relationship with God than about having a head full of religious facts; cf. 1 Timothy 2:4; 2 Timothy 2:25; 3:7; Hebrews 10:26) leads to godliness. The order is absolutely essential to note. Godly conduct itself does not lead to a relationship with God. Rather, the relationship with God that gospel faith establishes leads to righteous actions. God is not waiting to love us until we have gotten our own lives straightened out. Thus Paul makes clear *the means of grace: mercy alone.*

Grace's Duration (vv. 2, 3)

The duration of that mercy is another mark of God's grace. When he speaks of the "faith and knowledge" that are his purpose, Paul adds that these "rest on the hope of eternal life, which God, who does not lie, promised before the beginning of time" (v. 2). The convinced commitment of the Christian rests on our confidence (i.e., Biblical "hope") in the Biblical assurance that God grants a perfect relationship with himself to his people that extends infinitely beyond this life (cf. John 3:16; Romans 5:21; 6:23; 1 Timothy 1:16; 6:12). Paul goes on to say that at the "appointed season" (i.e., his present time) God brought this truth to light through the preaching entrusted to and commanded of Paul (v. 3). This is a quick reminder of Paul's specific commission to preach the message of God's grace to the Gentiles (cf. Acts 9:15; 26:15-18; Romans 1:16-18; Galatians 2:8). However, the apostle wants Titus to be certain of an even more encompassing truth: Though the message of grace for all the nations of the world comes through the apostle, it did not originate with him or in his time.

The picture being drawn by Paul's words is remarkable. He uses the cross-road in time marked by his own ministry to let us look both ways down the highway of God's grace. Not only does he point out that the highway of God's mercy for his people extends eternally into the future but also observes that God, "who does not lie" (as opposed to the Cretans who oppose him, v. 12), made the promise of eternal life "before the beginning of time" (v. 2). Grace began in eternity, and it extends to eternity. We do not have to worry about exhausting the supply of God's mercy because of *the duration of grace: forever*.

Grace's Effect (v. 4)

What is the effect of this grace that is so great, merciful, and enduring? It unites all believers in mutual dependence upon God regardless of experience or background. Paul speaks of Titus as his "true son in our common faith" and then offers him the blessing of "grace and peace from God the Father and Christ Jesus our Savior" (v. 4). Paul looks past the ancient antipathies between Jews (of which he is one) and Gentiles (of which Titus is one) and says that they are of the same faith and family. They are united in "grace and peace" that come from "our" Savior, meaning that they share a mutual need of being rescued by the work of another rather than by their own actions.

This "grace and peace" wording appears so often at the opening of Paul's epistles (with only slight variations) that its importance cannot be overestimated. When persons become absolutely convinced that their standing before God is based entirely on his grace and not on any goodness in themselves, peace comes. This peace that Christ's reconciliation provides is not only the end of antipathy between a rebellious heart and its Creator. Full understanding of grace also provides relief from the constant striving for status and affection that characterizes the natural human state. Assessments of who is more deserving of God's affection or acclaim go away in the recognition that "all . . . fall short of the glory of God" (Romans 3:23). Competition for recognition and regard fades in the realization that all the rewards of grace are unearned. We become equal members of the fellowship of those whose condition is desperate apart from Christ, and this humbling realization is the foundation of Christian harmony.

Our "common faith" — the recognition that all are in need of a Savior — removes any rationale for judgmentalism and any basis for pride. The need for comparison and competition dies in the recognition that Christ provides our only measure of glory before God. The necessity of Christ's pardon of us all prompts forgiveness, understanding, and love in the Christian community. Among conscientious Christians even the barriers of racial prejudice, national hatred, and ancient antipathies wither when the realities of grace blossom. This is evident when the former Pharisee named Paul calls a Gentile named Titus "my true son." That simple endearment powerfully states *the effect of grace: family unity*.

Grace's Application

Each dimension of the grace revealed in Paul's salutation to Titus reminds today's church leaders of the solace we must offer to those who have failed

God or fear they will. For the person who says, "My sin is too large or has persisted too long for God to forgive," we must say, "But his grace is great." For the sensitive soul that despairs in the face of personal weakness saying, "I am not able to measure up to God's requirements," we respond, "God does not save you on the basis of your ability but bestows his grace by mercy alone." For the tormented realist who says, "I can resist temptation for a while, but I cannot guarantee that I will maintain my resolve," we offer the assurance, "But his grace is forever." For the timid who fear, "I will not fit in," we share Christ's embrace, saying, "The grace of God our Father unites you to our family."

Each dimension of the grace Paul reveals not only answers the cry of sinners but reveals the nature of God. Paul characterizes the "grace and peace" of which he speaks as being "from God the Father and Christ Jesus our Savior" (v. 4). The sudden reference to the members of the Godhead may seem abrupt unless we recognize that the preceding discussion of grace has prepared us to see the significance of the divine references. Recently I was examined for a new pair of eyeglasses. I went through the process of reading an eye chart while the ophthalmologist dropped a series of lenses into a frame put before my eyes. As the proper lenses were sequentially dropped into the frame, the images on the chart became more and more clear. A similar process occurs in these opening verses. Each dimension of grace disclosed by the apostle acts as a lens to further reveal the features of God. Through the characteristics of his grace, we learn that God is great, merciful, eternal, and fatherlike.

What should happen when we see these features of the God of grace so clearly? To answer, consider what always happens when the people of God see him.

- When Isaiah saw the Lord on his throne high and exalted, he said, "Woe to me. . . . For I am a man of unclean lips, and I live among a people of unclean lips, and my eyes have seen the King, the LORD Almighty" (see Isaiah 6:5).
- When Moses approached the burning bush and understood that he was looking upon the great I AM, the future leader of Israel hid his face (Exodus 3:6).
- When Job ultimately faced the greatness of God, he said, "My ears had heard of you but now my eyes have seen you. Therefore I despise myself and repent in dust and ashes" (Job 42:5, 6).

Clear sight of God brings a keen awareness of sin, deep humility, and an intense desire to remove any source of shame from before the face of the Holy One.

It seems almost counterintuitive that a great vision of grace would bring a great commitment to holiness, but this is precisely what happens in the heart of the true believer. Paul will drive home the theme of grace-engendered holiness again and again in this book. His emphasis indicates the next priority that should characterize the ministry of Titus and today's Christian leaders.

LOVE GODLINESS

The ongoing verses of Paul's letter to Titus not only provide a greeting; they also set up the overall theme and content of the entire letter. Thus, in order to grasp the flow and purpose of this pastoral epistle, we will use these introductory words as a chart to navigate our study of all the material that will follow. As the letter unfolds, Paul will repeatedly press the theme of his opening words — "the faith . . . and the knowledge of the truth that *leads to godliness*" (v. 1, italics added). Godliness does not qualify us for faith, but Christian faith properly understood is lived. The grace that true faith receives stimulates a desire for godliness in believers, and this is no less true of their leaders. Thus the grace of Scripture never slights sin, never excuses laxity, never abandons the separated life, but always seeks the greater glory of the Savior.

The Key to Understanding (1:1 as Theme)

For Paul, the doctrine that rightly teaches the good news of Christ does not minimize the requirements of godly living but becomes precisely the motivation and foundation for such a life. Grasping this doctrine (i.e., that grace compels godliness) provides a necessary key to understanding much of the instruction that follows throughout this epistle.

> • Paul directs Titus to "appoint elders in every town" (v. 5) who "hold firmly to the message as it has been taught . . . [to] encourage others by sound doctrine" (v. 9). But it is not enough that an elder assent to sound doctrine. He must also live in accord with it. Thus an elder is characterized as "hospitable," "one who loves what is good," "self-controlled, upright, holy, and disciplined" (v. 8).
>
> • Elders must live in contrast to the false teachers in Crete who "claim to know God, but by their actions they deny him" (v. 16). Because grace never denies the need for obedience, actions must conform to expressed faith.
>
> • Elders must even demonstrate their deep knowledge of the gospel's truth in the way that their children's lives demonstrate consistency between faith and conduct. The children of elders must "believe," but they must also "not [be] open to the charge of being wild and disobedient" (v. 6).

• Titus himself is charged to "*teach* what is in accord with sound doctrine" (2:1, italics added). Then readers learn what is in accord with sound doctrine — teaching older men to be "worthy of respect" as well as "sound in faith (2:2), teaching older women to be "reverent in the way they live" (2:3), teaching younger women to be "self-controlled" and "pure" (2:5), teaching younger men to be "self-controlled" (2:6).

• Titus himself must not only teach these things but in everything must also set "an example by doing what is good" (2:7). What one believes must reflect in the way one lives, even for the teacher, Titus.

• Finally, the apostle, who has called himself "a servant [slave] of God" (v. 1), says that even slaves must "not . . . talk back" (2:9) and "not . . . steal" (v. 10), so that "in every way they will make the teaching about God our Savior attractive" (v. 10).

Life must conform to doctrine. The message is the same for leaders and servants, parents and children, male and female, young and old: Grace should produce godliness. At the end of Paul's numerous examples, the apex statement of this truth appears: "For the grace of God that brings salvation has appeared to all men. It teaches us to say, 'No,' to ungodliness and worldly passions . . ." (2:11, 12).

With the theme repeated so often, some readers might have grown tired of the message that a right understanding of grace leads to godliness. "Move this sermon along, preacher," they might think as they listen to Paul driving the point home from so many different angles. The reason for the apostle's persistence in this epistle to Titus, however, can be detected in a letter I received not long ago from another young preacher. He wrote:

It is with a heavy heart of discouragement that I write this letter. . . . I am so troubled at the number of men who are falling in ministry. I always knew that this happened, but these are no longer statistics, they are close friends and mentors that I have had in ministry. I look at these men who have walked far longer and deeper with God than I have, and I wonder how in the world will I be expected to make it if they did not. Most fell because of sexual immorality, others left under clouds of suspicion. In the last three weeks I have been told of four ministers, all friends of mine who have had to resign from ministry. . . . I fear becoming another statistic and watching my family suffer for my sin. Please forgive me for dumping these burdens on you, but at this point I doubt myself so much that I am not sure what is true and what is not.

When the message of the gospel comes unglued from godliness, faith shatters. No matter how commendable our intentions may be, the message of grace apart from godliness — or godly endeavor apart from an understanding of grace — destroys the hope that the gospel offers. This truth was powerfully and sadly demonstrated in the lives of many of my young minister friends after we graduated from seminary. As pastors in training we often challenged each other with the phrase, "We will live for the glory of God." Though the words sounded noble, they damaged us. What we were really saying to one another in our youthful zeal was that we would strengthen our resolve, bow our necks, and through our own goodness and grit march the kingdom of God forward. The focus was not upon our need for a dependence on grace but upon our personal determination to live more godly lives than those who had preceded us.

The results were devastating. We could not measure up to our own standards. Of those who graduated with me, very few are still in ministry. Many fell to sexual immorality, relational incompetence, or dishonesty. By trying to live godly lives without due focus upon God's pardoning and enabling grace, we had no protection from the despair that our own weaknesses and hypocrisies created. Such joylessness only exacerbated spiritual weaknesses that robbed us of spiritual health and credible ministry. Only those who discovered the power of grace found the strength to continue in ministry.

For these reasons, much ministry training in recent years has endeavored to follow Paul's example in making grace the foundation of pastoral training. As the epistle to Titus makes plain, Biblical grace spiritually strengthens for ministry by enabling leaders to acknowledge weakness and to depend upon the mercy of God rather than upon the strength of personal resolve. Because of the necessary bond between grace and godliness, however, these recent emphases upon grace will fail if they are interpreted so as to allow an easy familiarity with sin and/or the compromising habits of one's culture. Faith and knowledge of the truth that does not lead to godliness leads to sin and to doubting the most precious aspects of faith.

Crosscurrents of Conduct (1:1 and 1:10ff.)

Those who embrace grace must also learn to love piety, which is the fruit and fuller confirmation of the gospel in our hearts. Paul's challenging words caution, however, that such a love of piety is not automatic in those who speak of grace. Believers can get caught in the crosscurrents of attitudes about grace and godliness that tend to be present even in very healthy churches. Due to the evangelistic efforts of healthy churches, a portion of the congregation will probably have little Christian background. As they enter the life of the church, such persons will passionately and sometimes painfully assimilate (by formal instruction and by observation of others around them) what godliness means in terms of family relationships, material priorities, and personal habits. These new Christians probably will question whether what they have long allowed in their lives should now be rejected in terms of the entertainments they seek, the places where they socialize, worship observance, language, dress, monetary priorities, racial attitudes, child-rearing practices, and a host of other daily life issues.

While these newly churched persons are "putting on" the practices of daily obedience and holy living through questioning what they have long allowed, there are those long in the church who may be "putting off" what seem to be similar practices. Such persons may have followed a legalistic code of conduct for many years on the premise that adherence to such a code qualifies one to be a Christian — much as Paul's opponents taught on Crete (cf. v. 10ff.). When these long-churched persons finally understand that what God has done in Christ (rather than what they do in their own strength) is the sole basis of their hope, they may also question whether what they have long rejected is now acceptable. Such persons often begin to experiment with new patterns of conduct in terms of their language, dress, entertainments, and places to socialize. In certain sad cases, under the rationale that "We are now under grace," these people not only reject improper legalisms but also cast off standards of conduct that have long protected them from serious sin.

Where do Christians find balance so as not to get swamped by the cross-currents of those trying to put on the habits of legitimate Christian conduct and those trying to put off the baggage of false Christian codes? Paul explains by reminding us of the place and the importance of our conduct.

The Place of Our Conduct (1:10-16)

The apostle makes statements in this opening chapter that may have sounded very dangerous to the traditionalists in the church at Crete — for example, "To the pure, all things are pure, but to those who are corrupted and do not believe, nothing is pure" (v. 15). Does this mean for Paul that as long as you have claimed the grace of God, anything goes? Has Paul lost all concern for establishing standards of conduct? These statements must be placed in the context of Paul's condemnation of those in "the circumcision group" (v. 10). From Paul's comments here and other passages as well, we know that this group claimed that one's relationship with God is based upon the observance of certain ceremonial codes and cleanliness practices (cf. Galatians 2:12). Of those in this group Paul says, "Both their minds and consciences are corrupted. They claim to know God, but by their actions they deny him. They are detestable, disobedient and unfit for doing anything good" (vv. 15, 16). The apostle's strident terms should annul any thought that he has no concern about godly obedience.

Still, we wonder how Paul can say "all things are pure" and then be concerned that some people are being disobedient. The answer lies in the understanding that the apostle will annul the legitimacy of all codes that in themselves claim to make us holy or profane to God. Our conduct is *not* what makes us God's. Only grace does. In very strong terms Paul says any other claim is a lie that must be silenced because those who make such claims are rebelling against the truth of the gospel (vv. 10-13, 16). Conduct cannot be placed prior to or above grace in establishing our relationship with God. This does not mean conduct is unimportant. Grace has an effect upon its objects. Those who learn that God's love for them originates in forever past, extends to forever future, is proclaimed now at the command of God, required the blood of Christ, and allows repentance without fear of rejection will desire to honor the One who loves them so. Where such a desire does not exist, the presence of grace has no proof for the watching world or for one's own heart.

The Importance of Our Conduct (1:6 — 2:10)

Because grace leads to godliness, Paul will also say in the strongest terms that those who have real knowledge of the truth do not live as the world does. No code of conduct makes us God's, but lives indistinguishable from those not touched by grace deny the reality of God's work in us. The apostle will particularly stress that an elder in the church must live an exemplary life because he is "entrusted with God's work" (1:7). He should always remain conscious that the life of grace constantly seeks to glorify God for his unmerited kindness. This is not only true of church elders whose faith and life requirements are detailed (1:6-9) but also should characterize every other Christian whose life influences others (2:2-10) — older men and women, younger men and women, children, and servants. The conduct of all in the church should radically differ from those who are of the world. Something is radically wrong when believers' lives vary little from the unbelievers around them.

SHARE CHRIST

Knowing that our conduct is important leads to questions of how and why believers live as God requires. As Paul details his answer throughout this epistle, he not only organizes the actions of those in the church but also mobilizes their efforts for reaching those outside the church. Godliness springs from grace and spreads it. Thus we learn that Christian leaders have the mandate, and the privilege, to multiply the gospel as well as to reflect it. The multiplication efforts for which leaders are responsible involve more than the recitation of an evangelism plan. Verbal expression of what we believe is certainly included in what the apostle expects, but something far more encompassing is his real concern. All of what we are in Christ should express his love to others as godly living actually becomes the vehicle by which we take responsibility for the well-being of others in the Christian community and for witness to those outside the church.

Taking Responsibility for Community (1:1, 5 — 3:11)

Paul says that he is "a servant of God" and "an apostle of Jesus Christ" for "God's elect" (v. 1). Paul does not see his privileged position as intended for his benefit alone. He was called *for* the sake of others in the Christian community. Paul's service orientation is not supposed to be unique. All those addressed in his epistle have responsibilities for others:

- Titus's mission is to appoint other elders (1:5).
- The elders' mission is to encourage and instruct others (1:9).
- The sin of false teachers was their ruin of others (1:11).
- Older men, older women, younger women, and younger men were to set examples that influence others (2:1-8).
- Slaves are to order their conduct so as to promote the spiritual well-being of their masters (2:9, 10).
- External community attack is to be blunted by respectful and responsible behavior among all in the church (3:1-8).
- Internal community divisiveness is to be avoided and disciplined (3:9-11).

Against the tendency in our culture to privatize faith, these expectations of the apostle remind us that God does not intend for us to live our faith alone, i.e., in isolation from others. Though wonderful personal benefits accompany our relationship with Christ, his interests are not restricted to any one person. Our lives touch others and as a necessary consequence either communicate good or ill — more or less of Christ. A mark of maturity in believers is their sense of responsibility for others in the church community.

A teen recently approached a friend of mine who had just assumed leadership of a church youth group with a history of problems. Said the teen, "I will give you six months to get this youth group's act together or I'm out of here." The starkness of that consumer approach to a church's ministry strikes us as immature, but why? The young person was saying in essence, "I want a quality youth program." There is no sin in this. We cannot fault him for wanting to have a satisfying church experience. The problem is not in the teen's desire to be fed spiritually but in failing to see his own responsibility for spiritually nourishing others.

Paul's critiques of the false teachers in Crete make it clear that he had left Titus in a difficult situation (see 1:10-16). Titus's perseverance in that situation reminds us that the goal of our faith is larger than our personal benefit.

Were all of Christ's people to say, "Satisfy me or I'm out of here," then the church of Jesus Christ would never grow as God intends. Someone has to plow, water, fertilize, plan for the harvest — and faithfully pick up after the hailstorms.

Almost all begin the Christian life with the perspective that their walk with Christ is just between themselves and God. However, before we are equipped to lead in the church, a sense of responsibility for our community must mature in us. Such a sense of responsibility does not suddenly pop into our heart when we complete a leadership training seminar or even collect a seminary diploma. Whatever community of believers we currently share — whether it is in an academic, institutional, or social setting — is a training ground for the development of a heart of concern for others. If we limit our interest and involvement in such a community to what benefits us, we will stunt the growth of a mature faith in ourselves and will also deny the spiritual community the gifts we possess that would further its ministry. A commitment to sharing the blessings of Christ cannot develop by always deferring concern for others to some future evangelistic encounter. By giving our time, sharing our wealth, praying for the needy, forgiving each other, and living godly lives for the sake of one another in the church, we develop the selfless attitudes and expansive hearts that are necessary for effective witness to those outside the church.

The pursuit of godliness within the Christian community in some measure reflects one's willingness to take responsibility for the spiritual support of others. Striving for godliness indicates awareness that our choices, habits, example, and entertainments are instructing others. Because each Christian's life influences others in the church, we cannot view ourselves as living an autonomous life of faith. Though no particular action merits us God's love, we who know we are not responsible for ourselves alone are bound by the law of love (see Romans 13:10). Thus we should examine every aspect of our conduct not only in the context of whether we have a right to do it, but also in consideration of whether the action is loving toward others in our Christian community, given what we know about their needs, strengths, and weaknesses (see Romans 14:13-21; 1 Corinthians 8:9-13; 9:19-23).

Being only a taker or a consumer in a Christian community impoverishes one's own spiritual experience and that of others. Taking responsibility for community spiritually enriches oneself and others. These truths shone clearly in the life of the spouse of a ministry student who came to the United States for theological training after growing up in a communist dictatorship. Today this wife radiates joy and encouragement to others at the seminary where her husband studies. Some months ago I asked her about her remarkable radiance. I related that our seminary's experience with those who have grown up in oppressed countries is that they often are suspicious of authority, embittered by their deprivations, and abrasively manipulative with peers. I asked why she was so different.

She smiled and said that in her first few months here her attitude and actions had been as I described. She believed that American Christians were materialistic hypocrites who constantly compromised with the world because they had never faced persecution or sacrificed for their faith. She was angry about having to leave her homeland to study in a land so full of compromised believers.

What changed her was her need for others. She knew no English when her husband brought her here for his studies. Without language skills she was marooned in the loneliness of her apartment. So oppressive became the isolation that she ventured to take a seminary course with her husband in order to learn English and have some social contact. The course she chose to take, oddly enough, was New Testament Greek. Being a natural linguist, she managed to figure out the intricacies of English by hearing how the professor used it to explain Greek grammar. As remarkable as that ability was, more remarkable was what she learned from the New Testament when she studied her Greek — grace.

Reading the New Testament with the intensity her language studies required, she began to understand for the first time that God loves solely on the basis of his mercy, and not on the basis of our goodness. As a result, the Lord convicted her of the sin of her judgmental spirit that had so embittered her toward Americans (though their sin is undeniable), since she too was dependent upon God's mercy. As she began to realize the wonders of his grace, this young woman began to pray that God would lead her to others in the seminary community who were as lonely or isolated as she had been so she could share his love with them. New to the culture, hardly knowing English, and theologically naïve, no one would have had a better excuse than this young woman for simply absorbing what the faith community could offer her. Instead, she gave of herself in order to seek out the hurting, open her home, and ultimately begin a seminary choir to help those in the community share their gifts with each other. Soon she will return to her home country with her husband for a ministry of evangelism. Few here doubt her usefulness in that endeavor because the heart of care that developed in her community efforts is the kind of heart that God uses to reach others with the message of his love.

Taking Responsibility for Witness (1:1 and 2:10)

Through the conduct of those in the community of believers, God shapes hearts of concern for his most expansive purposes. Paul reflects these purposes in the opening words of this epistle as he calls himself "a servant [i.e., a slave] of God." Only one class of believers is directly instructed in this epistle to order their actions so as to make the faith credible to those outside the Christian community. Paul says that slaves must be responsible and faithful to their masters, "so that in every way they [i.e., the slaves] will make the teaching about God our Savior attractive" (2:10).

We tend to think that slaves should be more concerned about their own freedom rights than their witness to their masters. However, important as those rights are — as is always the case with those who have been truly captured by grace — gospel responsibilities take priority over personal rights. By identifying himself as a slave (Paul uses the same Greek word for "servant" or "slave" in 1:1 and 2:9) of God's purposes, the apostle not only identifies himself with the status of those suffering in the Christian community, but he also elevates their responsibility to the equivalent of his own. The message is clear: No matter what one's social ranking, there is no higher calling than making one's life a witness for the gospel of Christ. Furthermore, a chief means for this witness is constraint upon one's personal conduct as a tool of witness for those who do not yet find the gospel credible.

Limiting personal priorities and preferences for the sake of the credibility of the gospel is not a comfortable message today. We are a generation that even in preparing for ministry can become fixated on what will advance one's personal career — salary, comfort, position. Considering ministry where our service is needed rather than where our wants will be serviced has never been more important or difficult. The letter to Titus is a timely challenge to sense newly and deeply how important the gospel is for those who are in danger of Hell and who need to witness that gospel in the lives of God's people and their leaders.

PLAN FOR MINISTRY

Ultimately, Paul sees those of us in the church as responsible for sharing the message of God's grace to those outside the community by the love our lives evidence. This final dimension of our responsibility completes God's plan for mature ministry as outlined by the apostle for Titus. The plan encourages all in ministry to:

> • Embrace grace for the hope of Heaven it offers and the clarity of God it brings.
> • Love godliness for the beauty it gives our lives and the path to God it offers others.
> • Share Christ with our community and through hearts thus made caring for the lost.

I witnessed the beautiful reality of this plan one Sunday when I received word that Clifford, one of the elders in a church I had pastored, was now struggling with terminal cancer. Later that same day I participated in the installation service for a new minister in a new church. While preparing for that service I was struck by the realization that the new church, its expanding ministry, and even the young man assuming the pastorate were all products of Clifford's care. All his life he had been a leader in the historic church that I had pastored all of his adult life. Clifford had weathered immature pastors, divisions in the church, boring sermons, countless prayer meetings in his home, Sunday school class preparations beyond number, disappointing pet projects of passing youth ministers, petty accusations of disaffected members, exhausting discipline cases, draining session meetings, and not a few weddings and funerals of friends both close and distant. Once when there was a shortage of deacons in the church, Clifford even resigned his elder position for a time so the deacon board would have enough members to mow the grass, sweep the snow, and care for the mission budget.

By any human estimate one of the chief reasons this long-lived church had survived its many conflicts, disappointments, and crises was the faithfulness of Clifford. He was simply one of those people whom pastors come to recognize as cornerstones of the church. Through faithfulness to the gospel of grace and the community that should embody it, churches remain standing when controversy and complacency long since could have wiped away any witness to Christ's love. Not only had this church stood — with Clifford's selfless care it had thrived, becoming the largest church of its kind in the region and the greatest supporter of new churches such as the one that was now installing a new pastor.

There are few earthly reasons why church activities should be dear to Clifford, but when I was able to ask his wife if he were still able to go to church, she laughed an infectious laugh that I recognized echoed Clifford's own. Then she said, "No, Clifford can't get out anymore, and the one thing that we miss the most is church." The community of faith is the love of their lives. This dear couple so treasures God's grace that despite all the trials they have encountered in their church, they count as precious their opportunity to live for God and to participate in his expanding witness through the community of faith for which God has made them responsible. May God continue to multiply such Titus-type leadership among his people and in his ministers in order that grace, godliness, and the sharing of Christ's witness would be ever more present and powerful in his church.

35

Leading by Example

TITUS 1:5-9

The reason I left you in Crete was that you might straighten out what was left unfinished and appoint [or ordain] elders in every town, as I directed you. An elder must be blameless, the husband of but one wife, a man whose children believe and are not open to the charge of being wild and disobedient. Since an overseer is entrusted with God's work, he must be blameless — not overbearing, not quick-tempered, not given to drunkenness, not violent, not pursuing dishonest gain. Rather he must be hospitable, one who loves what is good, who is self-controlled, upright, holy and disciplined. He must hold firmly to the trustworthy message as it has been taught, so that he can encourage others by sound doctrine and refute those who oppose it.

We were on Ben Jehuda Street in Jerusalem. The tour day was over, but we still had some energy. So a number of us followed our guide to the street our travel magazines praised for its shops, street music, and Middle Eastern cuisine. We got more than we bargained for. The shop district was crowded with people, but some of them were on the seamier side. The food was plentiful but often unrecognizable. Most worrisome, the transportation arrangements for getting home were very confusing. The pickup point where drivers were to meet us was located down what seemed to be a maze of distant streets. Knowing where best to go, how to stay out of trouble, and how to get back to our lodging became serious questions. We resolved to stay in groups. Then we asked our guide to meet us at a specific time at an easily located intersection to direct us to the more obscure pickup point.

We were not prepared for our guide's reaction. "Please don't make me responsible for you," he said. "I have my own plans, and I am off duty. You are on your own." Not only were we unprepared for that answer — we were unwilling to accept it. He had brought us to this place, had knowledge we needed, and we were not safe without his guidance. Simply because he did not *want* to lead us did not in our minds relieve him of his leadership responsibilities. His knowledge and our situation obligated him to lead.

THE CHOICE OF LEADERS (v. 5)

Similar leadership obligations preoccupy this portion of Paul's letter to Titus. Through the instructions he gives to the new minister at Crete, as well as to those Titus will appoint as church leaders, Paul cautions mature believers never to act as though they are only responsible for themselves. The knowledge that Christian maturity brings, combined with the spiritual dangers that others face, obligate Christian leaders to lead. Before God, we do not have a right to say, "Others may be in spiritual need, but I'm not responsible for them." Leadership aversion for the sake of the "personal peace and affluence" that Christian philosopher Francis Schaeffer identified as the primary goals of most people in our culture is not Biblically defensible. God requires us to consider how our attitudes or actions will affect others.

So pervasive and persuasive is the self-orientation of our culture that even those who are considering "full-time ministry" may not be conscious of how their ministry priorities can be upended by personal considerations — such as obtaining a good salary, a nice home, and a respected pulpit. Years of sacrifice for a seminary degree can make virtually preeminent one's concern to find a position that provides well and is comfortable for one's family. Such concerns are not illegitimate in themselves. One would have to be crazy or callous not to think at all about them. Still, one of the requirements of those in ministry is the acquisition of a sense of responsibility for persons other than oneself or one's immediate family. The way a new husband has a growing sense of responsibility for his wife, or the way new parents suddenly realize that other lives are depending on them, parallels the responsibility mature Christian leaders feel for God's extended family, the church.

In 1:5-9 Paul tells Titus what should characterize mature Christian leadership. However, the apostle first says to Titus, "The reason I left you in Crete was that you might straighten out what was left unfinished and appoint elders in every town, as I directed you" (v. 5). Paul's words remind us that he had been in Crete previously but was not able to finish establishing the leadership for the church. Further, the lack of mature leadership now seems to have led to negative consequences that Titus must "straighten out." This is probably an oblique reference to the false teachers affecting the church, a situation that Paul will address in later verses.

Clearly there is a situation on Crete that demands leadership. Paul's willingness to have leaders appointed from among the Cretan converts to address the situation makes it clear that the leadership qualifications he will give do not solely apply to apostolically chosen leaders such as Titus. "Elders" (note the plural) were to be appointed "in every town." The plurality of elders in each place alerts us to the need for multiple persons in our churches who will assume responsibility for the spiritual care of others. How does one qualify for and express this responsibility? Paul answers by telling Titus the qualifications for elders.

THE GODLY EXAMPLE OF LEADERS (vv. 6-8)

Although the natural human inclination is to limit responsibility to one's own concerns, Paul makes it clear that church leaders live as examples for others. As exemplars, the elders that Titus appoints must be "blameless" (v. 6) in their *relationships* and in their *conduct*.

The word "blameless" needs careful examination since it is repeated twice in this text and explains much of the apostle's expectation for leaders (vv. 6a, 7). The word cannot mean "sinless," for then no one could qualify for leadership. At the same time, the apostle obviously has some measure of godliness in mind that requires definition from us. Scholars have long debated whether the standards for leadership in the early church were high or low. Although the list as it stands may appear daunting by modern measures, it could have been made far more intimidating. Note that among the Christian leadership qualifications there are no mountains to climb, no alligators to wrestle, no pilgrimages to make, no prophecies to utter, no ancient manuscripts to decode, no visions to conjure, no tortures to endure, and no miracles to perform. The standards for Christian leadership strictly relate to one's example before others.

Understanding that the requirements for elders relate primarily to how one lives before others helps explain Paul's use of the word "blameless." The Greek term is a technical word meaning "not chargeable with some offense." A "blameless" person in Paul's usage is one whom others have no obvious reason to accuse for living inconsistently with his faith commitments. Paul's "blameless" standard is based upon what others in the church see and observe. It is not so much a standard for one's own internal assessment (which would be required by a term such as *sinless* or even *good-intentioned*) but rather reflects the assessment of external community observation. What others observe about a man being considered for office bears on his qualification for office. In this passage the way a man is regarded by those in the church is Paul's primary concern, but his reputation in the community is also relevant (see 1 Timothy 3:7). Because his life should serve as an example to others, an elder should seek to live so as to avoid others' concerns that he is guilty of Biblical offense or neglect.

When blamelessness is properly understood as relating to one's community reputation, comfort may result for some and distress for others. There is comfort for those who realize that they are not disqualified for church office simply because their lives are not perfect, or else there would be no church officers. At the same time, there may be distress for one who does not want to be held accountable for what others think about how consistently he lives according to Scripture. Such accountability grates against our independent spirit. "Why should I have to worry about what others observe and think?" we question. The answer is that Christian leaders should always be concerned for the testimony of the gospel. Because we are responsible for the spiritual welfare of others as well as ourselves, we should seek to make the gospel credible to others by our example.

A Christian leader's readiness to accept spiritual responsibility for others becomes evident in the first measure of blamelessness that the apostle gives. Paul says that elders must be "blameless" (i.e., not open to community accusation of un-Biblical living) in their relationships.

Blameless Relationships (v. 6b, c)

Paul first says elders must be "blameless" in their marriage and family relationships. The relative importance of these particular qualifications is probably indicated by their placement in the list of elder standards. The precise meaning of these family standards has been debated through the centuries, and doing justice to the exegetical issues will require a more intense study of the original languages than this commentary is designed to accommodate. Thus, in presenting the briefest of exegetical sketches here, my purpose is not to try to present the final word in the arguments but rather to consider more broadly what these qualifications require every church leader to consider.

Marital (v. 6b). Paul says that an elder should be "the husband of but one wife." It is unlikely that by these words Paul means that all church leaders must be married, as has sometimes been argued. Paul was not married when he wrote this, and the best evidence is that Titus was not either. Paul even expresses a desire that in times of crisis persons with church responsibilities not be married (1 Corinthians 7:29-38). Still, the norm in the church is that leaders will be married. So Paul addresses that norm without requiring marriage of all elders. The same reasoning indicates that Paul was not requiring all elders to have children simply because he says that an elder must be a man "whose children believe." This standard applies to those who have children, but it does not necessitate having children as a qualification for office.

Paul says that an elder who is married must be "the husband of but one wife." First, we should observe that this is not likely a prohibition against having multiple wives. Polygamy was not normally practiced at the time and place where Titus ministered. If polygamy were being addressed, it would have been a peculiar addition to a list of elder qualifications — something akin to saying in this society, "An elder must not be a cannibal." We know what cannibalism is and do not want our leaders to be cannibals, but it would be strange to put it in a list of qualifications where the practice does not commonly exist.

Does the requirement of being the husband of one wife mean then that all men who have had more than one wife as a consequence of death or divorce are automatically excluded from church office? No. Few question that elsewhere Paul clearly indicates that a person is free to remarry upon the death of a spouse (cf. Romans 7:1-3; 1 Corinthians 7:39). The most troublesome questions we have relate to divorce. Can a divorced person be an elder? The question further divides into whether one divorced on Biblical or un-Biblical grounds can be an officer, and whether that Biblical or un-Biblical divorce occurred before or after conversion. The exegesis that could be brought to bear on each segment of this subject is massive, but a consolidated treatment must follow here. It seems unlikely that Paul specifically intended to answer all of these questions here or elsewhere. His intentions are more likely those indicated by the context and themes he has already established for this text.

The word "blameless" is an important touchstone for determining Paul's intentions. This word reminds us that Paul's marital standards for leaders relate to what their community observes about them. To this general concern we should add the precise wording of Paul's Greek phrase for the marriage qualification. Paul's precise wording in the Greek is *not* simply that an elder must be "the husband of one wife" as we translate it in terms familiar to us. The literal statement of the apostle is that an elder must be "a one-woman man." The literal phrasing seems less concerned with one's marital history and more focused on whether the man being considered for office is perceived as living in honesty, faithfulness, and devotion to his spouse. Taking these concepts of blamelessness and fidelity together as they are presented in the text, we should understand that they require those in the church to determine if the community perceives that an elder candidate is consistently living in faithful commitment to one woman. Recent or serial infidelity would annul one's eligibility for office, as would evidence that the man is not extending to his wife the unique obligations, privileges, and regard required in Biblical marriage (e.g., 1 Corinthians 7:3, 4; Ephesians 5:28-31; 1 Peter 3:7).

Determining an elder candidate's marital commitment is thus more than a technical question of whether he was Biblically, or even un-Biblically, divorced two months or twenty years ago. The morass of confusing and conflicting details churches encounter when they must determine such things indicates the challenges implicit in utilizing such standards for selecting church officers. Furthermore, determining the answers to these questions still does not resolve issues such as whether a man who un-Biblically divorced at age nineteen should be excluded from church office after being faithful and spiritually discerning for forty years. The cleansing and renewing nature of the gospel would seem to be at odds with any standard that does not recognize the reality of spiritual change and the benefit of leadership that has experienced it. This perspective robs us of precise marital-history or marital-status formulas for determining church officer eligibility, but it seems more in keeping with the kind of community assessment that the apostle is requiring.

Such non-formulaic assessments may at first glance seem only to loosen the standards for elder qualifications. However, conscientious consideration of community blamelessness may actually do the opposite. A man whose divorce(s) may satisfy technical grounds for Biblical divorce may yet be excluded from office because of community perceptions. A man who is married but whose marriage is wrongly troubled or whose spousal commitment is unhealthy should also be encouraged to step aside from church leadership consideration. Many a wise pastor has advised potential leaders whose marriages need attention not to seek church office despite the fact that they are technically married. God requires the church to determine whether a potential elder's marriage is whole, healthy, and solid as part of the assessment of whether that person is qualified for leadership in the church. As a corollary, men with damaged or deficient marriages should not pursue church leadership positions thinking that others will not care or notice. They will care and notice. This may drive some men to secrecy, but hopefully it will stir more to seek correction and aid.

Parenting (v. 6c). The other relationship Paul requires us to evaluate in order to determine the eligibility of elders for office is that of parenting. The apostle says that an elder should be "a man whose children believe and are not open to the charge of being wild and disobedient" (v. 6c). All parents of teens shudder at this. I have known pastors who have considered leaving the ministry because of their children's beliefs or behaviors, and I do not discount the importance of weighing such matters. Still, our hearts naturally resist this standard of blamelessness. We feel, "Why should I be judged for leadership appropriateness because of what my children do or by what others think about what my children do?" The answer, of course, is that parents are responsible for the proper nurture and upbringing of their children (see Ephesians 6:1-4; Colossians 3:20, 21). A person is not ready for the responsibilities of others' spiritual welfare if he is not willing and able to take responsibility for those in his own household (cf. 1 Timothy 3:4, 5).

While standing firmly for this parenting standard, we must ensure that we are operating Biblically and not on first impressions alone. A number of distinctions are important to note in the apostle's terminology. First, the term for children is *tekna*, and it generally relates to children in the home, under their parents' authority. We should not hold leaders as accountable for the actions of independent adult children as we do for children under their care and supervision. Second, the word for children is plural. We are not necessarily looking at the beliefs and actions of one child but at the character of the family as a whole. Finally, we are to evaluate whether the children are believing. The Greek term translated "believe" is derived from *pistos* and is probably better translated "faithful." This rendering better communicates the intended meaning that our assessment is to be based on observations of children's conduct and convictions made over time, not on isolated statements or actions. Paul's terminology is not so much requiring us to examine a child's professed testimony as to evaluate whether the child — in a manner appropriate for his age — is exhibiting evidence of consistent Biblical discipline and spiritual nurture.

We should all recognize that there are periods of life when raising children is more difficult and when beliefs of parents are naturally questioned. By encouraging us to examine the faithfulness of all a potential leader's children (and not, for instance, the temporary mistakes or commendations of one child in a family of five), the apostle is charging us to take stock of the home as a whole. We are to make an assessment of leadership appropriateness on the basis of overall patterns, not exceptions. The parallel passage in 1 Timothy 3 enriches our understanding of this standard. There Paul says that an elder should "manage his own family well" (v. 4). How could this be determined if there were never any struggles in the family? Good leadership is not determined in the absence of difficulty but in the prudent discipline and handling of problems when difficulties come. Patterns of disbelief and unruliness in a man's household should cause questions about his aptitude for church leadership, but occasional or exceptional difficulties well handled should not disqualify. Rather, they are precisely what do qualify.

Blameless Conduct (vv. 7, 8)

After dealing with the example of the elder as demonstrated in his relationships, Paul addresses the conduct expected of an "overseer" (or "bishop," as in some older translations). The interchangeableness of the terms "elder" (an honorary title) and "overseer" (a functional title describing what an elder does) in this passage indicate that these were synonymous titles in the early church. The interplay of terms also indicates that there is no second tier of qualifications among the ruling officers in Christ's church. An elder must exhibit the conduct Paul describes with five negatives and six positives (vv. 7, 8).

Before considering these conduct qualifications we should remember the reason for them. Paul wants the appointment of new elders in order to "straighten out" the situation in Crete (v. 5). These new leaders will be "entrusted with God's work" (v. 7). Each of these statements reminds us that an elder's responsibility extends beyond himself. Because leaders are expected to affect others, Paul consistently discusses their required conduct in other-oriented terms.

An elder is *not* to be:

• "Overbearing." Literally translated "pleasing himself," this term identifies one who is only concerned about his own rights and is unconcerned about the rights of others.

• "Quick-tempered." This is a reference particularly to the kind of temper that flares at others.

• "Given to drunkenness." These words mean overindulgent in wine, but the phrase was used idiomatically to refer to any kind of outrageous, unconcerned-for-others conduct, in the same way that we refer to people acting "stoned" or "out of their heads."

• "Violent." Older translations refer to a "striker" and help us understand that an elder should not be one who strikes out at others either in actions or with words.

• "Pursuing dishonest gain" indicates that an elder should not be known for taking advantage of people or situations for the sake of money.

Following these five negatives are six positive qualifications. Our understanding of the purpose of these positives is enriched when we observe that they are stated in the context of the apostle's concern for the influence of our conduct on others. Paul is not merely concerned for the personal implications of our conduct but requires that we examine all of our actions for their impact on others.

Concern for others is also obvious in the first three positives Paul says should characterize an elder's conduct. An elder should be:

• "Hospitable" — opening home and heart to others, the opposite of the first negative, "overbearing" — "pleasing self."

• "One who loves what is good" — particularly loving virtue or what promotes good for others.

• "Self-controlled" — controlling drives that lead to impulsive and damaging behavior.

There are three additional positive qualifications:

• "Upright" — living in accord with God's law.

• "Holy" — devout, committed to piety and godliness.

• "Disciplined" — a term probably analogous to the practices of an athlete in training, meaning rigorous application of the Biblical habits, means, and restrictions for growing in godliness.

These last three qualifications have a less obvious outward focus but should not be isolated from community concerns. Paul is not concerned about an elder being "upright," "holy," or "disciplined" for the sake of personal sanctification alone. These qualifications appear in the context of establishing an elder's observed blamelessness. The elder's example in the community bears on his eligibility for office because his actual and perceived spirituality will have consequences in the church. Individual godliness cannot be isolated from community responsibilities. Christian leaders should understand that because others observe one's piety, personal spirituality is always in some degree practiced for the sake of others.

A Christian leader's example demonstrates to others that the gospel and its power are real. Just a few verses later Paul will say that elders need to be able to communicate and defend the gospel — the message that by grace God frees us from the guilt and the power of our sin (see v. 9 and 3:3-5). However, this message has no credibility if the messenger cannot demonstrate the reality that the gospel has freed him from the kind of bondage to sin that the rest of the world experiences. Without question the apostle does not want leaders to portray themselves as perfect or free from all struggle (Paul surely does not portray himself this way). Nevertheless, the patterns and practices of obvious worldliness should not dominate the life of those who are church leaders.

Until one assumes the responsibilities of church leadership, there may be no real awareness of how messy are the lives of so many people in our churches for whom God makes us responsible. Beneath their surface courtesies, many people are burdened by dissatisfying marriages, enslaved to lusts and addictions, entangled in patterns of thought and habit that they desperately hope — but can hardly imagine — they can escape. They are ensnared in dead-end pursuits of money and power that control their lives without satisfying their souls. Such persons are desperate for the incarnation of the gospel in the lives of church leaders. A godly example demonstrates not that elders are more deserving of grace than others, but that One who is in us is more powerful than the one who is in the world (see 1 John 4:4). Godly leadership proves that freedom from the slavery of sin and selfishness is possible.

The awareness that a Christian leader's example helps *others* learn to hope that their lives really can be different should help us understand that blamelessness is a ministry and not "just something personal." Godliness, in addition to the blessings it personally brings, should be perceived as a gift of hope that we share rather than a burden of laws we assume. Our lives are incarnational lifelines of the gospel to those drowning in sinful despair. By our godliness we demonstrate that the gospel has real power, and we provide hope that change is possible — that tomorrow does not have to be like yesterday. The effects of one's example on others make it a glorious cause for living (and for dying to self) rather than a constraint upon privilege. The importance of this cause for the spiritual welfare of those dear to us and to the Lord wars against a lack of *discipline* in speech or habit, sloppy concerns for *holiness*, and merely self-considered brush-asides of others' opinions about what is *upright* in what we say, do, and see.

The apostle well recognized that the gospel's necessary emphasis on God's grace could make Christian leaders susceptible to using their liberties without concern for the effects upon others. This susceptibility is evident today in the "new legalism" that can pervade circles where fresh winds of grace are blowing away performance-based standards for God's love. The caricature of the old legalism existent among evangelicals taught, "You're not really a Christian if you smoke or drink or chew or go with the girls that do." The new legalism seems to counter, "You're not really a mature, grace-understanding Christian if you don't smoke or drink or chew or go with the girls that do. You need to cuss and cut up, at least a little — just to show that you really do understand your freedom from the law."

Clearly our salvation hangs on none of these matters. The apostle plainly condemns those who want to make special customs or practices qualify Christians for Heaven (see the critique of the Judaizers in vv. 10-14). Clear also is Paul's unwillingness to make any substance or stricture an automatic test of spiritual health. "To the pure, all things are pure," Paul says (v. 15). We are not to judge one another's spirituality only on the basis of the use of material things. Still, the standards Paul has established for elders make it undeniable that Christian leaders are required to examine how their example affects others.

As Christian leaders, we are always obligated to exegete our culture as well as the Scriptures to determine what is legitimate for our own conduct. We must ask what struggles face those for whom we are responsible, what our culture is using and abusing, what are common temptations and what leads to them, where we have seen injury and how we might take steps to keep others from going there. Conscientious Christian leaders ask, "Where are our own steps leading others — toward or away from danger? Are we creating legalism by our prohibitions, or are we leading into harm's way by our freedoms?" The apostle obligates us never to answer these questions merely on the basis of personal desire, but to evaluate how our example will affect others and then to govern our lives appropriately. This means that we will — in different cultures, different regions, different churches — probably come to different conclusions about what we should do in matters the Scriptures do not specifically address. However, what we cannot do is come to conclusions solely based upon personal preference or individual consequence. Our instruction comes from the apostle who himself said:

Though I am free and belong to no man, I make myself a slave to
everyone, to win as many as possible. To the Jews I became like a
Jew, to win the Jews. To those under the law I became like one
under the law (though I myself am not under the law), so as to
win those under the law. To those not having the law I became
like one not having the law (though I am not free from God's law
but am under Christ's law), so as to win those not having the law.
To the weak I became weak, to win the weak. I have become all
things to all men so that by all possible means I might save some.
I do all this for the sake of the gospel, that I may share in its bless-
ings. (1 Corinthians 9:19-23)

We cannot simply shrug off as "old fogies" those in our congregations
who are concerned about the example of their leaders. Our own perspective
will change when we assume the responsibility of counseling young women
after their abortions, of rescuing individuals and their families from the
wastelands of alcohol and drug abuse, of repairing families scarred by
molestation and abuse. We cannot do this work effectively if we are not
also willing to examine root causes in our culture and forgo some personal
liberties the Bible affords us in order to keep others from being enslaved to
the sins of our day. As Christian leaders we are obligated — in addition to
examining Scripture — to discern what is negatively affecting our communities, congregations, families, and our own hearts and then to govern our
own lives so as to provide counterinfluence and example. Christian leaders
determine their own steps based on the knowledge that their choice of path
does not affect them alone.

My sister-in-law and her husband, a pastor, recently purchased an old
home in an urban neighborhood where they are planting a church. Their
house is old, but their children are young. It is important for their health (and
their parents' sanity) that the kids get all the sleep they need. For this reason the early-rising young pastor has learned where all the squeaky boards
are in their creaky hallway. Recently we got a kick out of hearing (and
watching) his wife describe how he walks down that hallway every morning. Contorting his body like a skilled oriental dancer, he snakes a path
down the hall to keep from stepping on any board that would squawk and
disturb his children. Of course, he has a right to walk anywhere he wants
in the hallway, but he adjusts his steps according the needs of those who
are in his care.

True leaders in Christ's church similarly adjust their steps, though
they have full liberty to walk wherever they want within the bounds of
Scripture, for the sake of those who are in their spiritual care. Paul requires
an elder to provide a godly example for others in his relationships and in

his conduct in order to show that the gospel is real, powerful, and able to make a difference.

All of this concern to provide a godly example may seem to run counter to much of what we hear about church leadership today. Pastors are encouraged to be vulnerable and transparent in acknowledging their own struggles and imperfections. Elders are urged not to project an image that will cause ordinary church folk to fear they will never measure up to the expectations of the "holy men on high who are in charge." I also teach seminarians that it is important for ministers to communicate their vulnerabilities. I believe that Paul would too, since he was willing to "boast of the things that show my weakness" (2 Corinthians 11:30). How, then, do leaders reconcile these encouragements publicly to confess fallibility with Paul's already articulated requirement to provide a godly example? The answer lies in the recognition that Paul did not merely require church leaders to provide a godly example but also required them to provide a gospel witness.

THE GOSPEL WITNESS OF LEADERS (v. 9)

Not only does Paul require an elder to behave blamelessly but also, "He must hold firmly to the trustworthy message as it has been taught" (v. 9). What is "the trustworthy message" (literally, "the faithful word") that has been passed on to the Cretan church? Paul's salutation has already provided a reminder — "grace and peace from God the Father and Christ Jesus our Savior" (v. 4). An elder must practice godliness but must not portray it as the reason that he is God's. The "trustworthy message" that has been passed from and proclaimed by the apostle is that peace with God results from his grace, not from our actions (cf. 3:5). While godliness in our lives indicates the reality and power of the gospel, godly church leaders constantly discount the ability of those actions to qualify them for Heaven. Our lives should express the power of the gospel, but our lips should express the hope of the gospel. The foundation of this hope is that God loves us not because of our goodness but because of his — not because of our work but because of our Savior's. Though the church's leaders live so as to give others the hope that changed lives are possible, they never point to their actions as the basis of God's acceptance.

This doctrine of grace becomes the foundation of faithful church leadership. Though *doctrine* can have negative connotations today as a source of unnecessary church division, Paul — speaking literally in verse 9 of "the teaching" (*didaskalia* with the definite article) of Christ and the apostles — says this "doctrine" enables elders to perform their church functions. When a godly leader "hold[s] firmly" to the "sound doctrine" that grace alone makes us right with God, he is able both to "encourage others" (v. 9b) and to "refute" opposers (v. 9c).

Encouragement of Others (v. 9b)

Paul says that an elder must "hold firmly to the trustworthy message" of grace so that "he can encourage others by sound doctrine" (v. 9b). People are not encouraged by the life of a church leader who shows that even he cannot escape worldly patterns. Neither are they encouraged by one who gives the impression that God loves him *because* he has risen above the world. What the church needs is leaders who show that it is possible to live above the common constraints of the world, while at the same time being willing to make the common confession that they are as dependent on grace as any other person. Where an example of godliness and a confession of the need for grace come together, there God's people receive powerful encouragement in their own spiritual growth.

At a combined meeting of several churches this past fall, a guest preacher surprised some of us staid Presbyterians. Not only did he offer the ordinary corporate confession of sin in his pastoral prayer, but he then encouraged people to gather in small groups in their pews to confess their sins to one another. My wife was seated in the front row of the choir. She later smiled in the confession that she simply hunkered down behind the choir rail, glad she could remain unnoticed. Feeling slightly guilty for not participating in the small groups, however, she turned toward her choir neighbor to see if there was some inclination to join in the joint confessions. The friend indicated her inclination by silently but very clearly mouthing the words, "No way!"

Then, to the horror of both choir delinquents, the visiting pastor followed his own instruction to confess sin to one another by turning to the people nearest him. Those nearest happened to be my wife and her friend. Without the slightest hesitation the pastor dropped to his knees in front of them and said, "Let's pray." Then he began to confess his own need of God's cleansing grace. His manner was so sincere and his words so appreciative of God's love that my wife said there was no choice but to join him. The humor in the situation should not obscure how aptly this experience demonstrates the way spiritual leadership should work. The leader's example combined with his confession of the need of grace encouraged others to seek the face of God.

The visiting pastor's actions also help answer earlier questions about the appropriateness of expressions of pastoral vulnerability. Openness about our vulnerabilities is *not* the display of a willingness to sin, *nor* a casual disregard for the effects of our actions on others. Rather, the pastoral transparency that benefits a church is a leader's consistent confession of the need for renewing and empowering grace as much as anyone else. Leaders in Christ's church demonstrate holiness while giving the credit for their holiness to God. They should express vulnerability with regard to their weakness apart from him but should never communicate an easy familiarity with, or comfortable participation in, sin or what leads others into it.

Refutation of Opposers (v. 9c)

Holding to the message of grace with a godly example backing the credibility of the message also enables church leaders to "refute" (or rebuke) those who "oppose" the gospel (v. 9c). Paul's opposers, as identified in subsequent verses (see particularly vv. 10-16), claim that the Cretans need to observe certain aspects of Jewish custom and law in order to be accepted by God (v. 10). The apostle says that those who teach such false ideas are "ruining whole households" (v. 11).

The reference to "households" indicates that Paul is not merely concerned about winning an intellectual argument or gaining a political upper hand. He knows that doctrine has real-life consequences. "Ruin" results when the message of grace is lacking or polluted. We must "refute" those who "oppose . . . sound doctrine" because without adequate expression of the truth and power of the gospel families come apart, young people are led astray, compulsions control, despair grips. The awfulness, commonness, and sordidness of the ordinary lives of people in our churches are barely graspable for those who have not yet been given the entrée of a spiritual physician. Even those trained to deal with spiritual diseases can fail to anticipate the nature and degree of "ruin" that concerns Paul. At a gathering of young pastors recently, the statement that got the most and loudest sympathetic "Amens" was this honest confession: "I was unprepared for, and have grown depressed with, the number and degree and repetition of messy sins in people's lives."

While there are mature saints in most churches who can give encouragement to pastors and elders, the mass of individuals committed to leaders' care are languishing in anxiety, hidden sin, frayed relationships, drivenness, despondency, spiritual pride, and humiliating compulsions. To give these people the impression that what will heal them is becoming more respectable or adhering to a more strict code of conduct is to offer medicine that is forever out of reach. None of us will in this life achieve the degree of holiness that obligates God to relieve us from our misery. The gospel requires leaders to refute any form of the message that behaving better and better is the means to get God to help you or love you.

When church leaders really perceive how great the depth and commonness of others' needs are, their sense of responsibility for others' spiritual welfare grows proportionately — and sometimes almost unbearably. A pastor called me recently. "In my small church," he said, "there have been three cases of adultery disclosed over the last few weeks." Sadly, adultery is almost the "common cold" of today's church. Awareness of the commonness of such sin could have led the pastor simply to dismiss the problem. He might have rationalized, "It's so typical that our secular culture infects our churches this way." In this manner he could have simply passed the blame and the responsibility to others. But he did not. Instead, he asked a question: "Am I the problem?" Facing squarely the ruin of families and communities being caused by the sin in his church, he bravely asked, "There is so little power of the gospel evident in my church. Am I doing something wrong? Is it possible that preaching the message of grace is not enough?" In the face of spiritual opposition, his own heart was refuting the sufficiency of grace.

I know this man is a very intelligent and sensitive pastor. No simplistic answer would do. No shallow attempt to give him comfort and assurance would have been accepted. So I told him the truth as best I knew it: "Yes, you are the problem — at least in part." Does that sound harsh? Does it sound as though I am removing spiritual responsibility from those who are actually guilty? To some I am sure the answer to these questions is yes. Still, no mature church leader will allow me to say anything else. If there is little evident power of the gospel in the lives of those for whom I am spiritually responsible, then I know that in some measure the problem is mine.

I am not denying others' responsibility for their own rebellion, nor failing to acknowledge that even those who walked with Jesus fell into miserable sin. Nevertheless, sin in the lives of those in my spiritual charge must remind me that my life is not all that it should be. My commitments are not as fervent as they should be. My example is not as unsullied as I wish or as my people need. My heart is not as tender as it could be. If I were more accepting and had less pretense regarding my own goodness, perhaps those who are now in ruin might have come to me sooner for help or could have been led in safer paths. Being a faithful pastor, parent, missionary, counselor, teacher, elder, or leader in Christ's church requires that I confess that, at least in part, the problems of others are mine.

So what do I do? What did I urge the pastor to do? To claim the grace that he knows those who are in ruin need. This is what each of us who would be leaders in Christ's church must do — confess anew our need of grace and then claim and proclaim its reality. God forgives our failures, even as he forgives others' failures. In the knowledge that his grace covers us and relieves us from the burden of our guilt, we will then serve him in greater joy and strength that communicates the reality and the power of the gospel.

At a recent Easter service, a student asked the professors at our seminary to gather together to sing before all the students. Knowing of their love for the Lord and his Word made it very moving to see these great men of faith stand shoulder to shoulder and sing about their God. There was something beyond sentiment, however, in what was being expressed that brought tears to so many eyes. It was captured in the words of the song that was sung:

"Faith of our fathers, holy faith, we will be true to thee till death." Those who sing this song pledge to proclaim the gospel of grace "by witness true and virtuous life" — by gospel witness and godly example. As the professors sang, we felt the power of these forces that the Apostle Paul said should be united in the lives of Christian leaders. Our hearts were stirred by the witness of those whose lives expressed the power of grace and whose lips proclaimed the need of it. It is a stirring that I pray none will soon forget, for our Lord does not want those men to sing alone. Their song was a joint invitation with these words of the Apostle Paul to join the ranks of God's faithful leaders. All in these ranks commit themselves by example as well as by witness to proclaim the grace that is the power and peace of God.

36

Leading by Contrast

TITUS 1:10-16

For there are many rebellious people, mere talkers and deceivers, espe-
cially those of the circumcision group. They must be silenced, because they
are ruining whole households by teaching things they ought not to teach
— and that for the sake of dishonest gain. Even one of their own prophets
has said, "Cretans are always liars, evil brutes, lazy gluttons." This tes-
timony is true. Therefore, rebuke them sharply, so that they will be sound
in the faith and will pay no attention to Jewish myths or to the commands
of those who reject the truth. To the pure, all things are pure, but to those
who are corrupted and do not believe, nothing is pure. In fact, both their
minds and consciences are corrupted. They claim to know God, but by
their actions they deny him. They are detestable, disobedient and unfit
for doing anything good.

His research made him famous. Max Sherman, a scientist who studies
energy efficiency in buildings, had examined the effectiveness of various
sealants for heating and air conditioning ducts. He came up with a startling
conclusion, first reported on the Web and then rapidly picked up by the
Wall Street Journal, the Associated Press, and a host of broadcast media.
Sherman's news was that most of the duct sealants on the market work well
with one notable exception — duct tape. In just a few days after its application, reported Sherman, duct tape "failed reliably and often catastrophically."
News show interviews with Sherman contained exchanges such as this:

> Interviewer: "How did duct tape get its name?"
> Sherman: "I don't know."
> Interviewer: "What can you use it for?"
> Sherman: "Anything but ducts."
> Interviewer: "Do you use duct tape?"
> Sherman: "All the time . . . just not on ducts."

What made Sherman's duct tape discovery newsworthy, of course, was that the product that our society jokingly refers to "as the force that holds the universe together," while good for many functions, could not fulfill the one purpose for which it was designed. This irony may reflect a fear more than a few of us share when considering our role in leading the church. Careful preparation and perhaps years of study may have led to our consideration of leading others. No one can deny there are potentially many good purposes for what we have learned. Yet we fear that we will be unable to fulfill the very leadership function for which we have trained. Religious training does not guarantee meaningful leadership. In fact, we learn from Paul's letter to Titus that those in Crete who claimed to be the most religious were often the least equipped for Biblical leadership.

How do we keep from "failing reliably and catastrophically" in the very leadership role for which we may have long prepared? Paul answers by providing in Titus 1:10-16 a study in contrast for Christian leaders. Paul graciously uses the examples of errant leaders in the Cretan church to identify a path leading away from the gospel and says to us, "Don't go there." In previous verses Paul has told us what characterizes godly leaders, but here he tells us what characterizes the ungodly ones. (Note: One way to trace the themes of Titus is through the progression of the dominant personal pronouns. The opening of Chapter 1 is marked by Paul's reference to himself, "I" and "me," and to the qualified elder, "he." Chapter 2 focuses on the "you" imperatives. The bulk of Chapter 3 unites the church in the purposes of "we" and "us." This highly personal nature of the epistle makes the negative contrasts to "they" and "them" all the more striking in this passage.)

Wrong words, *wrong motives*, and *wrong actions* mark the ungodly leaders' path of error. Perhaps Paul speaks so sharply of these contrasts with true leaders in Christ's church because he knows it is often easier to spot these characteristics in others than in ourselves. Thus, to help us refine our understanding Paul discusses these words, motives, and actions both in the context of *what* should concern us and for *whom* we should be concerned.

WRONG WORDS (vv. 10, 11a)

Paul never explicitly identifies the wrong teaching of those who are opposing him in Crete, but he gives us enough hints by identifying what is important to them to let us know what should concern us.

About What Should We Be Concerned? Damaged Doctrine (v. 10)

Paul has just identified the need for elders to "encourage others by sound doctrine and refute those who oppose it" (v. 9). Now he indicates why this qualification is necessary: "There are many rebellious people, mere talkers and deceivers, especially those of the circumcision group" (v. 10). Some are rebelling against the apostle's teaching (the Greek word translated "rebellious" indicates an unwillingness to be subject to control). They contradict his "sound doctrine" with words that he describes as worthless or empty (*mataiologoi* = "useless" + "words"), and they also engage in outright deceit. What is this emptiness and deceit about? The reference to these opponents as being of "the circumcision group" tells us. Paul uses such references elsewhere (see Acts 10:45; 11:2; Galatians 2:7-9, 12) to identify former Jews who joined the early church with a "gospel-plus" message. "Yes," they say, "what saves you is faith in the work of Christ *plus* special, religious knowledge, diets, rites, or practices that qualify you for Heaven." This unsound message has nothing to it. Rather, it exalts matters that are worthless to God, and it deceives people into thinking that their heavenly status is determined by human accomplishments.

Paul simply and stridently says about those carrying such a message, "They must be silenced" (v. 11). The word for "silenced" can also mean "controlled" or "muzzled" and reflects the apostle's identification of his opponents as those who are not subject to control — i.e., "rebellious" (v. 10). To modern sensibilities this does not seem like a very tolerant attitude, but the reason for the apostle's imperative explains his zeal. He alerts us not only about what we should be concerned (i.e., damaged doctrine) but also about who should be the focus of our concern.

About Whom Should We Be Concerned? Damaged Households (v. 11a)

Paul says that those with the gospel-plus message are "ruining whole households by teaching things they ought not to teach" (v. 11). The damaged doctrine is not just a philosophical divergence or a contrasting speculation of no consequence. As wise Sunday school teachers have said, "Thoughts are things." As a man thinks, so he is (see Proverbs 23:7, KJV). What the people in Crete have been taught to think has affected their beliefs, choices, and relationships. The unsound teaching of the circumcision group is "ruining" (literally, "overturning") entire families. Knowing that the damaged doctrine is damaging "whole households," the apostle's zeal to silence his doctrinal opponents reflects his passionate love for God's people, an affection that should characterize all who have a true pastoral heart.

The Rev. Steve Smallman, current head of World Harvest Mission, for many years pastored McLean Presbyterian Church outside Washington, D.C. During one of his vacations from the church, a nationally known speaker filled the pulpit. The man talked plainly about the gospel of faith in Jesus Christ but then went on to suggest that anyone whose faith was genuine also had a particular view of American history and a certain political party affiliation. When Smallman returned to the church, he heard about the damaged doctrine that had been preached in this gospel-plus message. He then considered the damage done to the households of newer believers particularly, and he wasted no time. Although the visiting speaker had traveled to another city, the caring pastor wrote a pointed letter to him. The letter carefully reviewed the necessity of teaching the doctrine that we are saved purely by faith. Then the pastor added, "You may think that courtesy would restrain me from speaking strongly to you about what was said in my absence, but when it comes to protecting my people from a gospel polluted by human conditions, I am like a she-bear protecting her cubs." Smallman then distributed a copy of the letter to everyone in the church.

Why would a pastor speak so vigorously and vigilantly regarding a passing-through-town speaker? Because damaged doctrine damages people. If we ever add anything to the work of Christ as the basis of our security with God, we inevitably entrust our eternities to the work of human hands. There are only two possible results from such an error — spiritual pride and personal despair. If our spiritual security depends on anything that we do, then our standing with God is ultimately a matter of comparison — of being better than someone else. Because our actions will never be entirely pure or holy before God, the doctrine of gospel-plus creates the Christianity of competition with others. Even if the behaviors such a doctrine advocates are morally good, the results are spiritually ruinous.

The simple premise that we have to add something to faith to make it genuine — or ourselves worthy — results in arrogance, hardness, and envy. In the race to exceed the goodness of others, some who live the gospel-plus doctrine discover the need to tear down others in order to build themselves up. Gossip, backbiting, and power plays result. In the need to avoid negative assessments, others convinced of gospel-plus justification become driven, exerting inappropriate control of employees, subordinates, spouses, or children. Such patterns naturally follow where there is a need to cover and minimize our own sin lest we fail to meet our, or others', expectations. For those who feel they cannot cover or minimize their shortcomings (to others or to themselves), the doctrine of gospel-plus leads to despair. Teaching that God loves us because we are better than others in knowledge, practice, or lineage creates intolerance, bitterness, dissension, and despair. Households are thus ruined.

Despite the clarity of Scripture, gospel-plus attitudes exist in every church or Christian organization. Regularly in our counseling rooms, homes, and pews are those who really believe that because they do not measure up in some dimension, they are not as valuable to God as someone else or as valuable they could be. Gospel-plus thinking is virtually a human reflex. A recent graduate said, "When I went into the ministry I had no idea how little people think of themselves spiritually. They think that because they do not measure up they are worthless to God, and because they think they are worthless they abandon themselves to the temporary relief of sin." Our tendency when facing such thinking as church leaders is to blame others. However, Paul's warnings to Titus should alert us to examine whether our own teaching by word or behavior is communicating a gospel-plus doctrine that is doing the damage. When we confront lives abandoned to sin, our reflex reaction to correct others is also to make the gospel conditional upon something that will leverage people into new obedience. It is difficult to act consistently on the premise that what truly conforms us to Christ is the same thing that converts us to Christ — the gospel plus nothing.

Tommy Allen is a pastor in a formerly decaying urban setting that is now being rehabbed and repopulated by young professionals and homosexuals. Responding to a simple expression of compassion from Tommy, a gay man began to attend church. For months the man cried in every service but would not commit his life to Christ. Finally he came to speak to the pastor about the condition of his soul. The man said that he had not confessed his need of Christ because he assumed that his life of sin would disqualify him from Heaven.

"I know that I cannot measure up," he said, "so I have not asked God to accept me."

Tommy acknowledged that his first inclination was to tell the man to correct his behavior and to obey Scripture so God would receive him. Instead he remembered the lessons of the gospel that his situation has taught him. A number of former homosexuals attend Tommy's church. What they said drew them from the gay community to this church was not regular condemnation of the evil of homosexuality. What intrigued them and ultimately won them was preaching that undermined the concept that goodness qualifies you for Heaven. Tommy does not preach this message simply to appeal to those who have been put off by the condemnations of the church. He says the pure message of the gospel that God is not bought by human goodness touches something deep in the homosexual conscience.

"Many gays," Tommy says, "believe their lifestyle is wrong but can be compensated for by being good in other areas of life. Teaching that no human goodness qualifies us for God jars against the gay conscience, but it resonates as true in the heart." As a result Tommy confronted the man who was protesting that he could not be good enough for God with a pure gospel challenge. "Stop trying to be good enough," Tommy said. "When you come to God through faith in Christ, he makes you as righteous as Christ. God does not receive you on the basis of your work, but because you trust in Christ's work in your behalf." The words made sense and gave hope. The young man trusted in Christ.

The pure gospel sounds almost too simple to be effective, but it is the power of God — and the only true hope we can offer. Four days later the young gay man's commitment wavered, and his resolve faltered. He prepared himself to go out for an evening of "cruising" for sexual encounters. But the Holy Spirit was battling in his conscience, and the young man called the pastor:

"Tommy, I'm getting ready to go out and cruise."

"Oh?" said the questioning but not panicked pastor.

"I suppose you think that's wrong."

"Of course."

"Well, what am I supposed to do?"

"What do you think someone is supposed to do who is as righteous as Christ?" said Tommy.

We are made righteous not by our goodness but by Christ's. This means God in his goodness provides us with Christ's righteousness even when our goodness fails. We know this truth, but its reality and power can seem insufficient when we confront evil in our lives and others'. We want something stronger or quicker — a formula for correction. Of course, commonsense measures of intervention and prevention remain important. Warnings of God's discipline for unbridled sin also may dissuade some from wrong behavior. It may even be necessary to remind someone that there is no assurance of salvation where there is no obedience. Still we must resist the human reflex to say that our goodness qualifies us for Heaven. Such a gospel-plus message may provide temporary compulsion against sinning, but ultimately pride and/or despair result.

The unpolluted gospel that God loves us in our imperfection because Christ's righteousness has been applied to us holds the only true hope for turning from ourselves to God. The sin-damaged young man hung up the phone after talking with Tommy Allen and days later reported to his pastor that he did not go cruising that night. Instead, after the phone call the young man wrote down on a piece of paper over and over again, "I am as righteous as Christ, I am as righteous as Christ, I am as righteous as Christ." The words were not a claim that he was better than anyone else because of his personal goodness. He was too aware of his sin to make such a claim. Rather, the words were an attestation of his faith in the Savior of sinners. In that faith there was joy that provided the strength to resist sin. This member of the household avoided damage to his soul because of the undamaged gospel presented to him.

WRONG MOTIVES (vv. 11b-15)

Paul cautions church leaders to guard their words so that the gospel remains pure and undamaged in their ministries. Yet words are not his only concern. His epistle to Titus makes it clear that Paul is also concerned about motives. In the context of discussing the motives of leaders, the apostle again tells us about what we should be concerned, and about whom we should we concerned.

About What Should We Be Concerned? Ministries Focused on Gain and/or Garbage (vv. 11b-15)

Focused on gain (v. 11b). A certain kind of ministry comes under Paul's condemnation when he contrasts his ministry with those who not only pollute the gospel but also do it "for the sake of dishonest gain" (v. 11b). Their actions are "dishonest" in the sense that their true motive is to gain a profit rather than to serve the hearers. Older translations speak of Paul's opponents seeking "filthy lucre" (KJV) and "base gain" (RSV). These varying expressions all communicate the mercenary intent of those "teaching things they ought not to teach." What drives such men is the base motive of selfish advantage.

Being so basely motivated may seem far from us, but such motives easily entrap. In my position as a preacher who travels to many churches, I regularly have to make decisions about where I will go. I must confess that it is hard for me not to let the amount of the honorarium become a prime motivator. While many future leaders are in ministry training, they may think such matters are far away for them. Yet more important matters will face them almost immediately. Going where they are most needed, rather than where they will be most rewarded, is a decision most must make as their ministries commence. Some will make wonderfully sacrificial choices only to discover that the need to choose will return again in each chapter of their ministry. Each time a period of service terminates or a place of ministry grows wearisome, Satan will whisper, "You've already done so much — isn't it time others served you?" Whether we will be motivated by others' need rather than our own gain is a ministry decision that will not go away.

A young seminary grad recently was rejoicing that in the church that had just hired him, people volunteered their time and resources to renovate and expand an older house for him. The gift sounds wonderful, but what made it even more special was a visit that followed from the senior pastor. The experienced minister lovingly advised the new assistant to learn to appreciate such favors but not to solicit, expect, or grow dependent on them. Said the experienced pastor, "Too many of us in ministry develop what business people outside of our presence call a 'missionary motive,' the expectation that others need to do us favors and serve us because we are 'sacrificing our lives' for Jesus." When ministry is about gaining and expecting personal favors, gospel power dies. Service of self rather than the Savior will soon become the driving force of the labors of one who expects, or demands, the perks of pastoring. Should we be concerned about a fair salary and the care of our families? Of course. But even our families will ultimately discern if love for Christ and his people or advantage for us and our accounts is the Lord of our decisions.

Focused on garbage (vv. 12-15). Keeping Christ the absolute Lord of one's ministry is also Paul's concern in the further contrast he draws for those whose leadership is truly Christian. In addition to his concern about motives that focus on gain, we see the apostle's concern for motives that focus on matters he considers rubbish. Paul now becomes much more specific about what "those of the circumcision group" (v. 10) are teaching in order to gain their own advantage. He commands that they be rebuked "sharply" (v. 13) so that they "will pay no attention to Jewish myths or to the commands of those who reject the truth" (v. 14), nor be concerned about practices that supposedly make one pure or impure (v. 15). Apparently Paul's opponents were using Jewish fables (cf. 1 Timothy 1:4; 2 Timothy 4:4; 2 Peter 1:16) to bolster speculations that certain traditional rituals (literally, "commandments of humans"; cf. Matthew 15:9; Mark 7:7; 1 Timothy 4:1ff.; Colossians 2:20-22) were necessary for Christian purity.

Paul's bold statements that extra-Biblical practices do not ensure purity place the gospel in stark relief. The apostle has just finished saying that the leaders of the church (elders) should be "blameless" in behavior and belief as assessed by the communities in which they live. Further, his words charge elders to govern their conduct out of consideration for the effects of their habits, practices, and pleasures on others. But now, in these closely following words, Paul says that such leaders should put no confidence in any human practice as the basis for one's standing with God. Neither knowing nor observing the implications of certain myths or commands or cleanliness codes ensures high Christian spirituality or status. In contrast to those advocating these pursuits of status, Paul asserts (in essence), "This stuff does not come from 'God, who does not lie' (v. 2) but from your own human culture. And you know the credibility of what comes from your culture. One of your own prophets has said, 'Cretans are always liars'" (v. 12 — a quote from the sixth-century B.C. Cretan writer/philosopher Epimenides). The idea that special knowledge, behaviors, or background makes us right with God is a lie, having a human — not a divine — origin.

Paul's argument here in Titus should remind us of his appeal in Philippians:

> *If anyone else thinks he has reasons to put confidence in the flesh, I have more: circumcised on the eighth day . . . of the tribe of Benjamin, a Hebrew of Hebrews . . . a Pharisee . . . as for legalistic righteousness, faultless . . . but . . . now . . . I consider [all these things] rubbish that I may gain Christ, and be found in him, not having a righteousness of my own that comes from the law, but that which is through faith in Christ — the righteousness that comes from God and is by faith. (3:4-8)*

To focus on human observances as the basis for elevating one's Christian status is really just to focus on garbage. To press his point, Paul writes what must have elicited gasps from around the room the first time this epistle was read in public: "To the pure, all things are pure" (v. 15). This is entirely counterintuitive. If you have something pure, virtually anything else will make it impure. Yet Paul contends that for those whose motives are pure in Christ, virtually nothing makes them impure. In fact, their purity invades the supposedly impure and purifies it. Paul probably is speaking about such things as eating meat offered to idols. Thus his words echo those of Jesus:

> *"Nothing outside a man can make him 'unclean' by going into him. Rather, it is what comes out of a man that makes him 'unclean. . . . What comes out of a man is what makes him 'unclean.' For from within, out of men's hearts, come evil thoughts, sexual immorality, theft, murder, adultery, greed, malice, deceit, lewdness, envy, slander, arrogance and folly. All these evils come from inside and make a man 'unclean.'" (Mark 7:15-23)*

Neither Jesus nor Paul is unconcerned about our conduct, but they are deeply concerned about our knowing that neither physical nor material nor edible things in themselves sanctify or de-sanctify us. Already Paul has cautioned about cavalier disregard for community standards and congregational needs in determining one's habits and entertainments. Now Paul drops the other shoe of gospel concern, saying, "And if you think your abstinence from something or your discipline regarding something else makes you better than others before God, you still do not understand."

God's mercy alone is what makes us right with him. Deeply believing this truth will make us merciful toward others both in curbing conduct that would cause others to stumble and in refusing to assert that this action of ours in itself gives us any special status with God. Perhaps Paul balances the message best when he says, "All food is clean, but is it wrong for a man to eat anything that causes someone else to stumble" (Romans 14:20). These words reflect a wonderful pastoral balance — being concerned for others but not letting one's personal restraint be judged as the basis for God's favor of oneself or his disfavor of someone else. Judging our merit or someone else's demerit on the basis of such externals is giving too much value to garbage.

Most pastors can identify issues in their churches today that supposedly distinguish the regular Christians from those spiritually elevated by their special knowledge or practices — vitamin supplements, uniforms in school, political party affiliation, non-mutual fund investing, syncopated music, use of alcohol, movie attendance. I spoke at a convention recently in which two brothers, both preachers, would not appear on the podium at the same time because one held to a 1644 Confessional perspective on the law and the other held to a 1689 Confessional perspective on the law. I will not in these pages seek to defend or condemn anyone on the basis of these issues. Sincere

Christians have legitimate reasons for being concerned for these issues in terms of their impact upon churches and homes. My reason for citing such questions is only to remind us that seeking to elevate our importance or ensure our acceptance by what we practice in regard to these issues is to seek to gain spiritual status through what Paul says is worthless for such a purpose.

For Whom Should We Be Concerned? Those Who Have Lost Their Focus (v. 13)

Verse 12 sounds unnecessarily harsh in virtually any translation of Scripture: "'Cretans are always liars, evil brutes, lazy gluttons.'" Some allowance can be granted the apostle because the originator of this Cretan accusation is himself from Crete. However, though the apostle is quoting someone else's words, the apostle adds, "This testimony is true" (v. 13). Such a characterization of an entire nation of people is poor courtesy and definitely would not pass the politically correct speech requirements of our day. Honesty may compel some of us to admit that this may be one of those passages we wish were not in Scripture. Some relief may come to our troubled consciences, however, in considering the paradoxical nature of what Paul has said. If "all Cretans are liars," then the Cretan who wrote the statement is also lying, meaning that the sweeping condemnation of all Cretans is itself false. Rather than being a harsh assessment of all Cretans, Paul is probably expressing a wry humor at the expense of his Cretan opponents to undermine their credibility without actually saying anything damaging regarding Cretans as a whole. There is some conjecture in this explanation, but it is not the only cause to read Paul's words without an assumption of bigotry on his part.

What redeems these otherwise harsh words is the surprisingly caring statement that follows: "'All Cretans are liars.'. . . Therefore, rebuke them [i.e., the Cretan opponents] sharply." The surprising words that follow are, "So that . . . ." He does not follow with a "So there!" The apostle might have said, "They are teaching bad things — rebuke them. So there!" Instead, Paul follows these apparently harsh words with a gracious purpose clause — "so that they will be sound in the faith." Consider how gracious this is: Those who are involved in empty talk (v. 10), deception (v. 10), selfish gain (v. 11), and lies (v. 12) should be rebuked, "so that they will be sound in the faith and will pay no attention to Jewish myths or to the commands of those who reject the truth" (vv. 13, 14).

For whom do these words show Paul is concerned? Paul is concerned even for those who oppose him and whose words are ruining others. Those who are enemies of the gospel are included under the umbrella of Paul's care. This perspective should provide for a marked contrast between the world's attitudes and the attitudes of true ministers of the gospel. Just as "when we were God's enemies, we were reconciled to him through the death of his

Son" (Romans 5:10), so we should be willing to look past personal hurt and pain in order to seek the progress of the gospel even among those whose actions oppose our purposes.

Some months ago a new pastor called from a major urban center where he hopes to minister with his young family. He reported that he had been walking in his neighborhood and saw a man trying to break into a home across the street. The pastor quickly ran to the door of the nearest house to report the crime in progress. He soon recognized that the people in this house were a couple to whom he had been witnessing. Though they were married, the man was having an affair with another woman who was carrying a child conceived with yet another man.

When the pastor told the troubled couple that someone was breaking into the house across the street, the man of the house did not call the police. Instead, he headed out the door with a baseball bat and called over his shoulder, "Let's stop 'em." The pastor followed and then thought, "What in the world am I doing, following in the steps of this obviously unwise man? Without even a baseball bat in my hands, I am running toward a burglar who may be armed. For the possessions in the house of someone I don't even know, I am running the risk of leaving my kids without a father." The pastor stopped dead in his tracks, but fortunately the burglar was intimidated by the bat-wielding neighbor and ran away.

Unfortunately, the pastor noticed that the direction the burglar was running put them in the proximity of the pastor's own home. So he quickly walked to his own house and circled to the back door to see if there was any evidence of a break-in. There was no sign of the burglars. Instead, what the pastor discovered behind his house was an adolescent sitting on a bicycle, shooting up on some drug. The appearance of the pastor scared the kid — who sped away — dropping his syringe in the backyard where the pastor's children play.

Considering all the crime, immorality, sordidness, and danger to which this pastor had subjected himself and his family, and facing the reality of the opposition to the gospel evident in the people of the neighborhood to which he had come, the pastor came undone. He called me, disoriented from the assaults of his own fear and frustration. "Bryan," he said, "please pray that I will not hate these people." The words were said with a measure of despair, but they gave me hope because what they requested so reflects the gospel. People who were focused on their own gain and the garbage of this world were causing this pastor much pain, but he was still desiring their good. He was requesting prayer for the strength to restrain all the perfectly good excuses for turning his back on those who opposed him.

The Apostle Paul would surely commend this testimony of the gospel that so clearly reflects his own. Such a testimony instructs us of the importance and the necessity of caring for those who will oppose us and the gospel. As Paul's words make clear, even inside the church battle lines form, and factions press various agendas that will threaten the progress of the gospel. Still, to love the gospel, to fight for it and at the same time to desire that its truths capture the hearts of our enemies is what God requires of those who would differ from the world. The world understands hating those who oppose you. What contrasts those true to the Savior is the desire that all — even our opponents — would "come to a knowledge of the truth" (cf. 1 Timothy 2:4; Titus 1:1). We must mind our words — how we label people, how we characterize those who differ with us, how we phrase what we really want to happen to them.

We should recognize that there is no more powerful instrument for change in our opponents than true concern for them evident in us. We should not imagine that sometime in the future such love will characterize us if it does not now. I have no doubt that regardless of where we minister, or are preparing to minister, there are different attitudes, perspectives, and emphases among the people that can cause unfair and unkind characterizations and separations. While the apostle does not ask us to compromise our convictions, his example challenges us today to say a word of grace even to those with differing views, so that the gospel is more real in us and to us. I confess that I find this hard when people are attacking me, are saying what I believe is wrong, and are opposing the gospel as I understand it. I cannot contend that gracious living is easy, only that it is necessary if I am to understand how my God treats me. I am one who is also not always true to the gospel in thought, word, and deed, and yet God acts graciously toward me. My prayer is that we will populate the church with ministers who understand the same about themselves and that as a result such words and deeds of grace will flow from them that the church will be forged into a mighty, united force for the gospel.

WRONG ACTIONS (v. 16)

Though God does not accept or reject us on the basis of our works, he remains concerned about our actions. This is made clear in the final contrast that Paul will make with those who are opposing the progress of the gospel on Crete. After condemning his opponents' wrong words and wrong motives, he finally warns us from their path by identifying their wrong actions.

About What Should We Be Concerned? Deeds That Deny God (v. 16)

Paul says that his opponents "claim to know God" (the Greek terms reflect a public claim of a personal intimacy with God), "but by their actions they deny him." They are so "detestable, disobedient, and unfit for doing anything good" that their deeds inherently deny their knowledge of God. Furthermore, because these opponents claim to represent God, their actions also deny the holiness and goodness of God and thus betray him. The Greek word translated "deny" here is the same one used to describe Peter's renunciation of Christ (see John 18:25, 27).

These words that characterize the deeds of Paul's opponents do not challenge our minds so much for their definition, but they should challenge our hearts with the reality they are communicating. Word came recently of a minister who was called to the home of a grieving woman. He took advantage of her level of emotional need to fulfill his own needs sexually. Claiming to know and represent God, his actions instead denied God and are "detestable," "disobedient" and render this pastor "unfit for doing anything good." If our deeds do not conform to the gracious character of our God, then we deny his nature and deny ourselves the opportunity to serve him.

About Whom Should We Be Concerned? God (v. 16b)

The wrong words and wrong motives of those whose ministry should contrast with ours ultimately result in misdeeds whose description discloses the object of Paul's greatest concern. We are not told precisely what are the deeds of the apostle's opponents, but the deeds make those who do them "detestable." The term is probably ironic because it is the standard term used to identify God's attitude toward idolatrous practices. Those so concerned about detestable food offered to idols have actually made an idol of their purity standards and thus have made themselves "detestable" *to God*. The people who do these deeds also are "disobedient," the standard term for rebellion *against God*. These actions that deny God ultimately render their doers "unfit" to accomplish anything good *for God*. Concern for God is implicit in each of the terms describing the wrongdoings of the false teachers.

This contrast Paul has drawn should make it plain to true ministers of the gospel that our lives as well as our words should demonstrate a supreme loyalty to our God and his purposes. No one can promise that such loyalty to our God will make life easy, but the Lord promises that those who are preeminently concerned for him will be fit for the good for which we have been prepared in ways likely beyond our imagining.

The evening of the shooting in Littleton, Colorado, that claimed fifteen lives, my fifteen-year-old son prayed at bedtime that God would enable people to see some purpose in what had happened — that somehow God would use his people in Littleton for good amid all of the evil.

The next morning the *Today Show* interviewed Craig Scott, one of the students in the library at Columbine High School who survived by feigning death when students on both sides of him were shot. Craig ultimately led the survivors in the library to safety. Then he led them in prayer for their brothers and sisters who were still inside the school building. One after another brothers and sisters came out. Those praying cheered with each new arrival. "God did it." "God answered prayer." "I knew that God would protect my brother or sister." Again and again the cheers went up.

Craig told the details of the prayer time, and then he told of the one sibling of those praying who did not come out — Craig's sister, Rachel. She was one of the first to be killed — outside the building even as the two young gunmen were entering the school. Rachel had been a wonderful friend to many. She was popular, a starring actress in the school play, and she had planned to be a missionary — to give her life to the proclamation of the gospel. Craig told all of this even as his interviewer winced to hear him speak so lovingly of his sister. The interviewer then told local stations that the inevitable commercial break would be delayed to let Craig finish his story.

When the young man concluded the account, he affirmed his own faith that God would fulfill his purposes even in the death of Rachel and in the tragedy at his school. I knew that such supreme loyalty to God in the face of incredible personal hurt and cultural evil would be difficult for many viewers — perhaps most — to assimilate. It hardly made sense. Surely all who were watching wondered what this young man knew of God that could enable him to handle his pain and be at peace in the face of such senseless horror, sadness, and darkness.

The interview finally, almost mercifully, ended. The interviewer called for the overdue commercial break. I could not help but think of the prayer of my own son that God would somehow use all of this hopelessness for good. It seemed so unrealistic a petition — until the providence of God so powerfully and immediately displayed itself. Craig Scott affirmed his faith in God as the interview concluded. The commercial that played in my local area immediately on the heels of that testimony of God's faithfulness in the face of evil was an ad sponsored by a local church. These words scrolled on the screen immediately after Craig's urging others to trust God's faithfulness in a world whose obvious brokenness could make their lives seem empty and hopeless, unfit for anything good:

> *Dear God,*
> *You know everything.*
> *About me. . . .*
> *I know*
> *I've made mistakes.*
> *Please forgive me.*
> *Come into my life.*
> *Help me*
> *To follow You*
> *always.*
> *In Jesus name,*
> *Amen.*

If you confess with your mouth, "Jesus is Lord," and believe in your heart that God raised him from the dead, you will be saved. (Romans 10:9).

In the face of what the world can only see as misery and pain, young men — one on the *Today Show*, one in his evening prayers — were praying that God would yet minister for good. They were willing to see what only those loyal to God above all things can see — the great battle for eternity being waged all about us and in which we are warriors for God by our words, motives, and actions. The Puritan preacher Jonathan Edwards prayed for God to stamp eternity on his eyes so that all that he viewed would be seen in the context of its eternal consequences. May we too minister with eternity stamped on our words, motives, and actions, recognizing that as ministers of Jesus Christ there are eternal implications for the choices we make in every aspect of our lives. Such a realization that God is at work in, with, and through us will be the greatest joy of our life and will fit us for doing his good purpose, wherever he calls us, to do what he has prepared us to do.

37

Community Grace

TITUS 2:1-10

You must teach what is in accord with sound doctrine. Teach the older men to be temperate, worthy of respect, self-controlled, and sound in faith, in love and in endurance. Likewise, teach the older women to be reverent in the way they live, not to be slanderers or addicted to much wine, but to teach what is good. Then they can train the younger women to love their husbands and children, to be self-controlled and pure, to be busy at home, to be kind, and to be subject to their husbands, so that no one will malign the word of God. Similarly, encourage the young men to be self-controlled. In everything set them an example by doing what is good. In your teaching show integrity, seriousness and soundness of speech that cannot be condemned, so that those who oppose you may be ashamed because they have nothing bad to say about us. Teach slaves to be subject to their masters in everything, to try to please them, not to talk back to them, and not to steal from them, but to show that they can be fully trusted, so that in every way they will make the teaching about God our Savior attractive.

Two friends of mine are businessmen who meet weekly at a local sandwich shop to hold each other accountable for memorizing passages of Scripture. Both come from backgrounds in which Scripture was not a high priority. Now they reason that if they are to be responsible leaders in their church, then they need to have more of God's Word hidden in their hearts.

Challenging the good intentions of these men is the reality that both are quite a few years past their academic experiences. Memorizing no longer comes easily to them. They meet early in the morning at the sandwich shop when the crowds are light and the noise is low, so they can concentrate as they recite to one another. However, their efforts were made more difficult recently when some non-regular customers became a bit boisterous. The noise made it hard to focus on the Bible work, and ultimately one of the memorizers said to the other, "I'm getting a little ticked off at those guys." But, figuring this was not a very good attitude to have while memorizing Scripture, he shut his eyes, covered his ears, and spoke loudly enough to shut out any distractions: "O Lord, you have searched and you know me. You know when I sit down and when I rise up. You know my thoughts from afar. . . ."

As humorous as was the scene of this church leader shutting out everybody in order to concentrate on his Scriptures, it may be an apt metaphor for those who want to prepare for Scriptural leadership in the church by shutting themselves off from others. In contrast, in this portion of Titus, the Apostle Paul informs leaders of the importance of every believer's involvement in the community life of the church. As earlier passages have already discussed, God did not design the Christian life to be lived independently. Thus it is important for church leaders to know how God intends for the lives of the people in the church to interweave, to influence each other, and by these interactions to testify of the truth, power, and hope of the gospel.

GOSPEL TRUTH IN COMMUNITY (v. 1 AND OVERVIEW)

The apostle has just identified the negative characteristics of those who oppose him in Crete. Now, because of the negative influence of the false teachers, Paul says to Titus, "You must teach what is in accord with sound doctrine" (v. 1). The words are sobering for a number of reasons. Paul begins with an emphatic "you" (Greek pronoun *su* plus the disjunctive *de* plus an imperative verb), directed at Titus, as if to say, "Others are teaching what is wrong out of base motives, but *you* — by contrast — must teach what is sound." Even in an apostolic church the influence of false teaching was real and required vigorous countermeasures. If such influence could be present in that time, then we who are living in an era long separated from apostolic authority are cautioned all the more to see the necessity of teaching "sound doctrine."

The words "sound doctrine" are used by Paul to refer to the teachings passed on and approved by Christ's apostles, teachings meant to guard and guide the church (cf. 1 Timothy 1:10; Titus 1:9). No doubt Paul has in mind teaching the nature of salvation by unconditional grace, as well as the life of godliness that the apprehension of such grace stimulates — subjects that have preoccupied much of his letter thus far. But the doctrine alone is not to preoccupy Titus. He is to teach "what is in accord" (the single word in Greek means "consonant with" or "fitting with") this "sound doctrine." What follows "what is in accord with sound doctrine"? The apostle gives ethical instructions for personal conduct — not directed to the false teachers, but to all classes of persons in the church. These classes of persons in the church are identified by nearly parallel differentiations of age, gender, and station that typified descriptions of ancient households. The range of persons addressed by Paul's instructions indicate that neither "sound doctrine" nor the ethics that flow from it were for a spiritual elite. All true believers are expected to have their faith reflected in their conduct and to have their conduct affirm their faith.

Paul's emphatic imperative that Titus must teach "what is in accord with sound doctrine," combined with the scope of the groups to whom the instructions must be given, forces us to consider the state of the apostolic church at Crete. What was occurring in the apostolic church that would require such emphatic teaching, for so many, about such conduct? The list of issues that Titus must address in his teaching includes anger, immorality, immaturity in life and doctrine, lack of reverence, slander, meanness, substance abuse, idleness, family breakdown, crudity, dishonesty, frivolity, disobedience, back talk, and theft (vv. 2-9). If such matters had to be addressed in an apostolic church, we should not doubt that they would be present in the churches we now or will serve. Though such issues often lie beneath the surface, they are present wherever fallen people meet, and they vary only in degree.

A comment from a survey of recent seminary graduates reveals only one dimension of what is ahead for those in church leadership positions:

> Although you are told about it, although you have heard that it is going to happen, seminary cannot prepare you for the enormity of the complaining that you will hear. You are told that it will happen, but no one can prepare you for it. You have to realize that you will never make people happy. The myth is that you can. . . . The complaining that comes from church people is relentless. It is not the non-Christians who you will come in contact with, they don't complain, it's the children of God. . . . Unless your satisfaction is rooted in Christ, it will drive you insane. The complaining . . . will wear on you emotionally, physically, and spiritually. If you are not hiding in Christ, it will drive you out of ministry. I am not sure why we would expect anything different.[1]

And yet, we do expect things to be different. We want to believe that when our ministry preparations are over, life will simplify, getting less busy and less pressured. My wife tells of being at a dinner for the wives of graduating seminary students. She was sitting next to a young mother who gushed about being so glad that her husband had received a ministry call from a local church. "Now," she said, "our income struggles will be over, we will have mature leadership to shield us from problems, and my husband will be free from seminary studies so he can keep regular hours and spend more time with the family." My wife says she did not know how to respond. But what she thought was, "How can you get through seminary and not know that the fallen nature of people in the church will always present significant challenges for those who would teach others to live in accord with sound doctrine?"

While challenges are different in each stage of life, difficult days remain for any who minister in the church prior to Christ's return. I do not say this to discourage but to remove unrealistic expectations that can create excessive anxiety and to remind how necessary the gospel and its implications are even in the church. With unwelcome regularity I hear of friends and former students who are now out of ministry positions because of difficulty with supervisors, difficulty with fellow elders, difficulty with senior pastors, difficulty with senior high schoolers, difficulty with sexual impulses, difficulty with workloads, difficulty with spouses, difficulty with worship preferences. Easy street is *not* ahead.

Each day of ministry (and ministry training) is preparation for future difficulties. The early years of ministry are meant to equip us for increasing responsibilities and challenges. That is why it is important early in one's ministry training to develop the spiritual resources, expectations, and disciplines that will be necessary to function in ministry — to fill up your spiritual canteens, as it were, for the long and trying journey ahead. Another pastor responded this way in the aforementioned survey of recent seminary graduates:

> A professor of mine once said, "I can tell what kind of pastors you students will be by the way that you handle seminary life now." It was not that the guys I was in school with thought that seminary was a joke, but for many it was just a necessary hurdle they had to jump in order to get a job. . . . That is a terrible view. What you are doing right now is . . . preparation. The way you live your life now, the way you handle things now, is not going to change significantly when you get out. You are going to face greater pressures and demands when you get out. Things are going to get worse, if you are not living [faithfully] now, you will not do it later. The discipline that is required of you now is nothing like what will be required of you later.[2]

The disciplines that we normally consider essential for ministry preparation and practice are prayer, study of God's Word, and worship. Paul's letter to Titus hints at another discipline as well. Paul tells Titus to commit himself to teaching others who will in turn teach others the implications of the gospel. As a result, Titus's life and teaching are committed to the welfare of the church community, which further promotes the work of the gospel. It seems that the church community not only consists of those who trouble the ministry of the gospel, but within the community are also those who empower the gospel's influence.

GOSPEL POWER IN COMMUNITY (vv. 2-10)

Paul's identification of how gospel power flows through a spiritual community is important because it is a necessary correction of the way many approach the church today. Undoubtedly a large percentage of people in the modern church are driven by a consumer mentality. They value only what is beneficial to them and partake only of what pleases them at the times that are not disruptive to their schedules, at costs not significant enough to burden their lifestyles. Such persons will pick the church activities that are attractive to them but never think of the impact of their actions on others. Only the most mature have a sense of personal investment in regular fellowship, disciplined worship, and church community life. Paul is determined to make sure that we know what characterizes this mature perspective and participation.

For Older Men (v. 2)

Lest we compartmentalize our lives and faith from the lives and concerns of others, Paul first tells Titus to teach the natural leaders of the community, the older men (v. 2), "what is in accord with sound doctrine" (v. 1). The Greek term for "older men" is from the same root as that used for the office of elder (presbyter), but the context — and the contrast with older women — indicates Paul is likely referring more generally to men mature in years (cf. Luke 1:18; Philemon 9). Paul says that Titus should teach such men "to be temperate, worthy of respect, self-controlled" (v. 2). To be "temperate" means to be sober in thought or clearheaded. The phrase "worthy of respect" is derived from a single Greek word that means being so sensible or seriously considered in one's deportment that honor or veneration naturally come. One who is "self-controlled" prudently curbs his desires and impulses. These terms are used elsewhere in the Pastoral Epistles for the spiritually mature (cf. 1 Timothy 3:2; Titus 1:8) and might be interpreted as merely requiring personal discipline if Paul's language were not carefully examined.

The phrase "worthy of respect" hints at the importance of a community's regard and thus implies involvement in others' lives. This implication becomes explicit in the clause that follows. New Testament scholar Phil Towner explains:

> What the NIV has interpreted as three additional aspects of acceptable behavior (*and sound in faith, in love, and in endurance*) could by virtue of the participle "being sound," express instead the cause or means of the behavior described above [i.e., being "temperate, worthy of respect, self-controlled"].[3]

In other words, what enables the behavior expected of the older men is "faith . . . love . . . endurance" (cf. 1 Corinthians 13:13; Colossians 1:4, 5). "Faith" describes a personal relationship with God. "Love" describes relationships with others. "Endurance" describes steadfastness for the sake of these relationships, especially in the face of opposition such as Paul himself faced in the Cretan churches (cf. 1 Thessalonians 1:3). In the light of these three terms, mature Christianity is defined as a commitment to the maintenance of both the vertical (to God) and horizontal (to others) relationships that comprise the Christian community. From these initial instructions for older men, Paul's "Titus 2 Plan" for making grace ripple through the church community now begins to flow.

For Older Women (v. 3)

Titus "likewise" (or in the same way) is to teach "older women." These mature women, also "in accord with sound doctrine" (v. 1), are to be taught "to be reverent in the way they live." The word *reverent* refers generally to honoring God, but its source in Greek culture characterized the conduct of priestesses. The Greek Christians would have understood Paul to be saying that a mature Christian woman should demonstrate the holiness of a heart that is near to God. Thus Titus was to teach the older women "not to be slanderers or addicted to much wine." The first behavior cited there (malicious gossip) relates to lack of control of the tongue. The second (drunkenness) relates to lack of control of both one's appetites and purposes. Either out-of-control behavior commonly associated with indolent women in the decadent Greco-Roman society would damage the credibility of the life-changing power of the gospel. In this light it is apparent that Paul expected that the self-control of the older male leaders would positively influence the behavior of older female leaders with the result that their reputations would promote the gospel.

The godly conduct that Paul required of older women was not only for the sake of their reputations. After identifying the negative behaviors spiritually mature women should avoid, Paul identifies their positive pursuits. The apostle says that Titus should "teach" them "to teach what is good." Here the ripple effect of godliness is obvious: Good teaching leads to more good teaching. The simplicity of this plan may cause its profundity to escape those of us in modern society. For the ancient world this was a very bold plan. For a man to teach women to instruct others broke societal barriers and elevated the status of these women. It is possible that Paul only means that as a general consequence of Titus's teaching, these women should learn godly conduct. Nevertheless, he communicates a definite responsibility to them. At the same time that he gives mature women new responsibilities, Paul places a constraint on the teaching of male leaders. The specific reason Paul gives for Titus to teach the older women is so *they* will teach the younger women (v. 4).

At least two observations should be made about this pattern. First, Paul's words again affirm the importance of community contribution for mature Christians. The older women are not to hoard their knowledge but rather should pass it on to younger women who need the advice of those with greater experience. Second, Paul does not tell Titus to teach the younger women. This non-instruction probably reflects Paul's concern that a young woman perceive her husband as the male who is her primary spiritual instructor (cf. 1 Corinthians 14:35). Paul also apparently desires to establish a pattern of instruction in the church that does not lead to sexual temptation. The "good" things that the older women are to teach the younger seem to relate primarily here to matters of marital and family life (although they may relate to religious matters also; cf. 1 Timothy 2:9, 10). Paul's standards do not rule out the possibility of those with wisdom and appropriate safeguards giving personal counsel across gender lines. Still, the apostle's normal pattern for the church is to have older women advise younger women in daily matters of family and Christian lifestyle.

Paul's instructions for older women caution church leaders not to be cavalier about: 1) proper lines of family authority; 2) the real dangers of sexual temptation even for those with religious zeal; and 3) the great advantages to the church of having those with marital, child-rearing, and church experience understand how valuable is their willingness to communicate the daily responsibilities of the faith to those with less experience. Teacher and student will grow in the realities of grace as spiritual truths are reflected upon, organized, and passed along. When my children were young, my wife and I often sought the advice of Christians we respected regarding their child-rearing practices. Now that my children are older, I note that young mothers often approach my wife with questions about how to raise their children. And though she is not usually aware of the observation, we are told that others watch her to see how she deals with our older children. As I reflect on the ways that my wife teaches others, I recognize that she mothers many in our church. Further, I am immensely grateful that our family also benefits from her thoughtful reflection and consistent modeling of what being a spiritually mature woman means. When these dynamics are multiplied many times through the spoken and modeled instruction of mature women throughout the church, the entire body is nurtured by the spreading influence of these spiritual mothers.

For Younger Women (vv. 4, 5)

Paul specifically states what influence he wants the older women to have on the "younger." (Note: Paul actually does not insert the word for women or

wives, although it is assumed to be in his thought since he was just referring to older women and now speaks of the younger's responsibilities.) The
mature women are to model and teach godliness. "Then they can ["in order
to," '*ina*] train the younger women to love their husbands and children, to
be self-controlled and pure, to be busy at home, to be kind, and to be subject to their husbands" (vv. 4, 5).

The responsibilities of younger women are first outwardly oriented.
They are to "love their husbands and children." In that day of formal and
arranged marriages, a woman who truly and deeply loved her husband would
stand out as a representative for the gospel in Greco-Roman culture. Thus
Paul makes commitment to family the highest priority of a young wife.
Further, the apostle places commitment to one's husband first in the order
of duties and highlights its priority by offsetting it in the grammatical construction of the sentence (literally, "train the younger husband-loving to be
child-loving, self-controlled . . ."). The wording is a gentle reminder that
even more important than love for one's children is love for one's spouse,
because children will not readily understand the greatest of God's earthly
gifts (i.e., the love shared by Christian spouses) unless a mother's love for
her husband is evident in the home. Because the false teachers in Crete
were "ruining whole households" by their teaching (1:11), these seemingly
obvious household instructions may have needed special emphasis.

The next set of responsibilities specified for younger women underscores the ripple effect of godly leadership in the church. Just as elders
(1:8), older men (2:2), and older women (in the control of their tongue and
appetites; see 2:3) are to exercise self-control, so are younger women. Their
self-control is linked here to being "pure" (or chaste). This term hints at the
sexual constraint aspects of self-control, although it also refers to fidelity in
one's relationship with God. Love for one's spouse would seem naturally to
produce fidelity and restraint on one's ungodly passions, but perhaps Paul
speaks of the need for these controls because of the next instructions.

The older women are also to teach the younger women "to be busy at
home." We need to be careful not to impose modern debates about women's
roles on our interpretation of these words. It is unlikely that Paul had in
mind concern about "career women" or mothers in the secular workplace.
The Greek phrase literally says that the younger women should be taught to
be "home workers." The emphasis (particularly in light of the earlier instruction to the older women not to be caught in the vices of indolence in the
church community) is not on the location of a wife's work but on being
productive in the normal occupations of a wife each day.

This instruction still has bearing on modern discussions even if it is not
the absolute command for women to stay at home that some may desire.
The apostle without question ranks a wife's obligations to care for her husband and children over her personal benefit or fulfillment. Any woman who

makes career status or financial advantage a higher priority in her life than the welfare of her marriage, children, or home transgresses Scripture as well as the signals of a heart sensitive to God's Spirit. Perhaps this is the reason Paul urges that young women not only be taught to be productive at home but also to be "kind." A sensitive heart will not get so caught up in the routines of homemaking that compassion for a husband's or child's needs gets lost, nor will such a heart be dissuaded by the callousness of the secular world regarding the value of the homemaking routines. (Note: The word translated "kind" [*agathos*] literally means "good" or "useful for a purpose." This nuance underscores the emphasis on productivity in these clauses and may indicate that this word should be attached to the preceding to complete the thought that women in the home should be "*useful* home-workers.")

Finally, Paul says that younger women should be trained "to be subject to their husbands." This is one of five New Testament passages that uses this or similar language to refer to the relationship that a Christian wife should have with her husband. Perhaps because of the numerous other references Paul abbreviates his explanation of what the term means here. After all, here he is expecting the instruction of the older, godly women to be the chief vehicle for communicating Scriptural expectations to the younger women. Still, because we do not have the advantage of such experiential instruction in this commentary, it is important to clarify Paul's teaching on what it means for a wife "to be subject to" or "to submit" to her husband. Paul's more expansive treatment of the husband/wife responsibilities in Ephesians 5 make it clear that the Bible does not permit a husband to have a "Me dictator, you doormat" mentality. All persons in the Christian community are required to submit to proper authorities in their lives (Ephesians 5:21). This does not give anyone the right to be unfair, selfish, or abusive. Rather, a husband is to love his wife "just as Christ loved the church and gave himself up for her" (Ephesians 5:25). This sacrificial love of husbands is complemented by the love of wives who are to "submit to their husbands in everything" (v. 24).

The Greek term for "submit" (*hupotasso* = "to arrange under") does not mean that a wife is to suppress her intelligence, talents, and gifts in the home. Rather, she should fully express these gifts in the purpose of supporting her husband in the spiritual leadership of the home. The comparison Paul draws in Ephesians 5 is to how the church honors Christ (vv. 23, 24). Just as the church arranges the expression of her gifts so she can give maximum support to Christ's purposes, so a Christian wife should fully use her gifts to honor the spiritual purposes of her husband. Suppression of gifts is not the point. Proper expression of them is. A Christian wife arranges her gifts and talents under the higher purpose of supporting the spiritual nurture of the household. In this sense a wife's need to be useful and productive in the home not only applies to material duties (as in the earlier "busy at home" clause) but also to spiritual duties. The consequence of such conscientious care for both material and spiritual concerns is that "no one will malign the word of God" (v. 5b). As opponents in the church and potential faith seekers in the culture examine "what is in accord with sound doctrine" (v. 1) through the behavior of the young women in the church, the Word of God gains credibility. The wonderful message implicit here is that what happens in the home as a result of a woman's care is a powerful tool for the progress of the gospel.

For Younger Men, Including Titus (vv. 6-8)

Paul instructs Titus himself to instruct the younger men both by word and by example. Thus, just as the older women are to instruct the younger, the influence of Titus's life is to spread among the less mature men. Paul first tells Titus to "encourage the young men to be self-controlled" (v. 6). The issue of control over one's own conduct has now arisen among all the groups of the church (earlier: elders, 1:8; older men, 2:2; older women, 2:3; and younger women, 2:5), underscoring the contrast between those controlled by the gospel and those who are rebelling against it (cf. 1:10).

The contrast is heightened in that Titus's example for the young men is to be the antithesis of those opposing Paul's teaching in the Cretan church (cf. 1:16). The false teachers are "unfit for doing anything good," but by his example Titus is to teach "what is good" (v. 7a). The false teachers deceive (1:10), lie (1:12), and "reject the truth" (v. 14) for "dishonest gain" (v. 11). But Paul says to Titus, "In your teaching show integrity" (v. 7b). The word "integrity" probably refers not only to the character of Titus but also to his uncorrupted message. This is in further contrast with the false teachers who with their polluted gospel are "corrupted," and to whom "nothing is pure" (1:15). The false teachers are "mere talkers" (i.e., uttering empty, senseless things, 1:10), but Titus is to show "seriousness and soundness of speech that cannot be condemned" (vv. 7c, 8a). What the false teachers say and do causes them to "deny" God (1:16), but Titus's words and example should cause no one to deny the validity of his message or the character of those who deliver it (cf. 2:8).

Paul says that Titus should show "integrity, seriousness and soundness of speech that cannot be condemned, so that those who oppose you may be ashamed because they have nothing bad to say about us" (v. 8). At least to some degree, these statements reveal how Paul intends for Titus to carry out his earlier imperative ("they must be silenced," 1:11) regarding those who oppose him in the Cretan church. Titus's sound words and godly example should render the false teachers speechless, silencing them. Since this conduct of Titus is also to provide an example to the younger men, there should be a multiplication of silencers as the godly influence of Titus spreads among the young men and helps to heal the embattled church. Since even the young men are to follow the example of the speech and conduct of one as spiritually mature as Titus, the apostle makes it clear that godly responsibilities apply to all members of the Christian community.

For Slaves (vv. 9, 10)

No one is excluded from community responsibilities regardless of their station in the church or society. Even slaves have conduct and witness responsibilities. Paul tells Titus, "Teach slaves to be subject to their masters." Again the term for "subject" is the Greek *hupotasso* (i.e., arranging one's gifts under the purposes of those with proper authority — see earlier discussion on v. 5). For the moment Paul does not deal with the legitimacy of slavery. While this is difficult for those of us who only think of slavery in the context of the despicable practices of chattel slavery in early America and in other nations even today, our context does not necessarily parallel Paul's.

A slave (i.e., a servant, *doulos*) in the Greek world included those in miserable conditions, but it also included those in apprentice or indentured relationships, domestic workers, and some who held high government office. Additionally, as the context of this passage indicates, a slave could be considered a member of the master's household and a member of a religious community with freemen. The scope of responsibilities and positions was vast for slaves in the Greco-Roman world. Yet, what was common to all slaves was that in some measure each was subject to the control of another person. Such control makes it surprising to our minds and distressing to modern sensitivities that the inspired apostle does not directly annul the legitimacy of this control.

Undoubtedly, concern for the reputation of the gospel in the ancient society to some degree explains why the apostle wants slaves "to try to please them [their masters], not to talk back to them, and not to steal from them, but to show that they [the slaves] can be fully trusted" (vv. 9, 10). Such instructions must be meant to muzzle critics and to defang persecutors who accused Christians of inciting rebellion and threatening the stability of society (cf. 1 Peter 2:15-21). The apostle ends his instructions to women and to younger men with statements that the mandated conduct will blunt attacks, and it is natural to surmise that such a motive would remain in view here.

The more startling (and definite) motive for the instruction, however, Paul himself specifies: "so that in every way they [the slaves] will make the teaching about God our Savior attractive" (v. 10b). With these words Paul entrusts to slaves the ministry of making the gospel appealing to their masters. By giving this responsibility to slaves, the apostle makes their masters' eternity subject to the slaves' good-hearted willingness to live for gospel priorities. The slaves become the Savior's representatives, responsible for conduct that can lead to their masters' salvation. This perspective makes a master's ultimate welfare dependent on his slave and makes a slave the master of his superior's future.

This inversion of master/slave roles makes Paul's statement in the following verse all the more striking: "For the grace of God that brings salvation has appeared to all men" (2:11). We tend to think of this phrase as giving a rationale for extending the gospel down to all classes of persons, including the disadvantaged and despised. In context, however, the words encourage slaves to remember that even societal superiors who have been corrupted by their worldly privileges are objects of the grace of God and thus should not be denied the message of salvation by slaves who already possess the higher privileges of eternity. From a gospel perspective, the unbelieving master is the disadvantaged one who should not be discriminated against by withholding from him a hand up from the believing slave. While this is not a frontal assault on slavery, the leveling of privilege and the condemnation of discrimination are ways that the Bible effectively undermines the premises that would seek to legitimize slavery in any society (cf. Philemon 15, 16).

In addition, the responsibility for gospel witness given even to slaves becomes the ultimate statement of the apostle that everyone in the church community has a role in the progress of the gospel. The responsibility of Christians to participate in the church community flows from an understanding of how powerfully the gospel progresses when all persons live according to the principles of grace. Not only does such godliness conform the community members to the standards of God with ever-increasing numbers and depth of insight, but the testimony of the community as a whole (and of its individual members) radiates outward across social and class barriers. The progression of Paul's instructions to the various segments of the church indicate that community dynamics are instrumental in influencing others in the church, silencing opponents in the church, and reaching unbelievers outside the church. This is power from which no believer should cut himself or herself off.

GOSPEL HOPE IN COMMUNITY

Our corporate worship, prayer, and teaching times are not nearly so much about learning more facts as they are about experiencing and communicating the reality of God. There are times, of course, when church seems dull. Yet there also are moments that none of us can anticipate — when a family in crisis needs prayer, when God so inhabits the praise of his people that our fellowship with him becomes unmistakable, or when a sermon so causes us to see the majesty and intimacy of Christ that we are changed. Our collection of these moments is a spiritual mantle under which we are made stronger against sin, more fit for the daily battles against Satan, and more conscious of the realities of grace.

These corporate dynamics indicate why Paul expects ministry to occur through more than the leadership of the church. Yes, elders are to lead, but the apostle has clearly assigned to all in the Christian community a role. The older are to reach the younger, and the experienced are to pass along their experience to those coming after them — parents to children, those inside the circle to those outside the circle. Everyone has the role of making God real to someone else.

Prayer, praise, instruction, fellowship, and the service of the church do not fulfill their purposes if we do not function corporately and in community. There is always the temptation to privatize and individualize our faith experience. We tend to make decisions about whom to hear, what to do, and where to serve largely based upon what will be good for us personally. Paul's instructions to Titus thus prick our consciences in order to make us sense the importance of being responsible for others and living our lives in community. The hope we possess and pass in community should force us to consider the interests and needs of others more than our own (cf. Philippians 2:1-5).

If the hope we can give to others is not enough to motivate our involvement in the church community, the hope we ourselves receive should stimulate our mutual care. Elsewhere Paul writes, "I pray that you may be active in sharing your faith, so that you will have a full understanding of every good thing we have in Christ" (Philemon 6). Thus if we are really to understand all the goodness that we have in Christ, we must share our faith with others. This is not merely an evangelistic call but a call to live for others in whatever situation God has placed us. We should not confuse being a knowledgeable Christian with being a faithful Christian. In order to see clearly the realities of grace, we must be willing to give of ourselves for the nurture of others.

John Buchanan writes of another person trying to do ministry who has the world shut out in a different way than my sandwich shop friends whom I mentioned at the beginning of this chapter. She is an elderly woman shut into her home by age and blindness.

She lost her husband early in their marriage. With two daughters to raise, the menial jobs that she could get would not provide enough income. So she supplemented her small salary by baking wonderful, melt-in-your-mouth sourdough bread. When the daughters grew up and left home, the baking did not stop. The woman who had given herself so much for others was simply in the habit of putting others first. She kept baking bread and giving it away to friends.

Then something began to affect her sight. She progressed from weakened sight to total blindness very quickly. With so much against her, and so much pressure simply to survive, no one would have blamed her for calling it quits on everything except what was needed to take care of herself. But instead of submitting to the darkness, the elderly woman made an important decision. Baking bread was what God had given her to do to express her love and care to others. She would not give it up simply because she could not see.

So she mixes the flour and water she does not see, finds the dials on the oven in the dark, bakes the bread by instincts long developed in the light, and gives the loaves to people whose faces she can only imagine. She cannot tell you entirely why she bakes blind — only that God has given her love to share with those whose future and present need the yeast of her selfless love in order to share the bread of life with others.

Whether we are attending church or a Bible study or offering fellowship to another family or are baking blind, we do not physically see the spiritual effects on others. But what we share with each other in these settings is spiritual life, nourishment, and protection more sustaining than earthly eyes can estimate. Still, Heaven sees and blesses through such selfless sharing that prepares us for the future, protects us in the present, and shapes hearts forever.

38

"Intolerant" Grace

TITUS 2:11-15

For the grace of God that brings salvation has appeared to all men. It teaches us to say "No" to ungodliness and worldly passions, and to live self-controlled, upright and godly lives in this present age, while we wait for the blessed hope — the glorious appearing of our great God and Savior, Jesus Christ, who gave himself for us to redeem us from all wickedness and to purify for himself a people that are his very own, eager to do what is good. These, then, are the things you should teach. Encourage and rebuke with all authority. Do not let anyone despise you.

When El Nino's rain deluged Southern California one recent winter, the potential dangers of mudslides became a real nightmare for one family. While the family was still in their home, a wave of mud tore through the house, severing it and sweeping a sleeping baby out into the night. The parents began to search through the darkness for the child. Tromping through the mire that had descended upon their whole neighborhood, they searched, dug, and called for their child throughout the long night — without results. When morning came a rescuer, himself covered in mud, came to the parents with a mud-caked bundle in his arms — the baby, filthy but alive. You know what the mother then did. She clung to her child despite its filth, washed the muck away, and determined to keep the child out of the mud in the future.

The account helps me understand concepts in this passage that are so opposed to our common thought about the nature of God's grace. Grace, we know, annuls our works as the means of securing or maintaining God's affection. The natural human inclination, as a result, is to suppose that if our good works do not determine God's affection, there is no reason to do them. Why be concerned about godliness since we are saved by grace? Because, say the Scriptures, when the filth of my sin was sweeping me in my helplessness to eternal death, my God covered himself in the muck of this world to rescue me, embraced me despite my filth, and now wants me to remain out of the mud. Such grace should make us so in love with God that we cannot stand whatever in our lives re-soils us and offends him. Biblical grace makes us intolerant of evil in our lives. The apostle here underscores this truth, saying that the grace of God "teaches us to say 'No' to ungodliness and worldly passions" (vv. 11, 12).

Grace — rightly perceived — compels holiness. This is not a natural logic, we must confess. In the popular mind those who are full of grace are supposed to say, "Okay, that's all right. Fine. Never mind. Go ahead." But for the apostle, grace means we say no. What kind of grace is this? The apostle tells us by disclosing the power of Christ's rescue, the nature of his requirements, and the character of his redeemed.

THE RESCUE OF GRACE (v. 11)

The apostle begins to explain the nature of transforming grace by reminding his readers of what God has accomplished and for whom. In the preceding section of this letter (2:1-10), Paul told Titus to make sure that what is "in accord with sound doctrine" (v. 1) is taught to all kinds of people — older men, older women, young women, young men, slaves — who will pass along "the teaching about God our Savior" (v. 10) to others. The reason for these imperatives follows: "For the grace of God that brings salvation has appeared to all men" (v. 11). The context makes it clear that Paul is not contending that worldwide evangelism has already occurred, but rather that the message of God's grace has been made available to all kinds of people. By reminding his readers that the message of the Savior has not been withheld from anyone on the basis of age, class, or gender, Paul defuses the discriminatory objections of those who would deny their testimony to others on the basis of societal barriers.

Basis for discrimination is further removed when Paul reminds his readers of their own undeserved deliverance. The "salvation" (a predicate adjective describing God's "delivering" or "saving") made available to all kinds of people has been brought by "the grace of God" (a phrase used fifteen times in Paul's letters to describe unmerited divine favor). No one has been saved by what they have themselves accomplished or vanquished. We are saved not on the basis of our goodness, station, or class, but solely on the basis of God's sovereign action on our behalf.

Paul underscores this truth of our unearned deliverance and expands its implications by saying that this grace has "appeared" (v. 11). In Greek literature this word can function as a technical term to describe a hero (or a god) breaking into a helpless situation to rescue someone from danger. Paul typically uses this terminology to refer to the past or future coming of Christ to rescue his people (cf. v. 13). When the apostle uses the same word to describe the coming of grace, he so intertwines who Christ is with what Christ provides that the two become inseparable in our consideration. Grace is not some abstract doctrine or theological construct. Grace comes as Christ does. Grace is as personal as he is. In fact, Christ is grace. The unmerited favor of God is what Jesus is about, but it is also who he is. We should thus see grace as a personal action by a personal God who saved us from our helpless condition out of pure love.

Intimate affection by a majestic God is Paul's message, but intimacy is not the entire message. The ancients would have understood a god who came to rescue a person, a group, a city, or even a nation from a personal crisis. The ancient Greek and Roman plays included the *deus ex machina* by which a god intervened to rescue from a specific crisis. But as has already been made clear, Christ's appearance is not limited in scope to a man or clan. The unique Christian message is that God's rescue is offered and is sufficient for "all men" (v. 11) regardless of their human designation or demerit. Thus the rescue that God our Savior engineers is both intimate and immense.

THE REQUIREMENTS OF GRACE (vv. 12, 13)

Paul intends for the combined message of such an intimate and immense salvation to have an effect upon us. Our hearts should flood with wonder, thanksgiving, gratitude — and one more thing — determination. When we realize we have been rescued from the clutches of evil against which we were helpless, our resolution is strengthened never to go back there. We never want to allow the evil to take hold again. That is why the rescue of grace results in requirements. Not because the requirements rescue but because the rescued, who truly recognize the danger they were in, desire and strive to be forever free of its clutches. What the grace that has appeared requires is phrased in both negative and positive implications (v. 12).

Saying No (v. 12a)

First, Paul says that that grace "teaches us to say 'No' to [the nuance is to renounce on an ongoing basis] ungodliness and worldly passions." "Ungodliness" is a reference to the Christian's conduct — or, in this negative phrasing, his misconduct. One commentator refers to Paul's use of *godliness* as "reverence manifested in actions" — our external behaviors. But the ungodly externals are not all that Paul has in view as deserving our no. We are also to say no to "worldly passions." This means we are to deny ourselves not only external conduct that betrays God but also similar internal impulses, what the *King James Version* simply describes as "lusts" and other versions variously translate as worldly "appetites," "desires," or "cravings." There is no question that sexual compulsions are included in the term, but there is also concern about anger, hatred, ambition, and other urges that result in uncontrolled speech or behavior.

Now consider precisely why these prohibitions are given. They are not the means to get to God. Rather, they are a consequence of the appearing of grace that is God in Christ. As was mentioned in Chapter One, when Isaiah saw the majesty and holiness of God, the prophet fell down and cried out, "Woe to me! I am ruined." When God revealed himself to Moses in the burning bush, the deliverer of God's people hid his face. Paul expects the effect of seeing God so clearly in the grace revealed through Christ Jesus to affect us no differently.

When we have seen God clearly in the appearance of his grace, we have an intense awareness of our unholiness. Grace in this context "teaches us," as Paul says in the opening phrase of this verse (v. 12). A true apprehension of grace instructs us of the magnitude and repugnance of our sin. That is why Paul says that the grace of God that has appeared "teaches us to say 'No' to ungodliness." We want to be rid of what stained us before the radiance of his glorious grace. But saying no is not our only obligation. Isaiah rose asking God to use him. Moses walked from the burning bush to do as God required. There are positive compulsions that also arise from grace.

Living Yes (v. 12b)

Grace "teaches us to say 'No' to ungodliness and worldly passions," but it also instructs us to live in assent to God's requirements. Such assent constrains Christians "to live self-controlled, upright and godly lives" (v. 12b). The first two terms in this list could fairly be called the antithesis of ungodliness and worldly passions (mentioned previously in the verse). The earlier, negative terms were about unrighteousness and the lack of restraint. These first two of the positive terms are about control of passions (i.e., righteous constraint on one's own impulses) and uprightness (i.e., righteous conduct in dealing with others). Because the emphasis in the verse thus far is on controlled behavior, the third term ("godly") in the list of positive characteristics taught by grace has particular significance.

If being a Christian only involved self-control over our passions and "upright" behavior before others, we might get the idea that the Christian life was only a matter of living according to certain rules or performing in an acceptable way. By adding the word *godly* to the ways grace teaches us to live, the apostle reminds us that the Christian life is one of dependence on God. Godliness is not a consequence of human resolution or willpower. It is a relationship with God that results in a life honoring to God. Thus, taking the three positive characteristics taught by grace in order, we learn that the life of grace is comprehensive — involving oneself, one's relationship to others, and one's relationship with God.

Acting Now (vv. 12c, 13)

How long are we expected to live according to these standards? Is holy living a matter only of the past when people were under the law? No. Paul says that grace teaches us to live so as to honor God "in the present age, while we wait for the blessed hope — the glorious appearing of our great God and Savior, Jesus Christ" (vv. 12c, 13). We are not allowed to say that in this age of grace there are no standards for us to follow. Godliness remains our obligation until Jesus returns.

The future grace of Christ's return, when his "glorious appearing" will mark our deliverance (see earlier discussion of "appear" in v. 11) from the evil and suffering of this world, is also identified here as "the blessed hope." "Appearing" and "hope" are introduced by the same definite article, indicating that they are the same event. What Paul adds by introducing "the blessed hope" phrase is a definition of what the glory of the "appearing" will include. When the elements of this phrase appear elsewhere in Paul's writings, they refer both to the multiple aspects of the deliverance that believers will know at Christ's return (cf. Romans 8:24; Galatians 5:5; Colossians 1:5) and to the renewed presence of the Deliverer who will bring those blessings — he who is "the hope of glory" (Colossians 1:27). Thus the elements of this "blessed hope" include Christ's return, the resurrection of those who have died in Christ, the union of living believers with Christ, the reunion of the faithful living and dead, and eternal life with Christ (see 1 Thessalonians 4:13-18).

The certainty of this hope is underscored by Paul's identification of the Deliverer as "our great God and Savior, Jesus Christ." Though the natural reading of this phrase has often been challenged for its direct affirmation of Christ's deity, it remains one of the most powerful New Testament proofs of Christ's divine nature that grants believers assurance of blessing (cf. 2:10, 11; 3:4, 6). Not only is Jesus the Christ (i.e., the Anointed One who came to fulfill past promises as our Messiah and to provide present grace as the Lamb of God), but as our "great God" he is also able to deliver the blessings of future grace for which the faithful hope. The knowledge that our God is coming creates expectancy in believers that stimulates faithfulness in daily endeavor and grants perseverance in times of trial. Because Christ is coming, we desire to live in fidelity to him. And knowing that he will deliver us from trial and will vanquish all his and our enemies, we can live in faithfulness to him. "The glorious appearing of our great God and Savior, Jesus Christ" is our cause for godly living "in this present age."

In summary, the grace God provides in our past, present, and future requires that we say no to the world and yes to God *now*. Grace does not change the requirement of godliness in the Christian life. Still, because the categories of conduct the apostle has addressed are so comprehensive, Christians may be tempted to affirm their general obedience without really having examined the particulars of their lives. To force us to answer whether we are, in fact, willing to say no to the world and yes to God *now*, we need to consider specific areas of our lives where the world commonly challenges Christian faithfulness. Determining what God requires in a specific area such as the entertainments we enjoy will provide guidance for godliness in other areas of life.

A few weeks ago my teenage son went to see a popular movie. Unbeknownst to him and to us due to the posted rating, the movie included a scene with nudity and a following sexual encounter. My son walked out and took his friends with him. I was very proud of him for his principled leadership. Yet, what happened to my son afterwards has left me flabbergasted, discouraged, and occasionally angry. Over the next several weeks the Christian friends and adult leaders in his life, almost without exception, told him he was wrong. They said that such sexual material was not a valid reason for any really mature Christian with a well-developed world and life view to not see a movie. The result, of course, is that my son felt confused and alone in his commitment

How should Christians respond to such entertainments in the light of Paul's exhortation to respond to God's grace with godliness? Hopefully we will all recognize the folly of trying to establish a yardstick for flesh exposed (or lists of words used or themes addressed) in order to determine the appropriateness of works of literature and art for all Christians in all times. At the same time, the Bible requires that Christians *now* — in this place, culture, and time — answer to God regarding whether their entertainments, habits, and appetites exhibit a true commitment "to say 'No' to ungodliness and worldly passions" and yes to "self-controlled, upright and godly" living. Our inability to draw hard and fast lines regarding artistic expression for all historical and cultural conditions does not remove our responsibility to determine if what we are consuming, and encouraging others to consume by our example, is damaging the cause of Christ.

Many knowledgeable evangelicals will question a challenge to examine the appropriateness of our entertainments. They remember the warnings of Christian philosopher Francis Schaeffer that we not live in a "corner culture." Schaeffer rightly contended that we should not shut ourselves into a Christian ghetto, listening only to ourselves and losing our ability to understand our culture, to dialogue with it and ultimately to penetrate it with the message of the gospel. Such principles are profoundly true to the ethics and imperatives of Scripture. Still, Schaeffer was neither unconscious of the dangers inherent in our culture's values nor without warning about the indiscreet indulgence of what it offered. Schaeffer did not want freedom from legalism to lead to bondage to the intoxicants of the world. He wrote:

Often, after a person is born again and asks, "What shall I do next?" he is given a list of things, usually of a limited nature and primarily negative. . . . The true Christian life is not merely a negative not-doing of any small list of things. Even if the list began as an excellent list of things to beware of in that particular historical setting, we still must emphasize that the Christian life, or true spirituality, is more than a refraining from a certain external list of taboos in a mechanical way.

Because this is true almost always there is a reaction: another group of Christians begins to work against such a list of taboos; thus, there is a tendency toward a struggle in Christian circles between those who set up a certain list of taboos and those who, feeling there is something wrong with this, say, "Away with all taboos, away with all lists." Both of these groups can be right and both can be wrong, depending on how they approach the matter.

I was impressed by this one Saturday night at L'Abri, when we were having one of our discussion times. On that particular night everybody present was a Christian, many of them from groups in countries where "lists" had been very much accentuated; they began to talk against the use of taboos, and at first, as I listened to them, I rather agreed with the direction they were going. But as I listened further to this conversation, and as they spoke against the taboos in their own countries, it became quite clear to me that what they really wanted was merely to be able to do the things which the taboos were against. What they really wanted was a more lax Christian life. But we must see that in giving up such lists, in feeling the limitation of the "list" mentality, we must not do this merely in order to be able to live a looser life: it must be for something deeper.[1]

With Schaeffer there was certainly a push to make Christians aware of the values, concerns, and trends of our culture, but we must not forget why. Beneath the evaluation was outrage and grief. Schaeffer was outraged that the sophisticates of culture could take the noble things of creation and use them in rebellion against the Creator. Schaeffer's grief about young people being led astray was intense and compelling. A life committed to their redemption (on their terms, if necessary) was the zeal of Schaeffer, and it must remain ours. We must ask each other, "Is the reason we are partaking of the entertainments that are poisoning the minds and morals of many in our society truly so we can redeem them?" The Bible says we must cling to the good but hate what is evil (Romans 12:9). While we cannot read one another's hearts, we should be willing to examine our own hearts as to whether we truly hate what is illicit, immoral, or indecent on the screen.

Are we outraged, out for redemption, or just out with the rest of culture for the Saturday show?

The ethics of grace require us to ask honest questions even about our own entertainments. Are we redeeming or simply imbibing? Are we being informed or simply being tranquilized regarding evil? Are we evaluating or simply enjoying? Are we living as though there is no division of the sacred and the secular? Specifically, are we watching, reading, and listening to entertainments conscious that whether we are in a bright church, darkened theater, or secluded room we are before the face of God? Do we act as though wherever we are, we are on holy ground? Does what we are doing really reflect the conviction that a holy God who rescued us from the death grasp of sin is with us in every place and is coming back in power and glory? In light of his past, present, and future grace, do we live in gratitude to him with every thought, motive, and action? Are we doing everything in word and deed to the glory of God (Colossians 3:17), or does our God go away when the lights go out?

These are hard questions even for the one who now asks them. I struggle to know all the answers in my own life, and I look for the means to evaluate my habits in these words. How do we examine and, if necessary, re-sensitize our consciences? How do we know if we have moved beyond the boundaries of God's requirements in our own lives and are again in danger of being swept away by the mud — the filth of this world? Honest questions based on the apostle's instructions will help here, if we dare to ask them.

1) Have we lost the ability to say no?

We must honestly assess our internal compulsions — "worldly passions." Do they control us? Do we see certain movies, watch certain shows, read certain books, listen to certain music not because of their aesthetic excellence but because we need a sexual fix? No one can answer for us — we must each examine our own hearts with candor and rigor about these matters if we are to honor our Lord. Christ takes every idol of culture (sex, power, money, and all the rest) and requires it to bow before him. If those idols are beginning to control our thoughts, actions, and anticipations, then we are bowing before them.

We may have difficulty determining our idols because our thought can be so influenced by what culture approves that we have lost the ability to say no. Pervasive sin has the ability to make us callous, and part of the evidence of its desensitizing effects is that we lose a sense of distinction between godliness and ungodliness. There is a difference between what the world approves and what God approves. If we are in large measure simply accepting what the world accepts, something is amiss.

Spiritual blindness is inevitable if we become increasingly indistinguishable from a culture that denies itself nothing. Francis Schaeffer cautioned us about such a culture more than three decades ago:

> We are surrounded by a world that says "no" to nothing. When we
> are surrounded by this sort of mentality . . . then suddenly to be
> told that in the Christian life there is to be this strong negative aspect
> of saying "no" to things and "no" to self, it must seem hard. And if
> it does not feel hard to us, we are not really letting it speak to us. . . .
>
> We have a society that holds itself back from nothing. . . . Any
> concept of a real "no" is avoided as much as possible. . . . Absolutes
> of any kind, ethical principles, everything must give in to afflu-
> ence and selfish personal peace. . . .
>
> Of course, this environment of — of not saying "no" — fits
> exactly into our natural disposition, because, since the fall of man,
> we do not want to deny ourselves. . . . And this natural disposition
> fits in exactly with the environment which surrounds us in the twen-
> tieth century.[2]

If our understanding of the grace of God fails to teach us "to say 'No' to
ungodliness," then we are living in the same condition as the rest of the
world.

2) Have we lost the concern about living a yes?

I well expect that the reaction of many Christians to a renewed plea for
purity in our entertainments will be, "You cannot take my liberty away. I
am under grace. I am not under the law." I agree that I cannot judge the
thoughts and motives of others and that this limits my ability and right to
draw hard lines for others where matters are not directly addressed in
Scripture. This limitation, however, does not allow me or any other Christian
to stop being concerned for the effects of our actions on others. The Christian
life cannot be lived autonomously. Our assent to live godly lives requires
us to consider others as we make our choices.

When Paul outlines the behavior God expects of those in the household of faith, he reminds each member that he or she is not alone — the
actions of each touch others. Older men are to set an example for other
believers. The older women are to be reverent so they can teach the younger
women (2:3, 4). Titus himself is to be an example to others (v. 7). The
Christian life does not function independently. We are part of a community,
and our actions must be considered in light of their effects upon others.
Said Schaeffer, "We are to be willing to say 'no' to ourselves, we are to be
willing to say 'no' to things in order that the command to love God and
men may have real meaning. Even in things which are lawful to me, things
which do not break the Ten Commandments, I am not to seek my own, but
I am to seek another man's good. . . ."[3]

It is not enough to argue in the face of an immoral entertainment, "It
doesn't bother me." Maybe you are untouched by the intended stimulation of
ungodliness and worldly passions, but the church is not untouched. The

incidence of promiscuity among young people in evangelical churches is nearly equivalent to that of those in the rest of society. The abortion rate is not significantly different among those in evangelical churches from those in similar socioeconomic categories in the general culture. The frequency of unfaithfulness among pastors is epidemic. Sexual disease, dysfunction, addiction, and abuse are "the common colds" of the church. Something is terribly wrong among us, and no one can seriously deny that at least part of the problem that has stripped away moral reservation, inhibition, and respect is our society's entertainment norms.

The impact of these culture forces on God's people requires the concern of godly leaders. We should see the evil of explicit sexual expression in the entertainment media as the lure of Satan that it is. We must acknowledge that sexual expression on the screen is evil for those participating. We should consider what our dollars support and what our example endorses in the light of Scripture (cf. 2:7). Will history judge contemporary Christians any less harshly for paying to see sexual acts on movie screens than we judge ancient Christians who participated in pagan rituals? Christian leaders concerned for the future of marriages, families, and the church really must consider the long-term effects of young people longing, lusting, and learning in the darkened-theater-classrooms of Hollywood what marriage, sexual intimacy, and regard for another human being should be.

Perhaps you personally are untouched by the values of the culture evident in the sexuality and violence of movies, TV, and video games. Still, well-publicized tragedies in high schools and homes across this land indicate that others have been touched. As a result of the cultural forces dehumanizing people and/or turning them into objects of rage or personal pleasure, sexual and physical abuse are staggeringly pervasive. Awareness of what the morals and mores of our culture have produced forces us to ask the hardest question of all: We may be concerned about our community, but as we see its devastation are we concerned about our complicity? The grace of God will not allow us to live unconcerned for those God loves. Our practices and pleasures are examples to others of our values and of God's expectations. Our lives must manifest our assent to his concern for others.

We must be very clear about all of the requirements of grace. If anyone says that what we do earns God's love, that is legalistic trash. If anyone devises standards for us to follow that cannot be proven from Scripture, that is the rubbish of Pharisaism. But if anyone says that it does not matter to God or his people what we do, that is selfish, un-Biblical, and damaging to the gospel of our Lord. All about us are those who are enslaved to the evil of this world. If we pursue our liberties primarily for our own sake, then we may profess a maturity that gives us rights, but it will not support the proclamation of God's grace toward those lost in the miseries of sin. The goal of the godly is to adorn the gospel with credibility and evidence of its power in their lives. The indulgence of "ungodliness and worldly passions" ultimately is a denial of the Word of God and the message of the Savior. If our lives exhibit no freedom from the passions of this world, then our lives implicitly say the gospel makes no difference.

3) Are we willing to act now?

Those uncomfortable with the notion that an ancient apostle might have something to say about our modern entertainments are likely to respond, "No one can take away my Christian liberty. My church will only run headlong back into legalism if we promote concern about these matters. Furthermore, why should I limit my activities when no specific Bible verse addresses a specific activity, habit, or practice?" The Biblical response to such statements is that of course no one has a right to bind another's conscience or judge another's actions where the Scriptures are not specific. But the principles that bind Christians in their love for God, his people, and his purposes are more about relationships than proof texts.

When consciences made sensitive by the Spirit convince us that our conduct damages our heart's resonance with the Savior or contributes to such damage in others' hearts, then we change our course. This is why godliness is so dependent upon God. Without the convicting and renewing work of the Spirit in our hearts, we will always rationalize our sin and continue in its path. Yet, as we grow in our affection for God because of his grace, we increasingly grow intolerant of anything that distracts us from him and seek to guard our hearts from all that would distance us, or anyone else, from him.

The concerns for our relationship with God and our witness of him that influence our entertainment choices apply also to every area of life the apostle addresses in this letter — employment, speech, church leadership, homemaking. The implicit message is that grace daily calls us to action, no matter what our activity or station:

• The businessman whose industry is characterized by compromises that are contrary to the gospel — though he knows that his challenge of "the system" will likely make no difference, will only cause him to suffer, and will deny him the success to which his career is dedicated.

• The young mother who is wrestling with what Scripture says about her commitments to her family and what her culture says about her value in the workplace.

• A young person considering promiscuity and/or drugs knowing that "Any stand I make against these things will make no difference to the vast majority of my friends, will only cause me pain, and will deny me what others enjoy."

• A family so caught in the subtle cords of materialism and social acceptance that they are barely able even to grasp the sin that is making every day more desperate financially, relationally, and spiritually.

Godliness in all the areas of life that the apostle specifies for instruction about grace will prove terribly costly. What can ignite sufficient zeal for such priorities and purposes? The answer is, overwhelming love for him who gave himself for us. The apostle sparks such love by reminding us of our status as a result of our Savior's actions.

THE REDEEMED OF GRACE (vv. 14, 15)

Having been explicit about the requirements God has for those claimed by his grace, the apostle now makes it just as clear that these standards are *not* the reason God loves us.

Our Status (v. 14)

We are awaiting the appearing of Jesus Christ "who gave himself for us to redeem us from all wickedness and to purify for himself a people that are his very own." The work of salvation is his, and we are his. The apostle designs every phrase of this beautiful verse to exude the wonder of Christ's work and the consequent status of his people. Paul first reminds us that Christ "gave himself." The words initially remind us that Christ's sacrifice was a gift neither earned nor deserved. Next we are reminded that the gift indicates that our God acted "for us." He became our advocate, acting in our behalf though we were yet sinners. This is some of Paul's favorite language, used repeatedly to indicate the nature of God's unconditional favor for his people (e.g., Romans 8:31, 32; Galatians 1:4; 2:20), and it prepares us to understand what Christ's sacrifice accomplishes for his people.

Ransomed (v. 14b)

Christ gave himself for us "to redeem us from all wickedness." The word *redeem* literally means "to release upon the receipt of a ransom." Jesus speaks of himself as our ransom (see Mark 10:45, probably reflecting Psalm 130:8 and Ezekiel 37:23), and Paul uses the concept explicitly (cf. 1 Timothy 2:6) to refer to our Savior giving himself to pay the price for our "wickedness" (literally, "every lawless deed"). The preposition translated "for" ("gave himself for us") can even be translated "in the place of" to drive home the concept of Christ rescuing us by becoming a ransom for sin in our place in order to satisfy divine justice and free us from our guilt.

Cleansed (v.14c)

Not only did Christ give himself to redeem us, but he also offered himself "to purify" his people "for himself." This phrase reminds us of the various sacrifices and disciplines God established for his covenant people to demonstrate to them the need for cleansing from the taint of their sin. As the fulfillment of all these practices, Christ's sacrifice and blood cleanses all to whom it is now applied by faith. These words remind us that God has cleansed us from the defilement of our sin by the sacrifice of his Son (cf. 2 Corinthians 7:1; Ephesians 5:26; Hebrews 9:14).

Treasured (v. 14d, e)

Having redeemed and cleansed us at such a terrible price, God's attitude toward us could be one of resentment or disdain. Instead, we are told that those he has purchased and purified, he now claims as "a people that are his very own" (v. 14d). The Greek phrase reflects the wording of Exodus 19:5 where God identified the covenant people as "my treasured possession" (see the earlier cited Ezekiel 37:23; cf. Ephesians 1:11-14). The attitude of the Redeemer toward the redeemed is that we are precious to him despite the sin that required such sacrifice from him. These words breathe the grace that characterizes our God and should inspire us to do the good works that please our Savior. The people that are God's own by virtue of his unconditional favor and sacrifice are to be "eager to do what is good" (v. 14e). Here again is the theme that grace leads to godliness.

These statements that characterize our status as a result of Christ's work are our great protection against legalism and our great propulsion toward godliness. Because Christ's work alone purchases our salvation through the redeeming price of his blood, and because Christ's work alone purifies us through the cleansing that his blood supplies, we do not look to our works as the basis of acceptance with God. Doing what God requires does not make us his own, but having been made his own by no work of ours, we now love to love him who first loved us (cf. 1 John 4:19). Such love has profound effects upon our attitudes and actions.

My youngest daughter sometimes says to her mother, "Mommy, I love you with all *your* heart." I realize why a three-year-old says such things. She tries to show her love by mistakenly echoing her mother's frequent endearment — "Katie, I love you with all my heart." But it is no mistake that here in Titus, God teaches us to love him with all his heart. He pours before us the signs of our Redeemer's love so we will love and respond to him at as high and close a level of affection as the human heart can sustain.

What does being a loved people do to us? It makes us more sensitive to sin. We should note well the order of the apostle's descriptions of God's work and response. God's people are first ransomed by his work, then purified to be his own, and *then* they are "eager" (zealous) to do good (v. 14). In some ways this message turns upside-down a common perception of how the Christian life operates. We tend to think that we cannot see the love of God until we perceive the degree of our sin, but Paul here makes the point that perceiving the love of God enables us to see our sin.

Apprehension of the mercy of God in Christ makes us so long to love him and to reject what hurts him that we become intolerant of the sin in our lives. I understand this as I look at my own marriage. The longer I am married, the more I marvel at my wife's love for me despite my early coldness and continuing selfishness. Now the more I see how much she loves me, the more conscious I become of my insensitivities and the more eager I am to please her. The more I perceive her love, the more I cannot stand distance between us. In the same way, when we see how wondrous is the love of Christ, we become more and more sensitive to the sin in our lives, and we long more and more to do what pleases him.

This dynamic of having the love of God create an intolerance for sin is what the Puritans called the "power of new affections." What will ultimately make us holy is not willpower, nor guilt, nor an inspiring message, but deep apprehension of the mercy of God in Christ. The resultant love for God drives out and replaces our natural love for sin. The Puritans taught this truth with the image of the live oak, a variety of trees whose leaves — though dead — stuck to their branches through the winter. What eventually forced the leaves from the tree was not the abuse of the cold or the beating of the wind, but the new life of springtime welling up within the branches and forcing out what was dead. In a similar way, though we are God's people, there yet cling to us affections for evil that we must confess. These evil affections are replaced by an eagerness for good only as apprehension of Christ's grace wells within us and ultimately drives out the old affections with the new life that is profound love for him.

Our Standard (v. 15)

So wondrous are these truths that Paul insists they must be the standard message of Titus. Paul says, "These, then, are the things you should teach [literally, "speak"]." What are "these . . . things"? The context indicates they are the message of grace that enables Titus to "encourage" (*parakalei*; cf. 1:9; 2:6; 1 Timothy 6:2) and the message of intolerance to sin that requires Titus also to "rebuke" (or refute; cf. 1:9, 13) when it is appropriate. Grace does not save from nothing, nor does grace teach that a past way of life is inconsequential. These truths are too important ever to minimize. Each of Paul's instructions to Titus concerning "these . . . things" (i.e., "teach," "encourage," "rebuke") comes as a present imperative, indicating the need for an ongoing emphasis of each in his ministry.

Paul's strident exhortation reminds us that if we teach "these . . . things" (i.e., grace despite sin and obedience through grace), some will accuse us of promoting license on one hand, and some will accuse us of being legalists on the other hand. Still, we must not cease from making the message of grace and godliness our standard. Whether accused of being a prude or a profligate, Paul says the leader of God's people should "not let anyone despise" him (v. 15b). The word *despise* can also mean "disregard," reminding us that our teaching may be made ineffective either by failing to speak with authority or by failing to live in accord with Scripture.

Extricating ourselves and our people from the mire of those cultural sins that have entered into our habits, appetites, and homes will not come without struggle within and without the church. Still, we must proclaim the unconditional grace of God as the motive and power for standing with an uncompromising commitment to godliness. As the darkness of our culture grows more deep, we must stand for the truths and standards of God's Word. The reason should be clear: Others will need the encouragement of being able to look through a misty dawn of revival with the assurance that God's leaders are still willing to carry more of God's children from the muck that threatens their eternal lives. We must not tolerate a gospel divorced from grace, nor a grace that abandons holiness. May we so powerfully believe and proclaim the love of Christ that affection for him drives out the affections of this world!

39

Priorities of Grace

TITUS 3:1-15

Remind the people to be subject to rulers and authorities, to be obedient, to be ready to do whatever is good, to slander no one, to be peaceable and considerate, and to show true humility toward all men.

At one time we too were foolish, disobedient, deceived and enslaved by all kinds of passions and pleasures. We lived in malice and envy, being hated and hating one another. But when the kindness and love of God our Savior appeared, he saved us, not because of righteous things we had done, but because of his mercy. He saved us through the washing of rebirth and renewal by the Holy Spirit, whom he poured out on us generously through Jesus Christ our Savior, so that, having been justified by his grace, we might become heirs having the hope of eternal life. This is a trustworthy saying. And I want you to stress these things, so that those who have trusted in God may be careful to devote themselves to doing what is good. These things are excellent and profitable for everyone.

But avoid foolish controversies and genealogies and arguments and quarrels about the law, because these are unprofitable and useless. Warn a divisive person once, and then warn him a second time. After that, have nothing to do with him. You may be sure that such a man is warped and sinful; he is self-condemned.

As soon as I send Artemas or Tychicus to you, do your best to come to me at Nicopolis, because I have decided to winter there. Do everything you can to help Zenas the lawyer and Apollos on their way and see that they have everything they need. Our people must learn to devote themselves to doing what is good, in order that they may provide for daily necessities and not live unproductive lives. Everyone with me sends you greetings. Greet those who love us in the faith. Grace be with you all.

I remember my first pastoral crisis. Within about three weeks of my being installed as a new pastor, one of my elders became very ill. I went to visit him in the hospital — my first pastoral visit of any sort. As I entered the lobby of the small-town hospital, the wife and daughter of the elder were exiting with his doctor. The wife introduced me to the doctor, whose first words were, "Pastor, you need to advise this family about whether they should with-hold life-support from your church member since he is so old and his con-dition is unlikely to improve."

I did not know what to do. I was only a third of the way through my sem-inary training. So I called one of my seminary professors and received wise advice about our Christian obligation to prolong living but not to prolong dying. In God's providence, the family did not have to make any difficult decisions. The Lord took the elder to his heavenly home without the com-plications the doctor had anticipated. This meant, however, that now I needed to do my first funeral. I did not know what to do. So I called a seminary professor who invited me to breakfast so he could explain what my obliga-tions were.

After the funeral, our little church needed to elect a new elder, but no new officers had been elected in a generation. I did not know what to do. So I called another seminary professor who gave me a cram course on church government in his home office. A few weeks later we elected new officers.

Hopefully most persons entering pastoral ministry are better prepared than I was. Still, no matter how good our training, we will face circumstances and issues that will require us to say, "I don't know what to do." Some ques-tions will relate to the kinds of circumstances just described, but persistent questions will also relate to how we spend our time or to what tasks we should apply our greatest efforts. Repeatedly we, along with others, will question what should be the focus and thrust of our lives. Leaders in the church now have so much information to filter and file, so many new tasks and patterns to learn, so many new people to know, and so many problems to resolve that they can easily become overwhelmed.

What should get the most attention, energy, and effort in our churches? Because no training can prepare us fully for the range of issues, personali-ties, and circumstances that our individual ministries will confront, we must make decisions based upon Biblical priorities that are not always self-evident in specific situations. In this section of his epistle Paul summarizes what should be the priorities of Titus's ministry and in doing so the apostle estab-lishes the godly priorities for all church ministry.

REMIND GOD'S PEOPLE OF THEIR OBLIGATIONS (vv. 1, 2)

The first priority Paul specifies for Titus requires him to remind God's peo-ple of their responsibilities. This is a continuation of Paul's thought at the end of the preceding chapter where, having established the doctrinal basis for grace-motivated obedience, he tells Titus to speak without reservation about what God requires of his people. The apostle now communicates those obli-gations in the context of our rulers and relationships.

Rulers (vv. 1, 2b)

Regarding rulers, Paul says, "Remind the people to be subject to rulers and authorities, to be obedient, to be ready to do whatever is good" (v. 1). The verb "remind" means "to call to mind what is already known." The need to be "subject" (again the verb *hupotasso*; cf. 2:5, 9) to governing authorities is not new, but perhaps the zeal of the Jewish false teachers has contributed to a rebellious spirit against the civil magistrate in the Cretan church (see 1:10). As indicated in the earlier discussions of submission, being subject does not imply mere passive subservience. Expression of gifts in support of a higher purpose remains implicit. Thus Paul defines being subject not only as requiring obedience but also readiness "to do whatever is good" as loyal and contributing members of society. (Note: The term for "obedient" means to obey a magistrate and clarifies the meaning of the more generic phrase "rulers and authorities," which can refer to spiritual as well as civil powers; cf. Ephesians 6:12 contra Luke 12:11 and Romans 13:1-3.)

Despite submission to governing authorities heading the list of Christian obligations in various apostolic instructions (e.g., Romans 13:1-3; 1 Timothy 2:2; 1 Peter 2:13-15), the apparent priority of this obligation in this context may initially strike us as curious. Why, in summarizing a minister's duties, does Paul list civil submission as the first duty that a Christian minister should emphasize? Titus's immediate need to protect the Cretan church from persecution as a result of the reputed, or actual, rejection of authority must be a contributing reason. The scope of the instruction and the implicit gospel intention further underscore why Paul would make this imperative a priority.

The scope of the instruction becomes evident when we consider concretely what it means for us to be "subject to rulers and authorities." In an age of "culture wars" we can grasp how much of life is affected by the charge to give proper respect to national leaders. How we vote, the ethics we use in political debate and action, the laws we obey, the legislation we seek, and the language we use to discuss governmental issues and officials — at church, at work, and around the dinner table — all of these areas of life are affected by Paul's instruction "to be subject to rulers and authorities." Then this subjection is further defined by the instructions, "to slander no one, to be peaceable [i.e., not contentious] and considerate [literally, "gentle"], and to show true humility [i.e., mildness or meekness]" (v. 2b). Lest we think Paul and the other apostles simply did not know what we have to put up with, we should remember that these were the times of Caesars, occupational armies, and coliseums.

National authorities are not all that we must consider, however, when applying these instructions. "Rulers and authorities" will concern our people when they try to build or repair buildings (including churches) according to city codes, conduct business according to laws of commerce, drive according to traffic laws, run schools according to state standards, pay workers according to government regulations, or pay taxes according to the laws of city, state, and nation. For people to subject themselves to civil authority according to Scripture will require examination and correction of virtually every area of daily life. We will not escape this because we happen to be in a church ministry. I have yet to work in a religious setting where we did not face unreasonable standards or officials that inhibited the progress of our ministry — and every time there is a temptation to think that because the authorities are not reasonable, our obligation to submit to them is annulled.

The Bible will not allow the inconvenience of proper authority to lessen our obligation to submit to rulers for two reasons that involve the progress of the gospel. The first relates to the reputation of the gospel, and the second relates to the authority of its proclaimers. The most obvious reason, already indicated above, that Paul would tell Titus to have the Cretans obey authorities is that he did not want the gospel to be identified with political agitation that would bring Christianity under suspicion as just being a counter-political movement. This remains an important consideration today when so many want to identify the moral stands of Christian leaders as being merely political. If our gospel positions are to have credibility, we must make sure that we do not sully our stance in the political arena with words or actions that indicate unwillingness on our part to be subject to proper authority.

A second reason that the gospel requires the people of God to honor authority is that the gospel cannot progress if God's people only honor the authority they find agreeable. Consider Paul's concluding word of the preceding chapter as he instructs a Christian minister to "encourage and rebuke with all *authority*" (2:15). Although the Greek words translated "authority" or "authorities" vary in these two verses, the root concept does not. We must submit to the authority God places in our lives, even if that authority rebukes us. If Christians routinely operate in the mode of respecting only the authority with which they agree or that does not trouble them, then the minister of the gospel who must correct, rebuke, and exhort will soon have no authority.

Recognition that the ministers of the gospel will have no authority if they do not teach the people of God to respect authority perhaps best explains Paul's priority on this instruction, especially in a church infiltrated with false teachers. We should not let the ancient particulars, however, keep us from considering how important these standards are for us. An anti-authority mind-set pervades our culture and infects the church. An increasing problem noted by seminaries is graduates struggling with authority. As the evangelical church matures and enlarges, more graduates are going into assistant and/or associate pastor positions. These young leaders seem to be having great difficulty submitting to leadership (i.e., senior pastors, sessions, or church councils), especially when those in authority may have philosophies, practices, or perspectives with which the graduates disagree. Many seem to think they have a responsibility to submit to authority only as long as they agree with it, or as long as it is fair in their eyes, or as long as it does not require too much inconvenience.

Despite all the studies that evangelical seminaries have students read about the anti-authority mentality of modern culture, we do not seem to recognize our culture's influence on us. While it is true that we should resist authority that requires ungodliness, we can hardly expect parishioners to honor the Scriptural authority that confronts their sin if pastors will not honor the authority that disconcerts them. And if the people of the church will not honor authority, the Word of God will have no credibility for those outside the church. Ultimately a church community that does not submit to governing authority undermines the authority of the Word of God for the church and for the lost. No wonder Paul places such a high priority on teaching submission to authority.

Relationships (v. 2c)

At the end of the one long Greek sentence describing our obligations to governing authorities, Paul adds a clause that has a dramatic impact on all that precedes it. The apostle tells Titus to remind the people "to show true humility *toward all men*" (v. 2c, italics added). The word translated "true" is actually the Greek term for "all" or "every kind of." Having described submission with various preceding terms, the phrase "show all kinds of humility" is a summary of all that has preceded. But the summary takes an interesting turn as the clause comes to a finish. All kinds of humility are to be shown "to all men." The attitudes and actions previously directed toward ruling authorities by committed Christians, Paul now says must be directed toward "all men." In other words, all our relationships are to be governed by the kinds of selfless words and actions that have just been mentioned in these opening two verses.

In all our relationships, the apostle requires us to submit (i.e., arrange our gifts under a higher purpose) for the good of others. In all settings we must be ready "to slander no one, to be peaceable and considerate [Note: These two terms are included in the list of elder qualifications in 1 Timothy 3:3], and to show true humility toward all men." This is not doormat Christianity — passively letting people trample all over you — but is rather the exercise of the greater strength of not responding to evil with evil (cf. 1 Peter 3:9). For the good of others, those in the church — including its leaders — must recognize how disappointing and defeating it is for the people of God to be at odds or to speak ill of each other or not to be considerate of the weaknesses in others that may have caused their failures, unkind words, or inappropriate actions.

Some of us will rise to positions of importance in the churches or organizations we serve. In such positions we discover that the higher one rises, the better a target he is for all sorts of attacks. People will speak out of jealousy, out of depression, out of political agendas, or out of malice. Some just like fighting. Others will try to incite differences among those in the Christian community out of the sense of importance it gives them to be able to create problems, be in the know, or watch fur fly. Some of the attacks will be for valid causes. Others will not. As a consequence, one whose character is as flawed as mine will be tempted to establish his own position by damaging the reputations of others, or to sacrifice community peace for the sake of personal pride or the proof of being right.

The world well understands infighting and backbiting, but what wins the gospel a hearing from unbelievers is a very different pattern in the church. Those in the church are to model peaceableness and consideration, especially with each other (cf. Romans 12:18; Galatians 6:10; Hebrews 12:14). How? The answer lies in a willingness "to show true humility toward all men." Such humility enables us to submit to authorities, care for communities, and love peace over personal gain. Where does this governing humility come from? From the next central priority of the ministry that Paul introduces.

RECALL THE MEMORY OF YOUR PAST (v. 3)

Two processes are simultaneously active in the words that follow to create the pervasive humility that is so important for the life and testimony of the church. First, Paul distinguishes the present Christian life from its past worldly counterpart, and then he unites Christians in understanding how dependent each is on grace as a consequence of that past.

Lives Distinguished (v. 3)

Paul distinguishes our former lives without Christ in roughly the same categories as he has just outlined the believers' obligations.

We were once wrongly ruled (v. 3a). Instead of submitting to proper authorities, at one time we too were "disobedient" and "enslaved [precisely the verb form of "slave"] by all kinds of passions and pleasures." Christians who remember what it meant to be ruled by one's own standards alone, or who know even now the power of addictive passions and pleasures, understand the apostle's concern that we teach others that the Christian life necessitates a radical separation from this wrong rule. Once our lives were governed by what is "foolish" (i.e., without understanding) because we were not directed by God's wisdom, and we were "deceived" (the word suggests a false guide leading us astray).

The words "foolish" and "deceived" both carry the idea of a wrong understanding. The first term identifies this wrong as a consequence of one's own limitations. The second term blames the wrong upon the efforts of others. Less obvious in our translations is that the word *disobedient* also carries a nuance of being "not persuaded" and thus culpably not compliant. As a result, the first three terms of Paul communicate that once we possessed no wisdom, resisted God's wisdom, and followed others' lies. This precisely reflects the past experience of many of us who determined that Christ should lead us because we had followed a path that the world called wise, only to discover that it leads to emptiness (see Ecclesiastes 2:1, 10, 11; 1 Peter 1:18). We must be careful not to return to such deceptive wisdom even in our Christian lives, for virtually all the temptations to find fulfillment in this world's positions, people, or pleasures remain.

We were once wrongly relating (v. 3b). "We lived in malice and envy, being hated and hating one another." Paul reminds us that in our relationships we were motivated by getting back at others for what they had supposedly done to us ("malice") or getting even because they had what we did not ("envy"). Such self-oriented attitudes damaged our relationships, making us "hated" (the word could also mean "hateful") and causing us to hate one another. These motives will not disappear when we become Christians. In some ways they may become even greater temptations, because our different levels and kinds of spiritual experiences can cause us to experience "malice and envy" in new categories.

Thus Paul reminds Titus that the Christian's present life must be different from the past in the way that we are ruled and relate to others. There is a strong caution here — the apostle's challenge for us to examine whether we are truly living a separated life or whether we have inadvertently (or willfully) drifted back into a worldly pattern of thought and conduct. Still, distinguishing the Christian's past and present is not the apostle's only motive.

Lives United (v. 3a, b)

Paul overlays the process of *distinguishing* the Christian life with the process of *uniting* Christians. Note the repeated use of the rhetorical "we" (v. 3). The apostle does not stand off and say to Titus, "Remind others that *they* were once like this," nor even "Remind others that *they* and *you* were once like this." The "we" encompasses everyone, including Paul: "*We* too were foolish . . . enslaved by all kinds of passions. . . . *We* lived in malice and envy" (v. 3).

Paul, the apostle, groups himself with Titus and the people of God in past error. The plain message is that no one is distinguished by superior character or accomplishments apart from God's work. We have been leveled, made common kin by a common past. Every believer is a member of the union of the once despised. Apart from the work of God "we" were all hopeless. Neither apostle, nor people, nor preacher can claim his position by virtue of his personal qualities. This humbling truth can be hard to remember, but it is absolutely essential to unite and advance the church.

A pastoral friend recently confided, "When I graduated from seminary, I truly felt I had met the qualifications to be a pastor. I was respected by my peers and praised for my gifts in the church. I would never have *said* that my talents were anything but a gift of God, but I *thought* that I had met the academic qualifications, had satisfied the character requirements, and possessed the people and preaching skills that would be needed. I really believed that I knew how to control my conduct, how to raise my family, and how to lead a church. I was not being arrogant or blind. I simply felt that I had done what was needed to deserve a ministerial appointment. Only now do I understand that my conduct has never been what God required, that I will never be able to control all that is necessary to raise my family as I want, and that I haven't got a chance of leading a church anywhere if God hasn't prepared the path in a thousand ways that I can't even fathom. I had no concept of how little I knew, and how little I deserved to be a pastor."

If we do not know this truth of our universal need of grace, then we are not prepared to pastor, counsel, teach, or lead in Christ's church. Those whom God calls to lead his people are those who can say, "I was at one time foolish, disobedient, deceived and enslaved by all kinds of passions and pleasures. I lived in malice and envy, being hated and hating others." When we recognize that we were rescued from a pit deeper than we could crawl from, that we were saved from a darkness greater than our light could penetrate, that we were delivered from sin greater than our resolve could control — only then are we prepared to lead others. Such humility enables us to proclaim the gospel eye to eye with those who believe they will never measure up to the goodness they think we have attained by our resolution and strength of character.

Only when we truly believe that apart from Christ there is no more hope of Heaven for us than there is for the worst sinner we meet can we minister the gospel to that one and others. Believing the leveling truths of the gospel creates a community where malice, envy, and infighting disappear along with the need to measure our righteousness against one another. In humility lies the key to living out our obligations to rulers, to one another, and to God — and what produces that humility is the message that Paul says must be our ultimate priority.

REPEAT THE MESSAGE OF GOD'S GRACE (vv. 4–11)

Humility does not come solely as a product of recalling our past. Remembering a desperate past from which there is no rescue can produce despair rather than humility. Also, if our rescue from that past in any measure comes as a consequence of our wisdom, will, or strength, then pride rather than humility results. Thus Paul makes it clear that our rescue is totally the work of Another. Our willingness to submit to authorities and to live peaceably with others hinges on this understanding of our total destitution apart from the mercy of God. Whereas verse 3 gives the personal basis for the humility that motivates the imperatives of verses 1 and 2, verses 4 through 7 give the doctrinal basis — sheer grace!

The expression of all that God has done in our behalf is so highly compressed in these verses that we can barely scratch the surface of all that Paul is saying. The essence is this: When we explain our eternal status, God gets the credit, and we get the blessing. At the conclusion of this explanation of grace, Paul says, "This is a trustworthy saying" (the phrase by which Paul bookmarks Christocentric truths in his Pastoral Letters that are already established truisms in the church), "and I want you to stress these things" (v. 8). These emphatic phrases confirm the importance of the grace that is the focus of this section and the apex of the entire epistle. The message of grace is the foundation of obedience and blessing.

Distinctives of Grace (vv. 4-8)

A proper understanding of grace requires that we first identify the distinctions of the gospel and then identify distractions from that message. In modern parlance we might say, "TMT-ITK-TMT-TMT (the main thing is to keep the main thing the main thing)." The main thing is grace, and Paul explains this by identifying the credit God should receive for our rescue from our past and the blessings we receive as a consequence of our rescue.

God's credit (vv. 4-7). God's credit is evident in the words that speak of the attitudes, actions, and instruments involved in our rescue. Our salvation is not a result of earning God's favor. Rather, we were "foolish" and "disobedient" (v. 3), but "when the kindness and love of God our Savior appeared, he saved us, not because of righteous things we had done, but because of his mercy" (v. 5). These words emphasize that our salvation is a consequence of what is in God's heart, not what is in our heart. The words "kindness" (*chrestotes*) and "love" (*philanthropia*) describe God's benign regard for his people. Further our salvation is not a consequence of what we do but of what he alone does. "God our Savior appeared" (the term for appearance again relates to a divine rescue by Christ, who is God; cf. vv. 4, 6 and 2:10, 11, 13). The sense of rescue by another is even more apparent in the twice-repeated phrase (v. 5), "He saved us" ("save," *sozo*, in New Testament usage not only means to rescue from danger but also from judgment).

Paul's emphasis on divine causality is apparent not only in the concepts he states but also in his pronouns and personal nouns: "*He* saved us, not because of righteous things we had done, but because of *his* mercy" (v. 5a, italics added). And in the next sentence, "*He* saved us through the washing of rebirth and renewal by the *Holy Spirit*, whom *he* poured out on us generously through *Jesus Christ* our *Savior*" (vv. 5b, 6, italics added), so that, "having been justified by *his* grace, we might become heirs" (v. 7, italics added). In these words, which Paul apparently adapts from a Christian hymn or liturgical recitation of the time, the focus is on God who, in Christ and by the Holy Spirit, is alone the cause of our salvation. We are strongly (with an adversative participle) and specifically told that our rescue is "*not* because of righteous things we had done" (italics added) but "because of his mercy" ("mercy," *eleos*, carries the ideas both of kindness toward the afflicted and clemency). The idea of rescue from judgment reappears in the statement, "having been justified by his grace, we might become heirs . . ." (v. 7). To be "justified," *dikaioo*, means "to render or declare righteous." "Grace," *charis*, is unmerited favor that results in God's exerting his holy influence to turn us to Christ, to remove the guilt and power of sin, to increase our faith, to enable our godliness, to keep us and to bless us eternally as joint heirs with Christ.

The instruments that secure us also emphasize divine causality. "God our Savior appeared" (v. 4). He saved us by "the washing of rebirth" (v. 5). Though the thought of baptism may come to mind, "washing" (*loutron*) refers to the inner purification God provides by grace that provides new spiritual life (i.e., new birth) for us.[1] The following clause makes this clear by indicating that our "washing" and our "renewal" are indications of our "having been justified *by grace*" (v. 7, italics added). (Note: The aorist passive participle of justify, *dikaioo*, indicates completed action accomplished by another.) The apostle is at pains to say that no human work or act is the cause of our justified standing before God. In fact, the precise language of the Greek text — though quite complex and much debated — most likely indicates that the "washing" along with the resultant rebirth and "renewal" are the work of the Holy Spirit (literally, "through the washing that produces rebirth and renewal by the [operation of] the Holy Spirit").[2] This translation fits more closely with the pervasive Biblical understanding that the Holy Spirit is the instrumental means of our inner transformation — cleansing sin (washing), providing new life (rebirth), and making us new creatures (renewal). This entire renewal by the Spirit comes through his *generous* (i.e., rich or abundant) pouring out made possible "through Jesus Christ our Savior" (v. 6; cf. Joel 2:28, 29; Acts 2:17, 18; 10:45). Thus, the whole of the Godhead — Father, Son, and Holy Spirit — joins forces in accomplishing our salvation.

Our blessing (v. 8). The result of this gathering of resources is that we are made part of the heavenly family even though we had no right, righteousness, or resources to make this so. The culmination of God's grace is that we "become heirs having the hope of eternal life" (v. 7; cf. Romans 8:17, 23, 32). Already we have learned that we are saved because of God's mercy, not because of our righteousness. Paul emphasizes that we are justified by God's actions, not by our accomplishments or resolve. Now he indicates the culminating blessing of this grace by saying we have "hope" (i.e., faithful expectation — v. 7) that we will be united with God in his kingdom through our adoption as heirs of "eternal life" (the New Testament promise not only of length of life but also of a life filled with rich enjoyment of God, his people, and the New Creation).

As indicated above, Paul's description of these processes and products of grace are adapted from an ancient hymn. Now Paul specifically refers to the hymn, saying, "This is a trustworthy saying. And I want you to stress these things" (v. 8a). The reason for prioritizing these concepts in the church then follows: ". . . so that those who have trusted in God may be careful to devote themselves to doing what is good" (v. 8b). As he has done throughout the letter, Paul carefully specifies the cause and results of our blessing in this summary. Those who are believers have "trusted in God," not in their accomplishments or goodness. Still, now that they have understood the richness of God's mercy toward them, the apostle's expectation is that those in grace will be "careful to devote themselves to [literally, "to guard or give attention to"] doing what is good" (cf. 1:8; 2:1, 3, 7, 14; 3:1, 14). Our duties never garner grace, but the doctrines of grace lead to the duties of gratitude.

Since true godliness flows from love of and for God, Paul ends this doctrinal justification for the practical instructions at the beginning of the chapter with further evidence of God's love. He says that the duties he has enjoined are "excellent and profitable for everyone" (v. 8c). What God has commanded is not onerous or punitive. Rather, those who pursue the godliness that only comes out of love for God will discover additional riches of his grace. His commands lead to what is "excellent" (beautiful, honorable, or precious) and "profitable" (resulting in blessing) for "everyone" (plural, *anthropos*, men, indicating people generically, not just the religious elite or those already converted).

Distractions to Grace (vv. 9-11)

So great are the benefits of our knowledge and responses to God's grace that Paul now must make it clear that no other priorities should creep into our ministries. He tells Titus to avoid divisive issues (v. 9; cf. 2 Timothy 2:23, 24) and divisive people (v. 10). Paul describes divisive issues in terms that remind us of the likely concerns of the false teachers in the Cretan church (cf. 1:10-16): "foolish controversies and genealogies and arguments and quarrels about the law" (v. 9). Whereas the doctrines and duties of grace are "excellent and profitable" (v. 8), these matters are "unprofitable and useless" (v. 9). Because those who engage in such debates distract the church from its mission and purpose, "ruining whole households" (1:11), Paul tells Titus to "warn a divisive person" up to two times and "After that, have nothing to do with him." In this compressed way the apostle reminds us of both the Biblical process and necessity of church discipline (cf. Matthew 18:15-17; 1 Timothy 5:19, 20).

The goal of such discipline is not only the protection of the church from quarrel and ruin, but also to turn the divisive person from his error. The seriousness of this error is evident in Paul's words: "You may be sure that such a man is warped [twisted or corrupt] and sinful [also meaning, "to be without a share in" the benefits just described]; he is self-condemned" (v. 11). It is interesting that Paul does not say God condemns such a person. Rather, one who tries to justify himself by besting others (causing foolish controversies), presuming on his background or family status (debating genealogies), or by wrangling holiness from legal strictures (causing quarrels about the law) instead cuts himself off from his only hope of justification — grace. And thus he is "self-condemned."

We struggle with these commands to "avoid . . . arguments" because we know there are things worth disputing, and because it seems divisive to separate from divisive people. Two perspectives may help. First, Paul is speaking about ministry priorities. His words require us to examine whether controversy and argument about secondary issues become primary concerns in our ministries. If so, then our priorities require realignment. Second, there is a difference between needing to divide and loving to divide. A divisive person loves to fight. The differences are usually observable. A person who loves the peace and purity of the church may be forced into division, but it is not his character. He enters arguments regrettably and infrequently. When forced to argue, he remains fair, truthful, and loving in his responses. He grieves to have to disagree with a brother. Those who are divisive by nature lust for the fray, incite its onset, and delight in being able to conquer another person. For them victory means everything. So in an argument they twist words, call names, threaten, manipulate procedures, and attempt to extend the debate as long as possible and along as many fronts as possible.

Divisive persons frequent the debates of the church. As a result the same voices and personalities tend to appear over and over again, even though the issues change. Paul's words caution us about the seriousness of being "divisive." Though ego or entertainment may be served by argument, such engagement damages the church and should be avoided unless absolutely necessary. These are not easy words for those of us who enjoy ecclesiastical debates or rationalize them on the basis of the need for the voicing of views or the advocacy of a cause. I confess there is a part of me that loves to debate. Competitive debate was my training before seminary, and in seminary I loved the give and take of a good theological wrangle. Still, I discovered quite soon when I became responsible for the spiritual well-being of others that what was fun for me was not healthy for the church, nor was it a good way for me to mature in character or understanding.

At times we must fight (1:9). But if we love the fight, we must question if we are following God's priorities. Do we really want to devote our lives to quarreling, criticism, and argument? The man of God must not strive (2 Timothy 2:24, 25). He is by nature peaceable and gentle (Titus 1:7; 2:1; 3:2). He stands where he must, but he takes no delight in debates among brethren and does not make them the priorities of his ministry. Nothing other than grace must be the priority of the gospel-centered church.

RENEW THE MINISTRY OF GRACE (vv. 12-15)

Paul Kooistra, seminary and mission leader, once distressed some of his listeners when he was asked why he preached so much on grace. He said, "There is nothing else to preach." Intellectual argument at once ensued. Several claimed, "There are many other things to preach in terms of our obligations, relationships, and personal character." Yet, what we should understand as we see the organization of this pastoral epistle is that all of these matters find their proper context and motivation in our understanding of grace.

The Apostle Paul makes this point well as he concludes this letter. He says, "Our people must learn to devote themselves to doing what is good" (v. 14). This is his reminder of the imperatives related to our obligations, relationships, and personal character. He reflects these concerns in his parting words. He commends the care of others to those in the church (vv. 12, 13). One more time he reminds the people of their duties (v. 14). Then he reflects his own relational concerns: "Everyone with me sends you greetings. Greet those who love us in the faith" (v. 15a). But his final words are, "Grace be with you all" (v. 15b). The apostle states this message last to let its implications reverberate in Christian hearts through the ages. May it be the message that all of us in church leadership ultimately want to leave as well. May the priority of our ministries be to forever renew in the hearts and lives of God's people the message, "Grace be with you all."

Grace be with you all!

Notes

CHAPTER ONE: GREETINGS TO ALL

1. It is possible that Paul may be referring to more than one mystery in these Ephesian references. However, it is reasonable to conclude, as does P. T. O'Brien:

   Christ is the starting point for a true understanding of the notion of "mystery" in this letter, as elsewhere in Paul. There are not a number of "mysteries" with limited applications, but one supreme "mystery" with a number of applications.

   Gerald F. Hawthorne and Ralph P. Martin, eds., *Dictionary of Paul and His Letters* (Downers Grove, IL: InterVarsity, 1993), p. 623.

2. Certainly, the primary way "the mystery of godliness" is proclaimed here must be verbal. It is essential to the church's *kerygma* and *didache*. However, communication in the secondary sense (by the way the church conducts itself) is very strong here — given Paul's emphasis on conduct in verse 15 and the persistent connection between doctrine and church order and conduct in his earlier letter to Ephesians, especially chapter 5.

3. Philip H. Towner, *1-2 Timothy & Titus* (Downers Grove, IL: InterVarsity, 1994), pp. 13, 14.

4. J. L. Houldon, *The Pastoral Epistles* (London, England: Penguin Books, 1976), pp. 64, 65, writes:

   Yet of course, if bourgeois, then certainly *petit* bourgeois. The interest of this writer's circle is not to take part in public affairs or to direct them, but to *lead a quiet and peaceable life,* and, we may suppose, not to distinguish too keenly between good emperors and bad, but to support the existing powers so long as this minimum condition is fulfilled. In his eyes, God himself is content with government on these terms and asks no more (v. 3).

5. George W. Knight, III, *The Pastoral Epistles* (Grand Rapids, MI: Eerdmans, 1992), p. 40.

6. *Ibid.,* p. 61.

7. Donald Guthrie, *The Pastoral Epistles* (Grand Rapids, MI: Eerdmans, 1957), p. 56, explains:

   The word *hope* (*elpis*) used in a Christian sense conveys an element of absolute certainty, an element generally lacking in the modern usage of the word.

8. John Stott, *Guard the Truth* (Downers Grove, IL: InterVarsity, 1996), p. 37.

9. "Man's Weakness — God's Strength," *Missionary Crusader* (December 1964), p. 7.

10. Towner, *1-2 Timothy & Titus*, p. 41.

11. Knight, *The Pastoral Epistles*, p. 28.

CHAPTER TWO: THE WRONG USE OF THE LAW

1. J. D. Douglas, ed., *The New Bible Dictionary* (Grand Rapids, MI, Eerdmans, 1962), p. 381.

2. Gordon D. Fee, *1 and 2 Timothy, Titus* (Peabody, MA: Hendrickson Publishers, 1984), p. 39.

3. J. N. D. Kelly, *A Commentary on the Pastoral Epistles* (Grand Rapids, MI: Baker, 1963), p. 44.

4. Fee, *1 and 2 Timothy, Titus*, p. 40.

5. John Stott, *Guard the Truth* (Downers Grove, IL: InterVarsity, 1996), p. 44.

6. *Ibid.*

7. Michael Drosnin, *The Bible Code* (New York: Simon & Schuster, 1997), from the dust jacket.

8. This is the interpretation of the majority of critics, but it is debated. However, I think the majority interpretation makes better sense with Ephesians 3:2, 9, which was, after all, written to the same church. See Kelly, *A Commentary on the Pastoral Epistles*, pp. 45, 46 who explains the two views but decides against the interpretation I have taken. Kelly writes:

   The Greek noun so translated (*oikonomian:* better attested than *oikodomēn,* i.e. "edification") originally connotes the management of a house or household, but with Paul it refers either to God's redemptive purpose accomplished in history (Eph. I. IO; iii. 9), or to the responsibility, or stewardship, which God entrusts to his chosen delegates to secure its realization (I Cor. ix. 17; Col. I. 25; Eph. iii. 2). If the latter is the sense here, as the majority of critics think, Paul's meaning is that the errorists' exegesis fails to promote the faithful discharge of God's stewardship. The former, however, seems preferable, since it makes a more effective contrast with the purely imaginary fancies with which the false teachers' heads are full. If this is correct, the divine plan works through faith in the sense that it is apprehended, and so becomes effective, through faith on the part of those who accept Christ.

9. John Piper, *Desiring God* (Portland: Multnomah, 1986), p. 96.

10. Kelly, *A Commentary on the Pastoral Epistles*, p. 47.

11. Philip H. Towner, *1-2 Timothy & Titus* (Downers Grove, IL: InterVarsity, 1994), pp. 46, 47.

12. William Barclay, *The Letters to Timothy, Titus and Philemon* (Philadelphia: The Westminster Press, 1960), p. 36.

13. F. J. Sheed, *Theology and Sanity* (New York: Sheed & Ward, 1946), pp. 9, 10.

CHAPTER THREE: THE PROPER USE OF THE LAW

1. James Davison Hunter, *Evangelicalism, the Coming Generation* (Chicago: The University of Chicago Press, 1987), p. 46.

2. *Ibid.*, p. 163.

3. John Stott, *Guard the Truth* (Downers Grove, IL: InterVarsity, 1996), p. 47.

4. Thomas C. Oden, *First and Second Timothy and Titus* (Louisville: John Knox Press, 1989), p. 38.

5. Philip H. Towner, *1-2 Timothy & Titus* (Downers Grove, IL: InterVarsity, 1994), p. 50, 51 explains:

   Against God's ethical standard revealed in the law, human sin stands out in bold relief. The heretic's interpretation of the Old Testament (used to support a gospel that promised too much too soon) obscured this revelation, so that sinners were no longer directed toward the genuine gospel. Their use of the Old Testament was illegitimate because it did not accord with God's purpose.

   The false "teachers of the law" saw in the Old Testament law, especially in its "genealogies" (see above on v. 4) and creation stories, the basis for their extreme manner of behavior and the justification for their superspiritual claims. Their teaching missed the law's emphasis on God's demands and human need. False teachers are lawbreakers, who, without necessarily personally committing the sins listed here, become responsible for such sins by causing others to misunderstand or ignore God's moral demands.

6. Stott, *Guard the Truth*, p. 48 argues:

    The key antithesis, that the law is *not for the righteous but for lawbreakers* (9), cannot refer to those who are righteous in the sense of 'justified', since Paul insists elsewhere that the justified do still need the law for their sanctification. Nor can it be taken to mean that some people exist who are so righteous that they do not need the law to guide them, but only that some people think they are. Similarly, when Jesus said, 'I have not come to call the righteous, but sinners to repentance', he did not mean that there are some righteous people who do not need to be called to repentance, but only that some think they are. In a word, 'the righteous' in these contexts means 'the self-righteous'.

7. Gordon Fee, *1 and 2 Timothy, Titus* (Peabody, MA: Hendrickson Publishers, 1984), p. 44.

8. J. Gresham Machen, *Christian Faith in the Modern World* (Grand Rapids, MI: Eerdmans, 1936), pp. 56, 57.

CHAPTER FOUR: GRATITUDE FOR GRACE

1. John Stott, *Guard the Truth* (Downers Grove, IL: InterVarsity, 1996), pp. 53, 54, quoting from *The Acts and Monuments of John Foxe* (1563), fourth edition, revised by Josiah Pratt, Vol. 4 (Religious Tract Society, 1877), p. 635.

2. J. D. Douglas, ed., *The New International Dictionary of the Christian Church* (Grand Rapids, MI: Zondervan, 1979), p. 132.

3. Stott, *Guard the Truth*, p. 54.

4. A. T. Robertson, *Word Pictures in the New Testament,* Vol. 3, *The Acts of the Apostles* (Nashville: Broadman, 1930), p. 113.

5. George W. Knight, III, *The Pastoral Epistles* (Grand Rapids, MI: Eerdmans, 1936), p. 96.

6. Stott, *Guard the Truth*, p. 51, who writes, "or literally, as Thomas Goodwin the Puritan put it, 'I was bemercied.'"

7. Knight, *The Pastoral Epistles*, p. 94.

8. John Blanchard, *Truth for Life* (West Sussex, England: H. E. Walter, Ltd., 1982), p. 239.

9. John Piper, *Desiring God* (Portland: Multnomah, 1986), pp. 120, 121, quoting "My soul, purified, today returns to the City of God."

10. David W. Torrence and Thomas F. Torrence, eds., *1st and 2nd Timothy, Calvin's Commentaries*, Vol. 10 (Grand Rapids, MI: Eerdmans, 1964), p. 199.

11. Knight, *The Pastoral Epistles*, p. 105.

CHAPTER FIVE: FIGHTING THE GOOD FIGHT

1. J. D. Douglas, ed., *The New International Dictionary of the Christian Church* (Grand Rapids, MI: Zondervan, 1979), p. 581.

2. *Ibid.*

3. Charles Spurgeon, *The Metropolitan Tabernacle Pulpit*, Vol. 10 (Pasadena, TX: Pilgrim, 1973), p. 407.

4. Ned B. Stonehouse, *J. Gresham Machen* (Grand Rapids, MI: Eerdmans, 1955), p. 477.

5. John Stott, *Guard the Truth* (Downers Grove, IL: InterVarsity, 1996), p. 57 explains:

   Although here 'faith' does not have the definite article in the original, it does at the end of the verse (literally, 'suffered shipwreck concerning *the* faith'). So surely we must assume valuable things which he must carefully guard, an objective treasure called 'the faith', meaning the apostolic faith, and a subjective one called 'a good conscience'. Moreover, they need to be preserved together (as in 1:5 and 3:9), which is exactly what Hymenaeus and Alexander have failed to do.

6. David W. Torrence and Thomas F. Torrence, ed., *1st and 2nd Timothy*, Calvin's Commentaries, Vol. 10 (Grand Rapids, MI: Eerdmans, 1964), p. 202.

7. *Foxe's Book of Martyrs* (Philadelphia: The John C. Winston Co., n.d.), pp. 243, 244.

8. *Ibid.*, p. 244.

9. George W. Knight, III, *The Pastoral Epistles* (Grand Rapids, MI: Eerdmans, 1992), p. 109 explains:

   The relative pronoun, ἥν, must have ἀγαθὴν συνείδησιν, and only it, as its antecedent: It is rejection of "good conscience," not rejection of faith, that causes shipwreck regarding faith. τινες is used here in the indefinite sense of "certain or "some" to refer to those who are in the wrong (cf. vv. 3, 6). ἀπωθέομαι, which generally means "push aside," is used here figuratively in the sense of "reject" or "repudiate." To reject or repudiate a good conscience is to be willfully and self-consciously disobedient to God's requirements because a good conscience bespeaks a self-conscious obedience.

10. Gordon D. Fee, *1 and 2 Timothy, Titus* (Peabody, MA: Hendickson Publishers, 1984), p. 58 explains:

    . . . with a typical change of metaphor, Paul adds, they have shipwrecked their faith. It is not their faith that is shipwrecked — although that, too, has happened — but *the* faith. By rejecting faith (their complete trust in God's grace), they are at the same time in the process of bringing *the* faith (the gospel itself) to ruin.

CHAPTER SIX: PRAYING AND LIVING FOR THE GOSPEL

1. Adapted from "The Life-Saving Station" by Theodore Wedel.

2. John Stott, *Guard the Truth* (Downers Grove, IL: InterVarsity, 1996), p. 61.

3. Gordon D. Fee, *1 and 2 Timothy, Titus* (Peabody, MA: Hendrickson Publishers, 1984), p. 63 explains:

   The concern here, therefore, is not that Christians should have a life free from trouble or distress (which hardly fits the point of view of 2 Tim. 1:8 and 3:12) but that they should live in such a way that "no one will speak evil of the name of God and of our teaching" (6:1).

   This understanding is supported by two other factors: First, in 1 Thessalonians 4:11-12 Paul uses identical language ("lead a quiet life") for the selfsame reason (to "win respect of outsiders"), where "busybodies" are disrupting things (cf. 2 Thess. 3:11 with 1 Tim. 5:13); and second, the language all godliness (*eusebeia*) and holiness (*semnotēs*: better, "proper conduct," as GNB), which is peculiar to these letters in the Pauline corpus (except for Phil. 4:8, *semnes*), has to do with behavior that can be seen.

4. William Barclay, *The Gospel of John*, Vol. 1 (Philadelphia: Westminster, 1956), pp. 76, 77.

5. Publicity brochure from St. Nicholas Church in Leipzig.

6. Fee, *1 and 2 Timothy, Titus*, p. 65.

7. Stott, *Guard the Truth*, p. 73.

8. S. M. Baugh, "A Foreign World: Ephesus in the First Century," in Andreas J. Köstenberger, Thomas R. Schreiner, and H. Scott Baldwin, eds., *Women in the Church* (Grand Rapids, MI: Baker, 1995), pp. 47, 48.

CHAPTER SEVEN: LIVING OUT GOD'S ORDER

1. Robert W. Yarbrough, "The Hermeneutics of 1 Timothy 2:9-15," in Andreas J. Köstenberger, Thomas R. Schreiner, and H. Scott Baldwin, *Women in the Church* (Grand Rapids, MI: Baker, 1995), p. 167.

2. Harold O. J. Brown, "The New Testament Against Itself: 1 Timothy 2:9-15 and the 'Breakthrough' of Galatians 3:28," in Köstenberger, Schreiner, and Baldwin, *Women in the Church*, p. 199.

3. Paul K. Jewett, *Man as Male and Female* (Grand Rapids, MI: Eerdmans, 1975), p. 119 unequivocally concludes:

   Both in I Corinthians and in I Timothy appeal is made only to the second creation narrative as the sole text for understanding the meaning of human existence as male and female. Thus this second, supplementary narrative is interpreted in isolation from the first. . . . Furthermore, in reasoning this way, Paul is not only basing his argument exclusively on the second creation narrative, but is assuming the traditional rabbinic understanding of that narrative whereby the order of their creation is made to yield the primacy of the man over the woman. Is this rabbinic understanding of Genesis 2:18f. correct? We do not think that it is, for it is palpably inconsistent with the first creation narrative, with the life style of Jesus, and with the apostle's own clear affirmation that in Christ there is no male and female (Gal. 3:28).

4. George Marsden, *Reforming Fundamentalism* (Grand Rapids, MI: Eerdmans, 1987), p. 282 reports:

   A special committee of trustees, administration, and faculty was appointed in January 1976 to deal with the Jewett case. Disciplinary action was a real possibility, though dismissal was unlikely. After lengthy discussion, the majority of the committee concluded that Jewett was wrong in claiming that the apostle Paul was mistaken. Nonetheless, they were also convinced that he sincerely subscribed to the statement of faith's article affirming that "Scripture is the only infallible rule of faith and practice." Jewett, they pointed out, defended his view by an appeal to the long-standing principle that "Scripture should be interpreted by Scripture." Even though the committee "sharply disagreed" with Jewett's specific application of this rule, they construed his purpose, however mistakenly carried out, to be to defend the overall authority of Scripture, not to undermine it. No disciplinary action was taken.

5. Richard Clark Kroeger and Catherine Clark Kroeger, *I Suffer Not a Woman: Rethinking 1 Timothy 2:11-15 in Light of Ancient Evidence* (Grand Rapids, MI: Baker, 1992), p. 54.

6. S. M. Baugh, "A Foreign World: Ephesus in the First Century," Köstenberger, Schreiner, and Baldwin, eds., *Women in the Church*, pp. 13-52.

7. *Ibid.,* pp. 17, 18, 50.

8. Gordon D. Fee, *1 and 2 Timothy, Titus* (Peabody, MA: Hendrickson Publishers, 1984), p. 73.

9. Andreas J. Köstenberger, "A Complex Sentence Structure in 1 Timothy 2:12,"

Köstenberger, Schreiner, and Baldwin, eds., *Women in the Church*, pp. 89, 103 where the author concludes:

The meaning of διδάσκειν in 1 Timothy 2:12 is therefore an important preliminary issue in determining the meaning of αὐθεντεῖν. As was argued above, διδάσκειν, when used absolutely, always in the New Testament denotes an activity that is viewed positively by the writer, to be rendered "to teach" (cf. esp. 1 Tim. 4:11; 6:2; 2 Tim. 2:2). If the writer had intended to give the term a negative connotation in 1 Timothy 2:12, he would in all likelihood have used the term ἑτεροδιδασκαλεῖν (as in 1 Tim. 1:3; 6:3) or some other contextual qualified specifying the (inappropriate or heretical) content of the teaching (as in Titus 1:11).

Since then the first part of 1 Timothy 2:12 reads "But I do not permit a woman to teach" and the coordinating conjunction οὐδέ requires the second activity to be viewed correspondingly by the writer, αὐθεντεῖν should be regarded as viewed positively as well and be rendered "to have (or exercise) authority," and not "to flout the authority of" or "to domineer."

10. Fee, *1 and 2 Timothy, Titus*, p. 72.

11. George W. Knight, III, *The Pastoral Epistles* (Grand Rapids, MI: Eerdmans, 1992), p.140 explains:

It has also been suggested that the present indicative form of ἐπιτρέπω indicates a temporal limitation and thus limits Paul's statement to the then and there of Ephesus. An examination of other occurrences of Paul's use of first person singular present indicative (Rom. 12:1, 3; 1 Cor. 4:16; 2 Cor. 5:20; Gal. 5:2, 3, Eph. 4:1; 1 Thes. 4:1; 5:14; 2 Thes. 3:6; 1 Tim. 2:1, 8) demonstrates that he uses it to give universal and authoritative instruction or exhortation (cf. especially Rom. 12:1; 1 Tim. 2:8).

12. Thomas R. Schreiner, "An Interpretation of 1 Timothy 2:9-15: A Dialogue with Scholarship," Köstenberger, Schreiner, and Baldwin, eds., *Women in the Church*, p. 115 answers:

The 1 Peter text refers to *nonbelieving* husbands (3:1). And in 3:7 husbands are addressed in terms of their specific responsibilities to their wives (cf. Eph. 5:25-30, 33; Col. 3:19). No admonition for husbands regarding their relationship with their wives is present in 1 Timothy 2. Finally, it is obvious that Peter has husbands and wives in view in 1 Peter 3 since he says "wives should be subject to *their own* (ἰδίοις) husbands" (v. 1; cf. v. 5). It is precisely this kind of clarifying evidence that 1 Timothy 2:8-15 lacks, with the result that most scholars detect a reference to men and women in general.

13. *Ibid.*, p. 117.

14. Krister Stendahl, *The Bible and the Role of Women* (Philadelphia: Fortress, 1966), pp. 32-37.

15. S. Lewis Johnson, Sr., "Role Distinctions in Galatians 3:28," John Piper and Wayne Grudem, eds., *Recovering Biblical Manhood and Womanhood* (Wheaton, IL: Crossway Books, 1991), p. 160.

16. Douglas Moo, "What Does It Mean Not to Teach or Have Authority Over Men? 1 Timothy 2:11-15," Piper and Grudem, eds., *Recovering Biblical Manhood and Womanhood*, p. 185.

17. John R. W. Stott, *Decisive Issues Facing Christians Today* (Old Tappan, NJ: Revell, 1990), pp. 269, 270.

18. Michael G. Maudlin, "John Stott Speaks Out," *Christianity Today*, Vol. 37, No. 2, February 8, 1993, p. 38.

19. D. A. Carson, "'Silent in the Churches': On the Role of Women in 1 Corinthians

14:33b-36," Piper and Grudem, eds., *Recovering Biblical Manhood and Womanhood*, p. 152 writes:

> By this clause, Paul is probably not referring to Genesis 3:16, as many suggest, but to the creation order in Genesis 2:20b-24, for it is to that Scripture that Paul explicitly turns on two other occasions when he discusses female roles (1 Corinthians 11:8, 9:2; Timothy 2:13).

20. Phillip Jensen, *To the Householder* (Sydney: Matthias Press, 1996), p. 47.

21. Thomas R. Schreiner, "An Interpretation of 1 Timothy 2:9-15: A Dialogue with Scholarship," Köstenberger, Schreiner, and Baldwin, eds., *Women in the Church*, p. 151.

22. John F. Walvoord and Roy B. Zuck, eds., *The Bible Knowledge Commentary* (Wheaton, IL: Victor, 1983), p. 736.

23. Gallup Poll. *Emerging Trends,* a publication of Princeton Religion Research Center, reports that a June 1990 poll revealed that 71 percent of women surveyed believed that religion can answer today's problems, while only 55 percent of men agreed. *Leadership Magazine*, Winter 1991, Vol. 12, No. 1, p. 17 reports that the typical church service has 59 percent females versus 41 percent male attenders.

CHAPTER EIGHT: THE GOOD ELDERS

1. Walter Lock, *The Pastoral Epistles (I & II Timothy and Titus)* (Edinburgh: T. & T. Clark, 1936), p. 35.

2. Gordon D. Fee, *1 and 2 Timothy, Titus* (Peabody, MA: Hendrickson Publishers, 1984), p. 78.

3. *Ibid.*, p. 80.

4. James Humes, *Churchill, Speaker of the Century* (Briarcliff Manor, NY: Stein and Day, Scarborough House, 1980), p. 291.

5. Robert Saucy, "The Husband of One Wife," *Bibliotheca Sacra*, July 1974, pp. 229-240. Saucy concludes:

> I do not think that this is in reality a lowering of the standard of qualifications. In placing an emphasis upon the positive characteristic of a faithful husband rather than simply upon the legal married status, this understanding actually exalts the requirement. While there are men who have been barred from eldership who on the basis of this interpretation should be permitted to occupy this position, there are others now serving as pastors or elders who under this understanding of being characteristically a one-woman man should be disqualified. Legally as far as their married state is concerned they are husbands of one wife, but their actions and attitudes demonstrate that they are not truly one-woman men.

6. George W. Knight, III, *The Pastoral Epistles* (Grand Rapids, MI: Baker, 1963), pp. 158, 159.

7. John Stott, *Guard the Truth* (Downers Grove, IL: InterVarsity, 1996), p. 94. Note that the heading "self-mastery" is borrowed from Stott. He also provided wisdom as to how to group the text under the headings.

8. Gerhard Kittel, ed., *Theological Dictionary of the New Testament,* Vol. 21 (Grand Rapids, MI: Eerdmans, 1968), pp. 339, 342.

9. E. Stanley Jones, *Song of Ascents* (Nashville: Abingdon, 1979), pp. 129, 130.

10. J. N. D. Kelly, *A Commentary on the Pastoral Epistles* (Grand Rapids, MI: Eerdmans, 1992), p. 77.

11. Arthur M. Schlesinger, Jr., *A Pilgrim's Progress: Orestes A. Brownson* (Boston: Little, Brown, 1966), p. 250.

12. Os Guinness, *The Gravedigger Files* (Downers Grove, IL: InterVarsity, 1983), p. 187.

13. Fee, *1 and 2 Timothy, Titus*, p. 82.

14. Stott, *Guard the Truth*, pp. 98, 99.

CHAPTER NINE: THE GOOD DEACONS

1. J. N. D. Kelly, *A Commentary on the Pastoral Epistles* (Grand Rapids, MI: Baker, 1963), p. 80.

2. John Stott, "The Foot-Washing Lord and Savior (John 13)," Urbana 70, *Christ the Liberator* (Downers Grove, IL: InterVarsity, 1971), p. 21, referencing B. F. Westcott, *St. John's Gospel* (Grand Rapids, MI: Eerdmans, 1950), p. 192.

3. *Ibid.*, Stott, pp. 21, 22, referencing Peter A. Wright, *The Pictorial History of the Royal Maundy* (1968).

4. Kelly, *A Commentary on the Pastoral Epistles*, p. 81.

5. Betty Radice, trans. *Pliny Letters and Panegyricus*, Vol. 2, The Loeb Classical Library, (Cambridge, MA: Harvard, 1976), pp. 288, 289 (Book XXCVI): "*Quo magis necessarium credidi ex duabus ancillis, quae ministrae dicebantur, quid esset veri, et per tormenta quaerere*" — "This made me decide it was all the more necessary to extract the truth by torture from two slave-women, whom they call deaconesses."

6. George W. Knight, III, *The Pastoral Epistles* (Grand Rapids, MI: Eerdmans, 1992), p. 172.

7. Walter Lock, *The Pastoral Epistles (I & II Timothy and Titus)* (Edinburgh: T. & T. Clark, 1935), p. 40 assesses "the parallelism between the qualities required for them and for the deacons σεμνάς = σεμνούς μή διαβόλους = μή διαβόλους νηφαλίους = μή οἴνω π προσέχοντας πιστὰς ἐν πᾶσι = μή αἰσχροκερδεῖς ... συνεδήσει)."

8. John Piper, *Desiring God* (Portland: Multnomah, 1986), p. 175.

9. Kelly, *A Commentary on the Pastoral Epistles,* p. 85.

10. Haddon Robinson, *Biblical Preaching* (Grand Rapids, MI: Baker, 1980), p. 24.

11. Gordon D. Fee, *1 and 2 Timothy, Titus* (Peabody, MA: Hendrickson Publishers, p. 90.

CHAPTER TEN: THE CHURCH'S CONDUCT AND CONFESSION

1. A. W. Tozer, *The Pursuit of God* (Wheaton, IL: Tyndale, n.d.), p. 97.

2. Robert G. Rayburn, *O Come Let Us Worship* (Grand Rapids, MI: Baker, 1984), pp. 29, 30.

3. T. A. Smail, trans., David W. Torrance and Thomas F. Torrance, eds., *Calvin's Commentaries, The Second Epistle of Paul to the Corinthians and the Epistles to Timothy, Titus and Philemon* (Grand Rapids, MI: Eerdmans, 1964), p. 231.

4. Leland Ryken, *Worldly Saints* (Grand Rapids, MI: Zondervan, 1986), p. 154.

5. Philip H. Towner, *1-2 Timothy & Titus* (Downers Grove, IL: InterVarsity, 1994), pp. 97, 98 explains:

   But what is this great *mystery of godliness?* "Mystery," as often used by Paul, denotes the appearance of Christ in history as the hidden salvation plan of God which, conceived before time, has been revealed and fulfilled in the cross and resurrection (compare 3:9). The content of the Christ-hymn in 3:16 confirms the deep theological meaning of "the mystery."

   The whole phrase *the mystery of godliness* needs some unpacking. It is commonly taken as the equivalent of the phrase in 3:9, "the mystery of the faith." This would make *godliness,* like "the faith," a reference to the objective content of Christianity — that is, "what" one believes. As such, the word here rendered *godliness* is often translated "religion." But although "the faith" does often bear this meaning in the Pastorals, "godliness" is a more expansive, less static idea. It includes "the faith" but goes a decisive step further to link a certain Christian manner of life to it (see notes on 2:2). The context, with its focus on conduct (v. 15) supports the broader meaning of "godliness."

6. John Stott, *Guard the Truth* (Downers Grove, IL: InterVarsity, 1996), pp. 107, 108 gives an excellent breakdown of the three couplets. Similar interpretations are held by Kelly, Knight, Liddon, and Towner.

7. Clarence Edward Macartney, *The Greatest Texts of the Bible* (New York: Abingdon-Cokesbury, 1947), pp. 180, 181, from which I adapted this description.

CHAPTER ELEVEN: BLESS GOD'S GOOD CREATION

1. Martin Gardner, *The Flight of Peter Fromm* (Amherst, NY: Prometheus, 1994), p. 192 where the author used this illustration to depict intellectual change: "Something like this happened to Peter as he moved through the intellectual corridors of Gray City" (i.e., The University of Chicago).

2. George W. Knight, III, *The Pastoral Epistles* (Grand Rapids, MI: Eerdmans, 1992), p. 188, explains:

   How, when, and where did the Spirit give this message? The numerous occurrences of τὸ πνεῦμα λέγει in Revelation (2:7, 11, 17, 25; 3:6, 13, 22) demonstrate that this phrase can be used to refer to the revelation given by Jesus Christ (cf. Rev. 1:1-3, 9-20, especially vv. 1, 19, 20). Such usage brings to mind the warning of Jesus concerning apostasy in Mt. 24:10, 11 and Mk 13:22. The warning of Jesus is conceptually the closest to this clause in that both speak of "falling away" (1 Tim. 4:1 with ἀφίστημι, Mt. 24:10 with σκανδαλίζω; these words can be used interchangeably as in Lk 8:13 [σκανδαλίζω]). It is therefore most likely that Paul has this source in view. That he writes τὸ πνεῦμα λέγει emphasizes the ongoing and present significance of this warning, which has been reiterated by the Spirit through him and others (cf., e.g., Acts 20:28-31; 2 Tim. 3:1ff.; 4:3, 4).

3. Philip H. Towner, *1-2 Timothy & Titus* (Downers Grove, IL: InterVarsity, 1994), pp. 101.

4. John Stott, *Guard the Truth* (Downers Grove, IL: InterVarsity, 1996), p. 111.

5. Thomas C. Oden, *First and Second Timothy and Titus* (Louisville: John Knox Press, 1989), p. 58.

6. John Stott, *Guard the Truth* (Downers Grove, IL: InterVarsity, 1996), p. 113, referencing Josephus, *Wars* 2.8.2; cf. *Antiquities* 18.1.5.

7. J. N. D. Kelly, *A Commentary on the Pastoral Epistles* (Grand Rapids, MI: Baker, 1963), p. 95 writes: "What we have to do with here is not so much thorough-going Gnosticism as an incipient tendency in that direction manifested by converted Jews in a syncretistic environment."

8. Towner, *1-2 Timothy & Titus*, pp. 103, 104.

9. Leland Ryken, *Worldly Saints* (Grand Rapids, MI: Zondervan, 1986), pp. 40, 41 provides all the information on the subject of Roman Catholic sexual asceticism.

10. *Ibid.*, p. 53.

11. *Ibid.*, p. 44.

12. *Ibid.*, pp. 53, 54.

13. C. S. Lewis, *Screwtape Letters* (New York: Macmillan, 1971), p. 47.

14. T. A. Smail, trans., David W. Torrance and Thomas F. Torrance, eds., *Calvin's Commentaries, The Second Epistle of Paul to the Corinthians and the Epistles to Timothy, Titus and Philemon* (Grand Rapids, MI: Eerdmans, 1964), p. 238 provides the thought I have paraphrased and enlarged: "For those who do not abstain from self-seeking, hatred, avarice, cruelty and such like, try to acquire righteousness for themselves by abstaining from those things which God has left free."

15. Stott, *Guard the Truth*, p. 115.

16. *Ibid.*, who quotes from Dudley Barker, *G. K. Chesterton, A Biography* (London: Constable, 1973), p. 65, from unpublished notebook jottings.

17. C. S. Lewis, *Mere Christianity* (New York: Macmillan, 1952), p. 124.

CHAPTER TWELVE: PURSUING GODLINESS

1. George W. Knight, III, *The Pastoral Epistles* (Grand Rapids, MI: Eerdmans, 1992), p. 197.

2. *Ibid.* As Knight explains:

   But the εὐσέβεια is no longer, as in Greek thought, a general religious piety. It is now a εὐσέβεια rooted in the mystery of εὐσέβεια Jesus Christ. It is now a distinctly Christian εὐσέβεια, which is not just an external form, but which has an inner power (2 Tim. 3:5). That inner power is appropriated in Christ (*cf.* 2 Pet. 1:3).

   Faithful Sayings, 70.

3. Gordon D. Fee, *1 and 2 Timothy, Titus* (Peabody, MA: Hendrickson Publishers, 1983), p. 103.

4. J. N. D. Kelly, *A Commentary on the Pastoral Epistles* (Grand Rapids, MI: Eerdmans, 1992), p. 99.

5. *Ibid.*, p. 98. See also Fee, *1 and 2 Timothy, Titus*, p. 103, who explains:

   The participle that follows is a metaphor from child rearing, having to do with nurturing (training or nourishing). By translating it in the past tense, "brought up in," the NIV quite deflects Paul's point. "Brought up" implies that Paul is reminding Timothy of his youthful training (cf. NEB "bred"), whereas Paul's present participle intends something concurrent with the main verb, "you will be." Thus Paul's concern is with Timothy's *continuing to nourish himself* (cf. GNB "feed yourself spiritually"), so that he will be a good servant of Christ Jesus, as he points these things out to the brothers and sisters.

6. John Stott, *Between Two Worlds* (Grand Rapids, MI: Eerdmans, 1982), p. 208.

7. Donald Buttrick, *Homiletic* (Philadelphia: Fortress, 1987), pp. 213-215 provides a penetrating discussion of the pathology of sermonic repetition. I adapted the repetitive dialogue from Buttrick's example.

8. Gerhard Kittel, ed., *Theological Dictionary of the New Testament* (TDNT), Vol. 1 (Grand Rapids, MI: Eerdmans, 1968), p. 775.

9. John Stott, *Guard the Truth* (Downers Grove, IL: InterVarsity, 1996), p. 117.

10. Billy Graham said this at the Congress on Discipleship and Evangelism (CODE '76), a gathering of 1,500 students during the Greater San Diego Billy Graham Crusade, August 1976.

11. Personal correspondence with retired Air Force Colonel William Waldrop, February 1991.

12. Knight, *The Pastoral Epistles*, pp. 198, 199 makes the case decisively that verse 9 refers to verse 1. See also Kelly, *A Commentary on the Pastoral Epistles*.

CHAPTER THIRTEEN: SUCCEEDING IN MINISTRY

1. J. N. D. Kelly, *A Commentary on the Pastoral Epistles* (Grand Rapids, MI: Baker, 1963), p. 104 explains:

   Timothy, who need not have been born before 30, may well have not been much beyond his middle thirties. According to the ancient usage the description 'young man' (Gk. *neos,* etc.) could be applied to a full-grown man of military age. Polybius (xviii. 12.5) speaks of Flaminius as 'young' because he was only thirty, and Irenaeus (*Haer.* ii, 22, 5) explicitly states that one could aptly be called 'young' up to forty. We recall that Luke designates Paul a young man at the time of Stephen's death, when he must have been about thirty (Acts vii. 58). As a much older man, probably in his sixties, Paul was therefore perfectly in order in addressing Timothy in this way. Moreover, if the situation is historical, quite a number of members of the Ephesian community, including no doubt some of the elders, must have been considerably older than Timothy, and may well have chafed at being lectured to, and at having their conduct dictated by, so relatively young an official, all the more so if he was not of a forceful, assertive character.

2. Gordon D. Fee, *1 and 2 Timothy, Titus* (Peabody, MA: Hendrickson Publishers, 1984), p. 107.

3. John Stott, *Guard the Truth* (Downers Grove, IL: InterVarsity, 1996), p. 121, who quotes Justin Martyr, *First Apology,* translated by A. W. F. Blunt, *Cambridge Patristic Texts,* Vol. I (Cambridge: Cambridge, 1911), I, p. 67.

4. *Ibid.,* p. 122.

5. Fee, *1 and 2 Timothy, Titus*, p. 108.

6. Stott, *Guard the Truth*, p. 123.

7. Philip H. Towner, *1-2 Timothy & Titus* (Downers Grove, IL: InterVarsity, 1994), p. 112.

CHAPTER FOURTEEN: RELATING AND LEADING

1. R. C. Lucas tape, Lecture 10, 1 Timothy 5:1-16, "Expository Lectures on 1 Timothy," St. Helen's Vestry, Great St. Helen's, London.

2. J. N. D. Kelley, *A Commentary on the Pastoral Epistles* (Grand Rapids, MI: Baker, 1963), p. 110.

3. Gordon D. Fee, *1 and 2 Timothy, Titus* (Peabody, MA: Hendrickson Publishers, 1984), p. 116, explains:

   The imperative "give proper recognition to" is not easy to translate, because in verse 17 the same noun implies some sort of remuneration, whereas in 6:1 it means simply "respect." But the context of the whole section, finally clarified in verse 16, suggests that "give proper recognition to" in the sense of "caring for" is what is in view.

4. John Stott, *Guard the Truth* (Downers Grove, IL: InterVarsity, 1996), p. 129 explains:

   Coming to 1 Timothy 5, we notice at once that the section on widows appears to be divided into two paragraphs, each of which is introduced by a different main verb. The widows in mind in verses 3-8 Timothy is to *give proper recognition to,* literally 'to honour, or rather support', whereas those in mind in verses 9-16 he is to *put on the list of widows,* that is, 'register' or 'enroll' them. Commentators differ as to whether Paul is referring to the same group of widows in both paragraphs, or to two distinct groups. That different categories are in view is suggested not only by the different introductory verbs ('honour' and 'register'), but also by the different conditions for admission into the two groups. In the first case it is destitution and godliness, while in the second it is a combination of seniority, married faithfulness and a reputation for good works. I shall take it this way, understanding that the former group of widows is to receive financial support, and the latter opportunities for ministry, alongside the presbyters and deacons of chapter 3, although no hard and fast line is drawn between the groups, and they will probably have overlapped.

Further explanation is offered on p. 132:

The focus in verses 3-8 has been on the financial maintenance of widows, which in the first instance is the duty of their relatives and only becomes the duty of the church if the widow has no relatives. This concern does not recur in this paragraph, except as a kind of appendix in verse 16. Instead, this paragraph introduces new concerns. We read now of a 'list', 'roll' or 'register' of widows (9a, 11), of a quite different set of qualifications (9b, 10), of a 'pledge' to remain single (12), apparently in order to give themselves to service and of the non-eligibility of 'younger widows' (11-15). From this it seems that the register is not for widows needing support, but widows capable of offering service.

5. Philip H. Towner, *1-2 Timothy & Titus* (Downers Grove, IL: InterVarsity, 1994), p. 111 explains:

The Greek phrase in verse 9, literally, "one-man woman," is the counterpart to the "one-woman man" which describes the overseer and deacon (3:2, 12; Tit 1:6). The NIV translates it accurately as referring to faithfulness in marriage. For it is this, and not a commitment to remain single after one's spouse has died, that is probably in view.

Also Stott on p. 133 comments:

As argued in the comment on that text, this cannot mean that she has not remarried, since in verse 14 Paul counsels the younger widows to re-marry, but rather that she has been faithful.

6. Fee, *1 and 2 Timothy, Titus*, p. 122.

CHAPTER FIFTEEN: REGARDING LEADERS

1. Philip H. Towner, *1-2 Timothy & Titus* (Downers Grove, IL: InterVarsity, 1994), p. 125.

2. Gordon D. Fee, *1 and 2 Timothy, Titus* (Peabody, MA: Hendrickson Publishers, 1984), p. 129.

3. David W. Torrence and Thomas F. Torrence, eds., *1st and 2nd Timothy, Calvin's Commentaries*, Vol. 10 (Grand Rapids, MI: Eerdmans, 1964), p. 261: "I have no objection to Chrysostom's interpretation of *double honour* as meaning support and reverence, and anyone who wishes may follow him."

4. John Stott, *Guard the Truth* (Downers Grove, IL: InterVarsity, 1996), p. 137.

5. George W. Knight, III, *The Pastoral Epistles* (Grand Rapids, MI: Eerdmans, 1992), p. 232:

κοπιάω, "work hard," "toil," is used by Paul more than by any other NT author (14x of 22x). He uses it of physical work (1 Cor. 4:12; Eph. 4:28; 2 Tim. 2:6 of the toil of the farmer), most often of his own mental and spiritual labors in the apostolic ministry (1 Cor., 15:10; Gal. 4:11; Phil. 2:16; Col. 1:29; 1 Tim. 4:10), and also the work of others as spiritual leaders (1 Cor. 15:10; 16:10; 1 Thes. 5:12; 1 Tim. 4:10; here). With this verb he is self-consciously designating the work of these elders as a vigorous and laborious work.

6. Torrence and Torrence, eds., *1st and 2nd Timothy, Calvin's Commentaries*, Vol. 10, p. 263.

7. J. N. D. Kelly, *A Commentary on the Pastoral Epistles* (Grand Rapids, MI: Baker, 1963), p. 27 writes:

   It is difficult to escape the impression that he has in mind a concrete case, or perhaps cases, of scandal arising out of the preferential treatment which erring elders have received. He invokes God and Christ Jesus and the elect angels because the final judgment will be in their hands; Timothy must exercise his judicial functions as their representative, and also as one who will himself be judged by them.

8. Torrence and Torrence, eds., *1st and 2nd Timothy, Calvin's Commentaries*, Vol. 10, p. 265.

9. Kelly, *A Commentary on the Pastoral Epistles*, p. 128 explains:

   The advice, 'Don't go on drinking only water, but take a little wine for the sake of your digestion in view of your frequent indispositions,' seems at first to interrupt the connexion between 22 and 24f., and critics have often assumed either that it has got misplaced or that it is a gloss which has crept into the text. There is no MS support for either of these surmises, and so far from being a likely intruder, the very banality of the verse strikes a note of authenticity. Believers in Pauline authorship have not been slow to point this out, adding that the Apostle's style is often disjointed.

10. Fee, *1 and 2 Timothy, Titus,* p. 132.

11. *Ibid.*, p. 135.

12. Thomas C. Oden, *First and Second Timothy and Titus* (Louisville: John Knox Press, 1989), p. 154.

13. Torrence and Torrence, eds., *1st and 2nd Timothy, Calvin's Commentaries*, Vol. 10, p. 267.

CHAPTER SIXTEEN: REGARDING SERVITUDE

1. Geoffrey W. Bromiley, ed., *The New International Standard Bible Encyclopedia* (Grand Rapids, MI: Eerdmans, 1988), p. 544.

2. John R. W. Stott, *God's New Society* (Downers Grove, IL: InterVarsity, 1979), p. 251 quotes *Nichomachian Ethics*, viii.11.6 and *Politics*, 1.2, 4.

3. Bromiley, *The New International Standard Bible Encyclopedia*, p. 544.

4. *Ibid.*

5. *Ibid.*, p. 545.

6. *Ibid.*, p. 544.

7. Gordon Fee, *1 and 2 Timothy, Titus* (Peabody, MA: Hendrickson Publishers, 1984), p. 136.

8. Philip H. Towner, *1-2 Timothy & Titus* (Downers Grove, IL: InterVarsity, 1994), p. 131.

9. *Ibid.*

CHAPTER SEVENTEEN: APOSTASY ANALYZED: A WARNING

1. Paul Seabury, "Trendier Than Thou, the Many Temptations of the Episcopal Church," *Harper's Magazine*, October 1978, Vol. 257, No. 1541, pp. 39-52.

2. *Newsweek,* May 11, 1970.

3. George W. Knight, III, *The Pastoral Epistles* (Grand Rapids, MI: Eerdmans, 1992), p. 249.

4. James Charlton, ed., *The Writers Quotation Book,* 3rd edition (New York: Penguin, 1991), p. 86.

5. *Ibid.*

6. Henry Fairlie, *The Seven Deadly Sins* (South Bend, IN: University of Notre Dame Press, 1979), p. 9.

7. Walter Lock, *The Pastoral Epistles (I & II Timothy and Titus)* (Edinburgh: T. & T. Clark, 1935), p. 68.

8. Gordon D. Fee, *1 and 2 Timothy, Titus* (Peabody, MA: Hendrickson Publishers, 1984), p. 142.

9. Knight, III, *The Pastoral Epistles*, p. 252.

10. Lock, *The Pastoral Epistles (I & II Timothy and Titus),* p. 68.

11. Fee, *1 and 2 Timothy, Titus*, p. 144.

12. Philip H. Towner, *1-2 Timothy & Titus* (Downers Grove, IL: InterVarsity, 1994), p. 139.

13. George MacDonald, *Creation in Christ*, ed. Rolland Hein (Wheaton, IL: Harold Shaw Publishers, 1976), p. 265.

CHAPTER EIGHTEEN: A CHARGE TO THE MAN OF GOD

1. J. N. D. Kelly, *A Commentary on the Pastoral Epistles* (Grand Rapids, MI: Baker. 1963), p. 139.

2. Gordon D. Fee, *1 and 2 Timothy, Titus* (Peabody, MA: Hendrickson Publishers, 1984), p. 149.

3. Philip H. Towner, *1-2 Timothy & Titus* (Downers Grove, IL: InterVarsity, 1994), p. 142.

4. John Stott, *Guard the Truth* (Downers Grove, IL: InterVarsity, 1996), p. 155.

5. *Ibid.*, p. 157 explains:

   It seems more probable, however, that eternal life is here a present possession, because Paul describes it to Timothy as something *to which you were called when you made your good confession in the presence of many witnesses* (12b). The reference to 'many witnesses' has suggested to some that the occasion recalled is not Timothy's baptism but his ordination (cf. 4:14; 2 Tim. 2:2). But the combination of the calling (inward and private) and the confession (outward and public) more naturally refers to Timothy's conversion and baptism. Every convert was expected to make a solemn public affirmation of faith.

6. *Ibid.*

7. *Ibid.*

8. Annie Dillard, *Teaching a Stone to Talk* (New York: Harper and Row, 1982), pp. 12, 16.

9. Gordon D. Fee, *1 and 2 Timothy, Titus*, p. 152, explains:

   It is often suggested that this last phrase implies that Paul (or a later author) is writing at a time when the imminence of the Parousia is no longer alive. But that is to read far too much into one phrase (read, of course, in light of 2 Tim. 2:6-8). It also misses the eschatological urgency of these letters (1 Tim. 4:1; 2 Tim. 3:1), as well as the ambiguity elsewhere in Paul. As early as 1 Corinthians, the very letter that has so much of the urgency in it (7:29-31), Paul speaks of "awaiting the revelation" (1:7; cf. 11:26) and in Philippians one finds the same tension between his readiness to die (1:21-23) and "awaiting the Lord Jesus from heaven" (3:20-21). If the present text implies anything, it is that Timothy will experience the Parousia, and that scarcely reflects the perspective of a church settling in for a long life in the world.

10. Robertson McQuilkin, "Let Me Get Home Before Dark," 1981:

It's sundown, Lord.
The shadows of my life stretch back
into the dimness of the years long spent.
I fear not death, for that grim foe betrays himself at last,
thrusting me forever into life:
Life with you, unsoiled and free.
But I do fear.
I fear the Dark Spectre may come too soon —
or do I mean, too late?
That I should end before I finish or
finish, but not well.
That I should stain your honor, shame your name,
grieve your loving heart.
Few, they tell me, finish well . . .
Lord, let me get home before dark.

The darkness of a spirit
grown mean and small, fruit shriveled on the vine,
bitter to the taste of my companions,
burden to be borne by those brave few who love me still.
No, Lord. Let the fruit grow lush and sweet,
A joy to all who taste;
Spirit-sign of God at work,
stronger, fuller, brighter at the end.
Lord, let me get home before dark.

The darkness of tattered gifts,
rust-locked, half-spent or ill-spent,
A life that once was used of God
now set aside.
Grief for glories gone or
Fretting for a task God never gave.
Mourning in the hollow chambers of memory,
Gazing on the faded banners of victories long gone.
Cannot I run well unto the end?
Lord, let me get home before dark.

The outer me decays —
I do not fret or ask reprieve.
The ebbing strength but weans me from mother earth
and grows me up for heaven.
I do not cling to shadows cast by immortality.
I do not patch the scaffold lent to build the real, eternal me.
I do not clutch about me my cocoon,
vainly struggling to hold hostage
a free spirit pressing to be born.
But will I reach the gate
in lingering pain, body distorted, grotesque?
Or will it be a mind
wandering untethered among light phantasies or
grim terrors?
Of your grace, Father, I humbly ask . . .
Let me get home before dark.

CHAPTER NINETEEN: CLOSING WORDS TO THE RICH AND THEIR LEADER

1. Leland Ryken, *Worldly Saints* (Grand Rapids, MI: Zondervan, 1986), p. 63 quotes Stephen Foster, *Their Solitary Way: The Puritan Social Ethic in the First Century of Settlement in New England* (New Haven, CT: Yale University Press, 1958), p. 121.

2. Gordon D. Fee, *1 and 2 Timothy, Titus* (Peabody, MA: Hendrickson Publishers, 1984), p. 157.

3. Boris Pasternak, *Dr. Zhivago* (London: Collins and Harvill Press, 1958), p. 160.

4. *Chicago Tribune*, March 11, 1991, Section 5 (Tempo), p. 3.

5. Frank E. Gaebelein, ed., *The Expositor's Bible Commentary: 1, 2 Thessalonians; 1, 2 Timothy; Titus* (Grand Rapids, MI: Zondervan, 1984), p. 162.

6. David W. Torrence and Thomas F. Torrence, ed., *1st and 2nd Timothy, Calvin's Commentaries*, Vol. 10 (Grand Rapids, MI: Eerdmans, 1964), p. 282.

7. *Ibid.*, p. 283.

8. Thomas C. Oden, *First and Second Timothy and Titus* (Louisville: John Knox Press, 1989), p. 106.

9. J. N. D. Kelly, *A Commentary on the Pastoral Epistles* (Grand Rapids, MI: Baker, 1963), p. 150, explains:

The noun translated trust (Gk. *Paratheke*) is found only here and in 2 Tim. I, 12; 14. It is a legal term connoting something which is placed on trust in another man's keeping. The suggestion is that the Christian message ('the faith' or 'the truth', as it is so often called in these letters) is not something which the church's minister works out for himself or is entitled to add to; it is a divine revelation which has been committed to his care, and which it is his bounden duty to pass on unimpaired to others.

10. Sermon LXXXV.3, NPNF 2 XI, 198, in Oden, *First and Second Timothy and Titus*, p. 127.

11. William Barclay, *The Letters to Timothy, Titus and Philemon* (Philadelphia: The Westminster Press, 1960), p. 161. Note: Barclay's excellent application has here been paraphrased and expanded.

12. Colin Brown, *Philosophy in the Christian Faith* (Downers Grove, IL: InterVarsity, 1986), p. 219.

13. Kelly, *A Commentary on the Pastoral Epistles*, pp. 151, 152.

CHAPTER TWENTY: MINISTRY: RETROSPECT AND REALITY

1. David W. Torrence and Thomas F. Torrence, ed., *1st and 2nd Timothy, Calvin's Commentaries*, Vol. 10 (Grand Rapids, MI: Eerdmans, 1964), p. 289.

2. Gordon D. Fee, *1 and 2 Timothy, Titus* (Peabody, MA: Hendrickson Publishers, 1984), pp. 13, 14.

3. Philip H. Towner, *1-2 Timothy & Titus* (Downers Grove, IL: InterVarsity, 1994), p. 155 writes:

The next phrase introduces the purpose or goal of Paul's apostolic ministry: *the promise of life that is in Christ Jesus.* It is the good news of that promise that he has sought to bring to the world through preaching. At the moment of writing, Paul in his circumstances probably thinks of "life" (eternal) as something yet to be fully obtained — thus the reference to a *promise* (compare 1 Tim 6:19). Elsewhere he focuses more on the Christian's present experience of eternal life (1 Tim 4:8). The main purpose of the gospel is to introduce people to the possibility of new life. Such a possibility is a compelling reason to persevere in ministry and a powerful source of personal encouragement and hope.

4. J. N. D. Kelly, *A Commentary on the Pastoral Epistles* (Grand Rapids, MI: Baker, 1963), p. 156.
5. Fee, *1 and 2 Timothy, Titus*, pp. 226, 227.
6. *Ibid.,* p. 227
7. Towner, *1-2 Timothy & Titus*, p. 161.
8. "Man's Weakness — God's Strength," *Missionary Crusader* (December 1964), p. 7.
9. William Barclay, *The Letters to Timothy, Titus and Philemon* (Philadelphia: The Westminster Press, 1960), p. 166.
10. Towner, *1-2 Timothy & Titus*, p. 161.

CHAPTER TWENTY-ONE: STAND TALL, SUFFER, AND KEEP THE FAITH

1. "Man's Weakness — God's Strength," *Missionary Crusader*, December 1964, p. 7.
2. Philip H. Towner, *1-2 Timothy & Titus* (Downers Grove, IL: InterVarsity, 1994), p. 163 explains:

The gift of the Holy Spirit is linked expressly to suffering, struggling, and what he provides for the believer is what is needed to keep one persevering in the midst of trials that come because of faith — not removal to some higher plane. This view of the Spirit was quite different from that of the enthusiasts that Timothy and Paul faced. It is also an understanding quite different from that held by those in our churches who equate "spiritual" Christianity with the immediate resolution of life's difficulties. Paul's view is the correct one; the other is escapist fantasy covered over with a thin coat of "spiritual" paint.

Cf. pp. 158, 159 for a lengthy explanation.

3. George W. Knight, III, *The Pastoral Epistles* (Grand Rapids, MI: Eerdmans, 1992), p. 373 explains:

It is striking that Paul refers to himself not as Rome's prisoner but as "his" (αὐτοῦ), i.e., "the Lord's" prisoner, with αὐτοῦreferring back to τοῦ κυρίου. His imprisonment is for no other reason than that he serves the Lord. Paul always refers to himself as a δέσμιος in this way (δέσμιος Χριστοῦ Ἰησοῦ, Eph. 3:1; Phm. 1, 9; δέσμιος ἐν κυρίῳ, Eph. 4:1). That he does so here gives Timothy perspective on Paul's imprisonment and thereby gives him reason not to be ashamed of the apostle.

4. R. Kent Hughes, *1001 Great Stories & "Quotes"* (Wheaton, IL: Tyndale, 1998), p. 405.
5. William Barclay, *The Letters to Timothy, Titus and Philemon* (Philadelphia: The Westminster Press, 1960), p. 167.
6. George W. Knight, III, *The Pastoral Epistles*, p. 375 comments:

Except for the rendering of the *RSV,* "ages ago," there is a consensus among commentators and translations that the phrase, literally "before times eternal," is best understood here as "from all eternity" (*NASB, NEB*) or "before the beginning of time" (*NIV, TEV*). This is in accord with Paul's perspective, which speaks of God's decision before time and the world began (1 Cor. 2:7: πρὸ τῶν αἰώνιων; Eph. 1:4: πρὸ καταβολῆς κόσμου.

7. David W. Torrence and Thomas F. Torrence, ed., *1st and 2nd Timothy, Calvin's Commentaries*, Vol. 10 (Grand Rapids, MI: Eerdmans, 1964), p. 300.
8. Hughes, *1001 Great Stories & "Quotes,"* pp. 61, 62.
9. Donald Guthrie, *The Pastoral Epistles* (Grand Rapids, MI: Eerdmans, 1957, p.133.
10. George W. Knight, III, *The Pastoral Epistles*, p. 380 convincingly argues:

In this context the deposit is more likely to be what Paul has committed to God, e.g., his own life, since the statement speaks of God as the one who "guards" and of the deposit as Paul's ("my"). These two factors taken together distinguish this passage from the other two occurrences of the word (1 Tim. 6:20; 2 Tim. 1:4). In them Timothy, a human being, is the subject of φυλάσσω; it is he who is to guard the deposit, which is not personalized as "my" deposit, as it is here. "My" with the deposit here seems more naturally to refer to what Paul has committed to another than to what has been committed to Paul.

This . . . view also fits this part of the verse, which is oriented to God's care of Paul, ᾧ πεπίστευκα, "in whom I have put my trust" . . . [which] has prepared the way for Paul to speak about the ability of the one in whom he trusts to guard "my deposit," that which Paul has entrusted to God, which in effect he has already identified as himself in the statement "*I* have put my trust." Furthermore, this perspective fits the letter as a whole and particularly this section, where Paul is encouraging Timothy to suffer for the gospel. Paul is concerned not only for Timothy's fidelity but also that Timothy be assured that God will take care of his suffering servant. Paul gives him this assurance by pointing out this reality in his own life (cf. Paul's references to God's care for his life throughout the letter, e.g., 4:8, 17-18, and the maxim that those who endure will reign with Christ, 2:12). For the appropriateness of this view of the "deposit" to what follows see below.

CHAPTER TWENTY-TWO: MERCY TO THE MERCIFUL

1. Clarence Edward Macartney, *The Women of Tekoah and Other Sermons on Bible Characters* (New York: Abingdon, 1955), pp. 64, 65.

2. J. N. D. Kelly, *A Commentary on the Pastoral Epistles* (Grand Rapids, MI: Baker, 1963), p. 169.

3. George W. Knight, III, *The Pastoral Epistles* (Grand Rapids, MI: Eerdmans, 1992), p. 383, observes that the "Aorist passive ἀπεστράφησαν recalls some event in which 'all' 'turned away from' him."

4. Macartney, *The Women of Tekoah and Other Sermons on Bible Characters*, pp. 72, 73.

5. C. S. Lewis, *The Four Loves* (New York: Harcourt, Brace, 1960), p. 59.

6. David W. Torrence and Thomas F. Torrence, eds., *1st and 2nd Timothy, Calvin's Commentaries*, Vol. 10 (Grand Rapids, MI: Eerdmans, 1964), p. 303.

7. William Hendriksen, *Expositions of the Pastoral Epistles* (Grand Rapids, MI: Baker, 1957), p. 239.

8. J. N. D. Kelly, *A Commentary on the Pastoral Epistles*, p. 170 explains:

'So too cheered my spirits' translates a verb (Gk. *anapsuchein*: lit. 'Refresh') found nowhere else in the N.T. (But cf. Acts iii, 20 for the related noun *anapsuxis*.) The meaning is, not that Onesiphorus helped the Apostle at Ephesus materially or with practical services, but that he braced his morale with his fellowship.

9. Gordon D. Fee, *1 and 2 Timothy, Titus* (Peabody, MA: Hendrickson Publishers, 1984), p. 237 writes:

Having already entreated mercy for his household (v. 16a), presumably because of their loss, Paul now desires (again in the form of a wish-prayer) for Onesiphorus himself: may the Lord grant that he will find mercy from the Lord on that day! "On that day," as in verse 12, can only refer to the Second Advent. Thus it is hard to escape the implication that Onesiphorus is now dead. Why else, one wonders, especially in light of verse 16, should Paul only wish him to find (a word play on Onesiphorus' having "found" him; v. 17) mercy at the End?

10. George W. Knight, III, *The Pastoral Epistles*, p. 386 writes:

It has been suggested that this reference to "that day" and to Onesiphorus separately from his family (v. 16; 4:19) means that he was dead (e.g., Bernard, Fee). This is, or course, a possibility, but the separate references may only mean that Onesiphorus and his family were apart from one another when Paul wrote, or that Paul wanted to express his appreciation not only for Onesiphorus's ministry but also for the support and understanding of his family. Paul speaks in 1 Cor. 1:16 about a man's household while that person is still alive and in 2 Timothy about "that day" in reference to those who are still alive, including himself alone (1:12) and with all believers (4:8). Furthermore, he can wish eschatological blessings for those who are living (e.g., 1 Thes. 5:23b). Therefore, that Onesiphorus was alive and separated from his family is as possible as that he was dead.

11. Gordon D. Fee, *1 and 2 Timothy, Titus*, p. 237 explains:

Does this, then countenance prayers for the departed? Many think so. However, before one builds Christian doctrine on such a text, one needs to be cautioned that such an idea is quite singular to this one, not totally certain, text and that it merely expresses Paul's sentiment toward, or desire for, Onesiphorus. It is not, in fact, intercessory prayer (cf. the difference with Eph. 1:17 e.g.); rather, it is an acknowledgment that even one like Onesiphorus has only God's mercy as his appeal.

12. Kelly, *A Commentary on the Pastoral Epistles*, p. 170.

13. William Hendriksen, *Exposition of the Gospel According to Matthew* (Grand Rapids, MI: Baker, 1973), p. 880 explains:

The very close connection between Christ and the genuine followers is shown here, as also in 10:25, 40, 42; Mark 13:13; John 15:5, 18-21; Acts 9:4, 5; 22:7; 26:14, 15; II Cor. 1:5, 10; Gal. 2:20; 6:17; Col. 1:24; Rev. 12:4, 13. Cf. Prov. 19:17. Whatever was done for Christ's disciples, out of love for Christ, is counted as if done for Christ.

CHAPTER TWENTY-THREE: ON GUARDING THE GOSPEL

1. Gordon D. Fee, *1 and 2 Timothy, Titus* (Peabody, MA: Hendrickson Publishers, 1984), p. 238.

2. Guy H. King, *To My Son — an Expositional Study of II Timothy* (Fort Washington, PA: Christian Literature Crusade, 1968), p. 39.

3. Charles Colson, *Kingdoms in Conflict* (New York/Grand Rapids, MI: William Morrow/Zondervan, 1987), pp. 95-108.

4. Philip H. Towner, *1-2 Timothy & Titus* (Downers Grove, IL: InterVarsity, 1994), p. 171.

5. William Barclay, *The Letters to Timothy, Titus and Philemon* (Philadelphia: The Westminster Press, 1960), p. 36.

6. *Ibid.*, p. 183.

7. C. H. Spurgeon, *The Metropolitan Tabernacle Pulpit*, Vol. 16 (Pasadena, TX: Pilgrim, 1970), p. 370.

8. J. N. D. Kelly, *A Commentary on the Pastoral Epistles* (Grand Rapids, MI: Baker, 1963), pp. 175, 176 explains:

There has been much argument whether these rules (the Greek has the adverb *nomimōs*, i.e. 'Lawfully': cf. I Tim. I. 8) are *(a)* the particular rules of the game in question or *(b)* the official regulations imposed on athletes taking part in public games, which in order to maintain high standards included prescriptions about training. As an example of the latter, competitors at the Olympic Games had to swear an oath before the statue of Zeus that they had been in strict training for ten months (Pausanias, *Graec. descr.* V. 24. 9). Either is possible, but since cheating is not relevant to Paul's theme whereas arduous self-discipline is, *(b)* seems much more plausible than *(a)*.

9. *Ibid.*, p. 176.

10. Fee, *1 and 2 Timothy, Titus*, p. 243, quoting C. K. Barrett, *The Pastoral Epistles*, in *The New Clarendon Bible* (Oxford: Clarendon Press, 1963), p. 102.

CHAPTER TWENTY-FOUR: THE ESSENTIAL MEMORY

1. J. N. D. Kelly, *A Commentary on the Pastoral Epistles* (Grand Rapids, MI: Eerdmans, 1957), p. 177. Also William Mounce, *The Pastoral Epistles* (Nashville: Word, 2000) explains:

   Paul suffers not only to the point of being imprisoned but to the degree that he is treated like a "serious criminal." κακοῦργος is an adjective used substantively, appearing in the NT elsewhere only as a description of the thieves crucified with Jesus (Luke 23:32, 33, 39). Etymologically it means "a worker (ἔργος) of evil (κακός)." Its meaning ranges from a "good-for-nothing" person (Spicq, *TLNT* 2:241-3) to "one who commits gross misdeeds and serious crimes" (BAGD, 398). Spicq gives many examples of this word's use, and most illustrate the harsher meaning of the word, being used of violent people without a conscience, mostly thieves, punished by arrest, torture, feet and hands cut off, and eyes gouged out. This is therefore another indication (cf. 1:17) that Paul's current imprisonment is much harsher than the one described in Acts 28.

2. William Barclay, *The Letters to Timothy, Titus and Philemon* (Philadelphia: The Westminster Press, 1960), p. 192, quotes Tacitus:

   But all human efforts, all the lavish gifts of the emperor, and the propitiations of the gods did not banish the sinister belief that the conflagration was the result of an order. Consequently, to get rid of the report, Nero fastened the guilt and inflicted the most exquisite tortures on a class hated for their abominations, called Christian by the populace. (Tacitus, *Annals,* 15:44).

3. F. W. Boreham, *A Bunch of Everlastings* (New York: Abingdon, 1920), p. 19.

4. Donald Guthrie, *The Pastoral Epistles* (Grand Rapids, MI: Eerdmans, 1957), p. 144.

5. Andria Wolfe, "An Answered Prayer from Stalin's Times," *The Chariot*, (The CoMission Newsletter), 1st Quarter, 1994, Vol. 2, Issue 1, p. 1.

6. Gordon D. Fee, *1 and 2 Timothy, Titus* (Peabody, MA: Hendrickson Publishers, 1984), p. 249.

7. *Ibid.*, p. 249:

   This clearly mirrors Romans 6:8 (cf. Col. 2:20; 3:1), and there is no reason to think that it means anything different here from what it does there. Using baptismal imagery, Paul is reflecting again on Christian conversion as a dying and rising with Christ. The future, "we will also live with him," has primarily to do with life in Christ in the present (as it does in Rom. 6:8-11), although such language always has latent in it the thought of the eschatological fulfillment yet to be realized. After all, the present life with him is the result of his resurrection, *the* primary eschatological event that has already set the future in motion.

8. Mounce, *The Pastoral Epistles*, pp. 516, 517.

9. R. Kent Hughes, *Luke*, Vol. 1 (Wheaton, IL: Crossway Books, 1998), pp. 233, 234.

10. Mounce, *The Pastoral Epistles*, p. 517.

11. *Ibid.,* p. 925, 926.

12. Edward Hastings, *The Speaker's Bible* (Grand Rapids, MI: Baker, 1971), p. 89.

CHAPTER TWENTY-FIVE: HANDLING GOD'S WORD

1. Daniel J. Boorstin, *The Discoverers* (New York: Vintage Books, 1983), p. 482.

2. *Ibid.*

3. *Ibid.*, p. 483.

4. Gordon D. Fee, *1 and 2 Timothy, Titus* (Peabody, MA: Hendrickson Publishers, 1984), p. 254, argues that it makes most sense in light of the context to understand that verse 14 is referencing verses 11-13. Mounce loc. cit.. provides extensive support for this view, demonstrating that "The Faithful Saying (2:11-13) is closer to v. 14 and fits the contextual needs of vv. 14-26."

5. Note that verse 14 begins with an imperative "Keep reminding" and that "Warn them" is a participle that is subject to the imperative, so that the sense is "Keep reminding . . . *while* warning them."

6. J. N. D. Kelly, *A Commentary on the Pastoral Epistles* (Grand Rapids, MI: Baker, 1963), p. 182.

7. Walter Lock, *The Pastoral Epistles* (Edinburgh: T. & T. Clark, 1936), p. 98.

8. Max Zerwick and Mary Grosvenor, *A Grammatical Analysis of the Greek New Testament* (Rome: Biblical Institute Press, 1981), p. 641.

9. Peter Adam, *Speaking God's Words* (Leicester, England: Inter-Varsity, 1996), pp. 102, 103.

10. William H. Willimon, "Been There, Preached That," *Leadership Magazine*, Fall 1995, p. 76.

11. John MacArthur, Jr., *Rediscovering Expository Preaching* (Waco, TX: Word, 1992), p. 348.

12. Fee, *1 and 2 Timothy, Titus*, p. 255.

13. Donald Guthrie, *The Pastoral Epistles* (Grand Rapids, MI: Eerdmans, 1957), p. 148.

14. Fee, *1 and 2 Timothy, Titus,* p. 256.

15. The LXX Greek of Numbers 16:5 and the NT Greek of 2 Timothy 2:19 are almost word for word, except that the LXX has θεὸς (God), the NT κύριος (Lord). The LXX reads ἔγνω ὁ θεὸς τοὺς ὄντας αὐτοῦ, while the UBSGNT reads Ἔγνω κύριος τοὺς ὄντας αὐτοῦ.

16. Kelly, *A Commentary on the Pastoral Epistles*, p. 186 writes:

    . . . the unshakeable core of genuine Christians at Ephesus. It almost certainly stands for the last, or at any rate for the Ephesian church considered as part of the great Church, since the Apostle is clearly contrasting the solid foundation with the unstable few whose faith has been undermined. This is confirmed by the content of the two inscriptions which the solid foundation has engraved on it, and which both refer to God's elect and faithful people.

    Similarly, Mounce loc. cit. concludes his convincing explanation saying, "Therefore, we prefer to see 'foundation' as the individuals who are firmly elect, not being swayed by heresy."

17. *Ibid.*

CHAPTER TWENTY-SIX: FOR NOBLE PURPOSES

1. George W. Knight, III, *The Pastoral Epistles* (Grand Rapids, MI: Eerdmans, 1992), pp. 417, 418.

2. Thomas C. Oden, *First and Second Timothy and Titus* (Louisville: John Knox Press, 1989), p. 71.

3. William F. Arndt and F. Wilbur Gingrich, *A Greek-English Lexicon of the New Testament and Other Early Christian Literature* (Chicago: University of Chicago Press, 1957), p. 293.

4. Gordon D. Fee, *1 and 2 Timothy, Titus* (Peabody, MA: Hendrickson Publishers, 1984), p. 263.

5. George W. Knight, III, *The Pastoral Epistles*, p. 421 explains:

Paul indicates later in this letter that all scripture is profitable "for training in righteousness" (2 Tim. 3:16) and thereby sets up scripture as the standard of righteousness, δικαιοσύνη as human ethical action "is almost always used in the NT for the right conduct of man which follows the will of God and is pleasing to Him . . ." (G. Schrenk, *TDNT*, II, 198).

6. Philip H. Towner, *1-2 Timothy & Titus* (Downers Grove, IL: InterVarsity, 1994), p. 188.

7. William Barclay, *The Letters to Timothy, Titus and Philemon* (Philadelphia: The Westminster Press, 1960), p. 208.

8. James Boswell, *The Life of Samuel Johnson* (London: Penguin, 1979), p. 94.

9. William Mounce, *The Pastoral Epistles* (Nashville: Word, 2000), p. 535.

CHAPTER TWENTY-SEVEN: HEARTS OF DARKNESS

1. William Mounce, *The Pastoral Epistles* (Nashville: Word, 2000), pp. 543, 544:

At first glance it appears that these "last days" are in Timothy's future. "There will be" (ἐνστήσονται) and "will be" (ἔσονται; v 2) are both future tense. However, context requires that the vices of vv 2-5 and hence the "last days" of v 1 be present for Timothy. (1) The imperative "avoid" (ἀποτρέπου; v 5) is present as are most of the verbal forms. As a non-indicative it has no time significance, and yet as a linear imperative context requires that Timothy "avoid" these people now in the present. The use of the present tense verb in v 6 assures us this is the case. "The people who will be lovers of self . . ." (v 2) are the same who are (εἰσιν) currently entering Ephesian households. (2) In the parallel passage, 1 Tim 4:1-5, we have the same time issue. The prophecy of apostasy in the last times was originally stated as a future event, but context shows that what was once future when the prophecy was made is now present for Timothy. (3) Although there is no prophecy explicitly mentioned in vv 1-9, the tenor of the passage and its parallel to 1 Tim 4:1-5 shows that vv 1-2 are stated from the time frame of when the prophecies were made about future moral decadence in the last days, and it is that future in which Timothy now finds himself embroiled. It is also possible that Paul sees the present days as the inception of the increasingly evil days to come, and the future tense therefore does not exclude the present inception.

2. J. H. Bernard, *The Pastoral Epistles* (Grand Rapids, MI: Baker, 1980), p. 130.

3. William Barclay, *The Letters to Timothy, Titus and Philemon* (Philadelphia: The Westminster Press, 1960), p. 270, and Bernard, *The Pastoral Epistles*, p. 130.

4. G. Abbott-Smith, *A Manual Greek Lexicon of the New Testament* (New York: Scribner's, n.d.), p. 65.

5. Walter Lock, *The Pastoral Epistles* (Edinburgh: T. & T. Clark, 1936), p. 106.

6. Abbott-Smith, *A Manual Greek Lexicon of the New Testament*, p. 37.

7. J. N. D. Kelly, *A Commentary on the Pastoral Epistles* (Grand Rapids, MI: Eerdmans, 1992), p. 194.

8. John Charles Ryle, *Formality*, a pamphlet from "The Inheritance of Our Fathers" series, XXXII, No. 2 (Grand Rapids, MI: The Inheritance Publishers), p. 7.

9. Gordon D. Fee, *1 and 2 Timothy, Titus* (Peabody, MA: Hendrickson Publishers, 1984), p. 271.

10. George W. Knight, III, *The Pastoral Epistles* (Grand Rapids, MI: Eerdmans, 1992), p. 434 explains:

    εἰς ἐπίγνωσιν ἀληθείας ἐλθεῖν, "to come to the knowledge of the truth," is associated with being saved in 1 Tim. 2:4; εἰς ἐπίγνωσις ἀληθείας is associated with repentance in 2 Tim. 2:25; and ἐπίγνωσιν ἀληθείας is associated in Tit. 1:1 with the faith of God's chosen and with godliness (these are the other three occurrences of ἐπίγνωσις ἀληθείας in the PE [see the comments on each passage], which appears elsewhere in the NT only in Heb. 10:26). ἐπίγνωσις ἀληθείας presents "the content of Christianity as the absolute truth" (BAGD s.v. ἀλήθεια 2b). "To come into" that knowledge is to acknowledge and embrace the truth of the gospel and be converted by it so that the things associated with this phrase in the other PE occurrences (repentance, faith, being saved, living in godliness) become a reality in one's life. The terrible consequence of the false teaching is that the women, who are so burdened, never really learn the truth that can make them free.

11. Fee, *1 and 2 Timothy, Titus*, p. 272.

12. Knight, *The Pastoral Epistles*, p. 435.

13. Thomas C. Oden, *First and Second Timothy and Titus* (Louisville: John Knox Press, 1989), p. 79.

14. James Davison Hunter, *Evangelicalism, The Coming Generation* (Chicago: University of Chicago Press, 1987), p. 69.

CHAPTER TWENTY-EIGHT: REMEMBRANCE AND CONTINUANCE

1. Gordon D. Fee, *1 and 2 Timothy, Titus* (Peabody, MA: Hendrickson Publishers, 1984), p. 274 explains:

    The paragraph is in two parts (vv. 10-13, 14-17), structured around two occurrences of *su de* ("You, however," v. 10; "but as for you," v. 14) and the central imperative of verse 14. The two parts hold the keys to Timothy's abiding loyalty: first, to recall the past, especially Paul's teaching and example, learned through long association, and second, to give heed to the Scriptures, with which he has also had long association, and which both lead to salvation through Christ and are useful for all the tasks of his ministry.

2. J. N. D. Kelly, *A Commentary on the Pastoral Epistles* (Grand Rapids, MI: Baker, 1963), p. 198.

3. Fee, *1 and 2 Timothy, Titus*, pp. 276, 186.

4. *Ibid.*, p. 276.

5. *Ibid.*, p. 277.

6. Kelly, *A Commentary on the Pastoral Epistles*, p. 199.

7. William Barclay, *The Letters to Timothy, Titus and Philemon* (Philadelphia: The Westminster Press, 1960), p. 227.

8. Thomas C. Oden, *First and Second Timothy and Titus* (Louisville: John Knox Press, 1989), p. 167.

CHAPTER TWENTY-NINE: CONTINUE IN THE WORD

1. Ethel May Baldwin and David V. Benson, *Henrietta Mears and How She Did It!* (Glendale, CA: Regal Books, 1966), p. 149.

2. Herbert Danby, trans., *The Mishnah* (London: Oxford, 1974), p. 458.

3. William Mounce, *The Pastoral Epistles* (Nashville: Word, 2000), pp. 564, 565 argues:

   While the message about a coming messiah and issues of faith are part of the OT, it seems doubtful that Paul would say the OT, by itself, can instruct Timothy in a salvation that is by faith in Christ Jesus; this would be anachronistic. In addition, vv 14-17 are yet another appeal that Timothy remain loyal to what he has learned, and earlier in this letter this means the gospel message (see discussion of ἐν οἷς in v. 14). Of course, in his childhood Timothy would only know the OT. Our conclusion is that the form of the phrase "Sacred Writings" is drawn solely from the vocabulary describing the OT, but since Paul is thinking of more than just the OT, because he is thinking about the culmination of the OT hope realized through faith in Christ Jesus, choosing the anarthrous plural construction allows him the freedom to develop his argument in this direction, joining the OT and the gospel.

4. J. N. D. Kelly, *A Commentary on the Pastoral Epistles* (Grand Rapids, MI: Baker, 1963), p. 203.

5. *Ibid.*

6. George W. Knight, III, *The Pastoral Epistles* (Grand Rapids, MI: Eerdmans, 1992), p. 448, who provides the evidence for my position, though he is more properly tentative in his scholarly conclusions

7. T. H. L. Parker, *Portrait of John Calvin* (Philadelphia: The Westminster Press, 1954), p. 82.

8. *Ibid.*, p. 83.

9. Ronald Wallace, *Calvin's Doctrines of the Word and Sacrament* (Grand Rapids, MI: Eerdmans, 1957), p. 105, which references Calvin's sermon on 2 Timothy 3:16, 17.

CHAPTER THIRTY: PREACH THE WORD

1. David W. Torrence and Thomas F. Torrence, eds., *1st and 2nd Timothy, Calvin's Commentaries*, Vol. 10 (Grand Rapids, MI: Eerdmans, 1964), p. 32.

2. John Calvin, *Selections from His Writings*, ed. John Dillenberger (Atlanta: Scholars Press, 1975), p. 28.

3. *Ibid.*

4. Thomas C. Oden, *First and Second Timothy and Titus* (Louisville: John Knox Press, 1989), p. 135.

5. George W. Knight, III, *The Pastoral Epistles* (Grand Rapids, MI: Eerdmans, 1992), pp. 453, 454.

6. Torrence and Torrence, eds., *1st and 2nd Timothy, Calvin's Commentaries*, Vol. 10, p. 333.

7. Clarence Edward Macartney, *Salute Thy Soul* (Nashville: Abingdon Press, 1957), p. 5.

8. John Eddison, ed., *A Study in Spiritual Power* (Suffolk, England: Highland Books, 1982), pp. 85, 86.

9. George W. Knight, III, *The Pastoral Epistles,* p. 454 explains:

   The fourth imperative ἐπιτίμησον (NT 29x, here only in Pl.*), is used here with the meaning "rebuke," i.e., censure or prevent an action or bring it to an end (BAGD s.v. 1). In the third imperative Timothy is charged to speak to those who are in error or doing wrong and to attempt to convince them of that; in the fourth he is charged to tell those doing wrong to stop.

10. J. N. D. Kelly, *A Commentary on the Pastoral Epistles* (Grand Rapids, MI: Baker, 1963), p. 207.

11. Oden, *First and Second Timothy and Titus*, p. 137.

CHAPTER THIRTY-ONE: PAUL'S TERMINAL PERSPECTIVES

1. Frederick Langbridge, *A Cluster of Quiet Thoughts* (London: The Religious Tract Society, 1896), n.p.

2. John G. Stackhouse, Jr., "The Gospel Song" (unpublished).

3. George W. Knight, III, *The Pastoral Epistles* (Grand Rapids, MI: Eerdmans, 1992), p. 458.

4. C. S. Lewis, *The Last Battle* (New York: Collier Books, 1956), p. 184.

5. R. Kent Hughes, *Ephesians: The Mystery of the Body of Christ* (Wheaton, IL: Crossway Books, 1990), p. 255.

6. Phrase attributed to John Masefield.

7. Ralph Earle, *1 and 2 Timothy* in *The Expositor's Bible* (Grand Rapids, MI: Zondervan, 1996), p. 186 explains:

   The word for "race" is *dromon* (only here and Acts 13:25; 20:24). It comes from the second aorist stem of *trechō* ("fun"), and so clearly means a racecourse (cf. KJV).

See also J. H. Bernard, *The Pastoral Epistles* (Grand Rapids, MI: Baker, 1980), p. 143.

8. George W. Knight, III, *The Pastoral Epistles*, p. 460 writes:

   This sense of "keeping" in terms of faithfully proclaiming and preserving the faith does not rule out the subjective sense, that Paul has "kept on believing" and even necessarily includes it: Paul perseveres in that which he preserves (cf. 1 Cor. 15:1-2).

9. Gordon D. Fee, *1 and 2 Timothy, Titus* (Peabody, MA: Hendrickson Publishers, 1984), p. 291.

10. *Ibid.,* p. 461 explains:

   Paul resumes the language of the games by speaking of ὁ στέφανος (NT 18x), "the crown" or "the garland" (elsewhere in Pl.*: literal in 1 Cor. 9:25; figurative, as here, in Phil. 4;1; 1 Thes. 2:19; cf. the related verb in 2 Tim. 2:5), which is qualified by genitive τῆς δικαιοσύνης. In the other NT occurrences of ὁ στέφανος with genitive nouns (1 Thes 2:19: "of exultation"; Jas. 1:12: "of life"; 1 Pet. 5:4: "of glory"; Rev. 2:10: "of life"; 12:1: "of twelve stars"[?]) the genitive is appositional and epexegetic. Furthermore, in 1 Cor. 9:25 the adjectival qualification "imperishable" is used in the same way: To receive an imperishable wreath is to receive imperishability. Therefore, it is most likely that here, too, the genitive is appositional, so that the phrase should be understood as "the crown, namely, righteousness." Rather than being "the crown which will bring final justification" (W. Grundmann, *TDNT* VII, 629) it is much more likely that it refers to the permanent and perfect "state of righteousness" (G. Schrenk, *TDNT* II, 210) into which the Christian is brought by God (cf. Phil. 3:12- 14, where Paul uses βραβεῖον, the "prize" in a contest, which is used interchangeably with στέφανος in 1 Cor. 9:24-25; cf. eschatological use of δικαιοσύνης also in Gal. 5:5).

CHAPTER THIRTY-TWO: TOUGH FRIENDS FOR TOUGH TIMES

1. J. H. Bernard, *The Pastoral Epistles* (Grand Rapids, MI: Baker, 1980), p. 144.

2. John Calvin, *1, 2 Timothy & Titus* (Wheaton, IL: Crossway Books, 1988), p. 340.

3. Guy H. King, *To My Son — an Expositional Study of II Timothy* (Fort Washington, PA: Christian Literature Crusade, 1944), p. 126.

4. William Barclay, *The Letters to Timothy, Titus and Philemon* (Philadelphia: The Westminster Press, 1960), pp. 245, 246.

5. Gordon D. Fee, *1 and 2 Timothy, Titus* (Peabody, MA: Hendrickson Publishers, 1984), p. 294 explains:

"Because he is helpful to me in my ministry" (lit., "he is useful to me for service"). The phrase "for service" (*diakonian*), although a favorite of Paul's for the ministry of the gospel (cf. 4:5; 1 Tim. 1:12; 2 Cor. 4:1), is ambiguous here and may refer to personal service (cf. 1 Cor. 16:15). Perhaps a little of both is intended, but the context suggests that at least ministry to his personal needs is involved (cf. 1:16-18 on Onesiphorus).

6. George W. Knight, III, *The Pastoral Epistles* (Grand Rapids, MI: Eerdmans, 1992), p. 467 explains:

To make his request more specific, Paul adds the words μάλιστα τὰς μεμβράνας . . . a loanword from Latin for the "parchment" used for making books (BAGD). There are two possible significances for Paul's phrase. The first is that it indicates which books, among all those that Paul asks for, he particularly (μάλιστα taken as "most of all, above all, especially") wants. The second possibility is that proposed by Skeat ("Especially the Parchments"), which understands μάλιστα as an equating or defining term so that the phrase is giving a further definition of all the books that Paul wants. On this view μάλιστα would be rendered "that is," and τὰς μεμβράναςwould refer to the same thing. Skeat's documentation of μάλιστα with this meaning (in addition to the more common meaning) elsewhere in Greek literature and in the PE is convincing, which makes it possible here as well (cf. 1 Tim. 4:10; 4:17; Tit. 1:10[?]).

7. Walter Lock, *The Pastoral Epistles* (Edinburgh: T. & T. Clark, 1936), p. 118.

8. Thomas C. Oden, *First and Second Timothy and Titus* (Louisville: John Knox Press, 1989), pp. 178-179.

9. George W. Knight, III, *The Pastoral Epistles*, p. 467 writes:

Paul does not specify the "much harm" (πολλὰ κακά) that Alexander "did" to him (μοι). It may be that Paul mentions Alexander here because the "harm" he did was to have Paul arrested; ἐνδείκνυμι, used here of what Alexander did, was used as a legal term meaning "inform against" (see LSJM), and Paul notes that Alexander "vigorously opposed our message" (so Fee and Spicq).

See also Oden, *First and Second Timothy and Titus,* pp. 180, 181.

CHAPTER THIRTY-THREE: FINAL CONFIDENCE

1. Gordon D. Fee, *1 and 2 Timothy, Titus* (Peabody, MA: Hendrickson Publishers, 1984), p. 296.

2. George W. Knight, III, *The Pastoral Epistles* (Grand Rapids, MI: Eerdmans, 1992), p. 218.

3. A. W. Tozer, *Born After Midnight* (Camp Hill, PA: Christian Publications, 1989), pp. 119, 120.

4. Archibald Thomas Robertson, *Word Pictures in the New Testament* (Nashville: Broadman, 1931), p. 683.

5. J. H. Bernard, *The Pastoral Epistles* (Grand Rapids, MI: Baker, 1980), p. 148.

6. *Ibid.*

7. William Barclay, *The Letters to Timothy, Titus and Philemon* (Philadelphia: The Westminster Press, 1960), p. 253. See also Philip H. Towner, *1-2 Timothy & Titus* (Downers Grove, IL: InterVarsity, 1994), p. 211 who comments:

   One has the feeling that Paul sees himself in his experience of imprisonment as following in Jesus' footsteps. Jesus (and the early church) made use of Psalm 22 in interpreting his own suffering (Mt. 27:29, 39, 43, 46), and Paul seems to reflect on that psalm and ideas associated with it in this final section. Desertion (Ps. 22:1 [21:2 LXX]), deliverance (22:4, 8, 21 [21:5, 9, 21 LXX]), salvation (22:5 [21:6 LXX]), the Lord's nearness (22:11, 19 [21:12, 20 LXX]), and references to the mouths of lions (22:13, 21 [21:14, 22 LXX]) and the supreme power of God all suggest that Paul was greatly influenced and encouraged by this psalm.

8. J. N. D. Kelly, *A Commentary on the Pastoral Epistles* (Grand Rapids, MI: Baker, 1963), p. 220.

9. Alexander Maclaren, *Expositions of Holy Scripture* (Grand Rapids, MI: Baker, 1974), pp. 127, 128.

10. Knight, *The Pastoral Epistles*, p. 473.

11. Merrill Tenney, ed., *The Zondervan Pictorial Encyclopedia*, Vol. 5 (Grand Rapids, MI: Zondervan, 1975), p. 806.

12. Fee, *1 and 2 Timothy, Titus*, p. 302.

13. Knight, *The Pastoral Epistles*, p. 478.

CHAPTER THIRTY-SEVEN: COMMUNITY GRACE

1. Ewan Kennedy, graduate survey for a Francis Schaeffer Institute project (St. Louis: Covenant Theological Seminary, 1998).

2. *Ibid.*

3. Philip H. Towner, *1-2 Timothy & Titus* (Downers Grove, IL: InterVarsity, 1994), p. 236.

CHAPTER THIRTY-EIGHT: "INTOLERANT" GRACE

1. Francis A. Schaeffer, *True Spirituality*, in The *Complete Works of Francis A. Schaeffer: A Christian Worldview*, Vol. 3 (Wheaton, IL: Crossway Books, 1982), pp. 201-202.

2. *Ibid.*, pp. 216-217.

3. *Ibid.*, p. 216.

CHAPTER THIRTY-NINE: PRIORITIES OF GRACE

1. George W. Knight, III, *The Pastoral Epistles*, in *The New International Greek Commentary*, eds. I. Howard Marshall and Donald A. Hagner (Grand Rapids, MI: Eerdmans, 1992), pp. 341-344.

2. Cf. Philip H. Towner, *1-2 Timothy & Titus* (Downers Grove, IL: InterVarsity, 1994), p. 256.

Scripture Index

General Index

Index of Sermon Illustrations

had "stepped over the line" and
would not "give up, shut up, let up,"
182-183

Transparency
Guest preacher in staid church asks
congregation to break into small
groups to confess their sins to one
another, 303

Unbelief
Unbelief often happens imperceptibly,
like walking through fifty rooms each
slightly bluer, 97

An Unforgiving Spirit
Boswell's description of a man who
would never forgive Johnson, 220

Unity
The poem that begins "To live above
with the saints we love," 90
A. W. Tozer's analogy of 100 pianos all
tuned to the same fork, and thus
being tuned to each other, 90
Two brothers, both preachers, who
would not appear on the podium at
the same time because they could not
agree which Confessional perspective
on the law to hold to, 315

Violence
The Swedish choir director who attacked
a woman for singing off key! 80

Weakness
Oswald Chambers on how God only
uses those who renounce human
strength and power, "nobodies," 22,
174, 177, 183

Wealth
Timex and Rolex both end in "ex" but
. . . 160
Dr. Zhivago on how wealth could create
an illusion of character and
originality, 160

Christina Onassis — a million dollars
per week didn't satisfy her, 161

Witness
"The Life-Saving Station," a modern
parable of our failure to evangelize,
57-58
Aldous Huxley was moved by the
personal witness of a humble servant,
60
The man who came to Christ after
carefully observing his newly
converted son and his church and
friends, 93

The Word of God
Nelson Bell's regular 4:30 A.M. Bible
reading, 108-109
Lt. General William K. Harrison read
the Old Testament seventy times and
the New Testament 280 times, 109
The painting depicting young Luther
poring over a Bible from which
hangs a broken chain, 203
The young Russian man who pilfered a
formerly forbidden Bible, only to
discover that it bore his
grandmother's signature, 204
Samuel Rutherford on how God always
stands by his Word, 206
Dr. William Evans tearing the Bible
apart as he preached, as an
illustration of what it means if the
liberal critics' theories are true, 235-
236, 240

Work
The Christian employee who bragged of
reading three chapters of John in the
john! 140
John MacArthur's eloquent quotation
regarding the preacher's work ethic,
210-211

About the
Book Jacket

The design of the book jacket brings together the talents of several Christian artists. The design centers around the beautiful banner created by artist Marge Gieser. It is photographed here on the jacket at about one-twentieth of its original size.

Concerning the symbolism used in the banner for *1 & 2 Timothy and Titus* Marge Gieser writes:

Paul wrote 1 Timothy soon after he had been released from prison. He wrote 2 Timothy when he was in prison for the second time. The prison bars on both banners remind us of that fact. Paul used his prison experience to promote the gospel of Christ. Paul speaks of two crowns that symbolize the goal of all believers—*the victor's crown* (the laurel wreath) and *the crown of righteousness*. The predominant color of purple is to remind us of Lydia, the "seller of purple" whose hospitality to Paul enabled him to carry on the work of the gospel. The use of scrolls on the banners is a reference to the fact that these were personal letters Paul was writing.

The other artists contributing their talents to the creation of the jacket were: Bill Koechling, photography; Paul Higdon, design and typography; and Cindy Kiple, art direction.